AF461855

Praise for Vivien Goldman and *Rebel Musix, Scribe on a Vibe*

'People talk *about* Brian Eno, Robert Wyatt, Can, Betty Davis, Sex Pistols, George Clinton, Grace Jones all the time – but Vivien Goldman actually spoke to them. Whilst they were making that music we are still talking about. Essential reading: the making of history as it was happening. Vivien was there. And "Launderette" is one of the best singles ever. Read it'
Jarvis Cocker

'Punk! New Wave! Reggae! Vivien Goldman never fails to get the inside scoop. She is the messenger who reveals the truth about our music and ultimately, ourselves. Viva Vivien!'
Chris Frantz and Tina Weymouth

'A friend, an ally, a fellow musician and creative who is articulate, on point, a trailblazer and a necessary pioneer. Thank you for all your words'
Gina Birch

'For those of us coming of age in the mid 70s, in love with rock 'n' roll, our brains were lit on fire not only by new radical voices emerging from the fallout of hippie, but the writers turning us on to it all. Like contemporary Patti Smith, Vivien found equal value in writing about music as she did in performing it, completely free from any creepazoid hoary old patriarchal permission. Punk was our great experiment of liberation, our forum of total communitarianism and inclusivity, and Vivien was a light which made manifest the ideals of its truth. She said it loud from the beginning – one love, one music. The power is in the words. Read them and sing out'
Thurston Moore

'Vivien Goldman has the uncanny ability to shapeshift into differing cultures, to hear the musical world through the prism of an inclusive celebration of song as it unlocks emotion. In these collected works from the seventies and eighties, she reveals the inner world of genre that transcends borders, becomes global, and speaks to us of our common humanity'
Lenny Kaye

'I am very happy that Island Records helped to start Vivien off on such a positive career in the 1970s, when she briefly worked on Bob Marley and the Wailers' PR and helped make a difference. Then she became a pioneer in writing about reggae. [. . .] It is great to have a book like this that captures our whole lives, brings things that happened ages ago to life again and connects them with today. It connects all the threads'
Chris Blackwell, Founder, Island Records

'Vivien Goldman is an indisputable OG of music journalism: she's been a Zelig-like eyewitness to the emergence of multiple music scenes, from UK punk to Nigerian Afrobeat to US hip-hop, and a writer-as-doula who helped introduce now-iconic artists like Bob Marley and Fela Kuti to the world. *Rebel Musix, Scribe on a Vibe* is a thrilling display of Goldman's fearless brilliance, savvy wordplay, insouciant wit and cosmopolitan curiosity. It also underscores her deep, enduring commitment to anti-racism, anti-fascism and progressive feminism – values that are more essential today than ever'
Jason King, Dean, USC Thornton School of Music

'Firstly, Vivien Goldman is genius, and no one writes quite like her [. . .] There is something about her being "often the only girl writer", smart as a whip, her point of view is just different, more personal, intimate, funny and so descriptive. Reading these articles is like watching a great movie, like the scene in *Goodfellas* where Scorsese's camera pans down the bar. Vivien notices every detail, nuance and character [. . .] reading her words, you feel like you are in the room with her [. . .] and lucky for us she is able to write it all down'
Janette Beckman, photographer and writer

'Vivien campaigns with musicians fighting against racism, against misogyny, against social injustice. She celebrates the best of black, white, and Jewish musicians. She was doing it forty years ago. She's still doing it now. And that ain't nothing!'
Daniel Rachel, author of *Too Much Too Young*

'Revelatory, sensuous and incisive, *Rebel Musix, Scribe on a Vibe* revels in music and its profound power to shape human hearts and shake down the walls of Babylon. Vivien Goldman is not merely a scribe of the highest order, but a vibe unto herself'
Aram Sinnreich, professor and author of *Mashed Up*

REBEL MUSIX,
SCRIBE ON A VIBE

Also by Vivien Goldman

Bob Marley: Soul Rebel, Natural Mystic (1981)
with photographer Adrian Boot

Kid Creole and the Coconuts: Indiscreet (1984)

Pearl's Delicious Jamaican Dishes: Recipes from Pearl Bell's Repertoire (1992)
with chef Pearl Bell

The Black Chord: Visions of the Groove: Connections between Afro-Beats, Rhythm and Blues, Hip Hop, and More (1999, reissued 2024)
with photographer David Corio

The Book of Exodus: The Making and Meaning of Bob Marley and the Wailers' Album of the Century (2006)

Cherchez La Femme: The Kid Creole and the Coconuts Musical (2016)
with August Darnell

Revenge of the She-Punks: A Feminist Music History from Poly Styrene to Pussy Riot (2019)

Vivien Goldman is a British writer, musician, broadcaster and educator. She has published seven books and was one of the first writers to champion artists like Bob Marley and Fela Kuti. Now she teaches about them and other Rebel Musix as a long-serving Adjunct Professor at New York University.

REBEL MUSIX, SCRIBE ON A VIBE

Frontline Adventures Linking Punk, Reggae, Afrobeat and Jazz

Selected Music Journalism 1975–2024

Vivien Goldman

First published in Great Britain in 2024 by White Rabbit,
an imprint of The Orion Publishing Group Ltd
Carmelite House, 50 Victoria Embankment
London EC4Y 0DZ

An Hachette UK Company

The authorised representative in the EEA is Hachette Ireland, 8 Castlecourt Centre, Castleknock Road, Castleknock, Dublin 15, D15 YF6A, Ireland

1 3 5 7 9 10 8 6 4 2

A CIP catalogue record for this book is available from the British Library.

ISBN (Hardback) 978 1 3996 0174 0
ISBN (eBook) 978 1 3996 0176 4
ISBN (Audio) 978 1 3996 0177 1

Typeset by Born Group
Printed in Great Britain by Clays Ltd, Elcograf S.p.A.

www.whiterabbitbooks.co.uk
www.orionbooks.co.uk

To all the revelatory artists in this book
who gave me the vibe to be a scribe

The articles in this book have been written over a span of forty-five years. Our aim is to faithfully replicate the original writing and interviews, and therefore some of the language, ideas and attitudes expressed at the time may now be outdated in a modern context.

Contents

Prelude

Any undertaking of this kind – collecting, assessing and making flow five decades worth of one's music journalism – is bound to be an abseil into the attic of your mind. Some of these pieces I had travelled with from England to my new home in America in the early 1990s, sensing that someday they could come in handy. As I was moving out of the Ladbroke Grove home where I had written most of these stories, I foraged in my actual attic and passed on all my old copies of my tenure as a features editor (barring those I had written myself) to my colleague, Barney Hoskyns, who was then launching the website rocksbackpages.com, featuring those articles as the museum-worthy media they would be, soon enough. A cycle was turning. Without Rock's Backpages' digitization, pulling this book together would have been a lot tougher.

To accomplish this book – not everything here is up on Rock's Backpages! – meant handling those brittle, yellowing pages once again, dusting them off from their box, now on a high shelf in my coat cupboard; a vivid reminder of a time when rock 'n' roll itself was still only two decades old. Being a music journalist was obviously easier then, as there was far less pop music to be expert about than there is today! And it was a wild frontier business, lawless and exhilarating – like any business in its infancy, like silent movies were in the 1920s when women directors were more common than they are even now.

Often the only girl writer, maybe one of two, I had the unique privilege of shuttling between the Big Three rock weeklies – *New Musical Express*, the venerable *Melody Maker* and the scrappy little underdog where I began – *Sounds*. First, I became features editor at *Sounds*, and helped it shift more to punk and reggae than its rivals; then, caught up in the sort of politics I describe in these articles, like the one where I infiltrate a National Front gig, I threw myself over the edge of acceptable bourgeois living and turned freelance, as I proudly still remain some four and a half decades on. The rock press gave me a safety net, and I started working for *Melody Maker* and then for *New Musical Express*, the last rag standing, online, as I write.

Whether full-time or freelance, my beat was always Rebel Musix (though that last, inclusionary 'x', which updates Marley's title, would not be invented for decades). Musical territories seen as the margins – punk, reggae, Afrobeat and jazz, uninteresting to my colleagues – proved to be my native habitat. Apparently, some people are surprised at the connecting of these genres; but they all share a formidably assertive, progressive energy, lyrically and/or sonically, grounded in that punk essential – a defiant attitude that refuses to be constrained by earthly limitations.

The reach of the music press was extraordinary, though we were not aware of it. Over the years, people have told me about queuing to buy our rags the day they came out, in places as varied as the Lower East Side's Gem Spa in New York, Paris's Les Halles, even Roppongi in Tokyo. Yet the information is delivered as if to an audience of intimates. Unlike today's more grown-up, "professional" journalism, in which every artist has to be introduced and contextualised, my colleagues' and my pieces of the time fling around band names with the in-crowd confidence of one who knows their significance will be understood; if you were reading this rag, you were either hip to them already, or were damn sure going to find out what was up before next week's edition hit the stands.

Many of these articles appeared in the few ferocious years from the mid-1970s into the early 1980s (though later years have also snuck in). Back then, punk flared up and burned its scalding flame to scorch our musical earth and clear it for a new crop of music – which turned out to be the more sophisticated strains of post-punk, soon segueing into New Wave, the best-dressed New Romantics and the pretty-boy synth-pop haircut bands that became emblematic of the Thatcher/Reagan era.

At this point, I rather dropped out of music journalism, partly because I began making post-punk music myself; first with experimental new-wavers The Flying Lizards, then with some of the artists featured in these pages, including John Lydon and Keith Levene of Public Image Ltd (PiL), Aswad, Robert Wyatt, The Raincoats and The Slits. Arguably my best-loved of those songs, "Launderette", can be heard four decades later on HBO's series *The Deuce*. (For the curious, my 1980s music is compiled on the LP *Resolutionary*; and my 2021 developments are on the Youth-produced *Next Is Now*.)

Thenceforth, the frequency of my "journo" production was tied like the tides to the moon of market forces plus my own creative restlessness. I started to produce and direct music videos and documentaries, write scripts instead of articles – like the *Cherchez La Femme* musical I co-wrote with an interviewee, August Darnell of Kid Creole and the Coconuts, and the movie script around Jamaican ska/dance innovators Don Drummond and Margarita Mahfood, whose origin story is here, for a film that seems to be going into production as I write.

But who knows? The film business is far harsher than the long-gone rockbiz press that, despite sexism, gave me a great berth in some of popular music's most exhilarating times. Generally, writing has been my constant companion and hopefully always will be. I would return to the fray when I was burning to write about, say, Pussy Riot or, most recently, the Trinibad artist Rebel Sixx. His 2021 assassination concludes the Marley section, because it echoes loudly with my experiences around the attempted killing of Bob Marley in 1976, described here.

Punk and its liberating ideals formed me. Truly I was blessed to come of age with punk, a movement that embraced outsiders and the marginalised – and that even meant women! Previously excluded from roles of significant agency within the music business and only permitted onstage when they fit the patriarchy's accepted mould, women could at last start to step forward.

For some years now they have called me The Punk Professor. So irritating when people come up with these tags, right? Well, this one is simply, literally true, as I initiated the punk course at NYU's Clive Davis Institute of Recorded Music in New York. The disciplines I had learnt, not only as a writer but as a documentary and video producer and director, powered me to structure my courses – along with the mind of my mentor in academia, Dr Jason King, my Pygmalion. Having lectured at universities but never taught a full course before, I truly was that punk professor; much like The Clash's bass player Paul Simonon, who stuck notes on his frets to help him remember their songs, as he was a novice when he hit the stage.

Like a rotation crop, every four years since 2004, I have tried to spread the seeds of these musical movements I write about here – sounds and ideas that have improved my life – to new students, who have become increasingly punk and activist themselves.

In general, what compels me and has endured since my first writings, what has given some meaning to my life and work, is the belief I learnt from mentors chronicled here, like Marley, Ornette and Fela – music, culture is our loving weapon. No matter how creative information is suppressed, as it is currently being, most brutally, in American states like Florida with their book bans of vital classics, ideas expressed in music will find a way to bubble through and permeate concrete walls, as did punk, reggae, Afrobeat and, years later, Pussy Riot.

In this, our world, musix, like the humans who make them, mutate, intertwine and inspire one another, creating new hybrid forms that express their creators' own reality, as it reverberates with the recordings of others living far away in distance and maybe time, too, whom they may never meet.

So my anthology wound up selectively, personally, telling a story; one that traces the connectivity between musix over time. It is also my hope that I have been able to transmit something of the excitement of the period when punk and UK reggae first blossomed, which turned out to be the crucible of Britain's comparatively happy multicultural community. The sounds resonated around my Ladbroke Grove neighbourhood, and those illicit late-night shebeens in abandoned houses gave me a social life that I now envy. Our own culture was being transmitted via the Dread Broadcasting Corporation, the first underground reggae station, and thus the big daddy of all the pirates and legal dance stations that followed – some of whose founders have now been ennobled by the same British government that used to chase them down and dismantle their *verboten* rooftop transmitters. All of this I try to communicate to my students in these very different times, and now to you.

Who knew, when I wrote the bulk of these pieces, that I would wind up teaching about their topics half a century later in prestigious academic institutions? Articles with answers to some of our contemporary debates have been included, for classes of the future! Where possible, when I had the good fortune to follow the arc of an artist journalistically, like Marley, Fela and Ornette, and my *sistr'en,* The Slits, I have tried to use as many as practical, to chronicle their contribution more fully.

Discovering internal cross-references connecting a few of these pieces across the years made me realise how writing them had touched me. As is my wont, in previous books, like my collaboration with photographer David Corio, *The Black Chord*, and *Revenge of the She-Punks*, I have approached them thematically rather than chronologically. Check the dates, but hopefully you will find that these articles build into an arc, from the combativeness of punk to the deep communication required by harmolodic "free jazz". I hope you enjoy following the trail.

Not only has much changed since most of these pieces were written, the world has undergone extraordinary, violent shifts since I began compiling this volume. To the best of my ability, in my introductions I have tried to reflect this turbulent moment while speaking to readers in a future that may well be quite different, again.

Here, I invoke the spirit of my late father, Max, jazz violinist turned ladies' garment manufacturer, whose homilies increase in depth the further I am from their delivery. Whether I was seven or seventeen, there I would be, whingeing away, and he would sagely say: "If you have any complaints, put them in the Complaints Book." Frustratingly, of course, there was none. Having escaped the Nazis across Europe during years of peril, his philosophy, I now realise, was: work with what you got.

So, fierce reader, I have. You do know what to do with any complaints, right?

CHAPTER 1

Pre-Punk: The Sound Before the Storm

The timing of my start in the music press in the mid-1970s meant that I arrived a few months before it all kicked off and thus experienced the sudden emergence of punk, seemingly fully formed. Previously, the dominant bands were the monsters of the 1960s, like Pink Floyd and The Who. One minute it was all about Genesis and which clan tartan Rod Stewart was wearing – and then, the sea change.

Managers/ideologues Malcolm McLaren and Bernie Rhodes and spiky-looking members of The Clash and Sex Pistols, or Elvis Costello, with his eccentric neo-conventional look, would lurk in wait for us rock scribes in the grotty grey waiting room. None of today's formality or appointment bollocks, as the punk watchword then was to break down the barriers. Hence The Clash famously let fans who hitchhiked to their shows crash on their hotel room floors – and not in a pervy way. The same inclusionary spirit impelled Riot Grrrlz, two decades later, to do a little gig in someone's house and ask the fans at the end: "Whose pad can I crash in tonight?"

Undoubtedly, the hugest thing for my own development was the advent of women on the scene and the first youth culture stirrings of racial diversification as musicians of my age – first-generation Brits like me – were developing UK reggae and dub. Their reverse cultural colonisation of a generation as reggae became our religion would change my life permanently – I am writing this in Jamaica, from whence came the sounds that so gripped me in the 1970s.

However, despite our Year Zero rejection of what had come before, there were some compatible sounds allowed to stick around – notably counterculture stalwarts hippy, free festival outfits like Hawkwind, of Lemmy fame, and those rampant hets, the Pink Fairies. Generally speaking, though, the watchword of punk was reminiscent of any cultural revolution: kill (metaphorically and musically) the old guard. But there were always some who remained acceptable, even revered, despite the adage: Never Trust a Rock Star.

And here are some of these outliers. Just before punk, Brian Eno was a fascinator with his androgyny, glitter and ostrich feathers. A friend and neighbour, he introduced me to Robert Wyatt, and I was glad when my housemate Geoff Travis of Rough Trade got him recording again, as Wyatt's approach is oblique, unique and gripping in its subtle quietness. Arguably the most "modern" of all were Can – leaders of the dissonant "krautrock" (the war was not long over and the somewhat racist moniker was taken in good part, at least in this case) – whose free jazz-inspired atonality exploded the bloated excesses of rock 'n' roll. I include this particular article as before his death, Holger Czukay told me it was his favourite. And certain unique tribal rituals remained, pre-, during and post-punk, being amphetamine-fuelled and hedonistically subversive as punk: the twenty-four-hour underworld of Northern Soul, whose obsessions revived the careers of previously obscure African American soul singers; and free-spirited she-punk foremother Betty Davis, whose PR I was lucky enough to do at Island Records before I became a full-time writer; an education in the public projection of women that I am able to share here, recollected years later.

Brian Eno

In 1999, when I cleared out my attic and gave all my back copies of Sounds *to Rock's Backpages for our digital future, I mysteriously came across an old-fashioned scrapbook with various articles about the early days of Roxy Music painstakingly pasted in by hand. The band would always be special to me, as theirs was the first record I ever bought, while I was still at school – a 45 of 'Virginia Plain' on the pink Island label with the palm tree. Seeing them perform on* Top of the Pops, *with Eno stabbing the exotic synthesiser, dressed like a glam alien, aroused an exciting sense of new possibilities in me. Being able to give Eno something of his past felt like completing a circle: I was about to leave London for New York.*

Due to living in the creative hive of Ladbroke Grove – a fact that colours many pieces here – I was able to phone Eno, as he was my neighbour. Delighted to get the scrapbook back, he duly popped round for a cup of tea and some choccie biccies.

Already, he had tackled the classics with the deliriously amateur orchestra, Portsmouth Sinfonia, alongside a flatmate and my future compadres *in the experimental group Flying Lizard (yes, I wear another hat as a musician).*

Back in the old neighbourhood, Eno was always good at being one of the girls and liked to hang around with my then crew of photographer Kate Simon, soon-to-be-rock star Chrissie Hynde and the duo Snatch, comprising Patti Palladin and his paramour Judy Nylon (she still asserts that she gave him the idea for ambient music, so presumably she did). Loving to discuss ideas, Eno was quick, self-deprecating, funny, far from one of those macho rock 'n' rollers. He always had intriguing thoughts, which would lead to his future role as global tactician and cultural activist as well as artist.

We meet as his ambient music and label is opening new vistas for music lovers; before his mega pop success with U2 and Fela-influenced collaborations with David Byrne of Talking Heads (who we will meet later in this book). He has completed his landmark work with David Bowie on Low, *and . . . and . . . and . . . because when it comes to polymath Brian Eno, there is always another 'and'. Eno always has more happening in more arenas, from art to activist philosophy, than most of us can imagine.*

"Eno: Extra Natty Orations"

First published in Sounds, *5 February 1977*

"I was trying to think of some inventions, so I tried to think of what I needed. But I don't need anything. That's the difficulty, really."

Ever heard of mnemonics? It's a word game, you can have fun with it. Brian Eno likes to play word games. This one's taken from his 1968 journal:

N nothing
O on
T this
E earth
B betrays
O our
O own
K karakter
S so

Brian rushed into the tranquil golden room overlooking the park, little black notebooks spilling from his hands. He stacked them in a neat rank on the golden carpet in front of me and began to pick over them with the single-minded devotion of a jumble sale addict in quest of the ultimate Fair Isle jumper.

If the mnemonic is right, Eno is the reincarnation of Leonardo da Vinci.

Ten years of journals. His favourites are Challenge or Oldwich notebooks, supple black covers, creamy lined pages; just the right size and shape: correct gradients and lineaments for absorbing the juicy emissions of a mind frothing with invention. Every page covered in tantalising word juxtapositions, perfect miniature diagrams and cartoons, flippant games, some more comprehensible than others. Disciplines collide, clash, overlap. There's sex and adventure and bravado and games, lots of games.

The Eno Illustrated Annuals.

In 1968 he referred to himself as an art kleptomaniac. Naturally, there's day-to-day stuff – one page has a list of places to go, people to see – "Richard Williams. Sign on."

"That was when I'd just moved to London . . ."

There's a revealing juxtaposition for ya – Richard Williams was an influential writer who picked up on a new band called Roxy Music; the rest, including Richard's move to A&R at Island and subsequent departure under less than happy circumstances, being . . . History.

Brian was signing on that day.

The rest is . . . His-story.

Flipping through a Little Black Book . . .

"Here's something I've been looking for for ages. It's an equation by Richard Moore – a mathematician who works in the anatomy department at Guy's Hospital. This – earth-shattering theory – I think it's the most important thing since the theory of relativity as a single observational idea. It's mathematical proof that many apparently random situations generate not only predictable results, but also precisely predictable results . . ." The equation not only throws the basic tenets of contemporary physics into disarray, but it also applies rather well to this interview – an interview is a deliciously random situation, at best. This one had precisely predictable results. I had a great time.

Brian Eno says he wouldn't mind doing a bit of travelling now. He says that for a long time he's been very keen on just staying home, but now he wouldn't mind going to Jamaica. Ritva, his girlfriend (Eno always uses the word in a declamatory way, like saying "my colleague"), says they never go out except to go to the Electric Cinema (mind you, if you only go to one place in London, that's the wisest choice).

They live in a perfect little environment – a sunny flat overlooking a recreation ground in an area of no man's land in West London, squats on one side, classy boutiques and delicatessens the other, pretty canals not far away.

There's a darkroom, with Eno's Patented Invention mounted on a shelf – a glass box, the front divided into nine squares in rows of three. Turn off the light and the squares flicker in a rapid crossfire of different colours. Purple, brown, amber, red, chase each other in a frantic *Keystone Kops* race in and out of vision, random flashes of rainbows juggle in an anarchic square dance.

The kitchen window overlooks a struggling garden, with a tree bizarrely wrapped in strips of brown sacking on the lower limbs, to keep the cats away. Ivy grows over the windows. Brian and Ritva eat omelettes and shoots with oatcakes, for breakfast.

Brian's embedded in a book about genes, while Ritva and I leaf through photos in a picture book. A placid scene, only broken by Brian's occasional grumble when he comes to a bit he can't understand. "And the book's two months overdue," he groans.

"I bet you it finishes at the end of the track. I have great luck with these things."

Brian's taping Rico's great Wareika Dub album while we talk.

"I do like talking, but I don't like chatting. I don't like to do anything on that kind of level. I really like to do things where I'm stretched a little bit. The reason I've been reticent to do interviews for the past few months is because I've found them grounding. I do read books on genetics at breakfast. I didn't do that to impress you. I read them because I find them incredibly exciting. Often I'll go and do an interview and it'll be so abysmally dull, and I think – here I am, at least capable of something intelligent. Why am I being asked what kind of boot polish I use, effectively?"

Might as well clear that one up once and for all – Eno spits on his boots while he polishes. And he still travels by Tube.

"I will Brook *no* Argument" – crisply teasing mock-pedant tones here – "about the matter. I refuse ever again to talk at what is called 'people's level'. I don't believe in that term.

"It's just the same with music. There's always been people saying, 'You've got a potential audience. You could, if you want, make successful records.' But I don't believe in that. It's not arrogance – just a sense of I Want To Do What I Want To Do."

He's pacing briskly up and down and up and down the room, passing the dreamy Peter Schmidt painting of a mountain swathed in clouds (the sleeve of Fripp & Eno's *Evening Star* album) with cuckoo-clock regularity.

Turns briskly to me. "I wouldn't mind making hit singles, by the way. I don't refuse to communicate with people on that level. What I mean is I refuse to force communication with people on that level – if it doesn't happen, it doesn't happen. Too bad. I can't speak German either, but it's nothing to fret about."

Brian's Great Luck extends further than hitting the end of the track while taping albums. Like Patti Smith, he's succeeded in transmuting

Art into Money; the most learned mediaeval alchemist would tear out every last hair in his grey beard in perplexity trying to pull off that little number.

Those crazy, whacked-out, spangled days when Roxy Music rose glistening on the horizon, disseminating rays of Style, Glamour and Art in a crisp winter light over a beat-up music scene now seem more distant than Fritz Lang's *Metropolis* deco/expressionist landscape of dreams.

In those days, Eno was arrogant, a messenger of vice, swooping down on black ostrich wings, central figure in a tableau symbolising the first and finest flourishings of decadence. Eno glittered, kohl-rimmed eyes, silken fall of hair, an angel dallying deliciously, dangerously with the Fall.

Today he's wearing a velour top from Marks & Spencer, jeans and well-polished monkey boots. His blond hair is cropped and thins daily; his incipient baldness is as much part of his current image as his Roxy-on-the-road exploits were.

After leaving Roxy to the lacklustre leadership of Bryan Ferry, Eno spiralled off into a series of evermore intriguing solo projects. With each successive album, you could feel his capacities flexing, stretching; putting on muscle as the music pared down to minimal grace. Surreal, witty lyrics hint at mind-bending concepts and scenarios. His notebooks demonstrate the familiar intelligence that joys in teasing every frontier, laced with a serious appreciation of the fantastic.

"I've got fed up of this thing that runs through the rock business that the audience are a bunch of dumb cunts. I refuse to do it. If they are a bunch of dumb cunts – which they might be, I'm not saying there's a group of repressed intellectuals out there – if they are, I'm frankly not interested in them. It's as simple as that.

"Because I also believe there's an aspiring level in everyone and you can talk to the aspiring level or to the static one. Most people talk to the static one.

"There are always plenty of options for playing safe in the world, but they're not normally the very interesting ones. And finally, I think they're not the commercial ones. They are in the short term, I know, but . . ."

We look at each other and start to laugh.

"I am optimistic, I know! But I have reason to be, because I get along all right. Things go well for me. I'm lucky. Like with that tape—"

Eno leaps to the tape deck, plays back a few seconds and then turns up the volume. I listen, suitably impressed, as the wildly syncopated track fades out and finishes, just before the tape clicks neatly to a close.

A Brief Backtrack:

"Mystique and credibility are such important factors, and critics are always unaware of that factor. It is something an artist can take advantage of, but I'll tell you where it hurts. People are always generous to first albums. If it isn't very successful and you make a second album, you're in no man's land, because you don't have the credibility of having been around for a while. You're really nothing in anybody's eyes.

"I experienced that with *Taking Tiger Mountain (By Strategy)* – with the exception of yourself and one or two others, the feeling was – well, he's done one, why does he want to do another one? Why bother?

"My first album, *Here Come the Warm Jets*, is my least favourite. It sold best of all. But a lot of people genuinely prefer it; another instance of mystique at work. They heard that under the condition of wanting to like it a lot, and that makes a difference.

"I prefer the third, *Another Green World*. It's less aggressive, there's less adolescent banging about. Although there's fast numbers on *Another Green World*, they're much smoother. 'St. Elmo's Fire' is more like a sledge shooting over snow, that kind of speed.

"I want to make disposable albums. Well, I suppose albums are disposable, but I want to make records to get up with for a couple of weeks – because it has a nice sparkle, a nice shimmer to it, and there's no pretence that this is – MUSIC." He announces the word very grandly.

"Just another level, like having nice curtains or nice lights in the room. I'd sell them very cheap in a plain package that says 'Waking-Up Music', 'Breakfast Music', that kind of thing. They'd be like ordinary records physically, they'd just not come with the aura of art, so one wouldn't be frightened of having the things for a couple of weeks and then getting rid of them.

"They'd be cheap to make in terms of recording. *Discreet Music* only cost three pounds to make and it's my favourite record. I made it sitting there" – pointing to the wall where the stereo, tape deck and Revox squat in an amiably mechanistic row – "in about thirty-five minutes.

"It's actually false to say that, because it's the result of three different lines of experimentation, going back to '66. Like when you get the

Japanese painters who grind colours all day, prepare the paper, get their seat set up and move it around, get the brushes organised and so on, and then at the end of the day, just at twilight, go 'ch-ch-ch!' – executing a rapid series of karate chops in mid-air.

"It's like saying that picture took a minute, which it did, but there's a lot of background of it."

Lo!

"I guess David Bowie did tune into me, but most people regard that as a rather cynical process. They imagine David going to record shops, seeing what's going on and saying, well, this looks like a good horse to back. It really isn't like that, he's just somebody who isn't too proud . . .

"I think he just arrived at the same point of thinking. When you do that you have the choice to pretend it didn't happen, like painters do. They say, 'God, I didn't know he was doing that! Blimey! Well, I did it first' – all that kind of thing.

"I was embarrassed when I read some of the reviews. It's embarrassing when you work with somebody and then get credited with what they did. It confirms the old position of keeping to yourself and being defensive about your invention. If you invite somebody in, you run the risk of it looking like they did all the work while you sat there scratching your bum.

"It wasn't like that – it was a collaboration weighted very much towards David. The influence I had was as much to do with what I'd released on records as what I did there. He was very interested in *Another Green World*, for example . . ."

Whatever false assumptions reviewers of Bowie's *Low* album made, they're not surprising. Basically, *Low* sounds like an Eno album. Fresh and stimulating.

"You know on *Another Green World* I had two types of tracks – second-side-of-*Low* type tracks (extended semi-instrumental pieces) and song-type tracks? Well, all I did was shuffle them in with one another so they weren't so obvious. What David did was a much better solution to the problem: put one type on one side and the other type on the other side. That's what I should have done, a positive statement: I'm doing two different things – they ought to relate because they both come from me but they're different.

"I'm much more into a record that's a homogenous mood for all of its length rather than this jumping up and down thing. Like, *Discreet*

Music is an evening piece and the other side, which I don't think is very successful, is an early afternoon on a rainy-day piece . . ."

Eno's been undergoing strange experiences playing *Low* to Bowie fans. Their interpretation of David's sudden transformation from springing, wiry funk to synthesised streams of sound and echo, drifting neo-classical explorations and wild-eyed, wide-eyed extra-terrestrial songbeams is far removed from the careful construction of *Low* as Eno lived it.

"I know how David made the album fairly well and it had nothing to do with the kind of mystique they're inventing about it. They see these extraordinary profundities and depths that I know weren't there – not to say that there weren't profundities and depths, but they weren't of the kind of literary nature people assume." So how would you describe the conceptual shift?

"All the concepts are visible in a sense. What David's experiencing is what I'm experiencing – a transition away from focal music. The way rock music is traditionally organised is to some extent ranked. You have voice, guitar, rhythm guitar, piano maybe – rhythm guitar and piano are interchangeable – bass and then drums. Then at the bottom you have the bass drum. It's a kind of hierarchy.

"Partly one of mixing, because normally it was done so that the voice was loudest and the bass was quietest, that was the concept. But that was also the concept of what importance the listener was intended to attach to each of those things. The melodic concept of music was considered very important; being literal and semantic and linear was important.

"It's very obvious to me why David could make the transition from black music to what he's doing now, because in black music the focal point stopped being quite so important. The drums and bass started to have much more vocal roles, to become important instruments. It's demonstrated partly by the fact that they were mixed very loud and also the voices started to have a less significant role, singing rhythm parts and percussion parts. So that hierarchy got suppressed.

"What you create is much more of an enigmatic thing. It's not obvious to the listener what the focus is, but there's obviously some kind of interacting going on between all these separate musical events. Reggae's very obviously the same thing."

Eno's wearing a straight groove in the carpet by now. I shouldn't wonder. His interpretations and explanations are as lucid as an unusually clear lecture (another sideline of his, incidentally).

"Now it strikes me as quite obvious that if you feel the transition and enjoy it, you should then go on to a music that removes focuses completely and say, here's a whole lot of elements. They float around between each other and sometimes one of them comes into focus, then it disappears, and then . . . it's dub music, but it's also what's on side two of *Low*.

"Now the fact is that no numbskull of a critic can actually organise themselves to think in this functional sense of what is happening to the music."

He shakes his head in despair, then resumes pacing.

"They can see what's happening to the personality, they can see what's happening to the clothes, but they're so bloody thick, sometimes I could drive nails through their heads.

"What is happening is *the focus is getting lost*. Obviously there are other things happening as well, but that's a predominant one that both David and I are involved in."

The phone rings. It's been doing that with aggravating regularity: Brian takes it off the hook, Ritva puts it back on to make a call, the phone rings again. This time, Brian leaps at it savagely, grabs the receiver and begins to scream a hideous yabbering yowl into the mouthpiece before throwing it at me. Thanks to years of netball, I field the shot expertly and fend off the hapless caller.

A leg whips out and Eno kicks the phone ferociously across the floor.

"That thing. I bloody hate it."

Aha, but if it didn't exist, you'd probably have invented it.

"I probably would have, actually."

Robert Wyatt

Once, while still at school, I had seen the Soft Machine, Robert Wyatt's jazzy-psychedelia former band, at the Royal Albert Hall Pop Proms and I recall feeling transported by their churning instrumentals, powered by Robert's thrusting drumming. But his album Rock Bottom, *recorded after the accident that put him in a wheelchair, ravished me utterly and still does. The world and home he and Alfie created – and would continue to create in other places – was one of energising colour and constant alertness as they are both serious thinkers; I was honoured when Alfie presented me with one of her original sketches for the cover. Robert's commitment and integrity make his straightforward, uninflected singing very moving and profound. In any collaboration he adds depth. Robert played on my 45 "Launderette" in 1981. As it was built round the sinuous bass line of Aswad's bass player, George Oban, I had no clue what he should do. Luckily, Robert did, and his samba-tinged, free-flowing percussion helped make it the favourite it still is (in certain circles!).*

"Up from Rock Bottom"

First published in Melody Maker, *15 March 1980*

Writing letters to political prisoners, listening to Radio Havana, thinking about music . . . Robert Wyatt hasn't been inactive during his five-year absence from the studios. Vivien Goldman finds out why he's finally decided to record again.

> *Your lunacy fits neatly with my own.*
> "Sea Song" by Robert Wyatt

"Don't be too hard on your old self," was his advice to me on the phone. I was castigating myself for some idiocy long past. "Try and be friendly to your old self," he said encouragingly. "After all, even if it seems really stupid to you now, you were doing the best you could at the time."

This little homily could well have been – sounded as if it was – learnt from life. Robert Wyatt says that it's only recently he's begun to miss the things he used to be able to do before his accident seven years ago. Robert fell from a window during a party at Lady June's flat in a mansion block of flats in Maida Vale.

"I was very drunk," he remembers. "I didn't fall out, I climbed out . . . it seemed the best way to leave the party at the time. Yes, I did a lot of punch and then a bottle of whisky and so on. Which was quite good, because if you're going to fall out of a window and you're drunk, it doesn't hurt quite so much. Soldiers and bullfighters do it all the time . . . people who are smashed getting smashed."

The particular window Robert fell from while trying to evade a typical party tangle is sealed up now. I thought that was symbolic, until I found out that all those windows are sealed up now; some painter's mistake. Perhaps it's still symbolic.

One other thing that's stuck: Robert's relationship with his wife, artist Alfreda Benge [Alfie]. She was at the party and it's a sticky web of emotions – guilt, loyalty, but above all, a simple bond of friendship – that welds them together as a creative unit.

Oddly enough, during the last five years, in which Robert has been passive/receptive – not making records, at any rate, while absorbing information from all over the place like a deep-sea diver gulps oxygen – Alfie's own visual output has been declining. Perhaps now that Robert's broken the five-year silence, Alfie's paintings will increase, too. As a music/visuals team, they're matched only by Don and Moki Cherry; like Moki, Alfie's sleeves for Robert's two solo albums provide such a deep-pile context for the music that it's almost impossible to think of one without the other floating into your mind.

Robert's lyrics tend towards surreal dream worlds. Sometimes they seem surreal simply because they're so colloquial and direct you'd think nobody would sing those kinds of words in a song. Calling the first album you make after being stuck in a wheelchair for the rest of your life *Rock Bottom* indicates a surreal/straightforward wit that's awesomely matched by Alfie's eye: a cross-section of a seascape, with a little Robert's top half popping out of the water's surface, waving a big bunch of balloons in one hand – you can almost see the bright lollipop colours speckle the sky, though it's a grey-and-white pencil drawing – but beneath the waterline, there's no matching pair of little

Robert legs. Just fronds, or tentacles of passing octopi. Presumably it's Alfie bending over backwards on that tiny island.

Behind her, more balloons float gaily towards a boat puffing across the horizon. Someone standing on the deck is bound to see the balloons and want to grab one down from the sky, but they might never know that the little man who held them is out there in the water; and even he doesn't seem to know whether he's waving or drowning.

Alfie's illustrations go colour for Robert's next, *Ruth Is Stranger Than Richard*. Two curious animals – actually people, heads shrouded in masks of gaudy ritual birds and beasts – examine their reflections in mirrors. Each mirror shows the same red sun, each sun sliced across by a razor-blade cloud. But the bird-man in the Fair Isle jumper sees a solitary gull swooping and diving across the green field in his mirror, while the beast-woman with the beads and hippy print dress gazes impassively into her mirror, at a solitary small woman figure trudging across her green field.

Behind the uncommon pair, a washing line hangs between trees, stringing miscellaneous items of household ware and underwear across a gypsy encampment: a brown cauldron on a tripod goes hubble-bubble by a comfy armchair, a book lying half read on the flat earth beside it. A green gnome's teapot on a grey tree stump, a deckchair, a little green TV, even an ironing board near the hole in the ground. A blue ladder sticks out of the hole, so that Things can easily climb in and out; there's even a small green wiggling Thing squirming across Alfie's wild world, heading in the direction of the bird's house slung from another tree. Ideal Home in the wilderness, peopled by beasts that can't see each other, only themselves. What's worse, only their innermost souls. No breathers for commercials.

This may be a dubious recommendation, but no record makes me cry as much as *Rock Bottom*. Robert concedes that "it's one of the only things I've done I would listen to myself. It's one of the only records of mine I've got, I think."

Each track reminds me of Robert's musical self-description: "Long, doleful, when-will-this-end songs." *Rock Bottom*'s full-frontal pain – at least as intense as any Lennon in his Primal Scream period – sears so deeply that it doesn't seem idle to assume he's referring at least partly to his accident.

"This sounds so silly – I can't really remember," says Robert. "Somebody said, 'Oh, this is a cry of pain from the accident.' It doesn't sound appropriate to me at all to the kind of accident I had. This is taking it too far. You make records instead of saying things. It's up to anybody who listens to put the lid on it. I reserve the old romantic right of ambiguity in art, nineteenth century though it may sound."

About *Ruth Is Stranger Than Richard*, Robert says: "I'm more fond of that, but in the way a mother might be more fond of her Down's Syndrome child than the one with all its faculties intact. It's got so much investment of ideas and thought in it that don't hang together, don't make a complete record . . ."

He specifies the "fan worship thrill" of working with now-dead South African trumpeter Mongezi Feza, hearing Mongezi's rhythms hook into Gary Windo's horns, "jazz, not jazz-influenced". Bill McCormick and Laurie Allan were the bass-and-drums-respectively rhythm slice, and Robert was on piano: "I got a vague inkling of how enjoyable it must be to be a pianist in a jazz group."

Both *Rock Bottom* and *Ruth Is Stranger Than Richard* are deleted by Virgin Records, heaven only knows why. There are, apparently, plans to bring out a compilation of the two; why a compilation and not a double album reissue I equally cannot imagine. I certainly wouldn't fancy wielding the anthologist's knife over either of these immaculate assemblages.

It only means that I lost faith in this song.
"Signed Curtain" by Robert Wyatt and Matching Mole

Robert Wyatt listens with interest to everyone; he can be almost painfully self-effacing, as if being in a wheelchair had entirely removed the onus of aggression – as in, "look at me, I'm an assertive rock star" – from his shoulders. Robert says: "I've always been one to shirk responsibilities if there was the opportunity to, and this meant there was a certain number of things I couldn't possibly be expected to do any more, which was quite a relief." He's not being facetious.

There was *Rock Bottom* and *Ruth Is Stranger* – and then the five-year silence. Why?

"I tried to do a couple of singles and suddenly my preoccupations started to go out of synch with my job. I couldn't relate things I was thinking about to my particular mode of expression. Virgin Records gave me a lot of freedom and opportunity to do what I wanted to do. I've never been prolific and I couldn't keep the momentum going.

"It probably wouldn't have shown if I'd been in a group. The group momentum keeps the thing going – at any given point, one or two people within the group are the ones with ideas, pushing. The others become interpreters and then someone else takes a turn. It's much harder to sustain output on your own.

"Having said that, I must have written about 2,000 postcards in the last four years – the most exciting creative project of my life! I wrote them because it's nicer than writing letters, so the postmen have got pretty pictures to look at and if they really want, they can read it.

"They're not absolute opposites, being creative and being receptive, but there's an emphasis on one or the other. And I became more interested in music than in making music. That's always been my problem – I've never enjoyed playing instruments, I've always enjoyed listening to records. I'm really a fan of music, so I get involved in listening – and, from that, observing and being interested without being obliged to make it.

"My feeling about music now is . . . I get in a panic about how much there is to hear and not enough time, so it's going to get wasted, all that unappreciated beauty. Which is the opposite of ten years ago, when I was thinking: 'How can I express myself?'

"Going back in the studio – I didn't do it because I thought that singing about things that mattered to me would make the world a better place. I think Linton Kwesi Johnson was quite right when he said singing about things doesn't change them. Changing things changes them. Singing is singing. Just as in art, I'm interested in songs by people who have preoccupations I sympathise with, and acknowledging some songs that I like and the ideas and thoughts they represent."

The result so far is three out of a projected five 45s, possibly to be sold in a set – Robert Wyatt's Paper Bag, perhaps, a humbler collection than PiL's 12-inches in metal, but no less cogent.

They're all cover versions, "because I can't think of anything to say coherently at the moment," says Robert, modestly ignoring the fact that his selections are a pretty good statement in themselves.

Each single is a compact two-step of ideas. The Spanish-spoken one, with a Violeta Parra song on one side about the extermination of the native Chilean Indians, asks questions of American imperialism. It says that there are elections coming up, the implication being: what's the point when most of the indigenous population's already been exterminated? The flip's a version of "Guantanamera", familiar to us all as MOR elevator muzak, here restored to its original, fiery rebel spirit.

Then there's the Stalin single – one side is a version of "Stalin Wasn't Stallin'", originally recorded by an acapella gospel group, The Golden Gate Jubilee Quartet. Robert heard it on Alexis Korner's Sunday morning radio show. Alexis said that the record was deleted, like the sentiments expressed in it, and sent a cassette to Robert on request.

"It was made, I think, during the war or after it, and it's a straightforward rally-round, anti-fascist solidarity internationally in a war against Hitler, in which it's pointed out that the war against Hitler and against fascism in Europe, the turning point and the major victories, were won through amazing sacrifices by the Russians.

"The turning point was the Battle of Stalingrad. And – this is an embarrassing fact for the West – it wasn't bombing the shit out of Hiroshima, it wasn't the English and the Americans charging round the desert, it was 20 million dead Russians. And, of course, dead Poles and dead Jews. It's a jolly little song to celebrate Joe Stalin, who represented the power that changed the direction of the Second World War, so saving the rest of Europe from domination by Hitler . . .

"I think the underlying exercise I see running through thoughts of Stalin in the West now is to replace the idea of the all-time twentieth-century monster of Hitler with the all-time twentieth-century monster of Stalin. On account of the fact that at the end of the war he didn't stop killing people, for example. He seemed to get a bit carried away . . . to be honest, I don't want to get heavy. I just thought it was amusing to realise that the song had been done and how impossible it was going to be to find a composer, because he wouldn't dare say he'd written it anyway, when it comes to royalties."

Historical interest aside, the record's a swinging finger-snapper, with four-part Roberts going ooh-ooh in the background and a touch of percussion to spank along the pace. The flip's a poem by Peter Blackman, father of the Steel 'n' Skin steel band Blackman, about the fall of Stalingrad.

Robert saw Blackman read at an Art Against Racism and Fascism show. "As that song on the other side points out, England and America were for five extraordinary and unlikely years anti-fascist countries, because they weren't being the fascists. I didn't know anything about Peter Blackman and when he read this poem, I was very moved. He's not young, he belongs to quite another generation, the Thirties Left movement, and he's stuck to it where others haven't. He hasn't made a career out of either being left wing or a poet."

Blackman is a short, dignified man who carries himself in his casual polo neck like a general in full honours. When he walked into the recording studio, it was the first time he'd had the opportunity to record his work. But he wasn't in any rush. He was cautious, wanting to know and understand more about Robert's preoccupations and intentions.

Robert displayed great deference and respect to the older man, who recites with what Robert describes as "unapologetic pride".

As to where Robert stands, he says: "I'm actually a caring member of the Communist Party, so I'm in a paradoxical position being in the record industry. But I think that things that are serious and things that people enjoy can be the same thing."

Which leads on to the other recorded single, an initially bizarre coupling of Billie Holiday's classic, "Strange Fruit" – about seeing the corpse of a black man lynched by the Ku Klux Klan swinging from a tree in the American South – and Chic's "At Last I Am Free". As when Robert made a parallel cover hit – The Monkees' "I'm A Believer" – all the ambiguities and tensions disguised by the original straight pop format stand naked.

"I chose that song because when I first heard it I was a bit pissed and it made me cry. I was interested in that, because though Rodgers and Edwards are acknowledged songwriters, they're not famous for writing songs that make you cry . . . I don't think it necessarily moves me the way it moved them when they were writing it. But anyway, there was a bonus in the fact that it was in my range."

Which is . . .?

"Well, I don't know – I'm still waiting for puberty and my voice to break and all that sort of thing. Then I'll start covering men's songs, that men sing. Just technically, I find myself singing along more with women singers.

"Yes, a Billie Holiday song. It's a bit inappropriate, like asking a Jew to sing from the Koran or something. Cross-cultural references, it's not my song . . . I thought it was relevant now, but instead of talking about southern America, we're talking about South Africa. And I thought, we're just going to go on doing this – we were doing it before I was born, and it's going to go on after I die, and there's nothing I can do about it. But you can't help noticing."

While Robert's fans thrill to the fact that he's working publicly again, and Robert himself seems to be measurably more cheerful lately (although he's racked with nerves about each succeeding move), his pleasure's tinged with other, more ambiguous emotions.

"Going back to work is in some ways a defeat. Because I've now come to the conclusion that I can only do what I used to do in the first place. I'd like to think that after the last four or five years I could now see further, do more and so on. But this isn't the case – I find I'm reduced to this built-in introspection and narcissism of being A Creative Person, and it's very hard to harness the amazing things I've seen or heard. Suddenly all the windows disappear and are replaced by mirrors.

"Everyone believes in something and I used to believe in Art, in truth with beauty. That if it looked good and sounded good and felt right, then that contained the main truth you need to know and intuition would guide you from then on. If it feels good, do it. I don't see any evidence of that now. I can see that the cruellest and most repressive peoples and societies can sometimes produce the most beautiful and astounding art – in fact, they need to.

"If another analogy is that art is make-up then the more of it you need, the more dubious your real life is. But I do need to at least pretend to believe in something. And religion's out of the question. I've found that talking to people who had political knowledge and experience provided the stimulus that I'd been missing, that I really needed, and I clutched on to that."

Robert always seems to assume personal guilt and responsibility for the history of Western colonialism, which can be seen from his selection of songs for the singles. He claims that the aesthetic – is it a nice tune? – comes before the moral in his selection process.

"Art to me is everything that isn't true, if you want to be glib about it. It's quite useful to actually care about something . . . but I do come, on my mother's side, from a long line of Kentish fascists, and on my father's side I come from a long line of missionaries going out to various parts of the world to intimidate the locals into submission to make it easier for Western European colonial expansion. Although they'd deny it.

"That doesn't make me kind or like people I wouldn't otherwise like. I just feel angry that I was born a receiver of stolen goods. My immediate parents were breakaways from family tradition . . . but no amount of masochistic search for my own evil cultural roots would make me actually want to have a relative like Woodrow Wyatt."

*

Paradoxically, many people think one of Robert's greatest musical contributions is the way he sings: not with a classic Good Voice, just straightforwardly, in a middle-class English accent. This, despite the fact that one of the main reasons he left the Soft Machine is because they didn't like the way he sang.

Hearing Robert talk about drumming – obviously, he can't use a full kit any longer, but he's a sturdy and sensitive percussionist – is one of the few moments that the word "tragedy" pops into your head while you're talking to him.

"I don't feel I can get out of myself when I'm singing. And what I remember about playing music was the way, sitting in front of a drum kit, you somehow got out of your mad skin into the outside world – a wonderful feeling of release which I don't get from singing at all."

Robert's everyman vocal technique – I'm just an ordinary bloke, why am I so sad? – he puts down to this: "I go blank when I sing, which I think makes it sound sad. That's my sincere-sounding technique. Just go blank and try and get the notes right."

He has evolved some flamboyant but not flashy vocal styles over the years – babbling rushes of overlaid noise, colloquial speech patterns eliding over lines of melody so you sing an up-and-down incantation.

As for the much-celebrated Englishness: "It wasn't patriotic in any way. I got the idea from listening to other people – Pink Floyd, Kevin Coyne, Noël Coward, George Formby, Stanley Holloway, Vera Lynn – but, apart from George Formby, I didn't relate to their material. I'd committed myself to syncopated music and I don't speak a syncopated language.

"It's just that hearing tapes of me trying to sound like Steve Marriott trying to sound like Wilson Pickett, or Stevie Winwood trying to sound like Ray Charles, or Joe Cocker trying to sound like Ray Charles, made me realise there had to be another way if I was going to get anywhere in this business."

There's a classic John Peel session from years ago where he sings a song and changes the words to say how nice it is at the BBC, where they let you play almost as long and as loud as a jazz group or an orchestra on Radio 3, and he continues to sing about the coffee machine in the hall . . .

"Yes, I also got into writing words where some of my preoccupations were purely technical, and they'd come out as human-being-not-interested-in-technique things, and others to do with expressing myself would come out calculated.

"I got fed up with songs where the main accents would make you emphasise the words in a way you wouldn't if you were just saying them and I got interested in the technique of writing songs where the melody line fits the way you'd say the words if you were just talking.

"I'd say things you'd say in conversation, not even serious conversation, just things you'd say to make a noise. And that meant singing about things that were true as far as I understood it. And if you're muddled, the only things you're certain are true are that there's a tea machine in the corridor and it works or it doesn't. This is true, it's not wishy-washy bullshit. It may be low-profile, but it's true. Then I abandoned that and later, I was quite happy to sing things that didn't match the rhythm of the words at all."

I'm the one face down in the mud on the ground.
"Team Spirit" by Robert Wyatt, Bill McCormick and Phil Manzanera

The house, bought for the Wyatts by friends after Robert's fall, is in a finely preserved street in a residential riverside area of West London. The Wyatts live on the ground floor. It's a circumscribed world for Robert in his wheelchair and so it has to be a complete world.

The flat's full of rich, glowing colours, the layout and design catering for the fact that Robert needs effortless access to as much information as possible.

I once suggested that Robert should get himself an invalid car, and up his independence and mobility a hundredfold. Robert laughed and said, no – he'd just go off in a daydream and be bound to crash. Alfie merely commented: "No, not Robert, he's a born passenger . . ."

So Robert's world has shrunk from that of the globe-trotting rock 'n' roller, free-forming it on the French Riviera or in Ibiza, touring across the States supporting Jimi Hendrix ("I thought he was a real gentleman").

Interesting correspondence lies around Robert's desk. Letters from Africans in detention, with whom he's carried on lengthy correspondences that started out as sending a Christmas card and blossomed.

Robert maintains a series of letter exchanges from his desk and spends a great deal of time listening to the radio; not just the BBC, for his dial twiddling has led him to uncover long-range frequencies that keep him in touch with far global corners. It's a form of obvious compensation for immobility, but by subscribing to an enormous amount of magazines and literature and listening to people talk from all over the planet, Robert, sitting in his chair at home, is probably more in touch than he ever was in his mobile existence.

When people are around, the only external indication of Robert's frustration is the way the former drummer is constantly drumming – cigarette packs, lighters, anything that's lying around is fiddled with and tapped, so that every conversation is punctuated by non-stop syncopation.

"I wanted to get out of this place, especially when I realised after the last election that the country was just full of Tories – I wanted to separate myself and I couldn't do it physically, so I started tuning into the short-wave radio . . . to anyone who was considered the enemy, with immediate strong bonds of sympathy pouring out to them.

"The result was that I spend my time hovering between the radio of the Islamic Republic of Iran and Radio Moscow. And Radio Havana, on 41 metres short wave, from ten to eleven in English, which means missing the first part of John Peel. That's a sacrifice, seriously – but I'm prepared to make it, so entertaining is Radio Havana. I found out there's more to life on the short wave than the enemy and it's very Eurocentric to call anyone who isn't us the enemy."

Can

Out of the blue, I got a message from Can's Irmin Schmidt in 2014, inviting me to his home in the South of France to discuss their work for a project he had in mind. It was prompted by this article, which tickled his fancy because of its incorporation of random chance – in this case, the malfunction of my cassette player mid-interview.

Machines and their personalities were an appropriate motif for the futuristic and forward-thinking Can; their music was a challenging, experimental surprise. In the coming years, the influence of krautrock would extend exponentially with the advent of Kraftwerk, ping-ponging like PacMan into disco, into hip-hop, and basically, all dance music that relies on a driving electronic beat.

"Tales of the Supernatural"

First published in Sounds, *6 December 1975*

I was sitting in a standard hotel bedroom the other day, chewing the fat with a citizen by the name of Irmin Schmidt.

This fellow is none other than the spokesman for Can, the German group whose work might be described as semi-jazz-funk, part free-form improvisation, with a nasty tendency displayed on their recent album *Landed* to veer towards the more headache-inducing area of rock and roll.

Anyway, despite the vague reputation these gents appear to have for being roustabouts, tearaways or at any rate mildly eccentric, Schmidt sits facing me over a G-Plan coffee table looking more like my ageing German GP than anyone I've ever met, minus a few years.

Instead of the sinister shades or outlandish eye patches publicity has always decked him out with, Irmin is wearing the Teutonic equivalent of National Health specs. Quickly whipping out my own NHS specs, I proceeded to cross-question him about Can, the new album, the old albums and all the other things that came into my head.

Firstly, why have Can descended from the deliriously spiritual heights of their earlier stuff, especially their last United Artists album *Soon Over Babaluma*, to the nasty loud noises of *Landed*? Smiling beatifically, Irmin explains that you can't please all the people all of the time.

"People have been saying that *Landed* is a new rock and roll direction for us. Well, the next one may be completely different, probably will be completely different.

"On the other hand, I realise that this record seems to a lot of people more understandable, less exclusive than the ones we made before. There is something around Can which has the flavour of being avant-garde and exclusive."

Well, nobody can deny that's true, but at risk of being labelled as a member of what Irmin described as the "exclusivity", I feel obliged to hold out for the old-style Can, which I stumbled across quite by chance at the movies. I was sitting there, watching a very good film called *Alice in the Cities* from Germany, and when the credits came up I registered that all those ethereal sounds that had been regaling my ears for the last hour and a half were courtesy of Can.

Falsely or not, my introduction to Can had linked them somehow in my mind with what seemed, from the distant fastness of Battersea, like a new lease of life for German culture. That is to say, everywhere you look, art movie houses and even Sunday evening TV are showing these great new German films by guys like R.W. Fassbinder, Wim Wenders (who made *Alice in the Cities*), Werner Herzog, etc.

Add to that a growth of articles, like the sprouting of a chin full of teenage acne, on the subject of something called "krautrock" – a genre whose satellite apparently hove into view at the same time as the films (i.e. at the dawn of this decade) – and it all adds up to something looking suspiciously like a "Cultural Revival".

"You're wrong," says Irmin Schmidt, and gives a wistful chuckle. "There are quite a lot of people who have good ideas, brilliant ideas, but actually it doesn't show in Germany. It shows in France or England but not in Germany. And a lot of them are leaving Germany. I'm not especially excited about living in Germany – I'd like to leave, too.

"But what's happening in Germany now, nobody really dares to put his finger on. For twenty years we got rid of culture. It wasn't just towns that were bombed. Culture was bombed, too. And you can't rebuild culture."

As I believe I mentioned before, Can have a reputation for being heavies of one kind or another. Apart from that boring old rock star mythology of ripping Lamborghinis apart with your bare teeth, throwing your kidney-shaped swimming pool into your hotel room and setting the receptionist on fire. Can have some kind of aura, a mystique about being Scanners of the Skies, advance guard of a new long-haired breed of Nietzschean superheroes playing bass by thought-wave control.

Well, chums, it's all true! Every word of it! And I can prove it! But more of that later. Let's stick with Irmin's words of wisdom for the nonce.

"We play differently from all other groups who compose sounds, then rehearse them and go into the studio and record them. We have no piece composed before we go into the studio. We go into the studio and kind of improvise. Nothing is ever planned, overdubbing, anything.

"When the recording's finished, the piece is finished. It wasn't existent (sic) before.

"It's the same thing on stage. Nothing is planned. We use a lot of – what is the word? – telepathy. That sounds somehow like the usual promotion mystics but it is not the case. Now, after seven years, this telepathy is part of daily life.

"It sounds strange but in this group, everybody is a telepath. Potentially everybody is. It needs acceptance first and then, like everything else, it needs training.

"For me there's nothing specially mysterious about telepathy. It's something that happens to everybody every day. If you're looking for somebody's phone number and they call, that's telepathy. They call it coincidence but it's telepathy.

"At the moment, this tension in the new record makes it different from *Babaluma*. We haven't felt anything like it since *Monster Movie* (the group's first album). You get to a certain level of telepathy and you have to take the next step. That's what I call a crisis point. That's the basis of creativity – it's always crisis. I take the word crisis as something very positive.

"Now, either we'll take that next step or we'll break up. I don't see the end of the breaking down of the walls between people. You get to that kind of level, you know, where all living things are one . . ."

Well, I promised earlier that I'd regale you with my incontrovertible proofs of that ol' black, white or whatever magic on the part of Can. I might as well tell you right now that while this magic made for a very interesting interview for me, it means an inaccurate one for you.

This is what happened: Irmin and I were getting into the headier waters of the cosmos in our idle Thursday afternoon chat. Being always hotfoot for something new and exciting to think about in the bath and suchlike, I pressed him eagerly for titillating stories of the world beyond the veil, otherwise known as peculiar things, to please the jaded palate of my worldly-wise readers.

Now, at the start of this interview, Irmin had barely woken up, having only returned from a gig in Brighton in the wee small hours and risen shortly before my arrival. Being confronted by a tape recorder when the day has only just dawned can be an arduous experience, as proved by the fact that at the start of the interview, Irmin makes every point at least four times in case I didn't get it. Know what I mean – out of it?

The level in the bottle of white wine, which I neglected to mention, stood next to the tape recorder on the G-Plan table, dropped steadily. Irmin grew more loquacious but was still hesitant about discussing the wonder of the unknown.

As he explained to me: "It is not good to talk about these things if you cannot control them."

Right on! Just like H.P. Lovecraft says (paraphrasing desperately from Charles Dexter Ward here): "Never call up that which you cannot put down." So true.

We did it and we failed.

I scored about five juicy anecdotes of the preternatural powers of Can in general, and Irmin and Michael Karoly (guitar) in particular. I was leaving the hotel, rubbing my hands in glee, when I thought I'd listen to some of the tape, just for kicks.

The tape was blank!

Right from when we started getting into the really heavy shit, ya dig, nothing. *Niente*, *nada* and *nichts*. Overwhelmed and not a little put out by my discovery, I sprinted upstairs to Michael's room, where I found Irmin resigned rather than surprised.

"See," he explained gently, "I told you I shouldn't be talking about these things. I'm very sorry but what can I do? I didn't realise my power was that strong . . ."

Especially that early in the morning, I added grimly to myself.

Anyway, once the shock of the mystic touching my life was over, I made a few jottings. So here, in my own words (which for the sake of narrative we'll pretend are Irmin's), is the Hot Poop:

1. "I was lying on my bed one day, when I decided to see how much I could control my heartbeat. I made it go slower, and slower, and slower, and suddenly I thought to myself that if I decided to, I could stop my heart, and then I would die. As soon as I thought of that, I lost control completely and suffered a heart attack."
2. "Our studio at Cologne is in the middle of the country and in the village nearby there is – what do they call it? – a village idiot. Though if anybody called him an idiot I would be very annoyed. One day Michael was playing guitar and he was wearing earphones. You couldn't hear anything at all – the sound was going straight into his ears. This man was chopping wood outside the studio and suddenly we noticed that he was chopping in a very peculiar rhythm, and sometimes he would stop and then start again, in these peculiar patterns. Then we noticed that he was stopping and looking confused when Michael didn't play for a moment, and then he'd start when Michael started. I put on some earphones and found that he was actually chopping in perfect time with what Michael was improvising on guitar – and it was impossible to actually hear a note."

Buzzing.

3. "Again in the studio, we had an old organ that always made a most peculiar buzzing noise whenever it was switched on. One day Michael became so annoyed with it that he went over and commanded it to stop the noise at once. It stopped! We were all very surprised and so Michael tried the command again, this time saying: 'Start the noise!' The noise started up straight away and Michael carried on ordering it to stop and start and it always obeyed instantly. Since that afternoon it hasn't stopped buzzing ever again."

Gentle readers, you may dismiss all the above if you wish, although you'd certainly be banishing the element of mystery if you did so.

But there ain't no gainsaying that right from the time we started to discourse on the unknown, my cassette player stopped recording. You could come round and listen to it, but with cassettes the price they are today, I'll probably have to do another interview over the top before you read this.

Well, that's fate.

Northern Soul

For a southerner – moi – penetrating the very particular world of Northern Soul, unfathomable and impenetrable to outsiders, required a passport to its enclosed, almost hermetic, milieu. Thanks to my editor at Black Music, *Tony Cummings, I temporarily infiltrated the ranks of this UK equivalent of* Saturday Night Fever. *Northern Soul means essence of authenticity – a true example of a time, a place, a sound, a people's movement, combusting and crystalizing into a unique and heady scene that is still being renewed.*

"The Road to Wigan Casino"

First published in New Musical Express, *11 October 1975*

Oop North, they don't like London journalists snooping about. Still, this was a special occasion at the shrine of the "Northern Soul Scene".

The young boy sitting cross-legged on the edge of the stage looked as if he was about to throw up.

It was 4.30 a.m. at the Wigan Casino. He looked as if he should have been in bed hours ago, but here he was, gazing plaintively up at slick cabaret master Tommy Hunt, as if the suavely dressed black man held the answer to all of adolescence's traumas.

You see, the jam-packed Edwardian-style venue that is the Wigan Casino has seen many, many events in its time, but nothing as strange as the weirdo phenomenon of Northern Soul. Wherein many youngsters, mostly of Anglo-Saxon origin, assemble at 12.30 on a Saturday night/Sunday morning, intent on forgetting the frowstiness of an existence that in weekdays consists of a boring dead-end job, or no job and no money.

They forget it all, submerge their sorrows in a whirlpool of high-energy activity, dancing the night away to singles long since forgotten by everyone except possibly the artists concerned. Singles that, good or bad, are the losers of the record world.

They are resurrected from the mouldering vaults of warehouses in Chicago or junk shops in Bury, Lancs., to live again as the focal point in the lives of thousands of northern working-class kids.

And the Wigan Casino is the temple of the hopes and desires of this race who seem (at least to this outsider) to find little or no satisfaction outside the steaming world of the dance floor.

It all begins in the fish and chip shop next door to the Casino, facing the Wigan ABC – probably the only chippy in the country to open up for custom at 11.30 p.m. and shut again at 2 a.m. It's crammed full of youthful Wiganites and the atmosphere is electric over the Hall's meat and potato pies. Also served is that peculiarly northern delicacy: squashed processed peas in gravy. Even in the interests of journalistic science I didn't bring myself to have a bash at the peas. But I hear they are good.

There's a small fortune to be made for some enterprising bag manufacturer wanting to break into the Northern Soul market. Everyone, but everyone, lugs around hefty portmanteaus emblazoned with badges and stickers with mottoes like "Major Lance – The Torch Lives" and other cryptic codes. You need them if you've hitched from Huddersfield or Reading, if not for a change of undies, then for the singles you hope to sell, swap or merely hear blasting over the speakers in a glow of possession.

All of the fans are extremely smartly dressed, no matter how far the journey or how uncomfortable the pilgrimage. Fellas are invariably kitted out with a singlet to sweat through, a pully to put on to prevent double pneumonia when you leave the Casino dripping hot into the nippy Wigan morn and, judging from the traditional aroma, at least three spray cans of Brut.

Tonight, the excitement is particularly intense. The first ever Wigan all-nighter was held two years ago to the day, designed to fill the gap left by the closure of the all-nighters at the legendary Torch in Stoke and the equally legendary Twisted Wheel in Manchester.

The fact that the Casino took off with a bang is borne out tonight by the number of punters prepared to queue for hours in a remorseless drizzle on the off-chance of getting one of the 500 tickets left for door sales – the other 1,500 sold out a fortnight before.

The representative from Spark Records (one of the only companies geared wholly to Northern Soul and proud purveyors of Wigan's

Ovation), himself a Northern singles producer, said with awe: "They murder each other trying to get in."

A comment like that is like a red flag to a bull for an ace cub reporter, isn't it? I immediately charged for the entrance, only to be pushed back by a solid horde of lads who once out of the rain were in no way going to be manoeuvred in the direction of the street. A surly bouncer gave me the once-over – "An' wot do you think you're doing?" etc. – so playing safe I nabbed an unsuspecting youth.

"So tell me, what's it like out there?" I ask conversationally. "Are they murdering each other to get in?"

"Not at all, nothing like that," responds the fresh-faced lad. Then, suspiciously: "Are you a journalist?"

I'm forced to concede. And he produces an NUJ card of his own. Would you believe, a journalist who's also a Northern Soul fan! Who actually lives the life! In the company of my new-found guide, I check out the upstairs cloakroom – a secluded spot where a steady stream of bedraggled Young England is forcing its way into the Casino free of charge via the roof, in a spirit of adventure worthy of Biggles himself.

Got to admire the initiative of these young people. They all seemed to be suffering from mild abrasions of one sort or another, but spirits rode high despite all.

"Well, you don't want to pay, do ya?" explains a well-turned-out youth. "I've been coming here ever since it first opened. Stopped coming here, mind, when all those journalists from London came down and it all got commercialised. And look at them now" – gesturing at a hapless youngster – "he ought to be home in bed! Can't be more than fourteen!" The inference appears to be that he knows everyone has to be fourteen once, but this is ridiculous.

Back at the dance floor, a steadily shifting mosaic of dancers is already glowing and blossoming strangely in the ultraviolet light. Each dancer is moving in a private pattern of his/her own, staring fixedly at the stage, where a top Wigan DJ like Russ Winstanley or Richard Searling is spreading the word. Basically, tonight is like every soul night at the Wigan Casino. As soon as the last rock fan from the evening rock session (featuring heavy English rock) has filed out, an army of cleaners descends and makes all pristine for the 12.30 invasion. And then the kids seethe in. And then they dance.

That's the regular pattern of the evening and that's what it's like tonight but more so. 'Cos there's gonna be surprise appearances. Who is it to be? Those in the know are confidently anticipating the Chi-Lites dropping in on their way home from a nearby gig. Well, I was waiting for the Chi-Lites more than eight hours and they weren't there when I was, that's for sure.

But there was a goodly number of people there that night who couldn't have cared less, either way. Among them were the "VIPs", safely ensconced in the VIP room with lots of booze, lots of nosh, and generally lots of room for a fascinating display of the noisome infighting, bitchiness and backbiting that the individuals who consider themselves to be the controllers or guides of "the Northern Scene" love to indulge in.

This particular night saw tensions in that cosy room that led to near fisticuffs. Producers, journalists, DJs, music biz types, all circled each other warily, occasionally lunging in for a quick snap and then retreating to eye one another and lick their wounds. This intriguing parade of human behaviour took place quite independently of the spirit of Northern Soul, which as we all know is to be found on a few feet of parquet flooring.

It's refreshing to pop back and forth between the two environments. The main dancing body of the enormous Casino building is divided into three main parts: the most important is the central dance section, with its stage and gilded balcony running right round. Walking into this central section has the same kind of impact as strolling into a tropical rainforest from an air-conditioned limo.

H-O-T. And WET.

The actual walls are sweating, great drops of condensation beading every surface, backstage as well. Every move is a struggle, and attempting to cross from one side of the Casino to the other means an exhausting and dangerous voyage, comparable to circumnavigating Piccadilly Circus Tube station at the height of rush hour in a sweltering heatwave. For six hours.

The second area is Mr M's. That's where I spent the first part of the evening under exceptionally bizarre circumstances.

My colleagues and I were ushered into this slightly smaller dance area, also with a balcony complete with tables. This was when the regular patrons of the Casino were indulging in their Saturday night knees-up. As we walked in, a burly Wiganite was laying into an ugly looking bouncer: ". . . Paid my money and now they won't even serve me at the bar!" With surprising patience, the bouncer explained that there was only waitress service and two peroxide beauties led the placated Blunt Northerner to his plush chair.

If you diverted your attention from this real-life drama, your attention was bound to be caught by a personage exchanging risqué banter from the dais with the assembled Wigan punters. This was a performer in the great British tradition: a drag artiste. And a dirty drag artiste. Quite frankly, there was such a crush in the hall that it took me five minutes to decipher from whence came those naughty wisecracks. By the time I adjusted my vision to peering through people's elbows and slightly to the left of their beehive hairdos, the drag queen was slowly beginning to go through the motions of a strip. Off comes the long glove, to delirious shouts of "Get 'em off!" . . .

Cut to the same room, two hours later.

Every figure in the room appears to be straining to dance in the face of opposition of sheer numbers. The room is now "Mr M's", the oldies area of the discotheque, where by popular demand DJs like Davie Evison spin "oldies"; faves on labels like Okeh, Ric-Tic and Mirwood – now-defunct labels that specialised in a quasi-early Motown sound.

Oldies DJs tend to regard themselves in a rather pompous light as educators of the youth of the Casino, with a sacred trust to turn them on to the grand old "oldies" and open their eyes to the inadequacies of modern manufactured Northern Soul sounds such as Simon Soussan's Moog instrumentals (Soussan is a big name in Northern Soul. A former major bootlegger, he now produces artists like The Sharonettes, released on the Black Magic label).

One advantage of being an oldies DJ is financial. Most DJs simply couldn't afford to emulate Blackpool's Ian Levine – who comes from a wealthy family and may be said to have independent means – and make regular trips to the States and dig out their own fresh new Northern Soul sounds.

Mr M's keeps itself to itself and the fact of the second anniversary doesn't seem to make much difference to the oldies freaks, except there is more of 'em.

And now to the third sector of the Casino, the backstage area. This isn't like a concert hall backstage – it's another regular meeting place for the DJs and the more long-standing fans.

It was there that I met the gentleman who proved to be the only live entertainment of the soiree.

It must be a surprise to Northern Soul freaks of long-standing that it was Tommy Hunt who appeared on that momentous anniversary, because Tommy has never yet had a Northern Soul biggie. Hunt is most commonly known for having sung the original version of Bacharach's "I Just Don't Know What to Do with Myself". He also sang in The Flamingos, who cut a classic version of "I Only Have Eyes for You" (currently riding high in the charts once more by A. Garfunkel).

Since those hits, Hunt has, in this country at least, been a fine performer on the cabaret circuit, where he was singled out by Mike Walker, manager of the Wigan Casino and associate of Wigan's Ovation, and Barry Kingston, the producer of Spark Records. Hunt has a single released on Spark, a re-recording of a big Northern Sound by the late Roy Hamilton, "Crackin' Up". It is definitely among the more mediocre Northern singles.

Tommy Hunt is a super-hiply skinny dude with a neat, if familiar line in argot: "You from the *NME*? Groovy! This sure is a groovy place" et al. As soon as he hits the stage, he does a couple of neat backdrops, a few flips and contortions here and there, just to show the kids he knows where he is.

And that's when I noticed the fat little boy on the edge of the stage. He seemed to me to sum up so much of the mood of the Wigan Casino that night: a surfeit of energy, just waves and waves of untrammelled force aimed at the stage. For this lad in particular, the emotion seemed to be more than he could comfortably handle. So he looked as if all this energy was going to churn and churn inside, till it found the most convenient way of expelling itself from his body – through the mouth.

Tommy's set wasn't designed to do this boy's digestion any favours. It was one of those wham-bam-thank-you-ladies-and-gennulmen acts that doesn't leave you room to think. The relentlessness of its flow was geared to match the metabolic rates (mostly artificially induced) of his audience.

With lots of encouraging asides to his excellent band – "This is it, brothers. Give me a hand and we're gonna tear this place up!" – Tommy galloped his way through everybody's favourite black music standards: "Walk On By", "Get Ready", "My Girl", "Hang On In There Baby" and so on. The musicians moved as if wired up to an invisible metronome. The crowd was utterly, uncritically receptive as The Man delivered what sounded as if it were his regular cabaret act sped up.

The feeling of the show was very different from the last live spot I saw there, when Herb and Brenda Rooney – The Exciters – were on.

The sense of mutual adoration on that occasion was almost insufferably intense. It was more like visiting Lourdes than going to a soul night.

Meanwhile, Tommy has discarded as many layers of clothing as complies with decency ("Now I feel cool!"), has flattered the audience ("This is where it's all at!") and delivered "Just Say Goodbye" (Esther Phillips' current Northern hit) in fine voice.

Then – a shock.

Hunt sang an exquisite "Help Me Make It Through the Night". He actually apologised before starting: "I know you kids like the fast songs, but let me do one slow one and then I'll get back to your favourites." All of a sudden, here was a *SOUL* singer. The difference was alarming. It made me feel sad that such a talented performer should be scoring financially through the more second-rate aspect of his talents – Hunt's gift is more suited to bringing out the depth in a ballad-style, emotional number than to injecting expression into a fast Northern stomper.

When the ecstatic audience finally let Hunt leave the stage, he staggered on his knees, towards his buddies. The Fantasticks waiting for him in the dressing room. Jesting (I trust), he gasped "I shoulda stayed in cabaret!!" . . .

The next, and final, high point of the evening's entertainment (apart from the touching moment when various feuding soul bigwigs gathered on the stage, temporarily reunited, to cut the cake decorated with "Heart of Soul") was the *DANCE COMPETITION*!

This took me back to my youthful days watching *Ready Steady Go!*, when the best and brightest of The Cromwellian would challenge their equivalents from some other hip niterie. In this instance, the winner was such a foregone conclusion it was ridiculous – a dryad-like slip of a lad with curly blond hair and a gamin expression. Rather like the *Death in Venice* youngster, this budding heart-throb instinctively upstaged everyone by hogging the front of the stage with his startling gravity-defying twirls and spins.

Instead of just being very quick and accurate as they all were, he managed to combine that incredible speed with lots of expression and feeling. His stylised fluttering hand movements alone marked him out instantly. (Hey, any of you out there *Come Dancing* fanatics, too?)

THE WINNER!

This prodigy, in case any of you wish to seek him out (and I wouldn't blame you in the slightest), is named Danny Daniels. He asked me not to reveal his age and he works in an engineering firm, which he thinks is "great". Did he expect to win?

"No, not at all," replied the boy with heart-wringing modesty. This lad could go far.

And that, with special mention to Dave Duncan for doing well, is that.

By now, it was 8 a.m. On a regular night, the Casino would be packing up, but today, the festivities were to continue till ten o'clock. But for those of us with a journey to London ahead, enough was sufficient.

Quite a few fans had complained to me that they reckoned a lot of people there that night came just to say they'd been *THERE*. Well, so what, really . . . it was a massive, hot and steaming event. A celebration of two years of staying up late, grooving all night long and keeping the soul flag flying up there in the freezing North. All I can say is MAZEL-TOV, which, translated from the Yiddish, means, roughly: jolly good show.

Selected Second Anniversary Playlist
"Ton of Dynamite" – Frankie Crocker (Turbo)
"You Sexy Sugar Plum" – Rodger Collins (Fantasy)
"Oh Baby" – Nolan Porter (ABC)
"I Thought You Were Mine" – The Natural Four (ABC)
"This Love of Mine" – Carole Waller (USA)
"Let Me Make You Happy" – Billy Woods (Sussex)
"Do the Pearl, Girl" – The Matta Baby (Penny)
"Just Having Your Love" – The Moments (Stang)

Betty Davis

Appearing as a space-age silver archer on the cover of her 1974 LP, They Say I'm Different, *music-lovers admired Betty Davis. But she was a future female, and the environment of the times failed to provide the support her brilliance deserved.*

When Davis was teaching Miles and Jimi Hendrix how to be cool, women in the UK and the US were just starting to have the right to buy a house or car without a husband's or father's approval.

Some years after I wrote this piece, Betty did re-emerge. A fond documentary was made about her pioneering prowess. We will never know where the arrow of her trajectory might have taken her, had she enjoyed a more appreciative context: folks who understood that you can smile while being wild. Before I got a full-time writing job, I spent seven months at Island Records, where I promoted Bob Marley and Betty. She was a funny, warm delight when I promoted her Nasty Gal *album in 1975 . . . nasty – OK, if you think that the sexuality with agency she projected as part of her arsenal, is nasty – but very nice. The contradictions of what we were not yet calling the male gaze and Betty's infectious free spirit haunted me, so I grabbed the chance to re-visit our encounter, almost thirty years later.*

"Blues for Betty Davis's Smile: The Betty Davis Lacuna"

First published in Rip It Up: The Black Experience in Rock 'n' Roll, *edited by Kandia Crazy Horse. London: Palgrave Macmillan, 2003.*

The Pennsylvania woman who now has the last known telephone number of the 1970s futuristic, fire-spitting funkster Betty Davis returned my call from a hospital – an appropriately ominous locale, considering that no one in the general media/musical round seemed to know where Betty had vanished to. Registered letters were returned to sender. Word had it that the singer had reverted to her maiden name, Betty Mabry; but that moniker meant as little to the phone number's bemused inheritor as Betty's marital and stage name of Davis, relic of her short-lived, fiery marriage to jazz creator Miles Davis (1968–69; she was twenty-three, he forty-eight). Davis's legend is marked by a particular composition on *They Say I'm Different* that was generally taken to refer to their complex relationship: "He was a big freak! / I used to beat him with a turquoise chain, yeah."

Evidently Betty, the sizzling young model about town, was Miles's muse. Her beauty adorns the sleeve of Davis's *Filles de Kilimanjaro* and its haunting "Mademoiselle Mabry". She is saluted again on a later track, "Back Seat Betty", long after their split. Young enough to be his daughter, she had already scored a writing credit on The Chambers Brothers' "Uptown". Betty wasn't in her native Pittsburgh anymore. A hip scene-maker, she plugged Pops into a new generation of her super-freak pals like Sly Stone and Jimi Hendrix, briskly vetted and edited his wardrobe of suits, and generally loosened up and remodelled the maestro. The result: Miles's watershed album, *Bitches Brew* (1970), wherein Miles internalises the vibes of his trophy wife's crowd, all the young dudes like Jimi and Sly. Whether it was her extra-intimate rapport with Hendrix that caused the rift or not, it took just one year for Miles to decide, as he explained to his biographer Quincy Troupe, that "Betty was too young and wild for the things I expected of a woman. Betty was a free spirit, she was raunchy, all that kind of shit."

What manner of superwoman is this, to out-freak the notorious Master of Cool?

How deep is a footnote?

Only the most ardent funksters of the early twenty-first century recognise Betty Davis now, in the 2000s that she used to invent, way back in the 1970s. Thrashing dildo swingers in Williamsburg electroclash combos attempt to emulate (maybe without knowing it) her space princess clothes; few attempt her audio recipe of squealing, screeching, punky/funky vocalising, riding that jazzy funk itching to be free, though Macy Gray's vocals can be said to swing like Betty's baton. Cognoscenti including Labelle's manager and co-creator, Vicki Wickham, thought Davis might be in Paris; writer Tom Terrell, who'd fantasised about her since he was a schoolkid in Washington, D.C. – always a hotbed of Betty fanaticism – wondered if her life had devolved into a long round of rehab. Or, it was said Betty Davis was dead. If so, does Betty Mabry still walk among us? There's no evidence for any of it, really; only Betty Davis was deemed wild enough for anything to be possible. Anything at all. But some way or other, somewhere, somehow, the general feeling seemed to be that surely Betty Davis had been tamed by now. Or has she?

Looking for Betty Davis was an almost uncomfortable process, because while people who'd never met her were wondering about her whereabouts and mental state, I was haunted by the question: what stopped Betty Davis's smile? While waiting for feedback from various sources, the practical level of my quest ended when I came across an article by journalist James Maycock, who had actually tracked down the elusive Davis. "Poignantly, her career stalled when her fun, mischievous spirit was overcome by chronic depression following her father's death in the late 1970s," he wrote in the British newspaper the *Telegraph*. "Today one senses she lives a quieter life in Pennsylvania, although she's still passionate about music."

Still passionate. That was a relief. But her absence from the scene, with zero visibility for that smile, was still a loss that I felt. Unlike most of the others, her career was still careening to its destination. A surprisingly un-diva-like presence, the sunny young singer's sweetness and dimples charmed the Island PR office where, fresh out of Warwick University in 1975, I was promoting the then little-known Bob Marley, Burning Spear, Aswad and *Nasty Gal*, Davis's third album. I remember Betty shrieking and panting, strutting and grinding, on the small stage of Ronnie Scott's jazz club; and her silver outfit, a curious amalgam of mid-twentieth-century futurism and eighteenth-century music hall "pantomime boys" (really, girls in drag). The business with the turquoise whip for her signature tune, "He Was a Big Freak", went down well. With each slash, Davis struck something deep in the British psyche; regular public-school beatings of the junior elite were, after all, part of what made the British Empire great.

At the round table of the press office, there was much excitement about the audacious, charming Miss Davis. She graciously signed the shiny white jacket of a *Nasty Gal* test pressing for me with a fat felt tip; her signature was looped like a daisy with a butterfly for the dot on the "i". There were no press pictures, so I ordered a photo shoot and had her sassiest, sweetest, most juicy smile printed up as black-and-white 8x10" glossies. Her Afro rippled round her dimples like a candyfloss halo. Proudly, I pulled open the box for her manager. To all of our amazement, he dramatically ripped one up. "Destroy them," he urged. "Lose the negs." "But look at that great smile," I stuttered. "That's the problem," he insisted. "She looks too nice. Betty has to look mean."

He watched me jettison the photos – though somewhere in a storage, a couple of rogue pics may still lurk, obstinately chronicling her lethal blend of blithe innocence, carnality and dark wit. It was offensive, his disbelief that a smiling young woman could shout and sweat hardcore funk to her bones. In a cocksure, muscular music, for Davis to be authentic and accepted, glowering was apparently compulsory. But after all, when Davis whipped Miles, if that was indeed the case, he'd no doubt asked for it. And by the sound of it, enjoyed the whole process.

I felt bleak as I systematically worked through two hundred 8x10s, like I was destroying the image of one of her most potent aspects as an artist – and as a female. Her smile was an invitation, and also a tool, and if necessary, a weapon in her defence. But that was all invisible to her manager, who reckoned she – we – couldn't smile and be wild. Playing the savage beast card had become part of Betty's MO by now; though really, she hadn't been all that animal or even outrageously wild. She just sang, vibrantly, what many a female feels on a Friday night, and did, exuberantly, what came naturally, her lust for life unrestrained by the girdle of anyone's expectations.

But there it was – her passion for being had to be characterised as angry and wild. She had to be *l'enfant sauvage*. Or she wasn't allowed to be free. Was her stirring of deep psychosexual fantasies less effective if she was smiling, not snarling? Personally, it seemed to me that a slap would have no less stinging if delivered with Betty's sunny grin.

Those flying fragments of Betty's beaming photos fluttered into my mind some ten years later as I rattled down fourteen floors in an elevator in an old building in Manhattan's Union Square, from the loft of singer Grace Jones's Svengali and husband, visual visionary Jean-Paul Goude.

Wearing an electric-blue lame hot pant one-piece, Jones huddled against the wall sobbing all the way down. Some months after doing Davis's PR, I'd become a full-time writer and I was now on assignment for London's *Harpers & Queen*, covering Jones's glamorous life with Goude. She, too, was a great man's muse. Goude's indelible, iconic interpretations of her lean, gleaming ebony torso summoned both the panther he saw in her and the gazelle; the Giacometti and the Benin mask. Above all, she exuded the Amazon energy that would later serve her well as the deadly nemesis in action flicks. Given her impermeable image, I was slightly surprised by Jones's volcanic freak-out. Her lack of inhibition in front of an unknown writer was alarming, but also disarming.

Of course, Jones was the co-conspirator of her own image manipulation: ringing endless variations on Sheena the Jungle Woman. A champion national long-distance runner in her teenage years in Jamaica, Jones was as athletic as the big cats she channelled. Any warm-blooded mammal would have been partial to that snarl of hers.

But though Grace was able to work and cash in on that leopard-spotted persona for years to come, I never forgot her in that elevator, moaning between deep sobs, "He only wants me to be an animal!"

Meaning being that she just wanted, at least every now and then, to be wild – with a smile. Because it wasn't being mad or bad, being wild. It just felt free.

Which brings us back to Betty.

As slender as her petite yet sturdy frame, Davis's recorded output consists of just four albums: *Betty Davis* (1973), *They Say I'm Different* (1974), *Nasty Gal* (1975), and *Crashin' From Passion/Hangin' Out in Hollywood* (1995/6; rec. 1979). The first two, in particular, are blazing entries from the psychological subtext of a free-spirited female, born in 1945, riding high out of the 1960s decade of the pill and free love, into the infinite possibilities of the 1970s – before the actual costs had come in and been counted, with the shock of herpes, then AIDS, in the early 1980s. It was in that brief window – post-pill, pre-AIDS – that girls generally began to claim the right to be as wild as the boys, to wo/manhandle love where they found it, at their own (in)discretion. "I said I'm wigglin' my fanny [. . .] If I'm in luck I just might get picked up" Though sensitive, these women were tough enough to handle rejection and choose solitude rather than half-arsed compromise: "Tonight I wish I had someone beside me [. . .] But in the meantime I'll make do with what I have."

Davis represented a break from all the singers who came before her. She was no big, grieving blues mama like Bessie Smith, nor a tragic goddess like Billie Holiday. Equally, she wasn't an elegantly gowned church lady, like Aretha Franklin. Even her closest archetype, the rockin' Miss Tina Turner, that perennial hot chick, didn't dabble in Davis's outré extremism. Perhaps only Labelle, glittering in their own galactic silver, with their sexed-up songs like "Going Down (Makes Me Shiver)", matched her in voracious, untrammelled life energy on their records; and there were three of them. Betty was solo. Perhaps too solo.

Says Labelle's Nona Hendryx, who still travels with Betty Davis's music in her headphones, "We had a strong black following, from the Apollo; Labelle had a community. Betty didn't, because she came right out of the box, fully formed."

You can hear courage in the way Davis worked her vocal register – ratcheting her pretty alto into a drilling, grating vibrato and an off-the-meter soprano screech – suggesting a woman pushing herself to extremes, testing her mental and physical endurance, refusing to accept limits. "Game Is My Middle Name," she boldly announced; and Davis sure did know how to play with the big boys. In her prime, she was backed by musicians who were the architects of the full-blooded, grinding West Coast 1970s funk, a music unafraid of intensity and the surreal. The elite sidemen from Sly Stone's band, Greg Errico and Larry Graham (the latter would later join forces with Davis' natural heir, Prince); Santana's Michael Carabello; the Pointer Sisters, and a sprinkling of Tower of Power members. They all supported Betty as she riffled through the deck of superwoman archetypes and added a few more bad cards: swathed in gold, she was one sexy Egyptian mummy; poised for flight in silver, she was a space-age huntress, Davis as the goddess Diana.

Davis's musical reputation is primarily based on her eponymous debut and its successor: *They Say I'm Different*. There, she paraded the brutal realism of her take on love on tracks like "Anti Love Song": ". . . I don't wanna love you [. . .] 'Cause you know I could possess your body too." But during the *Nasty Gal* period in which I threw away Betty Davis's smile, her songs began to be obsessed with stating and reasserting her position. It was as if she had succumbed and adopted tabloid values, agreeing that by virtue of being exuberant, sexual and confrontational, she was not just lusty, but "shocking", "outrageous"; and that her success depended on it. On her next and to-date final release, *Crashin' from Passion*, aka *Hangin' Out in Hollywood*, she experimented with more conventional pop/dance forms that didn't play to her strengths, like the mutant aspects of her shapeshifting singing.

Throughout this search for Betty Davis's smile, there is the nagging sense that she was a woman without a context. Her shows were banned by religious groups in certain American towns and many of her catchier tracks were too specifically sexual for radio. So many young lions are chewed up and spat out by the music business's greedily grinding maw; what does one silver space-suited lioness matter? But a large lacuna has been left by the absence of Betty's forceful, raspy-voiced, strong-thighed, sassy spirit.

The outrageousness of rap artists like Lil' Kim seems closest to Davis's template; but their infinite varieties of fetish gear suggest a specific, calculated correlation between flesh showed and money earned, pandering to male/femme fantasies, aiming to please to squeeze a few dollars more. But when Betty sings that people think she's different, she's not talking about her barely there outfits. She just likes to wear them and look good. Instead, she boldly claims her place as a daughter of the blues, and references Bessie and Lead Belly, not Gucci and Pucci.

To quote Betty herself – "Don't you call her no tramp, no skeezer." And so, don't call Betty no ho.

CHAPTER 2

And Then Came Punk

I remember the onslaught of punk time as zany, dodgy, sped up (as we so often were). Almost a slapstick *Carry On* film when anything went and usually did. The old pre-Second World War certainties were crumbling like a heap of fairy gold shattering to ash. Empire, gone; colonies, gone; jobs, gone; pound, devalued; IRA bombs, imminent; expectations, nebulous to none, not now. We were all caught up in what seemed the imminent collapse of everything, as a vortex of global forces, including the oil crisis, combined to snatch up our former "normal" and whirl it up into the ominous atmosphere.

Homework was done by candlelight. Garbage mountains rose uncollected in the streets. Our reckless, sometimes feckless existence was made possible by the dole and squatting. Many heady sensations gripped us, as the demands of the time seemed to be finishing the work of the 1960s in eliminating the dead hand of Britain's class structure (as if). This exhilaration was amped as we suffered none of that puritanical shame about sex that Americans seemed to suffer from, certainly in the Riot Grrrl time.

For me, the meaning of punk was always inclusion, communal action and, above all, at last, the start of a space for women, which still needs to be wider and deeper. The patriarchal types were right to bitch, as though their hold continues to endure. The first female-friendly cracks in the old boys' citadel wall were being drilled by punk. With collusion from friendly men, women were storming the parapets while the dodgy blokes tried to pull up the drawbridge . . . a tussle that continues to this day.

Instead, in this scribe's memory the punk explosion was a years-long rampaging party borne along by weed and speed and righteous indignation and revolutionary activism and let's-implode-all-music energy. The central tenet was always DIY – do it yourself – which was why hardcore punks were annoyed when the manager of The Clash, Malcolm McLaren's good friend, signed them to the multinational CBS. McLaren, however, exulted in playing labels off against one another, though the band themselves had no input or knowledge of his Machiavellian strategies and remained prey to his shameless manipulation. The following is a vignette from their saga.

Sex Pistols

The strained atmosphere at this press conference, which I tried to liven up, may have predicted the way the Sex Pistols' A&M deal, which was signed on 9 March 1977, would be terminated with a settlement on 16 March. Yet again, the Pistols were thought to be too hot to handle. The band barely got to play, ever, as their image was deemed so shocking that almost every gig was cancelled.

When we meet, bassist Sid Vicious has now been introduced to the band, replacing the one "melodic" musician, Glenn Matlock. Just two years later, Sid's fate – dying in New York having accidentally killed the love of his life, Nancy Spungen – would forever haunt the other members; he had been Johnny Rotten's close friend since school days. Malcolm McLaren's manipulation was great for sensation and attracting cash, but tough on the humans he was trying to play like chess.

"Sex Pistols: For Queen and Country"
First published in Sounds, *19 March 1977*

Vivien Goldman trades insults at a strange press conference.

"Don't I know you from somewhere?" Johnny Rotten enquired suspiciously. He leant forwards over the table, his face in the semi-permanent screw so beloved of Fleet Street photographers. "Oh yeah. Given any good parties lately?"

It was a press conference at a Big London Hotel, to mark the Pistols' signing to A&M Records. Plush neutrality, neutral chairs, neutral carpet, seemed to squeal in mute protest at this conspicuously guttersnipe invasion, as the Pistols slouched, lurched, slumped and generally did everything the Emily Post book of etiquette expressly tells you not to do behind a G-Plan teak job.

When I arrived, the press conference was eunuch limp. The usual gaggle of foreign and national press sat decorously in neat rows.

Johnny and the lads were obviously wearying of the trembling hacks' questions with stock responses.

"This music's meant to be fun," Johnny was spouting dutifully, making a brave attempt to keep talkin' in the face of overwhelming culture gap communication problems.

My colleague Giovanni Dadomo (the "D" is silent as in "devil") was in attendance, looking agreeably saturnine in his red leather bomber jacket. He enquired about the emergence of a Pistols' album.

"It'll be out soon," Johnny stated definitely, "in time for you to slag it off in *Sounds*, Gio, like I know you're going to."

That was the high point of the conversation as far as I can judge. From then on the repartee slumped to silence. About time this convention was put onto a more meaningful level of communication, I thought to myself.

"May I ask a question? Has joining the Sex Pistols improved your sex life?"

That was when Johnny started riffling through the index cards of his mental computer and finally located punch card 98.6, which refers to New Year's Night 1976, when I very politely asked Sid Vicious to leave my party (to which, incidentally, he hadn't been invited).

It's not that I'm inhospitable, but Sid's image blew it for him – when he walked through the door, the bred'ren who were unpacking the sound system clocked his swastikas, studs, leathers and raffishly thug mien, and started packing the system up again in double-quick time. It was a simple choice: welcome the uninvited Sid or have a party. You'd have done the same thing.

"None that I've invited you to, Johnny," I replied sweetly. The band were obviously exhilarated at having something, *ANYTHING*, to break the deadly monotony of the conference. Enthusiastically, Sid yelled, "SCUMBAG!" in my direction, while Johnny frantically worked out how many words of abuse he could hurl and started hurlin'.

My moment of glory, what can I tell you. Even the foreign press asked me what was going on. I mean, how often do journalists get a chance of notoriety? There weren't any blokes from the *Daily Express* around at the Roxy the night Sid tried to smash a (plastic) glass in my face to make us quits . . .

Anyway, joining the band has obviously done wonders for Sid's state of mind. He bounded up to me afterwards, beaming as he offered me a swig of vodka.

"Let's have a reconciliation," he offered handsomely. "Look, I'll give you a plectrum – not that one, that's special, but I've got another you can have . . ." He started searching through various black items of clothing, inadvertently opening his flies even further (red 'n' blue stripes, if you're interested in fashions in gents' undergarments), but failed to locate the missing item. No matter – was it Shakespeare or John Peel who said it's the thought that counts?

Sid even went so far as to give me hot tips on How to Play Bass the Pistols Way (I play strictly rockers, y'all), which involves holding three fingers of the left hand in an unwieldy clump, aiming at a sound in which you can't differentiate one note from another. The old white noise technique.

Not bad for three weeks . . .

Sid: *[indignantly] I've been playing eight or nine months!*
Vivien: *But I thought Malcolm McLaren said you've been playing three weeks! [He did. Got it on tape, too.]*
Sid: *Oh, that's just publicity stuff. You mustn't tell anyone.*
Vivien: *You kidding me? Being an accomplished musician is something to be proud of and your many fans deserve to know. It's even more relevant than the colour of your knickers. [Anyway, it did my heart good to see Sid in such fine spirits.] Seems to me you're more fulfilled since joining the band.*
Sid: *Suppose so. It's more fun than being on the dole. I mean, I actually have a bit of money now. Not much, but more than the dole . . .*
Vivien: *How much d'ya get? Are you all on a wage?*
Sid: *I can't speak for the others, but I get £25.*
Vivien: *That to cover your rent 'n' everything?*
Sid: *[flatly] I don't live anywhere.*

Aha, a homeless wanderer . . .

Homeless wanderers the Pistols might be, but they're having a good time. Paul Cook, John and Sid were gleefully hamming it up round the room, capping each other's insults with a vivacity that flashed me back to the playground in a trice.

"Spotty!" Paul yelled at Sid.

"Baldy!" Sid shouted energetically back.

"BLACKHEAD-Y!" trumpeted Paul triumphantly, thrilled at the deflowering virgin insult. "Look at 'im, he's covered in 'em."

Reluctantly, I examined Sid's complexion. Yup, the requisite smattering of trendy teenage acne and yup, some blackheads freckling a face that's actually good-looking, though Sid doesn't appear to want the world to find out.

What can you expect when the poor lad doesn't even have a roof over his head?

You can't expect him to lug a bottle of pHisohex round with him wherever he goes, can you? It's only recently that Sid's had any form of steady diet, it would appear.

"Eggs 'n' chips three times a day," he muttered fervently. "It's heaven."

It was only with difficulty that I restrained myself from offering to supply him with automatically refillable thermoses of chicken soup for the road.

Meanwhile, the press conference had well and truly degenerated around us. Johnny was engrossed in a chat with Giovanni. I called over, "Enjoy the press conference, John?"

"Course not. It was dreadful. If you came in here expecting anything else, forget it."

Well, why did you do it then? I thought the whole point about the Pistols was they did what they wanted to do.

"Why?"

Johnny tailed off. Stunned into silence.

"Well . . . I'm stuck . . . *WHY NOT*?" he offered, hot to re-gain lost ground.

Well, there's a million things that are more fun to do on a Thursday a.m. . . . anyway, I could give you a point-by-point description of our verbal sparring match, but Johnny wasn't much of an opponent that morning. Probably worn out by the conference. I can dig it.

Later, I watched the Pistols tumble into the waiting limousine, giggling hysterically as they showered the grovelling Fleet Street photographers with champagne. Some people just love to be humiliated, and some people dig doin' it.

The Clash

The Manichean duality of the Beatles and The Rolling Stones in the 1960s was reflected in the next decade by the rambunctious Sex Pistols and the somewhat more sophisticated The Clash, with their agit-prop pop politics stencilled on their combat gear. (The Sex Pistols, on the other hand, were dressed in garments they would previously only have been able to steal from McLaren and Westwood's pricey transgressive clothing line at the SEX shop on King's Road, where they met.) The role of the French in promoting punk is often forgotten, but this chaotic show was significant in the development of the movement and, for some musicians, marked their first trip beyond Britain. The P.S. is a reminder that despite the popularity of Can and krautrock, "edgy" post-war racial jokes still bubbled shamelessly on the surface.

"Clash in Euro-Rock Horror"

First published in Sounds, *20 August 1977*

"Bilzen? more like Belsen"
Clash, Damned: Bilzen Festival, Belgium

The Clash have a tendency to attract trouble wherever they go. Not because they're malicious troublemakers, but because there's something about their stance that authority can't tolerate.

Latest event happened last Thursday, at the Bilzen Jazz Festival in Belgium. Normally a staid trad jazzers bop, this year Bilzen were presenting their first ever punk night featuring Elvis Costello, The Damned and The Clash.

The audience were mostly hippies, with a sparse front line of punks who'd picked up on the fact that the iconography of today's teen rebels includes safety pins stuck through the ear, from the media.

In front of the stage there was a wide press enclosure, with a few press rattling round inside. Then there was a big barricade, a fence of (barbed?) wire. Behind that fence, the kids were enclosed, scrabbling to get a decent view of the bands. Elvis Costello commented on the obvious stupidity of the arrangement, while backstage The Clash and The Damned were laying bets about who were going to get the fences down first.

As to the kids – every time one of them whacked at the fence, one of the exceptionally heavy security thugs would literally slap them in the face . . .

The Damned onstage commented bitterly: "This looks more like Belsen than Bilzen." They were right.

The kids began throwing things, out of sheer frustration. As the guards' hostility grew more brutal, the missiles the kids hurled into the press pit grew more dangerous. From empty beer cans to full, from pebbles to rocks to bricks.

When The Clash started their set, the kids aimed at the stage, desperate to make their presence felt, desperate to get through, break down the barriers. Joe's guitar was ruined. Paul Simonon got hit by a brick on the shoulder and his cabinet busted.

"Halfway through the set I got a brick right through my cabinet – it's a drag 'cos it cost quite a bit of money. But we finished the whole set. We had to stop during 'Police & Thieves' 'cos Joe jumped down into the press pit 'cos guards with helmets were hitting the kids with barbed wire. We wanted them to pull down the barricades 'cos it was just like a prison camp with all that barbed wire fence round," said Paul Simonon, back in the safety of London.

"I was just onstage with all these things coming over . . . but it's different when you're there onstage with people watching you. You're there to do something and you get such a tremendous feeling, you feel like a god, 'cos you've got control over so many people who want to see you play. You feel invincible even when the bricks are coming over . . ."

After the fighting broke out during "Police & Thieves" (remember – ain't no such thing as coincidence), The Clash carried on into a crackling "Hate & War". One of those moments in music history when the medium and the message actually fused and ignited. It may have been just as well that, despite Joe Strummer's efforts, the fence stayed up. The security guards were waiting just behind the barriers, out to kill.

The worldwide CBS deal with The Clash means that they're the international messengers of punk, bearing the movement into virgin territory as a matter of course.

Hence the band hopped over to Bremen to appear on Germany's answer to *Top of the Pops*, *Musikladen*. After a series of mishaps involving missed planes and a day of frustrating waits at various airports (bearing in mind The Clash get stopped and searched at every checkpoint, just on looks), the band arrived in Germany. The CBS rep warned them in the taxi going to the studio that punks were absolutely unknown; this TV appearance was the first. *Musikladen* appears six times a year. It's a big family spectacular, this show featuring Paul Nicholas, Tina Charles, Dana and The Clash.

Rehearsal time. The band were gleeful at being on TV for the first time, enjoying running through their numbers on a platform up against a backdrop studded with 45s, go-go dancers shimmying in ironic visual counterpoint.

Back to the hotel, where they were informed that programme director Mike Leckebusch had decided to throw them off the show.

Reasons: reputedly that the band were late (through no fault of their own – they'd been held up in a traffic jam), because they didn't mime properly (the band had been having fun knowing it was a run-through after a day of waiting around in airports) and because the dressing room was left in a mess (total damage: two broken beer bottles that fell off a table).

Paul Simonon summed it all up: "The bloke just didn't think we were respectable. It's really mad. He just didn't know what punk was."

Incidentally, Dana, Paul Nicholas and co. were all for The Clash and were outraged at their abrupt dismissal. Some people stick to the theory that Leckebusch had mistimed the show in the first place and when he discovered his miscalculation, decided to lop it to length by using The Clash as a scapegoat.

Watch this space for more manifestations of what really goes on when the two sevens clash . . .

PS: Showaddywaddy, who were also scheduled to appear on *Musikladen*, missed the entire rehearsal through being held up at the airport with currency problems, but appeared on TV nonetheless. Very interesting. Also, The Clash were kicked out of their German hotel. The manager wasn't happy about Joe drawing little moustaches on the men on the beer mats . . .

Public Image Ltd

Public Image Ltd defined post-punk, which succeeded punk's primitive thrash with more jagged, experimental, unpredictable aspirations. Feeling exploited by Malcolm McLaren, still bruised by the death of his old friend Sid, John attempted to create a new paradigm for artists in the industry. Good luck, chum! But PiL did help bring a change of weather to our musical climate.

As I write in the mid 2020s, people discuss mental health and the strains of being in a rock band. Sid Vicious, whom we met earlier, was already dead when PiL formed, but his ghostly presence would always hover over everyone close to him; reading this article again today, guitarist Keith Levene's depression is beyond cynicism. Jeannette Lee seems to be the only "sane" or together member, and she went on to become one of the most influential figures in the music business as a partner in Rough Trade. Yet the Metal Box *LP PiL had just released articulated all that made post-punk so healthily provocative, challenging all that had gone before. There is a built-in poignancy to our fetishization of endlessly alighting on the (impossible) new. If light needs dark to exist, so PiL needed regular rock 'n' roll to define them by their resistance to it.*

Quick notes – the Matumbi casually name-dropped here is the band of legendary dubwize producer, Dennis Bovell, of the Jah Sufferer sound system, and Linton Kwesi Johnson, who we will meet here soon. And a word on Wobble, the bass player who replaced Sid. Wobble was a prankster, but he was alright, really. Nowadays, Wobble said in an email, he is a Buddhist and believes women and men are equal.

"The Meaning Behind the Moaning"

First published in Melody Maker, *8 December 1979*

The Public Image Ltd collective tell Vivien Goldman that they want their existence to be "the proof that you can have it on your own terms".

"Well I don't believe it! It's Johnny Rotten, as I live and breathe!" The woman's hair was piled on top of her head in an elaborate Mao-chic coiffure. She was painted and polished to a high gloss. She laughed, a high, nervous tinkle. She didn't stop to say hello but swept on down to the far end of the restaurant. Not far enough, though, to have avoided hearing "Shut up, you stupid old boot!" and "What are you talking about, you prat?" echoing cheerfully behind her from the assembled PiL company.

Inevitable, I suppose, that it should be John the woman chose to comment on. At the same table was PiL's bass player Jah Wobble, in many ways a more colourful character, certainly more extrovert than the man they used to call Johnny Rotten in another time and another place, with a different face . . .

Why, everyone had to be on their best behaviour that night, because it hadn't been long since PiL had been allowed back into this excellent Indian restaurant up the road from PiL's HQ after Wobble pissed into a few pint mugs he'd just emptied.

"It took us a year to get back in," groans John. "Watch it, Wobble, will ya?"

Wobble's antics are notorious. Until he found himself in a position to channel his awesome manic-depressive energy into formulating some of the most original basslines in modern music, he spent his time being a terror. The high-quality mugshot on Dennis Morris' original album cover for *First Issue*, PiL album number one, does some justice to his matinée-idol good looks – Wobble wouldn't look out of place in a brocade dressing gown, in a lounge lizard vein. But no photo can do justice to those manic light blue eyes, all innocence as Wobble utters another whopper.

We were both watching Matumbi at The Music Machine a couple of weeks ago, when Wobble took time out to tell me that he's a vegetarian these days and a feminist. Wobble says it's the last year that's made him see the light, ever since he was disappointed in love, and – hey, Wobble, you can't expect me to believe all this! Still, you can't never tell, eh?

"Honestly, Viv, it makes me really sick. That's one thing I can't stand, seeing all my mates treat women as objects. I used to be like that too, really disgusting."

Wobble has the rap well down. He explains to me how every man has a bit of woman in them and vice versa. How the world would be a better place if everyone felt what it was like to be the other sex and so on. Everything plausible, everything eminently sensible and – almost – credible.

With Wobble's light china eyes staring fully and oh-so-frankly into yours, it's sometimes difficult to remember that it's not lies, it's not even fibs, hardly. Wobble simply embroiders the truth instinctively, just to make it a bit more interesting.

For all I know, Wobble may be an ardent feminist – though if so, why does he crack jokes about finding women to work for him on a street level? Or maybe he's only kidding.

He's a good lad, our Wobble, and one thing I'm certain – positive – about is that he's one of the most inventive, hardest white bassies working today, as one listen to the solid-state swirl of his bassline on *Metal Box*'s "Poptones" will tell you. A bassline to drown in and to sing at the bus stop too, as is the bassline on the next formidable track "Careering". All on the indispensable second side of the three 12-inch box set. Hear and you will believe.

Wobble is also the author of three solo singles released on Virgin. The first, "Dreadlock Don't Deal in Wedlock", is toasted over a backing track by Wayne Jobson of Native, taken from tapes originally produced by Lee "Scratch" Perry in Jamaica. So Wobble has something pretty solid to deal with – and listening to it again, it's remarkably good.

"The original Milky Bar Rasta," John teases him. "Let me see, who else is there now? There's Ari . . ." referring to the dreadlocked Ari Up of The Slits.

"Well, Ari's a good kid," says Wobble reassuringly.

I used to be nauseated by Wobble's excursions into mock-Jamaican accent, but at this distance of time it's the accurate social satire, the penetrating piss-take and the spot-on delivery that stand out. Wobble screams ecstatically. "Natty dread . . . stay clear of trouble, him just play scrabble, and listen to Jah Wobble . . ." As the fade-out says, this 12-inch single is really rather special.

"I wouldn't buy it," Wobble says modestly. "It's just a laugh, really." But later, away from the typical PiL atmosphere of put-yourself-down-before-somebody-else-does self-deprecation, Wobble reveals that he thinks they're all bloody good singles, genuine outpourings of his spirit. I agree with him. Put together, they constitute a sufficiently interesting body of work to grant Wobble respect in his own right.

The second, an EP, contains "Steel Leg", an echoing wail of misery from a wretched bloke with no friends. On the flip, film-maker and long-time PiL associate Donovan Letts does a creditable deliberately derivative toast in patois on "Haile Unlikely", all about how he doesn't want to go to Africa, thank you, there's plenty enough going on in Brixton. Slightly too restrained, but still memorable and very good sense.

Wobble's most frequent opus, the white label "Dan MacArthur", is well weird. For no particular reason that I can gather, Wobble is doing a Nazi salute on the back, standing at a bus stop.

"Have you ever thought he might be hailing a bus?" asks John, sardonic.

On the vinyl is one eerie side of voice treated so you can hardly make out the words over the roughly reggae tune, but there's sadness and desperation in the line "Feeling isolated . . ." – whether Wobble would publicly admit it or not. On the flip, Wobble employs his harmolodic bass playing for the first time in his own work, relentlessly thudding through an oblique counter-melody to the synthesiser, with lots of strange squiggles whizzing in and out of the machinery soundtrack, sounds as of flooding toilets, etc.

Which all leads me eventually to agree with the Dan MacArthur quote on the sleeve: "Jah Wobble never got the recognition that he so richly deserved." By the way – who is Dan MacArthur?

"Oh, it was just a new name. This week the new name is J.J. Palestine."

Prior to joining PiL, Wobble used to ride around on buses all day, playing games like "Spot the War Criminal" and "French Gangsters". He'd do that till about 6 p.m., then he'd go home to his mum and dad on their council estate in Whitechapel and eat a fish supper, usually. Then he'd watch some telly. He used to spend some time down at the job centre too, making out he was interested.

In the past year Wobble's got the bass sussed: "This is the bass. The thicker the string, the deeper the sound. The higher up the fret, the deeper the sound. It's a very digital attitude. You play bass like a guitar or like a drum. I play it like a drum. The gaps are the most important thing."

And for all you would-be Wobbles, this is how he gets the sound: he puts one track through, say, 15-inch Ampeg speakers to get a deep amp sound, then another track straight through to the desk, so that he gets a two- or three-track sound all at once. He direct-injects a deep bass sound so that he gets a reggae-style bottom end and a Stanley Clarke-type twang, then he puts it through the flanger to get a swirling effect.

On "Poptones" the bottom string was out of tune, too slack, two notes too low – there you have it, one of those divine accidents.

Jah Wobble still lives with his parents on their council estate. He is twenty-one.

Jeannette Lee isn't sure whether Wobble's a feminist or not, either. She should know – she's the only woman in the PiL collective.

"Leave it out, will ya, Viv?" John shouts. "We're no bunch of commies!"

Jeannette doesn't appear on stage, but she's a crucial member. A long-time associate of PiL, she worked for a long time with Don Letts, co-managing the clothing shop Boy in the Kings Road after running their own shop Acme Attractions. In those days the style was very sixties, three or four years before the sixties sensibility filtered through to your local shopping centre.

It's Jeannette who does the bulk of liaising with the outside world as far as I can make out, though everyone in PiL refuses to say exactly what they do. I'll bet Jeannette does most of the phone work, arranging the, uh, managing side of things, though the idea of management is anathema to PiL.

Jeannette doesn't talk very much while the tape is on, but afterwards she shows me her new pride and joy: a new Super 8 camera, the first really professional kind. She's already got film-making credentials from working alongside Don, helping him to write the very good script for Don's as yet unmade film *Dread at the Controls*. There's even a part for her, should the darn thing ever get shot.

Jeanette likes working with PiL because she sees it as a unit of infinite possibilities: "Lots of different things that people don't expect," she says, showing me how the film cartridge slots on in a wonderfully new efficient way.

In case you hadn't guessed, Jeannette will be making a film record, a kind of diary of PiL. Jeannette's still shy of thinking of herself as a film-maker, but not for long. She'll get lots of practice, because it's all part of one of PiL's master plans: a mobile micro-studio, one that can be taken outside to record gigs, and used by PiL and other bands.

That's a favourite project of Keith Levene's. Keith used to be in The Clash till lifestyle/temperament conflicts separated them. After that "I didn't do anything. I just sat around, went to the odd gig . . . There were no bands I wanted to be in. I didn't really want to know anyone, anyway."

There's a joke poster on John's living room wall, saying something like "You may be paranoid, but that doesn't mean they're not out to get you."

Lydon's image, perpetrated by certain hostile elements within the music press, was of a paranoid wreck cowering in the privacy of a luxury townhouse. Patently ludicrous when you register the worn but serviceable decor and feel the house's bones rattle every three minutes as juggernaut lorries thunder past.

Hardly a cloistered residence, and any disinclination to hang out at ligs is more than understandable in the light of self-preservation from death by boredom, apart from anything else. The way John has his domestic set-up arranged, it's like being in a non-stop sound system anyway and the music (as much disco as reggae these days) is better than you'd hear in a club. There's a constant stream of people dropping in, so you could hardly dub Lydon anti-social, either.

No – the paranoia tag might be better applied to Keith, a very intelligent man but equally highly strung.

"In case you think Keith's difficult to work with – he's not," says John most definitely.

The comment comes when a slight strain appears during the interview. Keith's explaining something, talking about PiL.

"I see PiL, the band bit of PiL, as just me, John and Wobble. That's the way I like it, with no drummer. The mobile micro-studio's going to have maybe an eight-track machine with a sixteen-track desk. The 8 is the main part, because we're into vision, video. We've got this Super 8 camera. We want to use electronics as special effects, using electronics to condense the quality of the Super 8. It's a metal disc played with a laser, so you can make an infinite number of copies, and use slow motion and make stills . . ."

I'm sitting on the floor, trying to digest all this rapid-fire consignment of interesting new information, when Jeannette comes up to me and offers me a Brazil nut plus nutcracker. I nod, turn to her to grab 'em, when Keith suddenly bursts out: "I *HATE* talking to people when they look away! It's boring! If you're being like that – I like people being attentive!"

And John teases him: "What's the matter? Didn't your mommy love you enough when you were little?"

Silence across the room as I try to reassure Keith, who keeps on saying he's not being paranoid. The outburst shocked me for a moment. I suddenly saw Keith as a person who's liable to explode at any moment and thought of Richard Dudanski, ex-PiL drummer, saying how impossible Keith is to work with (although PiL all say the same about Richard, based on his performance at the Leeds Sci-Fi Fest).

Still, after that Keith became very communicative once more. The basic problem seems to be that Keith has very little respect for and interest in 99 per cent of the human population, hence the feeling of isolation.

"I don't think anyone out there tunes into us anyway," he says. "There's no one I can discuss my ideas with. Either I'm in fear they'll rip them off and use them wrongly, or they don't know what I'm talking about. There's not many people I want to talk to and there's very few who want to talk to me. I'm very interested in meeting a new person. When I go to the Rainbow, apart from wanting to commit suicide, I definitely don't want to be in PiL. I'd probably quite like to play the Rainbow just to do a gig, but when I see the audience regard the band and the bouncers pushing people around . . . if you walk from the door to the front of the auditorium, you encounter so many guys who check your ticket. All that humiliation – music doesn't come into it. The people who go there should buy the albums and go and listen to it quietly at home on their fucking quiet stereos. It makes me sick. It makes me think I must be into it for something else, apart from doing gigs."

What is Public Image Ltd's public image? At this stage, where their visibility hasn't been very high, much of it probably rests on the slender shoulders of John Lydon. You remember him – he's the one on the radio ads: "The Metal Box – twelve tracks of utter rubbish from Public Image Ltd."

After a baptism of fire in which – other than artistically – he made a high percentage of all the mistakes there are to be made, John Lydon emerged from the easily identifiable chrysalis of Johnny Rotten to set up a situation that would avoid the cleverly disguised pitfalls and booby traps laid by the music business.

Public Image Ltd is the result: a unit of five, three public (Wobble, Keith Levene and John), two private. A unit set to confound all expectations by moving independently and thus obliquely.

"PiL doesn't fit into normal procedures. In these times things are very one-way. We have to be wiped off. No, I'm not being paranoid, it's a fight, all the way," says John. "PiL should be proof that you can have it on your own terms, it's very easy. I must admit, it's not exactly like I was Joe Bloggs, but when PiL started we were bankrupt in a very bad way. No money whatsoever. But if you're determined enough, you get what you want. But it's not easy. I had a fucking great albatross round my neck."

People's expectations?

"More like demands! It's not easy to cope with, but fuck 'em. I'm no one's puppet. The record company follows the same slavish position. What they expected PiL to be and what it was didn't make signing a contract too easy. Plus, I come hand in hand bankrupt and in debt from the past lot. It'll be years till that's sorted out. Just going through the motions and, God, there's a lot of them. I mean, that court case with Malcolm McLaren had to start because when PiL began, Malcolm wanted 25 per cent, with him coming in as manager!"

Are you getting ready for the eighties? All over England, loins are girded as musicians grapple with the future.

This Heat sit at home and make tapes, occasionally sit in front of other people trying to come to terms with "performing".

Crass stay in their North Weald community and send out messages in the shape of magazines and astonishingly cheap recordings. They would play, "perform", but they are scarcely allowed to.

2-Tone tuss with the industry octopus. So far they appear to be winning, forcing their label, Chrysalis, under manners by refusing to play footsy unless it's a collective activity embracing spirits of like mind.

Mayo Thompson and The Pop Group find their dance steps don't match with RadaR/WEA Label's and waltz off into the welcoming arms of Rough Trade, where scarcely any bands have managers or intermediaries.

One step, two step, find a new step in the dance of 1) making a living, 2) moving your ideas ahead, and 3) communicating with other people via records and other means. Which includes the current dilemma: to play live or not to play live, and if you do, how do you go about it? Many people working with music have spent many hours trying to crack these various practical, ethical and creative problems.

PiL appear to feel very strongly that they stand alone, but in fact they are one strand in a very dense weave. However, they're a very crucial strand, because to anyone who cares about the survival of conscious, conscientious musicians (though PiL will doubtless roll on the floor with laughter at being so described), the moves that Johnny Rotten made after the Sex Pistols were very important.

The Clash are what they always wanted to be: a straight-ahead rock 'n' roll band (to me, a yawn), the other ex-Sex Pistols have emerged as full-blown straight-ahead rock 'n' rollers (likewise), but PiL are an obstinate vanguard who insist on making new music that, while there is nothing new under the sun and everything's an extension of everything else, is pretty damn new – they sound like no one else.

The penalty they pay for sounding like no one else is that the majority of record buyers are accustomed to liking more familiar sounds. The penalty they pay for maintaining their "no-tour" policy is that they seem removed to the audiences who like saving up to go out and see their favourite bands.

PiL still haven't reached what to me seems their ideal stage: sending out a constant stream of communiqués, records or otherwise, that would remove them from the pitfalls of the "PiL album – an event – articles in the music press soon to come" syndrome, of which this article is merely one manifestation.

All the best things happen when the tape's off. John says that when the tape's on, his self-consciousness quotient rises by around 300 per cent, and thus I can't give you the exact wording of what he said to me after the interview, but the essence is definitely there.

As Anita Ward's "Ring My Bell" flowed into the immaculate Blood Sisters version on the very high-fidelity cassette machine, he talked more emotionally about PiL. Said that from the outset they all thought they were going to fail in some way. Said they'd accepted it a long time ago but that failure's nothing to be afraid of, because it only means you've tried. It was up for all the other Joe Bloggses to learn from PiL's mistakes. PiL is the kind of agent, John is sure, that could eventually destroy the absolute power that record companies traditionally enjoy over artists in their employ.

"That's what ruined the Pistols. It was too much the opposite of what had gone before, thus it was too easily identifiable, too easy to understand and assimilate. No threat. All that idea of changing the system from within – I've been through it and I know it doesn't work. Maybe it's our fault that we suffer from no feedback. When you're inside something, working, it's very difficult to see your own mistakes. You've got to understand that's why it works, because we've known each other for years. I was at college with Wobble and Dave, known Jeannette and Keith for years, so none of us can fool the others. You've just got to be totally honest. But it's a challenge, every day is a miracle. But we're sick of being laughed at."

That's actually a very Keith remark, really – not that Keith is a paranoid wreck as such. In fact, in his brighter moments he volunteers that he feels sure that PiL will meet up with kindred spirits. He cites Robert Rental, Daniel Miller aka The Normal, and Thomas Leer as musicians he feels might possibly be among them.

John, incidentally, refers to Donna (of Donna & the Kebabs – a Fatal Microbes offshoot – the songwriter of "Violence Grows") and Killing Joke as new outfits he sees as "very determined, into themselves in a proper way: people doing what they want for a change, instead of slavishly following patterns."

I hope that Keith loses his sense of alienation, hooks up with inspirational souls, otherwise it's a waste of a highly original musician, overflowing with enthusiasm and ideas. He's the most articulate about the way PiL functions, reiterating their creeds of "no manager, no touring for no reason" (although PiL lay claim to several unannounced gigs around the country over the past months).

About six months before PiL started, Keith started doing some video work with The Slits and when PiL began, he finally got his hands on a synthesiser, a long-time ambition.

During half the interview, Keith's in the basement playing synth. When I arrive I see a rarity: Keith practising guitar. He says he never rehearses, though he's happy to spend endless hours in the studio putting down all his ideas on quarter-inch tape so they don't get lost. That was the genesis of "Radio 4", the lush, sweeping, melancholy synthesiser instrumental that surprise-ends *Metal Box*. The *NME* reviewer thought it was a joke, for some reason. I simply found it emotional, as touching as a Satie composition, as thoughtful if not perhaps as soulful as a Charlie Haden solo. A great mood piece, rocking gently on a wave of gentle bass.

Keith: *I'm totally into production. I've never been into rock 'n' roll.*

John: *That's one thing we've all got in common. We all hate rock 'n' roll.*

Keith: *I've always been into something new and different. And when it comes to PiL's music, I think it is. Instead of adding to the sound, we take away. We have a totally open approach. We get the sound at source, so it's mixed in advance, though this lot don't help me to get a guitar sound . . .*

I mention that it's almost invariably the guitaring that makes me annoyed/depressed in bands. There still aren't enough people experimenting to get away from the disgusting guitar clichés that rule most guitarists' ears.

Keith: *When I joined PiL I hated guitars. I thought they were redundant. But I just make sounds on it. I play three tunes on it at once. They may be pretty tuneless tunes, but I'm definitely making them on purpose. All the noises the engineers want to cut out I have to say "It's taken me half an hour to make that noise!" People in studios, it's always a battle. You have to make them think they thought of it or shove them out of the way. Now, I'm totally into synthesiser. I learnt the guitar the way everyone learns. I played along with records and got really good at lead, so I knew lots of chords – and I hated it! But it was a very good databank for me, so I could use the guitar. I didn't exactly de-learn the guitar, but with the synthesiser there's all these knobs, infinitely variable, and it's the same with guitar for me. So I don't make tunes, I make sounds that go with Wobble's basslines. I use harmonics a lot. Things that most people clean up on the EQ I normally bring out, like on "No Birds Do Sing" . . .*

Wobble: *He'll play a chord, then play another string which sounds really good because it creates a harmony – then the engineer goes "You hit a bum note."*

Keith: *With "No Birds", I recorded it, then I did an overdub on one string which didn't go with it. Then I treated the sound; I'm into treating sounds a lot. I call it "insect stick", because it sounds like a load of insects in the back or hydraulic machinery. But it's guitar.*

As Keith himself said at another point, he's not *trying* to do things with the guitar, he *is* doing new things with the guitar.

Wobble modestly describes his classical à la Robbie Shakespeare bass on "Poptones" thus: "It's all harmonics, the same note in different octaves. It's a bit old fart, but it does take it to a certain extreme."

That kind of pioneering attitude, meeting with Keith's manic quest for excellence plus forwardness, is responsible for the instrumentation behind PiL's sudden surge forwards on *Metal Box* from the excellence of *First Issue*.

John says: "The songs are a direct progression from the first album. It's all part of an ambition that shouldn't be talked about . . ."

I'll talk about it, even if he won't. Apart from the superb "Public Image" single, which had everyone think that PiL were going to be an insanely catchy poppy group, PiL's first album is a wild yowl, all whiskers and fangs. When Dennis Morris first visualised the sleeve, he talked about reversing people's expectations of John's punk band with a sophisticated high-gloss satirical fashion sleeve. The result was a perfect visual expression of the confusion engendered by the record's contents.

Keith says: "When we made the first album the feedback did affect us. Since then, I think there's a real lack of interest in PiL, which bums me out. I'm not in it for myself, I need feedback. The more interest we get, the more interesting we'll be."

The album may have alienated Pistols fans, but it certainly attracted a new hardcore section of PiL admirers, though Keith seems unaware of the fact. Many couldn't fail to love it for its boldness alone, the portrayals of angst and hatred of self and others, ripping through conventions of "good singing" in a great primal scream, the ominous basslines, forbidding while they hypnotise/pummel your natural rhythms, and Keith's guitar ripping through the sound.

The process is refined, purer on *Metal Box*. The same elements, fencing more delicately, probing more certainly.

Lyrically, John's gone deeper. His delivery is immaculate, all first takes. He makes the most of a limited range by injecting infinite subtleties of inflection. Mostly, John writes from other people's viewpoints – if you didn't know that you'd think he was a complete prat. He's not, but he's a great satirist. He's responsible for the most lethal nicknames I've ever heard and he's an old hand at the one-liner that wilts the opposition.

The lyrics had *Metal Box*'s critics extending themselves in directions that roused the PiL camp into a frenzy of their favourite hobby: intellectual baiting, though in my vocabulary, they mean "pseuds". Why, even Wobble admits that true intellect is a wonderful thing.

Sometimes John continues the narrative style of "Annalisa" from the first album, based on the girl whose parents starved her to death because they thought she was possessed.

Here, "Poptones" is the story of a man who was raped in the woods. "It's straight out of the *Daily Mirror*, so I can't guarantee its authenticity," John quips. It's the details – like "I don't like hiding in this foliage and peat, it's wet and I'm losing my body heat" – that get people confused. It's so precisely evocative that surely he must be talking about himself. Wrong, of course.

As Wobble says: "It's all lean lyrics, no fat on 'em. He's not some cunt writing about his hang-ups."

John tells me that he identifies with Bob Marley's lyric on "The Heathen": "He who fight and run away / Lives to fight another day." A line that Marley also feels is very important to him, incidentally. Both men have survived attempts on their life, which I guess gives them something in common. John can't roll a decent joint to this day, following an attack in North London around the time of "God Save The Queen", which left him with a damaged nerve in his hand.

John may reckon he's lying low in some way, but he's right there in the front line as far as music and the production thereof goes. I've heard lots of people complaining about how difficult it is to get records out of *Metal Box*, a film-can lookalike that reminds John of a landmine: "I've seen them on telly."

But PiL regard it as a triumph for their organisation. The making of the box itself was an endurance test, involving renovating defunct machinery. PiL took a deduction in their £27,000 advance and fought for more protective wrapping, which they didn't get, and for more than 50,000 being made. The first album sold more than 50,000, but John says Virgin regard that as a fluke.

"Bear in mind, it's not an album. You don't have to listen to the songs in any order. You can play what you want, disregard what you don't. Albums have a very strict format, the eight tracks, difficult to find – I hate all that. The quality is usually appallingly low, almost unlistenable. We can't get our sound on a normal record, you can't get the depths and heights. Virgin didn't like the first album. They're determined to get me back with Steve and Paul."

I say I find that hard to believe.

"They've thrown money down the dustbin on that trashy film," crows John. "Or else why do we get so many hassles financially? Virgin will tolerate you screaming and shouting 'Anarchy!' till the cows come home, because it's not really doing anything. But as soon as you start changing the business techniques, they don't appreciate that at all. They don't like bands to have control over their own destiny. That wouldn't help their pockets."

PiL isn't a band, Keith insists, it's a company. They supply Virgin with finished artwork and records and promotional stuff, and Virgin get it out.

But plans for PiL don't include new members. It's for the five directors – three band members plus Jeannette and assistant Dave Crowe – to take an equal percentage and expand themselves into new areas. Video, for example.

"There's not much point in having your own label," says John. "You'd still have to go to the record companies in the end. It would be the end of all six of us."

Including here, presumably, new drummer Martin Atkins, a twenty-year-old from Durham, still bedazzled at being in PiL after two years of trying to gain entry.

"I'm not a drummer, I just hit things," is his introduction.

"We're all quite capable of messing about with cameras. It's just as easy as a string synthesiser. It would end up with secretaries and floors and floors of boring offices. People you don't really like typing out ridiculous letters."

PiL's position may seem isolationist, but it's a valid survival technique. The last word on the subject is left to Wobble, who while I wasn't looking sneaked up to the tape recorder, wound back the end of the tape and said: "PiL is basically . . . basically, PiL is all about . . ."

*

. . . and then, some five decades later, Pitchfork *magazine gave me a chance to reflect back on those times . . .*

"The Flowers of Romance"

First published in Pitchfork, *6 May 2018*

Each Sunday, Pitchfork *takes an in-depth look at a significant album from the past and any record not in our archives is eligible. Today we examine the brilliant chaos surrounding PiL's* The Flowers of Romance.

The saga that led to the recording of Public Image Ltd's third studio album, 1981's *The Flowers of Romance*, was as lurid as a telenovela. It was hailed as a defiant tour de force, a pivotal forerunner of techno and industrial music, one that set the bar for post-punk, and all of "uneasy listening" to come. Making the record was an exercise in alienation, more painful than getting and removing the same tattoo in one afternoon.

The sickly-sweet irony of *The Flowers of Romance* hid a time bomb. In its thunderous, distorted drums, hear PiL tick towards their own explosion. If you feel at odds with the world, know there's a better way, but no one will listen to you – put *The Flowers of Romance* on repeat. It may not soothe your soul, but it will make you feel you're not alone in your angst or your need to keep going.

Incidentally, Public Image Ltd were actually an incorporated company. This professionalism was a big fuck-off to punk's chaos that had camouflaged how lead singer John Lydon (aka Johnny Rotten, the former lead singer of the Sex Pistols) was being ripped off by the Pistols' manager, Malcolm McLaren, financially and emotionally. PiL was to be a fresh concept, one based on trust, non-hierarchical, primed to supply the 360-degree needs of a music industry adjusting to videos and CDs.

Along with Lydon, PiL's directors included Dave Crowe, one of his old North London mates; the anguished, gaunt guitarist Keith Levene, who had helped start The Clash; and, in a brilliant stroke of Lydon's, sparky Jeannette Lee as a non-specific band member. Witty and level-headed, Lee was the glue, the friendly face, responsible for just about everything except actually writing and playing, and even then, her savvy imprint was palpable. The petite heartthrob had previously run Acme Attractions – a progressive style and culture stall/salon in King's Road, Chelsea's Antiquarius market – with her then-boyfriend, film-maker Don Letts.

She thought of repurposing the name, *The Flowers of Romance*; Lydon had suggested it for a short-lived band of Sid Vicious, future Slits members Palmolive and Viviane Albertine. Lee would quit the band in 1982, while PiL goes on, still compelling today; but her tenure is immortalised on the LP cover. A red flower between her teeth à la Carmen, she appears to be about to bash the photographer with a blunt object – actually the pestle from then Vivienne Westwood stylist, Yvonne Gold's kitchen. The hectic glamour that the uber-stylish Lee projected stopped PiL from being perceived as all grumpy white boys – and never forget that even a pestle can hurt. Today, Lee is one of the music industry's most powerful women, as co-owner of Rough Trade Records.

For two weeks in the fall of 1980, these hardcore Londoners were off to the exotic Oxfordshire countryside. The stately neo-Elizabethan seventeenth-century home that Virgin's Richard Branson had converted into an unusually grand studio was a ready-made stage for breakdowns/breakthroughs, both artistic and mystic; it came complete with a ghost, whose visitations were yet another good reason to put off recording. The cast of this musical mystery experience included myself some days; drummer Martin Atkins, younger, less tormented than Lydon and Levene, his bouncing presence let some air in; and a slight charmer nicknamed Shooz, aka the late guitarist Steve New. Years later, Shooz said he had been hiding from his transvestism; but then he shared Levene's career-stunting fondness for smack, contributing to the general tension.

The waking hours, which mostly happened at night, were a tug-of-war between everyone's chosen stimulants or deadeners. In those times, cocaine was non-existent and weed had not yet been genetically modified into its current monster testosterone THC; so we can blame the paranoia on the speed. Among other things. Lydon was well known for being paranoid; but then, sometimes they are out to get you, as life had shown him. That uncomfortable knowledge crawls through every bar of *The Flowers of Romance*. Has any other LP been dragged from its makers so slowly? The album is a breech delivery that needed forceps to scream its way into the world, those indentations on the skull, that bruising – you can hear it all.

Lydon's Pistols experience was always tainted by the contempt of coulda-been father figure McLaren. Naturally, Lydon had been impressed at first with the worldly older man's naughty charisma. Convinced that he had not only assembled the group (which, in fairness, he had), McLaren also thought he had invented Lydon's creativity. Wrong answer! Actually, McLaren had lucked out but did not appreciate Lydon, who was a true untapped performer and poet with his own concept of sound. This dismissiveness had caused Lydon to retrench and seek to surround himself with those he knew and trusted, in the new, equitable PiL model.

The old Pistols construct had become its own sort of prison, one that Sid Vicious had not escaped alive. The loss of Sid, known as Beverley when he befriended Lydon at college, could never really heal. And now, another key figure was also missing – banished, in fact: amiable bass player Jah Wobble, another long-time friend, whom Lydon had talked into learning to play because he wanted him around. Who knows what was in Wobble's mind, but he felt entitled to use some PiL tapes for his own recordings, without discussion. Off with his head!

There was a garrison mentality. You were pro-PiL or not. If punk meant a *tabula rasa*, a clean slate, Lydon now found it necessary to remake the slate. Without Wobble, a solution had to be found, and the fewer people who were let into the besieged inner decision-making core, the better.

Frankly, I benefited from their creative scramble. As a rock scribe, I had often covered Lydon, but having been an original Flying Lizard – the early eighties experimental new wavers – I was now invited to use PiL "down time". (In the hours when the studio was not in use, I recorded my own indie 45, "Launderette/Private Armies", which Lydon and Levene co-produced with me.) Did Lydon already suspect that the studio would often lie idle?

Lydon and I had first bonded over a shared passion for reggae bass. Bob Marley called the rickety liaison between the music of two oppressed tribes – black youth and white punks – the Punky Reggae Party. With the Rastas' numbering of corrupt, controlling capitalist systems as Babylon, and Jamaican dub remixes shattering predictable reality, reggae was our religion.

Back then, I was a music journalist, often covering reggae. My interviews with artists like Big Youth and Dennis Brown sometimes happened at Lydon's terrace house in Fulham's Gunter Grove, where dub pumped through giant speakers and the session never stopped, a playground run on vampire hours. Apart from work, and even then, people mostly stirred when day bled into night. I doubt any of us had ever had that much space to cavort in before. For a while, we took over the asylum.

Hence my presence at The Manor. We lived in a topsy-turvy twilight zone. Rather than milking every precious moment of studio time, there was a lot of sulking and/or deep thinking going on, with everyone alone in their bedrooms. Result being, for me anyway, that the glorious moment when I laid down my vocals for "Private Armies" (on which both Levene and Shooz play) was somewhat marred by the engineers' annoyance. Having waited for hours – days? – for PiL, they were underwhelmed at Lydon thrusting me upon them. (It all worked out OK in the end!)

But bit by bit, *The Flowers of Romance*'s confrontational, epic tracks assembled, despite it all. A musician would wander in, play a riff, amble off, then another would show up, add another dimension to the fragment and so on. Lydon had reams of notes and could scribble down and deliver a new song fast, if the track moved him. Thus, the nine songs were assembled, a bit like a big communal jigsaw left out in the living room. But two weeks at The Manor only produced one finished track: the ambient instrumental, "Hymie's Him". The rest of the rhythms were taken back to the city and moulded at Virgin's Townhouse Studios, in a somewhat more disciplined fashion.

Yet even while PiL members were brooding alone in their rooms at The Manor, subconscious work had been done, wrestling with a metaphysical question: when your entire aesthetic has been rooted in bass culture, how to even make sound without it? Those still newfangled synthesisers were part of the answer when the album was completed. Levene almost invented the jagged, jangly post-punk guitar sound. Now he was testing digitised music, with his cumbersome Prophet synthesiser. When it came to music, Levene was fervent, obsessive. The key to *The Flowers of Romance* lies in his anguished cry, so loud I could hear it in the early hours in my bedroom next door: "I only want to make music like no one has ever heard before! Or I can't be fucked."

Of course, that epic ambition has always meant tempting the gods. And Greek-wise, Levene – who left the band in 1983 – was Sisyphus, doomed to keep pushing, not a boulder up a mountain, but a guitar or synthesiser's sound, till the new is no longer novel and the cycle starts again.

Doom and how to deal with it is the message of *The Flowers of Romance*, which unsettles from the start: an itchy insect sound is swatted down with a harsh swipe of one drum, making the listener the mosquito, followed by Lydon's startling muezzin-like wail. Disillusion and rejection infuse the title track, caught in this exquisite banality: "I sent you flowers / You wanted chocolates instead." Attraction keeps tussling with repulsion, especially at women's bodies in the primal scream of "Track 8". Repulsion wins on "Go Back", when PiL tackles the Babylon system that tries to make us all trot down one narrow track forever, led by debt and doubt: "Number one, protect self-interest."

But the overall effect is not rage or despair. The music is on the attack. This was PiL fighting for existence, collective back against the wall. No wonder they felt almost paralysed. How to top yourself, if your first band had become a global culture-busting sensation; your own band's first two studio albums – 1978's *Public Image: First Issue* and 1979's *Metal Box* – were hailed as game-changers, crashing through the primitivism of punk to deepen the template for post-punk's angular experimentation. Then the live official bootleg album from 1980, *Paris au Printemps*, got a severe backlashing from the press. PiL had to get its groove back.

The Flowers of Romance spat at their critics with intensity and twisted clarity. In "Phenagen", Lydon stubbornly intones, "Repair the damages you made . . ." He massacres the Mass as only a Catholic can and the record's pain might be a form of expiation, cathartic confession of damage done.

It's an album that itches in its skin, restless for oblivion. Rather like punk's perverse mode of communication – insult your best mates the most – Lydon's lyrics at first appear misanthropic, certainly suspicious of other humanoids. But a doubly perverse flash of humanism nonetheless illuminates the work. To mess with our heads, Lydon offers us just enough light.

The remorseless "Banging the Door" shows this duality. It starts out curmudgeonly: "It's not my fault that you're lonely."

The track reads more autobiographical than the rest. Against the world, PiL and cohorts would often ignore people pounding. With no security cameras or minders, they were wary. Lydon had often been beaten up in the street. More than once, he came home to find his apartment ransacked by the police Special Branch. He was a subversive rabble-rouser with Irish roots; IRA bombs were a regular menace; perhaps inevitably, some people and authorities projected their racism and/or security fears onto Lydon's anti-leadership.

But for those who were there, "Banging the Door" will always be associated with the tempestuous early courtship between Lydon and his wife, the striking blonde German scene-maker Nora Forster, mother of the late Ari Up, singer of the Slits. In retrospect, Lydon, who was quite a shy guy, might not have wanted to be seen as slushy in front of our fiercely cynical free-thinking coterie. After all, "This Is Not a Love Song" would be one of the band's biggest hits two years later, in 1983. Yet, the barbed bouquet of their stormy young relationship has lasted almost half a century.

Which is a metaphor for the continued meaning of *The Flowers of Romance* today, for the mood of survival despite betrayal that it has bequeathed us. Come to that, it captures where we find ourselves now: all lurching through dark Babylon towards an uncertain future. But there is some light ahead, if we keep banging away.

CHAPTER 3

The Original She-Punk Sisterhood

With the advent of she-punks along with the boys, I finally had a girly community in the music world! The male musicians were supportive – but more broadly, on an industry and office level, I had been battling the rock cockocracy solo (with input from my wo/mentor Caroline Coon, activist, writer and painter) for some eighteen months and having my own posse was like finally reaching an oasis.

My own community. At last. Things were changing fast for females, as legislation was at last giving us unprecedented, though basic, rights in practical areas like housing, banking and the right to work (though not equal pay, we're still pushing for that). I was already in my early twenties; these punkettes were ten or more years younger. We went through the punk fire together and are still tight today.

So unprecedented was this phenomenon of women musicians that a poignant debate of the day was: if women did ever get to make their own music their own way, as some were just starting to do, how might it sound? These articles offer some answers – and we're still hearing more.

The First Women in Punk Rock

Go on, amaze me. From some mouldering attic or vault, maybe you can unearth an earlier "Women in Rock" article than this one, but, to my knowledge, this is the Ur-story that foreshadowed a whole "Women in Rock" industry of series, on TV and in magazines, which would always be both appreciated and resented for its implicit reductive ghettoization. When would we have a special "Men in Rock" edition? Never, as we had one every week.

In the 1990s, I was asked to write about the state of play for one of the first Rolling Stone *women's issues. My point was backed with quotes from top female artists – but the article was canned and its approving commissioning editor got promptly fired.*

Happily, conditions have much improved since then; the firing editor was himself dispensed with, or dispensed himself; and women have a more level field now, for sure. But speak to women in music today and you'll find that the bad old men/tality still prevails; even as I write, bookers and promoters, publishers and editors, still decree, "We've got our one or two women. Basta! Enough!" as if working with us was a chore to be fulfilled. Couple that with attacks on women from so many directions – governmental and social, physical and mental – and, well, it's a good thing that women musicians, stylistically she-punks or not, can flow like the water that wears down mountains.

I remember the editorial meeting where I pitched the idea for this article. Much muttering and amazement at this new phenomenon – girls playing musical instruments, in a band, singing songs they had written themselves! "Girls don't buy music! Girls don't make music! Surely it can't last . . ." was the amused response as the editor gave me the go-ahead. So I am very glad to report that some of the women interviewed here are still playing today. Plus many, many, many more.

"The Other New Wave"

First published in Sounds, *11 December 1976*

While the world's been getting its undies in a tangle over punk rock, another new force has been quietly emerging.

The bass player's wearing braids coiled round her head. Her hips sway subtly as she plucks out a churning bass riff – plump little fingers thread deftly up, down and round the frets; the bass looks two sixes too big, but she can handle it. She's tough, though she looks around sixteen.

A particularly inspired lead guitar line rips the sound apart from stage left, soaring in crazy spirals round and round the bass line. Higher and higher, faster and faster. The bass player looks at the guitarist and smiles warmly. Sisterhood is powerful. The guitarist grins back elated, tossing a growl – bends it, twists it, gives it a shake for good measure, finally releasing it in a scurry of dazzling super-funk riffs.

The drummer concentrates on the cymbals – her lipsticked mouth purses in a dainty frown, following the inspired wheeling, swaying lead lines. Just for a moment, there's a danger she might lose control of the build-up; but no, she's retrieved herself, and pouting prettily, she straightens in the seat. Palely glimmering long blonde hair – immaculately Silvikrin City – swishes round a serious oval face. The lead guitarist looks at the rhythm guitarist and they all smile with delight as the music builds up and up and up . . .

Loud applause and cheers drown the triumphant flourish ending Hendrix's "Hey Joe".

Just another Tuesday night at The Castle. Painted Lady are getting down, the boozy audience are getting off.

Suddenly there seems to be an awful lot of women musicians, or women bands, featuring in the *Sounds* gig list. It seems that a woman's music underground is emerging overground; the arrival of Joan Armatrading, Patti Smith and The Runaways has suddenly given a structure to what had previously been dispersed freak phenomena – women forming bands and going out on the road, just like men.

As you might expect, there is a community of women's bands, with many closely involved musicians swapping round from band to band within the movement. Every gig I went to seemed to have musicians from the other bands in the audience, checking out the opposition.

Some of the women I spoke to have been playing for years, some haven't yet played their first professional gig. But the same conflicts recurred in every interview – lack of respect/encouragement from boyfriends and families; how to overcome the general assumption that an all-female band is necessarily a gimmick or else an exhibitionist freak-out display put on by a bunch of raving dykes; how to look and feel good onstage without pandering to an audience out for tits 'n' ass; how to win over an audience alienated as soon as the band set foot onstage *not* wearing G-strings.

Sometimes the problem is as basic as persuading the doorman that you're the band and not the groupies so that you can get backstage and tune up.

Not everybody was keen to talk. Many musicians were suspicious of the concept of an article about women's music, feared that I would be checking them out on their sex appeal instead of as musicians. They were terrified of being misrepresented – not surprising, considering the quantity of male journalists out to attract male readers of a more – ummm – *unliberated* nature. Quotes have been known to mysteriously appear in unrecognisable forms, totally misrepresenting the original point, hinting at untrammelled depravity, lechery and perversions practised by women unnatural enough to want to make their own music. Equally, many were alarmed at the prospect of being labelled as a women's band – i.e. as "Ooh, just a bunch of women playing at playing."

It's only to be expected that I didn't particularly like all the music I heard, simply because I was working from the outside in, talking to bands because they happened to be women, rather than because I was into their music. It's obviously true that "Women's Bands" is a category riddled with fallacies; a perfect example of what Kurt Vonnegut calls a "granfalloon" in his classic book *Cat's Cradle*. His definition goes like this: "If you wish to study a *granfalloon,* just remove the skin of a toy balloon." Vonnegut goes on to say, "Other examples of granfalloons are the Communist Party, the Daughters of the American Revolution, the General Electric Company, the International Order of Odd Fellows – and any nation, any time, anywhere . . ."

In other words, a granfalloon is a false grouping, only bound together by external forces that are nothing to do with what's *really* going down. But I still feel there's a justification, a necessity even, for this article.

When Keith Richards first picked up his guitar, when McCartney saved his pocket money for his first bass, they were simply following in the well-trodden footsteps of their idols. But even today, there are no models, no precedents, for today's woman bands other than rarities like Fanny or male-moulded glam-rock bands like The Runaways.

Joni Mitchell, Carole King fit into a palatable feminine mould – sensitive singer-songwriters are socially acceptable, dealing mainly with emotions, with love, traditional "womanly" areas. Before that, there's The Supremes, The Ronettes and all the others, all controlled, shaped and inspired by men.

But when women perform a professional hard-rocking set, with no concessions to female stereotypes, they're an automatic threat. They're a threat to men because they challenge male supremacy in a citadel that's never been attacked before; they threaten women who have perhaps never dared acknowledge that *THEY* want to be onstage doing the energising instead of watching their boyfriends do it, in passive admiration.

At the same time, it would be a mistake to assume that all women's bands are political. Some, like Jam Today, are militant feminists. Others, like the twin lead singers in Emily Sway and The Shuffle Sisters, have no objection to coming on in cabaret chic à la The Three Degrees. They're not consciously exploiting the feminine mystique – they feel comfortable within those boundaries. To some musicians, an all-woman band *is* a gimmick, a way of getting attention. To others, it's simply the only outlet for playing without being shoved to the back of the stage, and suddenly finding that the male bass player has cut in and nicked your solo time.

Women like Suzi Quatro, Joan Armatrading and Patti Smith are the only authentic inspirations for the majority of these bands. Even though they all have male backing bands (Suzy said to me it was simply because no women turned up for auditions), they still project an upfront, uninhibited *woman's* image. If I were a woman musician, I'd probably find inspiration in Labelle, who rose from comparative obscurity with the help of another woman, manager Vicki Wickham, who herself had battled a male-dominated hierarchy to become the producer of *Ready Steady Go!* But then women have always had a more respected role in the area of black music.

All the more surprising, then, that the only area without a band composed at least partly of women is reggae.

The only woman reggae musician I spoke to is Candy MacKenzie, a very talented singer, pianist and songwriter who performs with Aswad. Within the band her talents are restricted to singing backup; a major flaw in the band's presentation and structure, to my mind. Candy was unwilling to talk, initially, claiming that she didn't think of herself as a "woman musician", that she was a musician because that was all she could do, that was why she had been put on Earth, and there was no point discussing it.

But when she finally did volunteer information, her answers pinpointed the reasons why this article exists.

It transpires that Candy *had* been looking for other woman musicians, to sing backups with at least. No luck. The few women singers she tracked down were loath to commit any of their time outside of conventional social situations. And when she *did* find women singers willing to go to rehearsals, give up dates for gigs and so on, "We didn't agree about what we should do onstage. They were only in it for the glamour. They wanted to wear – you know, like powder-puff things," she said, wrinkling her nose in disdain.

Candy herself is a model image for a new wave of women reggae artists, not content to sway decorously in floor-length African robes à la The I Three or to look glamorous in nightclubs like Sharon Forrester. Candy onstage is strictly militant; dressed in street clothes – khakis, jeans, T-shirts – she moves naturally, smiles without artifice, and sings with uninhibited passion and fullness.

Candy is the only woman with a record label (Island) who I spoke to. I wanted to concentrate on unsigned bands, partly to give them exposure they wouldn't receive otherwise, partly to spotlight the fact that there *is* an underground that deserves to be explored. I was interested to discover whether the challenge of going on the road without record company support was so hideously prohibitive for a woman that only the most ardently extrovert, tough woman need even consider the possibility. I suspected that if you're motivated, you can just do it. I'm glad to say that I was right.

The Castrators

Tessa Pollitt, lead; Angela Risner, lead; Budgie Caroll, bass; Louise, keyboards.

"You must think we've got awful cheek, coming to see you when we haven't all got our instruments yet," says Budgie. But she doesn't sound as if she means it; she's got too much bottle to worry about what I think.

The Castrators ("We chose the name because we want a reaction, even if it's negative.") spread out across my room comfortably. They might not look like a threat to Western mankind at first glance, more like a crew of zany *St Trinian's* madcaps, but check more closely. See that round Budgie's neck? Yup, it's a pair of scissors slung on a leather thong. These sisters mean business.

The Castrators today aren't much more than a concept. But it's a spontaneous concept, no behind-the-scenes mastermind persuaded these bouncy teenagers to start a band so blatantly designed to strike fear into the hearts of any desirable potential dates. Boyfriends? They don't stand a chance.

"I wouldn't want to see my boyfriend every night of the week anyway," says Tessa scornfully.

The Castrators listen to The Clash and The Ramones. Patti Smith is their heroine. "She's *really* cute," comments Budgie with a sly twinkle. Budgie's the talker of the band and she knows exactly where she's heading.

"We play crap rock," she announces, daring you to betray astonishment. "I was getting really put off by music, because nobody plays the kind of crap I like. I mean, I listen to Bob Dylan, but quite frankly, he bores me."

The Castrators are still at school and college (Chiswick Poly) or work in banks. So far, they've saved up enough for instruments for about half the band, but Tessa's already written piles of lyrics – "She writes the good stuff," says Budgie, "and I write the—"

Crap?

"That's it! People do try and put us down, but it inspires us. There's a lot of fighting egos in this band, and that's good. It inspires us, the arguments make us come out fighting."

Budgie's mop of black curls dance around heavily painted eyes, flashing pure fire.

"I know we've got the power and the energy. I'm doing it to please me, not anybody else. If they like it that's fine, but if they don't . . ."

The scissors swing lazily round and round in the sunlight.

Painted Lady

Tina Wolford, drums; Enid Williams, bass; Kim McAuliffe, rhythm guitar; Deirdre Cartwright, lead guitar.

Everybody in Tooting knows The Castle. As soon as you walk in, you know why; it's a sprawling, welcoming Edwardian pub that seems to have a monopoly on the drinking habits of Tooting's gilded youth. It's a bastion of South London hip, nabbing Rizlas off adjoining tables, chatting up midweek encounters vigorously, fighting at the bar.

People are ranged around a mini-stage in front of the pool table, chatting in a desultory way. Then – a hush, as four teenage girls climb onstage under the canopy, settling guitars comfortably across budding chests.

Painted Lady are in the middle of a season of Tuesday and Thursday dates at The Castle, and unquestionably, they've got the crowd sewn up. Wild applause greets favourite numbers in the selection of rock evergreens the band whip out energetically – "Knockin' On Heaven's Door", "Hey Joe, "Can't Get Enough", "All Right Now", "You Keep Me Hangin' On" . . . The band's second set of the night ends with a bang after an hour-long set that shone with a level of mutual sympathy and competence that surprises, considering they've only been together for three months.

Kim, short and lean, with a cascade of pre-Raphaelite brown curls surrounding a cheeky pointed face, did the links and intros. What she lacked in polish she made up for in natural charm. Tina is a dramatically untypical drummer, visually; a genteel dainty blonde, looks as if she's more at home eating cucumber sandwiches with the crust cut off than drumming in a rock 'n' roll band. Sitting determinedly upright on her stool, she drums primly, toying with the sticks rather than battering the skins into submission. But she's always there with the right fill at the right moment, rock steady. Her astonished look of ladylike gratification at successfully completing a flourishing roll (as if she hadn't known she'd do it right!) is a gem.

The whole band are competent, Enid's robust frame swaying sensuously to each bass lick, Kim's rhythm chattering effectively, but Deirdre's lead guitar is a revelation. When she launched into her first solo, Dennis and I shot each other meaningful glances. Authoritative, melodic lines slash decisively through the sound. Her guitar tone is full and rich, ringing exultantly. This woman has got *IT*.

After the set, we straggle into the back yard, the girls brushing off eager offers from a stream of males, and climb into the group van.

Kim's folks bought it for them, and her Telecaster. They're unusually supportive – Mrs McAuliffe executing delirious jive spins and reels to the band's rockin' rhythms was a joy to watch.

First, the band has one weak spot in the vocals. None of them has a particularly outstanding voice, although Enid is fine when she takes her attention away from playing bass. Dennis and I agree that a powerful lead singer would catapult the whole band to new heights. They say it's been suggested before, they'll consider it. Hope they do, 'cos until then, Painted Lady won't achieve their undoubted potential.

"People said, oh, girls can't do anything," says Enid, "which made us want to prove that we can . . ."

Deirdre, the feminist of the band (she's also a member of Jam Today), states, "There's two different kinds of women bands. Either together for a gimmick, or else as a statement. This band has mixed views . . ."

But they certainly agree about their music. Painted Lady got this pub season together by simply walking in off the street and asking. Women, it *can* be done . . . "When we started, the audience was booing and taking the mickey, but they booked us back. The audience was dancing before we left."

Why just rock covers?

"We're working on our own material and we do play a couple of our own numbers. But really, we play what we know people want to hear. We might want to do more complicated stuff, but the audience wouldn't appreciate it. They might like us to play more commercial stuff, but we wouldn't enjoy it . . ."

Jam Today

Deirdre Cartwright, lead guitar; Frankie Greene, drums; Alison Rayner, bass; Terry Hunt, rhythm guitar; Corinne Liensol, trumpet; Angèle Veltmeijer, sax and flute; Josie Mitten, keyboards; Diana Wood, vocals.

The gym (at least it looks like a gym) downstairs at the Ladbroke Hall, North London Poly, is packed full of the alternative society. It's a squatters' benefit, featuring Jam Today and The Derelicts, the two top community bands, and everybody's hot to trot.

The audience is predominantly gay; sisters hugging sisters with the determined, almost self-consciously upfront demonstrativeness of those who banged the closet door shut behind them long ago.

Jam Today play an interesting set, notable for the horn section's jazz/funk feel overlaying the basic rock base. Frankie and Jo on drums and piano/organ are in especially good form tonight. Women in the audience cheer as Diana dedicates a song to them. The mood is strictly solidarity. Deirdre Cartwright plays a series of stunning lead solos, as you would expect – florid, luminous Sanatan-esque musical moments.

After the set we retire to a convenient staircase and all nine of us sprawl on the cold steps. Jam Today, as they explained it, are determined to function independently of the conventional music biz male-oriented structure. Some members of the band would like to play to women-only audiences all the time; they don't like men helping them with their instruments. They say they only want to record for a woman-controlled company, like Olivia Records in the States. They're all very aware of the responsibilities of being an all-woman band: "We'd like to have discussions with women after each set."

Individual quotes got lost in a cheerfully rowdy free-for-all discussion, with lots of teasing and jovial interruptions. The band started up with the members at vastly different stages of musical proficiency. They practised on familiar rock songs, changing lyrics they considered sexist.

The second verse of "One of These Nights" by the Eagles, for example: "I've been searching for an angel . . ." became "Lovers that would let us be ourselves . . ."

The band range in age from eighteen to twenty-eight. They're concerned with developing a form of music that's specifically women's: "I think the group is moving from rock to a funkier kind of thing. We'd never play cock-rock, but we don't think women have to stick to traditional acoustic music either."

They were particularly concerned that any women who read *Sounds* should know about the Women's Monthly Event, an evening where all women can jam together or learn from other women. For further information call 01-836 6081, the Women's Liberation Workshop.

The Derelicts

Susan Gogan, vocals; Barbara Gogan, rhythm guitar; Dan Kelleher, bass; John Studholme, guitar; Richard Williams, drums.

The Derelicts aren't really a women's band any more, since they've got as many men as women. But they're one of the first bands everybody thinks of, partly because there used to be two more women in the band who have since left (one is Marion Fudger, a bass player who works as a journalist on *Spare Rib* magazine and has done more to help women musicians in this country than anybody else).

They're very much a community band, playing good-time dancin' rock 'n' roll in a straightforward bashing way. Susan in jeans and jumper is a no-frills sweet-voiced vocalist, never attempting to woo the audience.

"We never even thought of joining a band," says Susan in the next-door bar – they're playing in the Nashville Rooms that night. It was the squatters' movement that brought the band together – all the musicians lived in squats in Latimer Road, Ladbroke Grove.

They did experience trouble at one stage with previous male band members trying to push the women to the side, but now, they say, a good balance has been achieved. "But at the time it was definitely a male thing. The men had more experience and assumed that we had nothing to offer, which wasn't the case. We all got oversensitive, but it did help us define the band's politics very clearly."

Liz is The Derelicts' roadie, with some entertaining stories of male roadies' astonishment and occasional resentment: "Women have got to get over the idea of going to see a male band and fancying them. They've got to be conditioned not to be in love with rock stars."

Advice?

"Just think about the instrument you want to play, and go ahead and play it. You've got as much chance as anybody else. A lot of women wait for the approval of a man before they do anything. You've got to learn to do without that."

Emily Sway and The Shuffle Sisters

Julie Usher, lead guitar; Mary-Ann Hughes, rhythm guitar, vocals; Shelia Gill, bass guitar; Gail Shipley, drums; Annis & Anne Peters, lead vocals.

Probably my favourite band of the lot, but that's because they play my kind of music – funk as opposed to rock.

They're the strongest band we saw in terms of individual musicianship – every band member is hot, and the twin vocalists sway with professional assurance as they belt out the songs, soulful and direct.

"We haven't got our image sorted out yet. It's very difficult," they all sighed during a break as we clustered round the gas fire in the draughty L-shaped rehearsal room.

Three members of the band had been trying to get a woman band together for a long time and offered horror stories of being turned down for auditions *on the phone* simply for being a woman. The Sways are a perfect example of women who have got together because there wasn't any other outlet for women professionals to play without aggro from male musicians, rather than any feminist political motivation. They aim to please, not disturb; simply, they want to play. They've even written a song, "Sophisticated Lady", designed to placate any women in the audience who might feel automatic resistance at seeing women onstage.

"We want to be a sophisticated girl group," say the twins, Annis and Anne Peters. They started out singing backup on reggae records (Sharon Forrester, Johnny Clarke, many others), but gave up when they had to fritter their energy away on hassles for their money. Now they're happy, playing opening sets for The Chi-Lites, playing discos round the country.

The Shuffles play swinging, funky, funk, all original material (much of it written by rhythm guitar/singer Mary-Ann Hughes) and they're my tip for swift commercial success.

Mother Superior

Kate Buddeke, lead vocals; Jackie Badger, bass; Jackie Crowe, drums; Simon Fletcher, keyboards.

I was late for Mother Superior's gig at The Red Lion, Fulham – I got lost. But I saw enough to be agreeably impressed. The band veer towards jazz, dealing in extended lengthy numbers with an almost operatic flair for extravagant lyrics and breaks.

Lead singer Kate Buddeke flails a mane of fair hair and can shake ass with the best of 'em, singing with fire. Bass player Jackie Badger looks real mean, a bit like Nils Lofgren, a slight figure in fetching shades, close-cropped hair, wrenching a raunchy bass sound with a lean, elegant style of playing. Jackie Crowe is really hot on drums; probably the best woman drummer I saw on my rounds.

The night I saw them, their guitar player had run off to join Brandy, and a male friend filled in competently. There is also a male keyboards player, Simon Fletcher, who's heard all the wisecracks before, thank you very much.

But anyway, how come one man?

"If you're really into being female," says Kate in the boxlike dressing room upstairs behind the bar, "it's tragic. But we just wanted someone who could play. It just so happened that we were all girls before."

The Runaways?

"Nothing but girls being girls."

The two quotes may seem contradictory – let's face it, they are – but they sum up a major conflict for women musicians: how to be women without being womanly in the conventional all-out-to-please-the-fellers way.

I'd been particularly impressed by their finale – an excellent, vivacious version of The Stones' "Gimme Shelter" that more than stood up to the original.

"Yes, although we rely a lot on bass arrangements and we're jazzy, we don't fit into any specific musical category."

They'd played a bunch of rock songs I didn't recognise by famous rock bands, as well as their own stuff – after personnel changes, they're still building up an entirely original set, so to an extent they're in a state of flux. But even at this precarious stage of their two-year career, they've got solid saleable potential (A&R men take note . . .)

"All the women bands I know in the States aren't together because they want to play music," says Kate recklessly. "They want to say men are bullshit."

"It's just tough for anybody to start a band," says Jackie Crowe, when Simon offers that women bands are "good for a kick-off, to get exposure."

"It can be a disadvantage," explains Jackie Crowe, "especially if they want you to be in a real female image . . ."

Brandy

Cathy Feeney, keyboards; Jill Sawerd, vocals, flute, congas, guitar; Audrey Swinburne, guitar; Chris Leon, bass; Val Lloyd, drums.

I didn't manage to see Brandy through conflicting schedules. As it turns out, they don't fit in this story since Polydor are releasing their first single on 7 January, "Ooh-ya".

I spoke to bass player Chris Leon on the phone, and this is what she had to say: "The fact that we're all girls is obviously a gimmick, but that doesn't mean we aren't out to prove that women can do it. I always wanted to be a bass player, just because I like doing it. I've been in two-woman bands before, Bitch and Faith, Hope and Charity, but that's only a small proportion of bands I've played in.

"It's difficult to say whether it's better being on the road with all women or not. It's difficult because when you're on the road there's tension, and because you're all women you tend to get bitchy. But at the same time, it's good in other ways. You're all girls together, so you can have a laugh. The new single's a mid-tempo funky kind of thing. Cathy Feeney, our keyboards player, writes most of our songs, including that.

"Yes, she does write love songs" – [most women bands eschew that in horror] – 'but what did she say? Oh yes – "I'm inspired when I fall in love and when I fall out of love." It's natural, isn't it? I do it all the time!

"No, I hadn't realised we were the first woman band to be signed to a contract. You know, when you're involved you don't see it in that light – it's just normal. It's just life."

The Slits

Palmolive, drums; Kate Korus, rhythm guitar; Suzi Gutsy, bass; Arianna Forster, lead vocals.

As soon as you step into the squat, you're made forcibly aware of the presence of cats. Walk down a rickety staircase, avoiding planks missing from the floor if possible, and open the door with the loud noise coming from behind it.

Inside, it's a dank, dark basement. A cheerless environment, packing cases strewn about, gaping cracks in the floorboards, and three women blasting out incredibly speedy, driving new wave rock.

The Slits have formidable power and attack, even rehearsing in this ultra-gloomy basement, even without skinny fourteen-year-old Arianna belting out the heavy-message lyrics of their own compositions.

Palmolive is short and sturdy, with darkly flashing Spanish good looks. She's a vicious drummer. Kate's shapely, with dashing grey-black hair, an elegantly be-Oxfammed American with a tingling line in rhythm guitar. Suzi, a tawny wild rose with a thick mop of dark waving hair, rosy cheeks, brown eyes and rosebud-red lips, plays bass with dogged ferociousness. We adjourn to a sleazy cafeteria off the Edgware Road, where we all have cups of tea and Suzi eats a rather dubious jam tart.

Suzi has been trying to form a women's band for years. She was in a woman band called Chaos, "'cos of all the trouble we had." Suzi Quatro is her inspiration. Quatro's only fault, to Suzi, is that she beat her to it. Suzi's parents bought her brother a drum kit, but they wouldn't help Suzi buy a bass guitar. Suzi left home early.

"You've got to learn that everything they're telling you is bullshit," says Kate. "It's really hard not to feel silly because you're a girl and you're expected to think in a silly way, not know how to put lights together, or carry heavy things."

The Slits say that politics is boring, and they're writing songs about ripping off from supermarkets. And if that ain't politics . . . But Kate argues, "Politics are into making people think a certain way. We just want to make people think."

A couple of nights later, I meet Arianna for the first time; she'd been at school when I visited the rehearsal. It was at an Aswad gig at the Nashville Rooms. Joe Strummer was there and Johnny Rotten walked out early. Palmolive and Arianna were both wearing elaborate black weals of make-up slashed round their eyes, and the word "SLIT" painted on their necks and cheeks. They'd only just decided on the name and were justifiably excited about it.

"Are *you* Vivien Goldman?" Arianna asked with what appeared to be dismay. Why shouldn't I be?

"I don't know," answered Arianna, with her faint German accent lingering on the words. "I thought you'd be much – *younger* . . ." They'll be coming your way after Christmas – on all the best punk bills.

The Raincoats

Dub music, first Jamaican then British, was a ferocious influence at the punk time – with remixed, deconstructed vocal versions of reggae songs stripped and shuffled till they were almost unrecognisable. A magical sleight of sound, dub was born in an ecological recycling spirit when Jamaica was going it alone, allied with Cuba and Russia (who were being more friendly to the newly independent island than the USA). Vinyl 45s would be melted down and recycled in Kingston studios; rhythms would be "versioned" by different "toaster" DJs – the roots of hip-hop, it's generally held – and equally tracks would be torn up and re-stitched together – the producer as Dr Frankenstein – and the music's edgy unfamiliarity mirrored how punk time felt. With nothing stable or certain and everything up for grabs, the chorus of your life could suddenly be transformed into a tricky bridge or verse.

That spatial sense particularly infused women musicians, including The Slits and The Raincoats, more literally for the former; The Raincoats veered more towards free jazz, their songs rarely following a predictable format.

With songs titles like "Earthbeat", the punky reggae The Slits declared their fealty to natural rhythms and organic cycles. Their "sister" band, in being the other best-known mostly female combo, The Raincoats, were far more cerebral: their music less earthy, more experimental. They articulated post-punk's urge for innovation.

And they still are. They still play, together and separately; and Gina Birch's vivid art was used as the key image of the Tate Britain's powerful 2023–4 exhibition "Women In Revolt!" while she was hitting the road with new, avowedly feminist music. By the way, in this piece I misjudged Fanny, the hard-rocking Millington sisters. They too are still showing us how it's done.

"New Raincoats Don't Let You Down"
First published in Melody Maker, *1 December 1979*

Following the sun, Palmolive washed her hands of The Raincoats. But they're back on the road, singing and playing. Vivien Goldman took a long time writing this piece . . . and they took a long time talking

This article has been a long time coming. The first interview took place in July, when Palmolive was about to leave for India to study tablas. In the unlikely event that you've forgotten Palmolive, she's the punk drum star who used to play with The Slits before she swapped over to The Raincoats: a Spanish woman, square jaw and shoulders, sturdy peasant stock, the creator of a unique free-rolling, melodic drum style.

Since Palmolive quit The Raincoats (by mutual, amicable consent), they've never been able to find a drummer of either sex to slot into the combo. With this in mind, there were glum faces at the council flat of Ana Da Silva, The Raincoats' Portuguese singer and guitar player, in July.

Palmolive bangs in, wearing jolly fifties print skirt (it was a curtain once), flouncing. As a matter of fact, Palmolive didn't leave for weeks, but at the time it seemed as if she was about to head for the Indian subcontinent on the next bus. The conversation quickly zoned in on the many contradictions involved in keeping a roof over your head via music in the late seventies.

Palmolive: *[isn't messing about] I'm not happy with the surroundings. To me it feels restrictive, compromising too much, this rock business. It's the same old shit – with education and everything, you end up building a wall around you by the time you're nineteen. You say, I can see a way things could be better, then you realise that whatever you do . . . When punk started, there was room, then straight away you get conditions, people started thinking you had to be a certain way, like Sid Vicious or something. More building a wall . . .*

Ana: *But there have been attempts for some people to open new ways of doing something. So far we've managed not to fall into the things we thought were mistakes.*

Gina Birch [bassie]: *Me and Anna went to Hornsey Art School in '76, '77, when the Roxy was just opening and Patti Smith had just been over. We went out a lot to see The Slits play. It gave us a lot of encouragement . . .*

Listen once more to Viv Slit talking in a *Sounds* interview from 9 October 1976: "All the guys around me were forming bands and they had heroes to look up to. But I didn't have anyone. I didn't want to look like or be Joni Mitchell. I didn't even want to be in the group [Fanny]. Then it suddenly occurred to me that I didn't have to have a hero, I could pick up a guitar and just play. It's not so much why I started playing, as why I didn't play before."

Despite having a direct blood link to The Slits in Palmolive, The Raincoats sound nothing like them. The Slits' album is so polished and stylised that no un-doctored voice comes through, which is fine in its way. The Raincoats go for the windswept sound; free-fighting harmonies that startled me greatly when I first heard the album. It made me realise that it's taken me twenty-seven years of listening to music to hear a woman's rock album.

Why not Fanny or The Runaways? Because they're surrogate men, musically shaped, groomed, defined and controlled by male puppeteers, glad to be "dollied".

What is this women's music? I haven't heard enough of it, sadly, to be able to lay many handy guidelines, but it might have something to do with the way The Raincoats organise themselves and their music: no hierarchy of instruments, no lead singer or players, a conscious change from the top-dog/underdog pattern set up by the patriarchal structure.

The Raincoats underplay it. They are not aggressive onstage. On and off, they wear the same casual jumble sale anti-chic. They do interviews together and they're each so mindful of not outvoicing the other Raincoats that half the time they don't finish what they're saying. Irritating, this democracy.

Returning to last July's discussion: Palmolive is cheerful but adamant. She eventually reduces her argument to: "I feel like going to a place where people in the street are more friendly and there's a bit more sun."

Vicky Aspinall, the most overtly feminist Raincoat, is also the most prone to dialectic. She says: "I'm a bit in doubt why you're dropping out of something you see as positive. You're not going to criticise it by doing that, you're not going to change it or influence it."

Palmolive: *You can't change things. If society wants to go that way, let them go. The Slits wanted to go a certain way and I didn't want to. I said, shit, Malcolm [one-time Slits manager] would be terrible for us. Malcolm was saying things like, "I hate women, I hate music, you want to come with us?" – and they were saying, yeah, he's such an interesting person. To me that didn't make sense.*

The Slits are valuable, but it's all so messed up. I can't be myself unless I'm doing something I feel. You can become a commodity very easily. Music's nothing to do with money or business, music is wanting to give something, to say something.

Vicky: *But it is a commodity. The way it's passed on is as a commodity. You have to use the channels of communication open to you, which is records, otherwise you just play to a circle of friends.*

Palmolive: *In that case I'd rather not reach lots of people. I'd rather just live in a house and be responsible for something I can really cope with.*

Gina: *That's the problem once you become involved with popular music. You become something of a spokesman. People look to you and you have to take on certain obligations you maybe don't want. People want you to behave in a way they can look up to and admire you for. And maybe you're in a position you don't want, where either the fantasy has to take over, like Sid Vicious, or you blow your image and everybody hates you and you have a nervous breakdown . . . [General laughter.]*

Generalisations are dangerous and misleading, but here are a few anyway:

When I interview Stevie Nicks, Gladys Knight or The Raincoats, about 50 per cent of the conversation revolves around feelings, emotions – that's roughly 50 per cent more than when I'm interviewing men. The reason probably is that while men are trained and socialised to cultivate their aggression, force and ambition, women are socialised to have easy access to their emotions and encouraged to express them more freely.

Anna says The Raincoats' songs are all about feelings. Certainly their album contains a surprising number of love songs, the traditional domain of women's lyrics. Perhaps that's not what you'd expect from a group of New Age Steppers, to filch Ari-Up's expression.

Of course, the mere fact that The Raincoats are expressing an undiluted woman's view is a piquant change. Their extraordinary cover of Ray Davies' "Lola" (their only non-original) doesn't alter the lyrics at all, giving Ray's own swings-both-ways suggestions extra bite.

Vicky: *Sixties rock was all about male sexuality, male rebellion against parents through sex – the Elvis thing. Women's sexuality wasn't in the picture, except as the object of desire and the consumer of the record. Female singers always sang about that view of love and emotion.*

Palmolive: *I'd feel restricted not being able to talk about love. If you're writing, you can't have a level you feel and don't express.*

Ana: *Love is a strong subject, anyway – it does exist. You just have to write honestly.*

Vicky: *But there's a point in avoiding all that for a while, just to show that women think, too.*

Ana: *I've felt better this last year than I've ever felt in my life, but if you don't get on with the people you deal with, what's the use of anything?*

I was really depressed the other day because it's very difficult to be close to people and I think it's the most important thing in life. Relating near and close to people is almost impossible, so if your relationship with people doesn't work well, why do music and poetry? It's such a distant way of communicating.

Anything can happen in a group. It's very difficult to get on 100 per cent, but I think it helps being all women because there's a certain sensibility, which is a woman's sort of thing.

Gina: *Which we weren't aware of when we were working with men, before we became all women. It's obvious, in a way.*

Palmolive: *With a group of women, they're always checking the way the other women are feeling. It's much more on one level. The way girls relate to each other is – different . . .*

Gina: *I know men who behave the way we're saying women behave, and vice versa . . .*

Vicky: *The reason I relate to other women is because we share the oppression we've shared for all our lives. I always will, till things change – and things are always in a state of change. That's a positive statement.*

Ana separated herself from her most brutal excesses of oppression in Portugal by moving to London, just as Palmolive did when she moved here from Spain. Vicky and Gina come from middle-class English backgrounds in the Nottingham and the Hertfordshire commuter belts, respectively. But the several feelings of dislocation, alienation and all-round paranoia that suffuses The Raincoats' album come from wider, more general pressures.

Yet they aren't feminist separatists at all. Apart from Gina being a member of the Red Krayola's touring party, for example, she's also collaborating with the Krayola's Mayo Thompson on a script for a musical comedy. Vicky actually left the feminist jazz-rock group Jam Today partly because "they're non-commercial to the point of fetishism. The venues they would agree to play meant they were basically playing to the converted, so that they were separatist without actually wanting to be.

"But how many women are doing it, being in bands? Why are we one of the few all-women groups? There's not a single woman drummer to be had. All women sing or play bass – because it's easier to start playing bass than guitar. More men are in guitar groups at school. Women just have to be twice as good and twice as pushy."

Our third and final interview took place last week. The Raincoats had taken a long time to get the mix that they wanted on the album, then it wasn't cut right, then in the middle Ana and The Raincoats' colleague Shirley [O'Loughlin] had gone to Bermuda, and . . . and now they want me to meet a woman called Val Whitehead, who may be their new drummer, a former music student at Durham University.

All during the summer it had seemed as if The Raincoats had shut up shop. Now, to my relief, they've got dates coming up in Germany, they're supporting The Pop Group in Liverpool and the show's on the road again.

I'm glad because, as Ana's song says, all of The Raincoats have put their lives on the line; they've got to continue to be twice as good and twice as pushy.

The Slits

In my article on the first women in punk rock, "The Other New Wave", I share my initial encounter with The Slits – on the same night they claimed their new name and identity. Between these pieces, Kate Korus would leave, to be replaced on bass by Tessa Pollitt, last seen in The Castrators. Pearls that they were, the band was sufficiently irritating to the macho mainstream that when Ari was knifed while wearing a man's overcoat (its capacious folds saved her), the attacker shouted, "That's a slit!" as he ran away. The Slits expected to be an aggression. As you can see here, they confused and confounded the majority, who found it hard to believe that these four outlandish and outrageous females were simply being their authentic selves and they really didn't give a toss about blinkered people's opinions. At the same time, they themselves were not un-confused.

Years after her death, Ari's dreadlocks still cause consternation. In a class at NYU, a student objected that Ari, the first white woman many of us had ever seen to grow serious below-the-waist dreadlocks, was guilty of cultural appropriation. But beyond a 'do, Ari, the first white woman many of us had ever seen to grow serious below-the-waist dreadlocks, actually was a Rasta, students were surprised to hear. How could it be? In the Rasta group to which Bob Marley and many other artists belonged, the Twelve Tribes of Israel, you could be of any complexion, as long as you believed in Jah, His Imperial Majesty, King of Kings, Haile Selassie, Conquering Lion of the Tribe of Judah, Earth's Rightful Ruler – H.I.M for short. And Ari did. Moving the debate beyond essentialist divisions based on melanin (which ultimately serve to confirm rather than dismantle the very same racism it is meant to be responding to) seemed to be a novel concept for some of the class.

Sometimes the cultural appropriation debate is misdirected towards individual fellow artists when it is really about money: who gets it, how it is deployed and by whom, and the options, access, power and respect it represents. Artists uniting to consciously rebuild the biased structures that have held so many down has a more constructive ring.

Anyway, meet The Slits, and see how they fare navigating a new cultural context – America.

"And Lo, 'Three Wise Slits Take Their Temple to the West'"

First published in New Musical Express, *20 December 1980*

Games on Trains

It started as soon as we left the house to go on the subway. He was quite an old guy, Puerto Rican – they all work round that area in the Pepsi Cola plant; won't touch Coke in any neighbourhood bar – when he yelled out to us "Hey! You! Where you from? What are you?"

Now I was wearing my new (hot) designer coat, but I knew it wasn't me he was shouting at – it was Ari Up, taking me for a visit to her brothers and sisters in Brooklyn.

She didn't ignore him and flounce on; she's too keen on confrontation for that. And in any case, just a minute before, she'd been talking about her love for this neighbourhood and New York, because there are so many different races and cultures and you should snatch time with each exciting new variety.

So instead of the icicle-shoulder number, she turns round and yells, "I'M JUST THE SAME AS YOU!"

"No, you're not!" the middle-aged guy yells back. "I'm not as pretty as you."

"Pretty? What does that mean? I'm not talking about what things look like, I'm only interested in feelings." With that, we descend into the subway.

Things are less eventful on the train ride. We spend most of the time loudly singing Dennis Brown's "Rolling Down", trying out a few new harmonies. People don't seem to mind too much. Over in New York they have subway nutters like The Slasher to contend with; he's the loony who stashed an axe in a brown paper bag and thrust it through the closing doors of a train, wildly hacking and slicing, wherever his hand could reach. Some hangover. Compared to that sort of thing, our cover versions must have been light relief.

We get off the train still singing and we're sashaying through this fairly derelict part of Brooklyn with the great grey girders of the subway spanning the smouldering sites like giant spider legs. A couple more people yell, "What are you?" And Ari keeps shouting back, "I'M

JUST THE SAME AS YOU!"

The big encounter comes minutes later. We've been chatting about Ari's mum sending her away to boarding school in Germany when she was eight. Having already been transplanted from Germany to England, she wasn't happy about being put there; she was homesick. But now she has fond memories of the family feeling – sisters – in the all-girl dorms.

So it's a surprise when another voice yells out, "Hey, you! Sister! What are you?"

I think I've managed to hustle Ari past the new distraction, but no; this girl is determined to communicate with as many people as possible as much of the time as she can. She turns and greets these three youths, real dude-style guys, earmuffs and cocky hats with scarves under them, silly bobbles on top – that kind of thing. They're all holding dresses in plastic wraps, trying to flog them to passing street trade. These little beige suits are hotter than saunas, obviously.

Looking curiously at Ari's impressive dreadlocks (she's just about caught up with Bunny Wailer's by now), the one guy asks, "You a Rastafarian or something?"

"In a way. I just see the Creator in everything," Ari replies, sincerity evident in her friendly blue eyes.

"Can I see them?"

Ari grins, whips off her tall black crown. Her locks jut out at a startling angle, wound round and round with a red wool scarf to a vertical tower topped with a froth of matted brown hair.

The men are clearly taken aback. "What's that for? May I touch it?" the same little guy with a wool cap says.

Ari inclines her head graciously – she is, after all, of an aristocratic family – and answers, "I'm just growing a tree on my head."

A tree on her head. Right!

You can tell these guys are reassessing the situation, including the possibility that this white girl is plain crazy.

"You know, you have very pretty eyes. Are you in love with a boyfriend?"

"I love my brothers, yes. And my sisters, too. But," Ari says firmly, forestalling sniggers, "I'm not talking about sexually, I'm talking about universal love, the most important kind."

The guys try to press her for more conventional male/female reasons, but Ari keeps on insisting on universal love. The main man is beginning to regard her with near awe as she deflects the increasingly direct questioning.

The other guy with the earmuffs is just saying, "Hey, what he means is, do you have a boyfriend in New York, now?", when another woman approaches to check out the dresses. She catches sight of Ari.

"Oh, my Lord!" she says. "Let me have a look at that. This I gotta see."

She reaches forwards and tugs a loose lock. The topknot starts slipping to one side. Suddenly, Ari looks beleaguered.

She backs away. "I'M JUST THE SAME AS YOU!" she cries out, sounding oddly like the Elephant Man when cornered in the gents in a scene from the recent film. "I'm not in a zoo!"

The woman looks at Ari, laughs with the faintest trace of derision and walks off. We wait awhile before we start singing again.

Keep Your Hat On

The previous night, Ari, Neneh Cherry (Ari's unofficial sister and singer in her own right), The Slits drummer Bruce Smith and I all go to see Sun Ra play in a small club called The Squat.

It makes sense to see Sun Ra with this contingent. Sun Ra, who comes from Saturn, and his richly talented crew are all dressed in elaborate brightly coloured silk clothing, non-specific ethnic robes and the like. The Slits are quite possibly more involved in Hat Culture than any other band, so they go well with Sun Ra.

As Bruce explains it to me, hats are very important. They not only keep your head warm, but they also round off your corporeal being with an expressive flourish of your personality at little cost.

Bruce is young, eighteen, and a drummer of such sterling quality that musicians frequently tug a forelock at the mention of his name (in fact, Wailer Al Anderson does it tonight), regardless of their feelings towards the combos he's concerned with.

We're talking about drums in the break, after a four-hour set from Sun Ra's crew who believe in playing extended, chanting, extemporising tunes. Born in San Francisco, father an artist, Bruce moved to Bristol when he was eight. He says he sees life in terms of circles. Everybody is a circle, but these circles – like the big daisies you can draw with a compass – have areas where they're separate and areas where they overlap.

"Drums are circles, do you see? They all have their own sound, then they mesh together and interlock. You can relate that to people. There's bits they share with others and bits where they have to respect their own personal space. If we could all work on that, and work on the interlocking bits, we'd really be getting somewhere.

"It's all got to do with discipline and respect. Keeping the reins taut. Some people would object to those words, say they're moralistic, but I don't think so. I definitely like the idea of reins, riding with the rhythm but directing it this way and that."

Virtually every interview with The Pop Group (and many Slits interviews, come to that) are unrepresentative of the groups because, confronted with such a Niagara of idealistic energy, the journalist is thrown – just like the street hustlers were when Ari blanked out their ritualised pick-up technique and then shifted it to the plane of abstract philosophical reasoning.

This idealism can be irritating, because at first sight it seems undirected, just empty words; and anyway – some would say – who has time for youthful idealism when there's rent to pay?

But The Slits, if not The Pop Group, still pursue their ideal way, of a nomadic tribal society balanced between the sexes, a well-functioning microcosm of what may never be, on a planetary scale.

Bruce explains, "All that change-the-world stuff – we were looking forward to something that's totally possible. It's not bad to aim high. I do when I play drums – I want people to be able to lose themselves in the rhythm. It has to be as much as it can be, totally, every time."

Sun Ra is a stocky man, dressed in purple and yellow silk robes. He bulges out in the middle like a bumble bee. Antennae wobble on his space cap as he solemnly marches down the length of the tiny club where we're sitting. He holds high the hand of his robed woman singer. Her veil floats behind her. The theatre is an abbey and she is an empress. They chant: "You make your head [. . .] You need this medicine bad . . ."

Big Boys' Toys

Like that other bi-sexed group The B-52's, The Slits do a lot of shopping on the road. Dump your stuff at the hotel, then it's straight over to the local thrift shops, junk shops.

Steve goes to the toyshop. Steve Beresford (co-founder of the Musicians' Collective, original Flying Lizards team, writer, etc.) walks round the toyshop. He walks towards a thigh-high toy piano and perches himself on the miniature stool and begins to play, first some classical-sounding ripples, sonata-style. Then he breaks off into regular reggae side-to-side chops, cuts that and starts to blues it up, sad and a bit smoochy.

A sales assistant leaning against the counter says, "Yow, man, wheredja learn to play that thing? Can you give me some lessons?"

Steve replies: "No, that's very nice, but I'm not going to be around. Anyway, there must be hundreds of out-of-work musicians in New York."

The sales dude shrugs. "Well, I don't know any."

Steve asks, "Where's this piano from? East Germany, probably, they always make the best ones. Got any more? Smaller ones? I'd never be able to get this back. I've bought that toy sax already. I know – got any synthesisers?"

By now, there's quite a crowd checking out the free solo spot. The other assistant is building a heap of toy instruments. The manager reaches up to a high shelf.

Manager: "Ever tried one of these?"

He holds up a plastic pipe with coloured keys – kind of a flat melodica. It makes a skirling noise. The manager sits on the floor next to Steve and begins to play the theme from Rimsky-Korsakov's "Scheherazade".

Manager: "Pretty neat, isn't it?"

He switches to "In the Hall of the Mountain King" from Peer Gynt.

CUT to a shot of Steve's room in North London: there are neat stacks of singing bird toys, a couple of toy synths; and track round the otherwise sparse room with its bed and bookshelves, dotted with toy pianos.

CUT to the toyshop again: a woman sales assistant leans against the counter as if it were a grand piano and she were a torch singer. A few feet away, Steve is playing the large toy upright.

The woman croons, "Heard it through the grapevine, not much longer will you be mine . . ."

Then by the time we get out, Steve's talked me into buying a very useful set of Mickey Mouse matching luggage. Perfect for dwarves.

Do or Dare

We've been on a hat hunt down Delancey Street, the poor part of town. No luck, but bassie Tessa [Pollitt], who draws the spiky demons, devils and impish characters that express The Slits in graphic terms, has bought some brocade Chinese notebooks. I need to get to the bank. Tessa says she'll come with me.

We get halfway across the street, when there's a juggernaut lorry, eight wheels long. Tessa, her eyes sparkling, mouth set in a defiant smile, declares, "I've always wanted to do this."

Suddenly, she's scrambling down under the wheels of the lorry. Swept along by the sudden energy surge, I follow, thinking that perhaps I really am nuts as the sound of the engine thunders on either side, and the lorry still seems to have half a mile to go.

Tessa lives with her fascination with death in unusual ways.

CUT to Tessa five years ago, a polytechnic first-year student who was forming a group called The Castrators with other college girls. Tessa was plumper and seemed more assertive and confident then. She loved the idea of the group, loved the way their name freaked people out. Actually, the group had never played at all then, not even rehearsed, but she was sure they soon would.

Tessa wore something on a piece of string round her neck. She smiled triumphantly as she held it up to the light; her fingers moved and the miniature scissors round her neck flashed like a small samurai whirling for the kill.

CUT to Tessa's head bobbing up from under the truck, in the middle of a crowded New York street. The smile's the same.

Small Talks

One day we sit through the queue of interviewers who come to gawp at The Slits. Viv Albertine says, with some satisfaction, that nobody seems to be able to place The Slits, that they're never sure whether they're a religious sect or a wandering tribe, or what.

Those self-images appeal to The Slits women. They dismiss questions about how they got together.

"That's boring. Can't we talk about something else?" the group say repeatedly to the young girl from *Rolling Stone*, the English boy from a fanzine, the two radio interviewers. Viv lounges on the floor by her brown paper carrier of hats, sketching, looking down. She's the oldest and the most articulate; she, too, talks of going round in a wandering minstrel way, spreading the message wherever they go. When I manage to get all The Slits in one room, we talk about the competition they ran recently on a local radio station. The question The Slits posed was: "What are the colours of stains on a girl's knickers through the month?" It was inspired by a new Slits song called "Girls and Their Willies" (and, girls, if you don't know what that song is about, you'd better take a mirror and look for yourself).

One woman phoned up the station and got the answer right: snowy white, yellow, light red and so on. She was the only person to phone in.

Viv Albertine says "Girls and Their Willies" is an educational song. Once I did a radio interview with Viv where she talked about that song and they never used it. What about the half that's never been told . . .?

What else can you expect from a song itself as it goes along.

The two men-with-feminist-insight contribute a lot. Steve gives avant-garde/pop/soul/reggae playing experience. Bruce is one of that sophisticated drumming school for whom rhythm is more important than volume, who understands that a silent beat can be as powerful as the loudest thrash. He's learnt a lot from dubmaster Dennis Bovell. When Bruce and Tessa play together, the rhythm is something you live alongside, as opposed to being raped by. As Viv puts it, "We're all so fair!"

You can't lump all The Slits together into one entity. Ari's devotion to a mystic, spiritual, Rasta worldview tends to cloud the other identities, if only because her visual impact is so unusual. With little formal education, and her early days of shuttling between Germany and England, her vocabulary can't express her thoughts. She offers to draw a picture instead, but here are her (slightly manicured) words:

"Music comes automatically to everyone, and if you start playing music on stage or record it's to share what's coming from your own heart and root with other people. They're sharing your heart, in a way, so you mustn't just jam along. If you're doing it like we're doing it and making a tribe, it's a very serious thing."

Aha! Here's this making a tribe business again! The most irritating element of The Slits: their assumption that it's open for everyone, you can all join in, oblivious of the traps of circumstance.

Meanwhile, the nomadic Slits caravan has the luxury of being able to take off and leave the tedium of one town behind. They're not even nomads, though they describe themselves that way – somewhere in the world, these people have a base, even if it's a slightly insecure squat.

Steve doesn't want to get involved in the discussion. I push him.

Steve: *Oh well, I never use that word "tribal". There's a resonance to it I don't like. It's got too many overtones.*

Viv: *That's just because the whole ethnic thing became a trend, though.*

Steve: *It's to do with ethnic chic. David Toop's writing a piece about it, about oppressed minorities . . .*

Viv: *But Ari doesn't think like that.*

Steve: *Yeah, I know, but I do, and that's why I don't use that word.*

Ari: *I don't get it. I don't even know what that means!*
Steve: *[sounding beleaguered; snaps back] Fuck it, Ari, I've got my own point of view!*
NME: *Calm down. She's not criticising you.*
Steve: *But every time I open my mouth you tell me you don't understand me.*
Viv: *You're educated at university, this girl left school early.*
Steve: *Yeah. OK. But every time I start a sentence I'm stopped.*
Ari: *That's rubbish. I just didn't understand one word. I want to learn. I am learning from you.*
Steve: *Yeah, all right. There's a way of making people into parodies in order to turn them into gods, dehumanising them till they're more than people, but less than people as well. Rather than seeing them as people, i.e. not noble savages, with their own contradictions . . .*
Ari: *I don't think we're talking about us, we're talking about the guys who write the books on them . . . What do you call it? Groups of people, family, gang, team . . . I'm not one of them. I want to build a family. Human beings are just in a circle together. Within that circle, each individual has their own circle. I'll draw a picture instead . . . Every human has the right to live the way they want their temple to be set up, every tribe of the human race. I can hardly talk about it, it's so simple, but it's worth repeating yourself like a machine. You must never give up spreading the message . . .*
NME: *Ari, do you feel comfortable in any society?*
Ari: *No, I don't think I feel comfortable in any society at all. Whatever society is.*

The Pretenders

We did this interview at my home on Ladbroke Grove, which had been one of Chrissie's preferred crash pads while she was making her way. The three storeys set over a betting shop was a long-running bohemian commune, now I look back on it, whose former denizens are still my friends today, Chrissie among them. In that hinterland pre-The Pretenders, she must have still been posing for, while also taking, art classes; I don't know what happened to her bold, realistic drawings that were once consigned to the same attic where Roxy Music's old scrapbook inexplicably turned up, but I was excited when, having scaled virtually every height in the music industry, Chrissie returned to painting seriously. Her move was not untypical. Other punk painters of her generation pursued the same path, like Paul Simonon, Toyah Willcox, Gaye Advert, Gina Birch, Youth from Killing Joke and the writer Caroline Coon.

When she was crashing at my pad, Chrissie was the "It" girl who everyone knew to be super-talented, but no-one quite knew how to position. But her talent was unstoppable. Still a punk, though she would likely dispute the choice of word, Hynde is an activist, a militant vegetarian and an animal rights defender, who had no hesitation in being arrested for protesting at McDonald's.

"Hynde Sight"

First published in Melody Maker, *26 January 1980*

"I'll never feel like a man in a man's world." As The Pretenders' album and single rise in the charts, Chrissie Hynde discusses with old friend Vivien Goldman her macho image and private reality. Goldman wonders what happened to "Bud and Dee's little girl".

"I suppose we should have talked about that night," said Chrissie Hynde after the interview was over, "when I'd been at the Roxy with Captain Sensible and we got onstage and sang a duet of 'Me and

Mrs. Jones". After that I went back to the basement where we were rehearsing, but it was so cold and dark, I had to piss in a hole in the floor, so I had a couple of quid in my pocket and decided to come over here.

"But when I got here you were asleep and I started to climb up the scaffolding on the building next door, to climb in through the window. And a cop car was driving down the road and saw me and the cops started to yell at me to come down to the street again. And you woke up with the noise and came to the window to see what was going on, and the cops stared 'cos you weren't wearing anything and you were yelling at them to let me in. I was OK . . ."

We don't need to talk about that now, Chrissie. We should talk about what you're doing now. That's the most important thing.

Vivien: *Well, if we could start with the album – can you explain to me what this inner sleeve is all about? [It's a lithograph of a little boy with a toy robot.]*

Chrissie: *I have no idea. Dave Hill who is our manager – he collects toys. And he found that picture and just thought it was a gas to put it on the inner sleeve. Anyway, I didn't see the thing before it went to press, which is a big boner for me in this operation. I finally straightened it out by saying, "Look, you don't print things up until I've seen it." Anyway . . . it means nothing to me.*

I mean, basically with the sleeves and everything, it's got so over the top and clever that I'd like to get back to just a photo of the band, no big deal, just keep it simple. We really have no sort of style that we project. I don't think we try to do anything, we're just trying to go in and knock out good songs, and rehearse, and that's about as far as it goes. That takes up all my time. So I'm heartbroken when something goes out which I don't think is a gas visually, which I'm not proud of.

This year it's just been so hectic, and moving so fast, that I haven't been able to keep my finger on the pulse, on that pulse, all the time.

But nothing is an accident . . . I was thinking about it on the way over here – in the space of one year since the actual band has been . . . or just a little bit over since we did our first single, when we still hadn't done gigs or

> *anything, we've done three singles, and they've all been like in the thirties in the charts. Now we've got a number one single, the album went straight into the BBC chart at number one, we've done* Top of the Pops *about six times, five times . . .*
>
> *And, you know, we're real flaky onstage. I mean, I don't have an act together, I don't know what the hell is going on up there. I can never hear my amp . . . it still has all the problems of a very young band onstage. Just to get basic things done.*
>
> *But as long as the material keeps on coming in . . . I'm always in a panic about songwriting. But I was starting to write songs well over ten years ago, so it's not like . . . If I wasn't in this game, I'd still be obsessed with writing songs. But I'm always worried that we won't get the new material and stuff . . .*
>
> *I can't work under pressure and I don't like to work from a competitive point . . . you know, I'm not motivated by competition or anything. In fact, as soon as there's competition, I back off – I'm not interested in getting into any kind of race, you know? But I was thinking today that if we were going to go out and record another album right now, we probably have enough material.*

Like virtually every music press journalist who's written about The Pretenders' front person, my relationship predates her dawning as the eighties' first "star". Nowadays, Chrissie dreads the prospect of her (excellent) music journalism in the *New Musical Express* being aired again – despite the fact that the editor of this paper still cites Chrissie's piece on David Cassidy landing at London Airport as one of the finest pieces he's ever read in the rock press.

A few years back, Chrissie, along with other budding songstresses like Patti Palladin and Judy Nylon of Snatch, was a voice to watch on the punk scene; but while Patti and Judy, like most sensible people, sought as much publicity as possible in music paper gossip columns, Chrissie was the one who continually threatened never to talk to me again if I dropped her name in among the listed liggers, the "faces" and "names".

It's not long since 1977, but three years have seen names zoom like comets into the limelight, that light that swivels quicker than a searchlight, burying names in darkness just when they seemed to shine most bright. Patti and Judy, for example, are still trying to get their respective shows on the road – Judy with a band in New York, respected but still not signed, Patti perpetually promising. They released a "basement tape" via BOMP! Records, a fine B-side on an Eno Polydor single, "R.A.F." and one Snatch official 45 on Lightning Records, much talked about on the strength of its phenomenally costly 3D effect sleeve.

Chrissie, the restless one, always talking about how she was desperate to get a band – oh, if only she could get a band – has released three singles and an album, grabbing the ears of the nation now that the punk brouhaha has settled down for good and we're left with bands of that generation, some good, some bad, judged as musicians, not "punks".

The sleeve of every Pretenders artefact is visually atrocious; but the vinyl within is startling even to those who have known for three or four years that Chrissie could sound like Aretha or Mavis most days of the week. It startles because it's just so good. So good that all of her old mates have to resign themselves not to have Chrissie climb in through the window at 4 a.m. – the kind of harum-scarum escapade that was her everyday life – any more.

Her great talent has bided its time, grown, developed, blossomed, till Chrissie has to devote a lot of time to the world. Chrissie has gone clear.

Chrissie: *Of course, when I started singing professionally I was a bit green. I mean, the first band I tried to be in – when I was sixteen, I think it was – I met the guy . . . oh, ten years later – it was that Mark Mothersbaugh from Devo – and I said, "Hello, do you remember me?" And he said, "Yeah, I used to be in a band with you." And he turned to me and said, "You would never sing in the same room as us." We used to rehearse down in some guy's basement and I was so shy that I wouldn't stay in the same room as the band to sing. I'd take the mike into the laundry room and shut the door.*

I'll never let anyone in the studio – except for the engineer and the producer – when I'm doing a vocal. I'm very easily distracted and very nervous about it. But you get to the point where the shyness leaves a little bit and you do

> *open up as you keep working on it – it could be anything, playing the guitar or anything. You start to get your own technique and your limitations. And it only comes through actual work.*

It's not a matter of crowing "Toldja so" – everyone around Chrissie knew her as a brilliant singer and songwriter who simply hadn't come out yet . . . even when young punk boys like Mick Jones and various Sex Pistols jammed with her offstage and grabbed all the attention onstage – and maybe didn't credit or encourage her as much as they could have done . . .

That's why I remember so clearly Chrissie and me walking down Holland Park Avenue through the April blossom-covered trees when Chrissie suddenly says, "Sit down here," and points to a low wall. So we sit, and Chrissie pulls out a cheap old cassette player and says abruptly, "Hear this." It's a tape she's made with some musicians like Nigel Pegrum, the Steeleye Span drummer, a tune called "The Phone Call".

Right then, I thought – I'm going to remember this, one day; remember hearing this tune. The blossoming pink and white, and I'll remember this, because this song is exceptional, and Chrissie will make it heard, somehow.

It's on the album now and oddly enough, it still bears some relation to the taut, tense, tinny tune on the cheap cassette. The song was/is oblique, edgy, evocative – offbeat enough to be "weird" and to satisfy the most blasé, exacting tastes.

In "Private Life", Chrissie's extravagantly controlled vocals spin out tension like a bullfighter: "I hate anything official." And yes, that's our Chrissie, always the most truly beat/Zen individual I'd met – with the possible exception of Angus MacLise, the original Velvet Underground drummer, who used to send me strange epistles written on bamboo shreds from India, where his little boy was being brought up by the monks.

Like Angus, Chrissie believed in a spartan, ascetic life. Before she became a homeless wanderer, she lived in a cupboard of a room in Clapham, South London – a thin foam single mattress she rolled up in the days, ready to hit the road, a copy of *Bhagavad Gita* she treasured, given to her by the saffron-robed guys who normally sell them in the street – they gave her one, recognising a kindred spirit. A well-thumbed copy of Kerouac's *The Dharma Bums* (the prototype), some incense, old snapshots of Chrissie hanging well loose in Paris, riding big choppers – she always had a fondness for the Angels' style, high, wild and loose – nothing else but the guitar she cooed over, polished, stroked, played at a volume to drive her housemates wild, while she fretted and yearned – why the hell was it so hard to find a band? That's all she wanted, some boys to play with. Her own band.

So Chrissie eventually got her band. Dave Hill of Real Records turned out to be the one to stick by her, bankroll at the ready, after she and Tony Secunda gave up trying – he originally introduced her to Adrian Boot by saying, "This is Chrissie Hynde, she's a star," so he definitely knew what was going on.

Chrissie: *Dave just got more and more keen. I said, "Look, I've got a rehearsal place, but I'm about £70 in arrears and basically I've got fuck all, man, I haven't got a band or anything." So I expected him to say, "Well, come around when you've got something together," but he didn't. He said, "Look, I'll pay off the debt you've got here" – it was £15 a week – "and we'll just advertise for musicians and I'll leave you to it and I'll just aid you." And as he got more involved he decided to leave having the record label, even, and just manage us.*

Vivien: *Has he acted as a kind of buffer between you and Warner Brothers, or have you been very involved in Warner Brothers, too?*

Chrissie: *Very involved – like I am very, very closely involved with Clive Banks, who'll be our publisher when we sign the deal. And I've been on the phone to Moira Bellas (at WEA) and gone into her offices for hours and hours in the past for consultation . . . She's really stuck her neck out.*

So I'm delighted about the success for the people who have been working for us; personally, I'm not that bothered about the album or the single. I'm thinking about the next single and our next album, and I'm thinking about new material and the three months of touring that we have to do in a week. We don't even have a show together or anything, because we've been so busy with all this unexpected so-called success. But I'm delighted on behalf of the team . . .

Vivien: *That's what every band needs. That's what John Lydon tries to set up around himself, you know, a team. A band has to be like an extended family.*

Chrissie: *Absolutely. I've spoken to John at length about it and I totally agree with his position, being without a manager . . . That might be fine for him, but personally, there's no way that I'll ever do anything as far as the business goes. There's no way I'll try to negotiate, when it comes to money and setting up deals. In the final analysis, I'll put my finger on it if I don't think it's hip or a good deal. But my mind doesn't work in terms of figures, you know? At all.*

So I'm glad to have a team. I'm just going to stay in my room and write songs, play the guitar and sing, and there's no way I'm going to get up there and do anything else. It's too time-consuming.

Every single moment that I have free, which is hardly anything at all, is down to rehearsals and trying to work out our show and our songs and stuff. It's been like that . . . it's been full tilt . . .

Vivien: *How do you feel about that?*

Chrissie: *Neither here nor there. It's been chaos. You've got to go along with the machine . . . you've got all these people on the team and they're all doing their bit, and you've got to do your bit. Even if you don't like it sometimes. I would be perfectly happy not to see my mug in the paper ever again and never quoted again or anything. But that's just not . . . I'm just facing the music, basically.*

I'd much rather go home and write a song, and make a record, than do an interview that night. But sometimes you have to make sacrifices. You constantly have to make a sacrifice for your work . . . everyone has to do their work.

Vivien: *Because your work is all you've got.*

Chrissie: *It is for me. There is simply no other aspect in my life. And I'll make any sacrifice . . . anything. I don't care if I don't have a place to live and I don't care if my social life goes down the pan. You just have to get your priorities straight.*

Right now, I'm very excited, because we had a good rehearsal.

Vivien: *Just now?*

Chrissie: *Yeah. So I feel . . . this is the thing, we walk into Warners and they say "Congratulations," and we say, "What?" And they say "Oh, you're number one," and like, oh, that's good, fair enough. But if I'd gone into rehearsal that night and I'd had a lousy rehearsal, I would have been depressed . . . like, the fruits of the work are somebody else's – they've got nothing to do with me. It's the work itself that's the reward.*

Vivien: *Looking back, do you feel that you were very frustrated at the time? You were always saying you wanted the band, so I suppose that one could interpret that as being frustrated.*

Chrissie: *Well, I'm always going to be frustrated, because one's character doesn't change. I'll always probably be fairly depressive. I'd probably always go out and get pissed every two weeks and make a complete and utter fool of myself, and probably always be basically pretty lonely and on my own . . . and I don't see this that'll change whether I'm a cocktail waitress or doing this. But certainly the frustration of not having a band has gone. It's evaporated like a cloud, you know?*

Chrissie became immersed in pulling this band together, introduced me to various musicians. Some stayed – like Pete Farndon – and some went, and she was vaguely surprised and disappointed that they seemed like archetypal black-leathered rock 'n' rollers, not Zen dharma bum types. Then I remembered Chrissie's penchant for bikes and the stylised charcoal drawings of fantasy greasers she made between modelling sessions at St Martin's School of Art, and thought I understood . . . Then I was busy and she was busy, and we didn't see each other. Until I ran into her in the paper shop in Notting Hill Gate, just after I'd heard her first single, "Stop Your Sobbing", a cover of The Kinks song.

We went into the Tennessee Pancake House for a coffee. I paid, 'cos she was, as usual, skint. I tried to explain why I was disappointed – the vocals were good, of course, but she sounded so girlish. All that soul depth she'd had when we duetted along with The Staple Singers' "Respect Yourself" wasn't there. I said I preferred her song, "The Wait" on the flip. Chrissie accepted my thoughts – most of her friends had said the same thing.

She stuck by the old Kinks song – and, of course, the radio DJs laughed at all of her friends by playing it to death until even I had to realise that it was infinitely better than 99.9 per cent of things you hear on the radio.

I went to see her band play a few times, out of loyalty . . . I never could get used to seeing her play with such a conventional-looking crew. The guitaring always annoyed me – not hers but the other guy's. Still, Chrissie was always great, and improving. Her insouciance was natural and her intelligence kept your attention, once grabbed.

Chrissie: *I just feel that if one person out of The Pretenders left, we'd have to change the name of the band, you know?*

Vivien: *You do think that?*

Chrissie: *Absolutely. But this is strictly in musical terms, because there don't happen to be any personality problems in the band. It's not as if the three of us don't like the bass player, or the drummer doesn't get on with the guitarist – there's none of that. We're all like mates . . . we know each other too well. These guys have known each other for years and I get to know people really fast, really easily . . . I'm just lucky that way.*

The only thing that could possibly . . . I mean, who knows, it's always open for change . . . would be if there was a musical difference. If I came down to the rehearsal one night with a riff and Jim looked at me and said, "It's just not happening, Chris," then goodbye operation, goodbye team, you know? A million bucks isn't going to hold us together if we're not stimulated musically. 'Cause Jim'll be off – he can play with anyone. Any of these guys can.

They can drop me any minute because they can go and play with anybody – they're all proficient musicians and they're inspired enough that they have something to offer anybody, probably. I don't think that there's a band in town that if they needed a drummer and Martin Chambers went to audition, he wouldn't get the job . . . unless it was Chelsea [a punk band]. He went to audition for them and they didn't like the way he looked. So he didn't get the job.

Image might be very, very important in some bands. For example, these all-girl bands, the image is very important to them or they wouldn't stipulate in the paper "Female Drummer Wanted", which I've always thought was . . . well, to stipulate that you only want to work with another female is like saying, "Yeah, well, we don't allow any Jews in the operation" or "We don't want blacks" . . . It's not the sound that you're getting out of the grooves, then, it's the image, isn't it? Unless you're into some quacky political stance or something – girls together – which I can't understand.

But I've never actually spoken to a girl band about why they're just working with girls. I mean, personally I'd much rather have three little honeys to work with, y'know, than three other chicks. It's like a little bit of icing on top of the cupcake to have these geezers around – and that doesn't strike my ego, it's just delightful to have all these good-looking men around me all the time.

And they accept me as a bloke . . . no, not as a bloke, but when we're down at rehearsals the fact that I'm a chick has zero to do with anything – it simply doesn't come up – so it doesn't interfere. It is strictly a musical reason that we're all together. It's because of the band that I met Pete, that I met Jim, that I met Martin. So. That doesn't enter into it for a minute.

But what have I got to say? I'm not going to go out there and say, "Girls do this" or "Do that". I personally think that a woman's place, if she has kids, is in the home. If you have kids, your number one job – just like my commitment to this band – is you take care of them and you don't put anything else first, ever, ever, ever.

You might as well appreciate the little ironies life offers. Like the way Chrissie is up there singing songs of personal politics that delineate a woman's view no less clearly than the classic Slits songs; especially "Private Life", where Chrissie just is not interested in some guy's feeble excuses and pathetic, lying cover-ups: "I just feel pity when you lie, contempt when you cry."

She presents sex from a woman's viewpoint, the non-dependent woman who doesn't need a man for his car, his house, his job, anything that women of previous generations needed a man's validation for. She's precious, she's got to have some of his attention if she decided it's that way – or at least she'll make a try for it and be prepared to accept rejection, just like men have had to do.

This comparatively radical viewpoint is set in a frame of regular guys, straight ahead rock 'n' rollers – dare I say it, macho types as often found in bars. When interviewed, Chrissie's explanation of her line "No, I'll never feel / Like a man in a man's world" (in "Lovers of Today") has an odd resemblance to Margaret Thatcher's line on women – the classic line that says, on the one hand, "I've made it, so any woman can, now I'm one of the lads"; and, on the other, agreeing with the traditional male line that women are somehow dangerous, might rock the boat. In my view, until women and men can work together as women and men, we might as well as just watch telly and give everything up.

Of course, reality makes a mockery of theory; it may have taken Chrissie longer because she's a woman in a man's world, but the chemistry in The Pretenders obviously works, however it works, better than a pet theory that never gets onstage.

Vivien: *When Warners makes The Pretenders the number-one band on their priority list, are you aware of any pressure?*

Chrissie: *I just pay very little attention to that aspect of things. I know that I trust the people who I'm working with – if I don't trust somebody, I don't work with them. It's as simple as that. I trust that they're doing their job better than I could do it. If they make a mistake, that's fair enough. I leave it in their hands.*

I know that I can always fall back on cleaning houses – I've got the experience, I can waitress, I can type, you know? If it falls through, I've got loads of vocations I can go back to. Build picture frames, work for architects, anything . . . I'm equipped. Lead me to it, you know? I still have my old domestics agency number in my address book . . . if I need a job cleaning houses tomorrow, boy . . .

Vivien: *You've got to keep healthy . . .*

Chrissie: *Boy, don't I ever – I've really let it slide. You know how adamant I am about health – I've been getting so drunk, because you get very wound up, especially if you do a gig. You can't say, "Oh, that was nice. Good night, guys, see you tomorrow," and go back to your hotel and get a good night's kip. It takes a vat of wine to begin to unwind. It's like real dangerous and it's becoming a little bit of a problem.*

I looked in the mirror last week when I woke up and thought my God, not only are you rapidly becoming an alcoholic, but you're also rapidly starting to look like one – and I really curtailed my drinking activities after that. Because I don't drink for pleasure, usually, but to get completely smashed out of my brain, and it's so stupid.

One night, I felt very blue. Can't remember why, but I just wanted to see Chrissie really badly. It wasn't so easy to see her these days – not like the time I'd come home and she'd have made us a suitably frugal supper of brown rice and vegetables.

Those were the days when coming from Akron, Ohio ("Bud and Dee's little girl") was just an embarrassing joke. How funny it was when Stiff Records began their Akron hype, and suddenly it was cool to be from Rubber City and have a dad who goes bowling every week. The time Ma and Pa Hynde came to London on a visit and freaked out seeing Chris dressed like a rock 'n' roller, we were all pretty distressed by that . . .

But I phoned, on the off-chance, and Chrissie was home. Said "Come over," right away, so I scraped myself off the floor and grabbed a cab.

To find Chrissie in great shape, and slightly more terse. From time unlimited, she'd already begun to change into a person with No Time, like the White Rabbit in Alice in Wonderland . . .

Chrissie, it seemed, had suddenly become aware of material possessions. Two new silk suits from Strawberry Studios. She'd started to enjoy walking down the street looking fine. By that time I'd lent her old Portobello Road striped cotton skirt to a girl I knew who needed one – just till Chrissie wanted it back. Now, Chrissie looked like a rock aristocrat in her silk suit and new Johnson snap-brim hat. I made a mental note to tell the girl not to rush giving me back that skirt.

Indeed, it wasn't long until Chrissie was numero uno – for how long, of course, it's difficult to say. That limelight switches at a crazy rate. But Chrissie's durability stands a far better chance than most, simply because she can sing like Mavis and Aretha, even if she's got a cold.

So she came round to my flat again and we did an interview. Rush, rush, rush, like the White Rabbit, but it was great to see her again, though I couldn't say she hasn't changed. She's under pressure in all kinds of ways, but her resolve and humour have tempered, become stronger, under pressure.

Crisp, articulate, incisive, as she explains the whys and wherefores of what's going on. Highly professional, helping Adrian Boot to get the best possible shots. At the end of an hour and a half, she stands up to go – looks round the room she was trying to climb into at 4.30 a.m. a year and a half ago, and hesitates – should we have been talking about old times as if they were the Good Times?

That's totally OK, Chrissie, your future starts here.

Neneh Cherry

How prophetic the first lines of this article proved to be. At the time, her two eldest daughters, Naima and Tyson, were not yet joined by Mabel, the youngest. But all three have gone on to make music in their own style; while ex-Slit Neneh Cherry has progressed to become an icon of progressive, conscious, individualistic music and style. At the millennium, a few years after this article came out, her duet with Senegal's Youssou N'Dour, "7 Seconds", was voted Song of the Century by the nation of France.

Moving naturally between genres, Neneh's popularity grew when she explored hip-hop; and thus, very human connections grow new branches on the tree of music. We meet her here as she is recording the tracks that will help anoint her in the US hip-hop/dance world, like "Buddy X"; and asserting her primal womanhood.

"Neneh Cherry: Back on Track"
First published in ELLE UK, *1992*

A Home Brew from Ms. Melting Pot.

"I'm a girl breeder," announces Neneh Cherry, chuckling. The staff of the record store in San Francisco grin appreciatively at Cherry's comment on her capacity to produce daughters (she has two). This is a woman-run outfit and her quip has the effect of rallying the troops – finally, here's an artist who understands.

It's Cherry's only day to talk with the media and music industry people of San Francisco on the first leg of a meet-and-greet marathon to reintroduce the artist to America. Her new *Homebrew* album has broken the three-year silence since her landmark release, *Raw Like Sushi*, and its hit single, "Buffalo Stance". Her schedule's so tight she barely fits in an hour with her stepfather, famous jazz trumpeter Don Cherry, a Bay Area resident she hasn't seen for months.

Cherry won hearts the world over by performing as a serious, sensuous superstar, dancing "wind-and-grind" style in a second-skin mini, while pregnant with her second daughter, Tyson, now three. But when first announced, her pregnancy caused consternation at her record company. "No one really insinuated that I should have an abortion," Cherry remembers. "But there was this look of 'Omigod, what're we gonna do now?' It was the best mistake!"

Then she pulled her disappearing act. When what may have been Lyme disease, or just utter exhaustion, forced Cherry to cancel a 1990 American tour to promote *Raw Like Sushi*, she took a tactical and creative retreat from the public eye. In true goddess tradition, she went through that age-old mythic cycle: Death and Rebirth. "It was obviously time to take a break," she recalls. "It's really interesting what I picked up from reading the press. Their reaction was almost gleeful . . . That's why men can be sick and women will always soldier on with their flus, because if you get sick, you're perceived as defeated."

Renting an old farmhouse outside Bath, in Britain's verdant West Country, Cherry found herself surrounded by a loveable, unruly tribe of friends and family. Soldiering on didn't work, so a doctor prescribed his then-famous sleep cure: a healing, total immersion into sleep, aided by generous amounts of sleeping pills – a veritable descent into the underworld.

Cherry, however, heeded her own instincts, shunned the pills and simply took to her bed. A good thing, too: now officially discredited, the sleeping-pill cure was revealed as quackery by a vigilant British press, once reports started emerging of debilitated patients awaking from hibernation hooked on downers.

"I'm a bed person anyway, so being allowed to lie in bed for two weeks reading five books was bliss," Cherry says. "My head opened up; I had lots of ideas. It was strange, because I'd been around people constantly, surrounded by complete activity. First of all, not having to do anything was a complete relief. Then I had all these weird emotional explosions."

From these explosions come *Homebrew*, which Cherry co-wrote and co-produced once her recuperation was complete. Certain moments on the release transcend pop, inhabiting instead the still intensity of deep meditation, such as "Move With Me" and "Red Paint", a moving and disturbing depiction of a scene witnessed by Cherry's mother, Moki, in a New York City supermarket: although a young man had just been shot dead, grocery shoppers continued making their purchases, casually stepping round the corpse, their footprints red with his blood on the supermarket floor.

"Twisted", the most personal song she's written to date, also emerged from her big sleep. The lyrics from a wry love song to her husband, Cameron McVey: "Will twisted tongues bring us down?" As her co-producer, colleague and lover, McVey plays a central role in Cherry's life.

"It's reputedly difficult to work with your husband," says Cherry, anticipating the question. "I don't think we'd make it if we didn't work together. Through and with him I've blossomed in another kind of way. In a lot of relationships people take away from each other. You end up doing crazy things like running off with other people. I've never sacrificed anything. I'm on an equal footing."

Fittingly, for such a close-knit couple, *Homebrew* was actually recorded at home. Their current London residence centres around a well-equipped studio, which is next door to a big and welcoming kitchen. "When I got stuck on lyrics, I'd pick up a knife and start chopping something, just to relax my head," Cherry says with a laugh. In her kitchen, such artists as Michael Stipe of R.E.M. and Guru of jazz-rappers Gang Starr have enjoyed Cherry's "crusty" cooking: her honey-baked chicken with stir-fried broccoli and tofu.

Says Guru, who collaborated on *Homebrew*, "She's a great cook. She represents hip-hop and she represents womanhood. Plus, she's beautiful. And very lyrically motivated – she writes constantly. Although I'm older than her, she's like an older sister. She's got a lot of wisdom."

Womanly wisdom, rather than wiles, also drew Stipe to sing with Cherry about sex education. "Neneh's a woman's woman. She's very strong and that's obvious in her art and in her personal life. Women respect that, and men see and respect it as well. I'm one of the men who saw it and I jumped at the chance to work with her."

Not that Cherry comes without role models. Her Swedish mother, Moki, is an acclaimed artist, whose work with fabric and wood sizzles with colour, passion and meaning. Her father, Ahmadu Jah, who lives in Sweden, is a dancer and drummer from Sierra Leone. And her stepfather, Don Cherry, forged free jazz alongside Ornette Coleman in the sixties. Also, as might only be expected from such a remarkable family, her brother, Eagle-Eye, a dreadlocked actor and musician, has a new band, Love and Life, that is currently a hot property.

As children, Neneh and Eagle-Eye accompanied their parents, touring Europe and North Africa with Don Cherry's Organic Music on a bus with beds built into it. When not on the road – or visiting their extended family in Sweden, California and Sierra Leone – Cherry's time was divided between the colourful homes Moki had created: a Long Island City loft, with a spectacular view of Manhattan, and a rambling old wooden schoolhouse in Tågarp, Sweden. A centre of creative activity, the big schoolroom also housed the nationally televised children's theatre founded by Moki.

It was this home that Cherry, a state-of-the art punkette with a shock of wild red hair, left, at sixteen, to move to London and become a punk reggae rocker. She scored odd jobs in a hippy badge factory before singing backup for the prototypical wild-women, punk-dub group The Slits. Their token male, drummer Bruce Smith, became the father of Cherry's daughter, Naima, now nine.

Now a biracial citizen of the world and a partner in a racially mixed couple, Cherry has marked experience with America's tribal wars. "It's more tense here than it is in Europe," she states. "Over there, you see a lot more mixed kids, mixed couples. Here, I always get the most open grief from black men: 'You sold out to the white man.' 'She's denying her blackness.' On a day-to-day level, I ignore it. I've got pride in myself as a black woman. There's always been a strong black culture, it screams out in the music, but now there's a lot more anger. It's been shit for the black male in this country. It's been the white American man's business to make sure they had no pride left, because they were too sure they had no pride left, because they were too dangerous. But when I found someone I loved, that was gonna rule!"

Punk Fashion

Watching a cutter flow with the scissors, to me, is like hearing a jazz solo; I was raised in my folks' garment workshop. Writing for the enfant sauvage *of punk high style, Alexander McQueen, was a chance to express the fashion developments I had lived through . . . the original thrill of pulling together an appropriately inappropriate punk ensemble from various unlikely sources, including the infamous black garbage bag that Poly Styrene used to cinch with a belt and wear onstage. Call it reverse snobbery, but such inspired scavenging – which is now becoming its own eco-movement of upcycling – in some way feels superior to merely being able to buy anything from the Collections. Back then, we weren't being eco-conscious, we were just broke and working with what we could get our hands on. The thrill of the hunt demanded originality, imagination and improvisation. Delightful though it is, it's just not the same when a stylist hands it all to you on a rail.*

Writing this has got me flashing back to a black satin knee-length pencil skirt – kick slit in the back, just my size, a one-off from the 1950s – that I found in a (then downmarket) Battersea junk shop in 1976. How its discovery made my pulse race! When it was first made, you were only really expected to wear such an item with (equally risqué) fishnet tights, while hanging round on street corners, soliciting men for a quickie.

In fact, what became of that satin knee-length pencil skirt? Hopefully someone else is wearing it now, cut down into a mini, with laces up the sides.

"Neon Is the New Navy Blue"

First published on www.alexandermcqueen.com, 2019

Neon is the new navy blue. Fashion eats itself, gobbling decades like it was stoned rather than anorexic. In the beginning, in the first wave mid-seventies UK punk time, there was no neon in the drab, shabby London streets (apart from Soho strip joint signs). There were no elite, pricey vintage boutiques, nor glittering high street racks of garish leopard-skin and studded vinyl motorbike jackets, mass-produced tropes of punk style. There was not much "vintage" concept back then. Instead, we had jumble sales and second-hand clothes that your mum would sniff at – who knows where it's been? Might have germs!

Such treasures we would score in church hall scrums, junk shops or street markets, everything from Great War military jackets to 1960s op art shifts. We could pillage back through fashion's archaeological layers: a 1930s velvet tea gown; tweed suits straight from a 1940s Hitchcock flick. Oh, that long-lost 1950s eau de Nil chinoiserie dressing gown with massive shoulders! There were shrunken school blazers and baggy overcoats galore to take home. And then you could cut them up. Rip off the sleeves, pin up a hem, make darts with safety pins. Because you couldn't buy the gear we wanted to wear. All the looks we liked, we had to put together somehow ourselves, customising old owners' discards, just as we were cobbling together a new culture from the seeming crash of all that had gone before.

That included the previous bit of the twentieth century, like two World Wars and the sixties happy hippies. Instead it was a grey grind of no jobs, IRA bombs, power cuts, garbage strikes, constant street fights with the racist National Front and the infamous police "sus law", which meant young black boys could be picked up on the Orwellian charge of suspicion of loitering with intent. Arguably, today's anti-terrorist laws are less amorphous and all-encompassing.

It was not long since Britain had supposedly said goodbye to its colonies in Africa, Asia and the Caribbean, when punk first snarled. The nation's traditional all white, all right face was changing to reflect the countries it had "kept in their place" for centuries. Often spread by the first generations of kids whose folks had arrived from Jamaica, the island's deconstructed dub sound saturated punk music by people like The Slits, The Police, UB40, Generation X and The Clash, who used to say, "Like trousers, like brain."

Dub challenged our preconceptions of what music could be. It rearranged the regular reggae heartbeat riddim the way we restitched our clothes. Our dress codes were cut-ups, like our music, like our lives. The key thing was to mismatch, showing our disconnect from typical expectations. Here's the start of wearing "inappropriate" trainers or bovver boots with a frilly frock. Of wearing a First World War jacket with athletic clothes.

And the more taboo, the better. Stuff that was always worn by the opposite sex to whatever you were. Clothes that had only been flaunted by sex workers – fishnet tights and leopard skin – were ours by outsider right. Anything from the shady fetish demi-monde: rubber, vinyl, chains, studs. Punk claimed garb from the wild side, like the teddy boys' bad attire. The scourge of the 1950s streets, their sharply cut drape coats held a special seam to hide your razor blade in case of a "ruck". Like the instability we felt, we craved unfinished garments, inside out, rough, still in progress; wonky hems and zips. Clothes were a canvas and people spray-painted or stencilled stirring words on army surplus. Bondage trousers aside – they were a cute symbolic provocation – punk gear should always be ready for a mosh pit, for fight or flight.

Of course, Vivienne Westwood and Malcolm McLaren were flogging their bondage trousers and big mohair jumpers with pre-ripped holes at SEX on the King's Road – but not even punk rock stars could afford them. So they either nicked them or, like most of us, kept on foraging and inventing.

Then a street high-style generation arose from within the punk ranks: hatmaker Philip Treacy, catsuit queen Pam Hogg, Jean Paul Gaultier and of course, Alexander McQueen. The Versace siblings never looked like actual punks. But it was their slinky, safety-pinned uni-shoulder gown worn to a 1994 premiere by then little-known actress Elizabeth Hurley that seemed to set punk style pogoing into our high streets and malls.

It was considered "edgy" in 1975 when photographer Robert Mabblethorpe shot punk poet Patti Smith in a man's shirt and tie on the sleeve of her *Horses* LP debut; but now it's normal. When not just wearing another gender's clothes, but gender evolution itself is a prime-time TV staple – is any style still subversive? Since the 1980s, neon was always a reliable sign of hard-core "raverdom". Where is the abandon implicit in neon, now that Queen Elizabeth has worn it for her ninetieth birthday shindig?

Mallification and commodification and yes, a sort of style gentrification has happened to all the aforementioned once transgressive looks. Can fashion still be resistance?

In a world that often seems set up to make us conform or die, what you wear is still something you can control and use to project yourself, who you are and hope to be, how you feel about the world and the sort of change you want to make.

But how to be individual, express rebellion, even, when everything is so available, scarily manufactured who knows where by who knows whom?

The original solution is still the greatest. Whatever you find, whatever you buy . . . you can flex it. The long can be short and the short long(er). Dye it. Tie it together in a new way. Try it back to front. Change buttons, change mood. Adjust it, jazz it up. Wear it like only you can. Slice it, stitch it, frock it – rock it.

Pussy Riot

Eastern Europe has always been a fertile breeding ground for punk. Ironically or not, their playing was often more sophisticated, as many benefited from a classical music training to mess around with, courtesy of their socialist regime – even as the US was cutting its school music programs. At the time of Pussy Riot's court case, I pitched the New York Times *on a story, but the Music department passed. The collective's activism had overshadowed their exuberant, cutting sound. Happily, the Style section understood their significance as artists more generally; how Pussy Riot pulled their unmistakable look together is also eloquent about their needs, desires and demands. Unusually, the group had to project their music, message and personality without showing their faces – the reverse of the usual process. So often in the early twenty-first century, militant music lovers would wonder, has music lost its potency as a vehicle for uniting people and progressing society? Where are the great protest musicians, today's Bob Marley, Fela Kuti, Nina Simone or The Clash?*

The courage and integrity of Pussy Riot certainly gave them an answer. As events unfolded after the appearance of this article, some members found themselves paying the price for their outspokenness in brutal gulag prisons – but still refusing to be silenced.

"The Riot Girls' Style"

First published in the New York Times Magazine *blogs, 8 August 2012*

It has been a shock to see the bravely smiling faces of three girls from the Russian punk collective Pussy Riot locked in a glass cage in a Moscow courtroom these past two weeks.

Ordinarily they are dressed in shots of clashing colours, their faces hidden behind bright balaclavas. Stripped of their costumes and dressed in plain clothes (graphic tee, button-down shirt, day dress), they are unrecognisable. Hearing their names and seeing Nadezhda Tolokonnikova (twenty-two), Maria Alyokhina (twenty-four) and Yekaterina Samutsevich (twenty-nine) exposed and vulnerable on national television seems only to emphasise the band's slogan: "We Are All Pussy Riot." After all, if women who look like Tolokonnikova, Alyokhina and Samutsevich are Pussy Riot, why can't I be, too?

The women are on trial after being arrested in March for performing an anti-Kremlin "punk prayer" inside the Cathedral of Christ the Saviour in Moscow. Already imprisoned for five months on charges of hooliganism, the three women were initially facing up to seven years behind bars. (It's looking, today, like the sentence will be closer to three years.) The Russian journalist Sergey Chernov said, "This case reminds us of both the 1930s Stalinist show trials and medieval witch trials." It's suspected that Vladimir Putin's relentless pursuit of the Pussy Rioters is a reaction to their criticism of his cozy relationship with the Russian Orthodox Church. As a piece of political performance art, Pussy Riot's confrontational demonstration seems to have worked brilliantly. And their style – so noticeably missing from their appearance in court – is as big a factor in their effectiveness.

"The way they present their performances is a bright, feminist splash in our gray Russian politics and society," said Pyotr Verzilov, Tolokonnikova's husband.

Pussy Riot's communally conceived fashion attack is clearly visible in the YouTube video of the group's performance on the altar of the church. All the elements are there: gaudy, ripped-to-fit minis and shifts in contrasting solid colours with bright tights, boots and those haunting balaclavas. "Different colours explode when the action is performed," said Bullet, a member of the collective who helps the girls to make sure they look ready for the stage . . . or barricades. Indeed, the video proves you can always spot a Pussy Rioter in a crowd – kneeling in prayer or being dragged off by police, she's a flash of moving colour, never an individual girl.

Right now, the trademark balaclavas that keep the members anonymous are being worn at demonstrations around the world. Some of their most famous supporters – Mike Patton of Faith No More, Kathleen Hanna, Bikini Kill and the members of Rage Against the Machine – have fancier balaclavas than the girls themselves. But in the true spirit of punk DIY, anyone can make a similar balaclava. Simply unfold a wool beanie to its full length, then cut out the eyes, nose and mouth. "It's just a detail, but we use small stitches around the holes to make it fit better," Bullet explained. Pussy Riot's balaclavas are any colour but black. "We don't like the terror style. Colours have a different energy," Bullet continued.

"No more heroes!" has always been a popular punk slogan, so it's appropriate that Pussy Riot embraces a look that achieves collective identity via individual anonymity.

"The principle of our image is that no personality should stand out in the show and no identity of a particular girl can be recognised," Bullet said. "It's close to the ideas of Guerilla Girls, who had nicknames and masks. It's very important to us that there are no designers or labels to fetishize around us, because we do everything ourselves."

The one exception to this rule are the Dr. Martens they sometimes wear. "The girls have to be able to run at all times," as Bullet put it.

"When we get together to work out our clothes, it is like a feminine punk game," Bullet said sombrely. "The girls meet and we show each other the dresses, and say, 'Look what I've found!', just as if we were going to a cocktail party. But it's not for cocktails, it's for a performance that could be dangerous." Selections are made based on size. "They can be any clothes you find in the garbage, or steal from an expensive boutique or a thrift store," Bullet said. "My friends and I combined our dresses. We all had party outfits that we hadn't felt like wearing, because these days we don't feel very festive in Moscow."

Last night Madonna showed her support of Pussy Riot's actions during a concert in Moscow. It was announced today that the verdict of the trial will be delivered on 17 August at 2 p.m. Moscow time (6 a.m. EST). One hour before the verdict is to be released, supporters plan to organise what Sergey Chernov calls "a peaceful, nonviolent solidarity action" around the world. Balaclavas welcome.

CHAPTER 4

The Crisis Can't You See: Identity, Punk, Rasta and Rock Against Racism

(This chapter title is inspired by Poly Styrene of X-Ray Spex, the first ever Afro-Punk . . .)

Much of punk's glory was the ability to shed the old Babylonian patriarchal identity and transmute yourself – via name, outlook, lifestyle or attire – into another, free-er being. No doubt the organisation of Rock Against Racism (RAR) meant so much to me, among so many others, because it made sense of the post-war, post-colonial aftermath and fresh stirrings we were living through. It gave us the sense of a more positive and just future being possible, and maybe not even that far ahead in the future. Like the young Rasta bands, I was first-generation British – surely the world had learnt something definitive about the need for peace, after two world wars in such short order, each with its own sickening sort of carnage?

We, as young artists and writers, all had much to learn, but that punky impulse towards agency, freedom and individual expression, combined with a comm nal outlook, still sustains us. But despite the contradictions inherent for any freethinkers in the Old Testament-based 1930s Rasta faith, as evidenced in Peter Tosh's woman-belittling tirade (yet another revolutionary where it suits, alas – but he is still a revolutionary!), Rasta artists did give the protest movement of that time a sense of pride, of a positive ideology of equal rights and justice. It was a pan-African movement, not only Black-centric, but also inclusionary, along the JA lines of "Who Feels It (Knows It)".

I have tried to show here how the neighbourhood and the times we lived in tended towards making a multiracial society where everyone enjoyed everyone else's culture and calendar as well as appreciating "their own" and our community's celebrations. We were happily free of the crass, philistine, brutal extremism and fundamentalism, usually woman-suppressing, cultural invasions that have given multiculturalism a bad name. Let's enjoy every culture's festival we can, and our own celebrations as a community, in a broader togetherness! Ignore the threats of divisive naysayers. Citizens of different creeds and complexions can live together and appreciate one another in harmony, as has been proven over centuries, if the will for co-existence is there – and we had it. We still have it and if it seems to be lost for a while, we can find it again.

Here, I hope to draw you, the reader, into the exhilaration of that underground world created by first-generation Black British artists and entrepreneurs in a way that welded all of us tribes together, skanking to the heartbeat rhythm and spacey sonic extravaganzas of those late-night shebeen blues dances. Close dancing was signalled in the early hours by playing lover's rock, the UK's first Black music genre. You could wind your waist to Janet Kay, Carroll Thompson, or hit-making teenage girl harmony trio 15 16 17 mentored by Jamaican mastersinger Dennis Brown. (Lover's rock was also pioneered by Dennis Bovell, who plays with Linton Kwesi Johnson.)

The big tribe of dub was welded by men like DJ Weasel, who made sure our local all-night shebeen, held in an abandoned house, was a safe space for women. Turns out they were to be some of my best dancing nights ever, skanking alongside The Clash, The Slits, Aswad, The Cimarons and others of the punky reggae alliance. Dennis Bovell's Jah Sufferer sound system and Jah Shaka, the Zulu Warrior, could take a community centre, or even a bigger venue, and make it a sanctuary for the night.

In England, the essence of what Bob Marley called the "Punky Reggae Party" is interwoven into the DNA, and is understood to be the foundation for grime and all sorts of underground dance sounds since. For other readers, the post-colonial, post-war, first-generation kids of folks from the recently freed colonies were developing their own type of reggae and dub with Black British groups like Aswad. Jamaica's conscious Rasta reggae of that moment was at a peak of recording excellence, a golden era, and those sounds of the generation I cover in "Jah Punk" (see page 141) became the dominant punk UK soundtrack of choice. Always something of a one-sided love affair, the punks adored the Rasta sounds – while mostly the Rasta contingent welcomed the energy and the appreciation. And a new Black British sound did arise, not only with lover's rock, but with reggae that had a more citified, polished swing and sheen than the roots sounds which inspired it.

The constant threat of fights with the National Front (NF) was not at all existential, as my own encounter with them proves. But they could never win the fight, and they galvanised the grassroots anti-racist organisation Rock Against Racism, whose stages were first to have Black and White bands perform on the same bill. However, did we realise that the same fight would still be on, as I write, some five decades later? As Fela said, "Music is the weapon", and our grassroots culture-on-the-hop created the Dread Broadcasting Corporation. The first reggae radio with its own transmitter, it challenged and eventually transformed the rigid feudal overlord hold of the BBC on the UK airwaves forever.

Rock Against Racism

Three years before this 1979 article, "guitar god" Eric Clapton had reviled the Black culture that had given him a career from the stage, leading to the foundation of landmark grassroots movement Rock Against Racism. The following year, the British fascist party National Front got thoroughly trounced in a street struggle with locals and the police, known as the Battle of Lewisham. However, through the late 1970s, the National Front were a very real threat to anyone who wasn't a WASP (White Anglo-Saxon Protestant), as they were fielding a significant number of candidates for election, and in certain areas were gaining as much as 40 per cent of the vote. At the time, I naively thought that after the respective carnages of World Wars I and II, we as a planet might finally find a way to live in peace. Such was the uplifting energy of those mass multicultural Rock Against Racism marches. Alas, the same old battle is rising, not receding, as I write (often, cosmetically modulated platforms camouflage the evil old agendas).

After the publication of this article, I received a letter at the office from the National Front guy I spoke to, one Tony Williams. He was devastated – because of it, he had been asked to leave the National Front. I can't say I felt any remorse. To this day, I shudder as I can still hear his revolting voice in my head, spewing his bigoted hate. Joe Pearce, mentioned here, has apologised for his political career with the NF and written a memoir detailing his conversion to Catholicism. Looking back on it, did any of us really understand that we were entering an epic, seemingly infinite confrontation that would not just disappear, but force us to struggle to overcome ignorant bigotry, philistinism and ruthlessness anew in each generation? But overcome we must, time and time again, and there is no doubt to me that art and music play a vital role in the struggle, which is even hotter now than when I wrote this. The rôle of art and music may seem subtle to some, but it is real.

"Seeing Red at RAC"
First published in Melody Maker, *25 August 1979*

What's white and thinks it's all right? Yes, the NF's new rock offshoot. Vivien Goldman infiltrates the racist ranks.

There were two, three, sometimes four policemen chatting to each other with walkie-talkies at every corner of the peaceful Holborn square and at the back door of the Conway Hall where Rock Against Communism were about to start their first gig.

The idea of an organisation called Rock Against Communism (RAC) has a familiar ring – why, yes, it must have something to do with opposing Rock Against Racism (RAR)! Yeah, that's it – anti-racist equals commie equals reds-under-the-bed equals . . . in this case, the Young National Front, in the person of their führer, Joe Pearce.

Now, according to my sources, of whom more later, the youth are coming to the forefront of the NF because the older stalwarts have been forced to retire by public pressure from "commies" or "reds" from the Anti-Nazi League. Hence, it's up to young sparks like Joe Pierce to realise that music is the rallying cry for youth, regardless of colour or creed.

And hence this RAC gig – the first, the pass-out says, presumably of many.

Those conversant with London venues may remember the Conway Hall as a home of humanist gatherings, lectures and the like. The posters dotting the Ethical Society Hall draw attention, ironically enough, to the plight of Sri Lankan refugees. Some very odd doublethink going on somewhere in the Conway Hall.

That same Saturday night, London offered several events of several natures. There was the Black Prisoners' Dance at the Acklam Hall and the pre-Carnival Jump Up at the Commonwealth Institute. This Heat were supposed to have been playing at an Anarchists' Ball in Wapping – but, being anarchists, they forgot to book a PA, so that was out.

Which partly explains why I was trailing a strange sound in a green square in Holborn. Oddly, it sounded like the Balinese monkey dance with heavy reverb – just percussive slashes of sound.

As we turn corner after corner, the sound grows more and more distinct – it's rock 'n' roll! The big RAR truck blares through the neighbourhood, a very audible opposition to RAC's nearby presence, drawing snap-happy American and Japanese tourists to grab a quick Polaroid of a large phalanx of cute British bobbies.

In fact, the dark green shadow-windowed Special Patrol Group vans are parked not very discreetly here and there suggest a less cuddly scenario to the locals in the RAR march. A true seventies blend of styles: genuine-article turquoise-haired punks, hippies who looked straight out of a *News of the World* special on social security scroungers, Asians in crimplene strides and turbans. The group Charge were on the RAR truck, performing great acts of heroism as leads fell out, amps played up and so on. Their lead singer, looking like a miniature blond-haired Elvis Costello in a pork-pie hat, serenaded the SPG while the policemen marched alongside trying to maintain the patented police Great Stone Face as much as possible.

"Leave me alone," the singer warbled, "they won't just let me be what I want."

RAR main man Red Saunders, typically bubbly, yelled: "It's the first time there's ever been an electronic picket!" – a cheerful observation that lost some of its impact when the police called a halt two corners on, before the truck reached Conway Hall, and strolled alongside until they'd packed all their charges off safely down the Tube and out of harm's way.

I'd vaguely assumed that the left-wing element would somehow infiltrate the RAC show and express their sentiments, the way the British Movement are fond of doing these days, but it seemed like I was the only one with pinko tendencies walking towards the Conway Hall. The fresh-faced young cop who stopped me seemed to think so.

"Excuse me, which side are you on?" he asked with a charming smile. "If you don't mind me saying so, you look like you're on the other side. I wouldn't like to go in there, miss, if I were you. There's a pretty rough lot in there tonight – skinheads and all that."

Without wanting to damn every skinhead, I agreed with him. But what I'd noticed with alarm about the Conway Hall clientele was a super-abundance of beefy, red-faced, beer-bellied, thuggish types in black leather jackets with NF and swastika armbands giving myself and (black) photographer Vernon St Hilaire some flame-thrower glances as we got out of the cab.

Inside the Conway Hall, there were about 150 youths – I say youths specifically because there were only about five women, including a couple of skins and a punkette in a Ramones T-shirt. The lads were mostly skins with steel toecaps and braces fresh from seeing Chelsea draw 0–0 or burly-looking characters in NF T-shirts looking like mercenaries gone AWOL 'cos the army life was too soft. The DJ was playing Devo, the Sex Pistols and – heaven help us – Tom Robinson.

I got talking to a gent in a black leather jacket and jackboots pulled over his forage trousers. He was wearing a badge of NF supremo John Tyndall, taken from a youthful shot of the NF Oberführer in full Nazi regalia. "Tyndall in his romantic days," quipped my companion, one Tony Williams, the organiser of the Ipswich branch of the NF. Williams, twenty-two, looks suspiciously Latin but assures me he's of pure Welsh stock. He works in a wine and spirits firm, and informed me that the beer had already run out and that it was only shandy, anyway.

Williams reckoned it was a magnificent event: "The first time British men have ever been able to get together and enjoy themselves like this! It's different from anything I've ever seen!" I remark that it looks like all too many (rather unpleasant) skin gigs I've been to – chaps bouncing up and down at 45-degree angles and butting one another. The only difference was – no women. Women, Williams explained, are frightened of coming out politically because of social pressures to be feminine. "We do have some nice girls in the NF, but not enough. I mean, look at that one!" He pointed to a skinhead girl in braces. "Isn't that the ugliest thing you've ever seen?"

What did Williams think of the popular conception of the NF as British Nazi Party?

"Well, of course, you do get all kinds of elements within any political party," said Williams smoothly, obviously well versed in "the party line". "I mean, frankly, we're probably surrounded by Nazis tonight," he added conspiratorially.

Just then, his friend Simon, an ultra-Aryan tub-like hulk in a forage jacket, came bouncing up to us excitedly. "I say, did you hear those lyrics? 'We are the Master Race!' Isn't that terrific!" White Boss were onstage, a combo best described as sub-punk. I was only astonished Simon had been able to hear the words. The group were suddenly swamped in wave after wave of shouts of "*Sieg Heil! Sieg Heil! Sieg Heil!*" from the audience. Simon bounded away, overcome. Williams gave me a weak smile.

Williams expressed great admiration for the lads who had agreed to play. He prophesied: "They'll probably never be able to get a record contract now. Those Reds can get up to some pretty nasty tricks, you know. What did you vote, by the way? I know it's a personal matter. I," he whispered, "voted Tory." Yes, well, so did my mother.

During the course of the evening, Williams gave me "the party line" on all number of things. He expressed some sympathy with Chinese, Rastafarians and Jews – he appreciated the way those ethnic groups liked to stick together, close to their culture. He evoked the world of urban decay and squalor, forgetting that the rest of the planet is in exactly the same position, and laid it fair and square on the heads of those black youths who terrorise and beat up that favourite NF archetype, "harmless old ladies".

I say that I wouldn't necessarily feel all that comfortable alone in a train carriage with some of the NF members in attendance. Williams takes my point, but says, "Don't you see? They're all looking for something! If there was a National Front government, all these types would have to be disciplined anyway. You'd be sure to be safe then."

We adjourn to a pub, after Dentist deliver their "The Nazis are innocent" message from the stage. ("I say!" says Simon happily. "Did you hear that? Great, eh?") The pub is full of NF men, wearing their Anti-Commie League badges with the arrow logo directly ripped off from the Anti-Nazi League design – in fact, this sudden cultural explosion of the NF is remarkable for its total unoriginality.

Williams expounds his theories of the irrelevance of the concept of equality, based on the highly dubious statistic that all blacks have a 16 per cent lower intelligence rate than Caucasians. "Eight per cent, actually, old chap," grins Simon.

Williams says that he doesn't object to foreign travel as such; it's just that he likes to go to Kuwait or Hong Kong or wherever and see the native culture, and he reckons all expatriates should be back in there contributing; this despite the fact that he numbers the proprietor of one Indian restaurant among his acquaintances.

It's not so bad if the "alien culture" works hard, makes money and keeps themselves to themselves, but nonetheless, he invoked an eighties world of endless battered, crippled old ladies in fetid slums and a population of "coffee-coloured mongols" – the hideous end result, he claims, of interbreeding. I later discovered he'd lifted that colourful phrase from Enoch Powell's recent rant.

About now, my tolerance level was pretty well worn down, amiable and chatty though my companions have certainly been. I say it's time to head home.

"By the way, what do you do?"

"I'm a journalist from the *Melody Maker*."

"Oh. Well, do write nice things about us, won't you . . ."

"By the way, what's your surname?"

"Goldman."

"Oh." Pause. "Isn't that a Jewish name?"

"Yes."

"Oh. Well, the NF line is that if you're not a Zionist, you won't have to be sent to Israel."

On the way out, Williams asks if he can come back to my place. I am, as I tell him, genuinely shocked – it would have been more understandable, more worthy of respect, if he'd walked away in disgust, let alone after telling me about Jewish financiers and the anti-"goy" bias of such reputable Jewish firms as Marks & Spencer.

"Well," says Williams with a cheerful shrug, "you can't think about politics all the time."

Punky Jews

As I write in mid-2024, the world is in the midst of political turmoil and unspeakable human tragedy in the Middle East, as two tribes fight over a comparatively small strip of land they both claim as home, whether they call it Palestine or Israel. But round the world, throughout time, Jews and Muslims, Arab, African, European and otherwise, have lived peacefully side by side. When you read this, the world may look quite different; at this specific moment, however, due to a war over which they have no immediate control, the people's multicultural British idyll I just described is being tested, and sometimes seems fractured, though happily, not at all beyond repair. Generally, England enjoys being multicultural; we hate extremists, but know that they are a different thing. Nonetheless, in cosmopolitan, diasporic urban centres, like Paris, London, Los Angeles and New York, terrible physical manifestations of both Islamophobia and Jew-hatred have risen dizzyingly. Someday maybe I might write about the brutality inflicted on Muslims, and the unforgettable response of the uplifting Imam who, with his north of England community, decided to feed the fascists who were threatening them. The tactic worked. The men finally ate the delicious halal food, a dialogue ensued, and communication would be somewhat different in those streets in the future. However, this particular article is specifically about Jews and punk, so . . . Some cry that the Holocaust is being weaponised, even while the more reputable mainstream media show that one in five adults in America, and one in twenty in Britain believe it never happened. Should you be one of those doubters, fierce reader, trust me. It did. What happens next remains to be written, as hate stirred and manipulated for the economic benefit of the powerful is a force we must continually resist.

But at the time I wrote this piece, in 2014, we were simply considering regular, everyday anti-Jew-isms, the kind one might run across as a member of any minority.

How will we overcome the generations of hate being seeded ever more deeply by successive seasons of destruction? Arts can certainly help project the need and possibility for a fairer future, and music does connect people who otherwise might share little else than, say, their love of punk.

"Never Mind the Swastikas: The Secret History of the UK's 'Punky Jews'"

First published in the Guardian, *27 February 2014*

Punk Svengalis Malcolm McLaren and Bernie Rhodes were Jewish, and the faith had an influence on both UK labels and journalists. For Jewish kids, meanwhile, the subculture was an "inclusionary haven".

Who put the Oy in Oi? Surprise is the default reaction, and sometimes even disapproval, when I mention the "Jews in Punk" panel I am moderating for London's Jewish Book Week. And no wonder. Punks and Jews really are a contradiction in terms. Orthodox Judaism means following a body of rules as closely as possible, whereas punk is the reverse.

But being a first-generation Brit, first-wave punk and Jewish in a time still closely touched by the Second World War did have its conundrums. Witness an incident at my New Year's Eve party 1976/77, held in my basement flat in Ladbroke Grove in West London. The reggae sound system had started playing, rather late, when my friend Viv Albertine, the guitar player of The Slits, turned up with her pal Sid Vicious. Not yet a Sex Pistol, poor Sid's insecurities were camouflaged by black leather and a large swastika. When he walked in, the Rastas took one look and started packing up the speakers. Sid was no Nazi: his dying love was a Jewess, Nancy Spungen. But understanding the price of style, Sid and Viv left for a less sensitive gathering.

A lucky break for me, as the Rastas saved me from one of those ghastly confrontations I avoided where possible. Being of refugee German Jewish descent, I saw concentration camp numbers on the arms of my parents' friends. Swastikas made me feel sick, even though I told myself they were an ancient Aryan symbol and that punks just wore them to piss off their parents. It was hardly worth debating, anyway, as the pat response was always that they were simply cool and anti-establishment; genuine believers in the swastika rarely gave their true identities away. The swastika also caused an argument between two Jewish manager/theorists of punk, the Pistols' Malcolm McLaren and his friend, The Clash's Svengali, Bernie Rhodes. Fast-talking McLaren embraced being what my late mother called "a disgrace to the race".

Activist, artist and punk chronicler Caroline Coon recalls rehearsals for the 100 Club's first punk festival in 1976. Malcolm started handing out swastika armbands he'd had made. Siouxsie of The Banshees put one on right away and some of the Pistols seemed ready to follow suit. Aghast, Rhodes blurted out that if anyone wore swastikas onstage, they couldn't use The Clash's instruments as planned. The Clash backed him up. The gig went on. No swastikas.

The subverted symbol might not have been of much concern, had it not been for the growing reach of the NF, which at that time of social crisis was gaining traction and used punk for youth recruitment.

Writing for *Sounds*, the punk rock weekly, I infiltrated a NF fund-raiser gig by the band Skrewdriver and wound up in a Holborn pub with a leather-clad NF spokesman, eager to recruit girls. Blithely, he ranted against immigrants, Jews and the "coffee-coloured morons" who would soon ruin England. When he asked me for a date, I had to say: "Maybe not a good idea. I'm Jewish." A beat. "Oh, well, we can always make an exception," he replied cheerfully. Which made it sweeter when he wrote to me, complaining that after the article was published, the Front had kicked him out.

So the NF united Jews in opposition and located us on barricades alongside our fellow tribal Brits. Despite its general whiteness, punk's bond with reggae made it the first artistic expression of the new multicultural society. Having been the main "other" in WASPy England for so long, maybe Jews were finally one British tribe among many.

Apart from Mick Jones of The Clash, Jon Moss – who drummed with several punk bands before Culture Club – and a few others, our UK punk input was more on the ideological, art, media and business side. Judaism was not discussed much. I knew that Geoff Travis, the founder of pioneering indie label Rough Trade, was inspired to structure its socialist business model on the time he had spent on a kibbutz. In a rare moment of same-faith bonding, *NME* writer Charles Shaar Murray told me that his grandmother had to scrub pavements for the Nazis in Vienna, which he felt drew him to the blues and all sufferers' music, such as punk.

As for the two managers, McLaren's charm was the flip side of a master manipulator. Both he and Rhodes aimed to control their teenage musicians absolutely, like dictators. Nonetheless, they helped to create and project the free-thinking conceptual climate in which punk spread ideas, made money and delivered enduring music. These days, punk is established as the international sound of rebellious youth, grown locally in any trouble spot. That is not because of New York's garage rock and artistic forays. It's because of the sort of UK punk energy those managers encouraged.

I happily embraced punk's ungodly Year Zero. My musician father, who always said he had escaped from Gestapo HQ in Berlin, cautioned me to remember that I was British, not English; never to feel too safe, even at home. That sense of life on a fault line made UK Jews, us first-generation ones anyway, perfect candidates for punk, an inclusionary haven for marginalised misfits and outsiders. Belonging to a generation that launched Rock Against Racism made me feel more secure.

In a classically angst-ridden Jewish ambivalence about identity, the New York punk Richard Hell – of Television, The Heartbreakers and the Voidoids – has said he doesn't like to be defined by the fact that his father is Jewish. But he's one of many Jewish (or Jewish-ish?) artists on the New York scene, such as Joey Ramone, Lenny Kaye of the Patti Smith Group and Blondie's Chris Stein, who overcame his Holocaust paranoia by collecting Nazi artefacts. (The concerns of punky American Jews are documented by Steven Lee Beeber in his book *The Heebie-Jeebies at CBGB's*).

In a documentary I made for BBC 6 Music, "A Tale of Two Punk Cities", Talking Heads bass player Tina Weymouth recalled that New York punks thought people who talked politics were a bore. But to us, the ideas expressed in "Anarchy in the UK" and "White Riot" were real. The G2 or Second Generation theory, whereby children of Holocaust survivors are often socially conscious activists, could have had something to do with it; however, it was never discussed. But the Yanks were trying to forget Vietnam, while we were still living among bombsites in our own civil war zone, fighting teds, skinheads and rockers, as well as the sus law and the NF. Our punky Jew experience was also different because British punk mostly inhabited a shared political landscape, as well as views of the kind that McLaren and Rhodes helped to spread, which manifested in organisations such as RAR.

Nowadays I teach about punk in universities, to sophisticated New York students. Many of them regard LGBT rights as the last remaining major social issue of their generation (and that's not to diminish their importance). Getting the correlation between, say, The Clash's "White Riot" and the group's own experience of conflict, and seeing how it describes the street fighting Britain of the time, sometimes comes as a surprise. The immediacy of pop reacting in protest is not dead, but it is no longer necessarily expected and the life support is beeping; but, traditionally, artists do stir themselves to protest and the glorious tradition cannot die, even if it dozes for a while.

So the whole idea of Jews in punk arguably now has a quaint ring to it; the sound of a time when music responded quickly to battle lines that were clearly drawn and nervy underdogs were fighting in the streets for a cause, then singing about it. Today's enemy is diffused via infinite surveillance cameras and servers, not as easy to smash with a brick; and militant music is less fashionable than vinyl. But the war that began with the 7 October 2023 Hamas attack on an Israeli music rave and other sites ushered in a different social reality outside of the Middle East as well. While Palestinian civilians were dying in their thousands, attacks on Jewish citizens in some parts of the world rose by around 400 per cent.* Even before that disaster, our old foes were on the rise again in Europe; a toxic stew of unemployment and anger feeding the microclimate in which they flourish, as it did in the 1930s.

This grim vortex, of course, is an ideal condition for punk and what I like to think of as a Jewish contribution. Take the inherited trauma of generations of exile and suffering, use it to up your empathy, and channel it energetically, using culture, for the world you want. In short: be as punk as possible.

---

* Reuters, 31 October 2023. 'How the surge in antisemitism is affecting countries around the world'. Reuters.com [online]. Available at: https://www.reuters.com/world/how-surge-antisemitism-is-affecting-countries-around-world-2023-10-31/ [accessed 8 July 2024].

Jah Punk

Quite regularly, I am called on to teach about the particular scene I described for the first time in this article: the patchy but pivotal mid-to-late 1970s alliance that Bob Marley described as the Punky Reggae Party. Again, I was lucky enough to live in West London's Ladbroke Grove, which was almost Punky Reggae HQ, with its blend of Rastas, punks and all-purpose bohos. A sense of excitement always surged through this crucible of creativity, and everyone felt it. And it was all accessible, all populist. Different types of people enjoying living side by side.

Punky Reggae Party was a rather one-sided love affair. Generally, punks loved dub and reggae more than Rastas liked punk, though they did enjoy the attitude, energy and being appreciated. British reggae often had a slicker texture and wilder dubs. Even at the time, all concerned knew the combined energy was special. So these key artists were often friends, too. Again, there was no velvet VIP rope dividing writers from musicians in those days; we all participated in a grand artistic community – although admittedly, due to "Babylon system", some of us made a better living at it than others. Joe Strummer of The Clash and the lead singer of Aswad, Brinsley Forde, were neighbours on an adjoining road to my place. The only difference was that former squatter Strummer now owned his four-storey terrace house, while Brinsley's was a rent-controlled council flat. But neighbours they were, and both definitely appreciated the proximity, which was a great leveller – and in some ways, both knew they shared a unifying mission. The red, green and gold Patti Smith button that summed it all up was by local activist institution Joly MacFie's Better Badges.

The movement still reverberates in much popular music – and will continue to do so.

"Jah Punk: New Wave Digs Reggae"

First published in Sounds, *3 September 1977*

> *No boring old farts will be there . . .*
> "Punky Reggae Party" by Bob Marley and the Wailers

It was the red, green and gold Patti Smith button that clinched it for me. I was walking into the lumbering grey Hackney Town Hall for the RAR gig with Generation X and The Cimarons on the same bill, and there was this regulation blue-haired punk with the above-mentioned button on, and there was Dennis Morris, the Jamaican photographer, formerly reggae-pix-a-speciality, fresh from snapping Scandinavia with the Sex Pistols, walking into this punky reggae party with me, and . . .

One of those divine flashes where all the energy lines fuse and the outlines stand crystal clear. It goes something like this:

1. Basic premise: Jamaican music is to punk music what R'n'B music was to sixties beat groups. The Rolling Stones cut The Valentinos' "It's All Over Now", The Beatles cut Barrett Strong's "Money (That's What I Want)", The Clash cut Junior Murvin's "Police & Thieves" and Generation X do a reggae-style dub version of their own song "Listen" on the *John Peel Show*, guitars showering in shattered fragments on the airwaves.
2. Yet more evidence. Patti Smith bouncing around clapping her hands in excitement in her bedroom at Blakes Hotel, when Lenny Kaye walks in the room to say they've tracked down their favourite reggae toaster Tapper Zukie, and he's gonna come and visit 'em backstage for their second night at the Hammersmith Odeon. In the event, Tapper joins them onstage and toasts along with 'em, with Don Letts, Rasta DJ at the Roxy, the original punk club, helping out on drums. Later, Patti and Lenny fly Tapper out to New York to be a kind of roots consultant for their projected revival of the MER label.

The Clash go into the CBS studios with Lee Perry, the magical mystery Jamaican producer, whose crystalline star war productions are impossible to reproduce, and cut "Complete Control".

That same week Bob Marley's in town recovering from yet another football injury to his big toe. I walk into the room carrying a copy of The Clash album with their Westway rocka "Police & Thieves" on it – remember, Lee Perry (let's call him Scratch) not only worked with Marley, but also cut the original version of "Police & Thieves" with falsetto-swooping Junior Murvin.

Marley grunts, clocking the long player and my newly bleached hair. "Wha' 'appen, Viveen? You turn into punk-rocka?" he teases, inference being it couldn't be more uncouth. "You shoulda change your hair to red, green and gold!"

That's next week, Jah B. Now, just check these sounds awhile . . . Marley and Scratch are both surprised. Impressed.

"It good, t'raas claat!"

And the week after that I'm in a listening room at Basing Street Studio, and Bob's voice is rolling in magical command out of the huge speakers: "It's a punky reggae party . . ."

I'm not sure how many punks, in it to have fun, would recognise themselves in Marley's typically emotion/politics charged description, but it sums up the crucial reason why punk and reggae are linked – when you get right down to it, punks and dreadlocks are on the same side of the fence. Bluntly, who gets picked up in the street by the police? Answer: those natty dreads and crazy baldheads. Girl choruses syncopate behind Marley's throbbing, dangerous lead vocals "new wave, new craze, Jah Punk . . ." Thanks for the title, Bob.

Bob Marley and Lee Perry both said it, sitting in the thick white carpeted luxury of Basing Street. "The punks are the outcasts from society. So are the Rastas. So they are bound to defend what we defend." Marley pauses, flexing his arms. He's wearing a bright blue tracksuit, and he's just finished telling us why he wears just tracksuits and faded denims onstage. It's because he doesn't want to wear flash clothes that the youth will admire, envy and feel frustrated 'cos they can't have.

Remember all those declarations in the early days of punk that echo his sentiments? Anti-chic, poor people's fashions, dustbin liner chic. If you can't afford a packet of safety pins, you can pick 'em up in the street . . .

"In a way, me like see them safety pins and t'ing," Marley continued. "Me no like do it myself, y'understand, but me like see a man can suffer pain without crying."

DO YOU KNOW WHERE YOU'RE GOING? DO YOU KNOW WHERE YOU'RE FROM?

Apart from the fact that all the original safety-pin brigade faked it, that comment spotlights a heavy difference in punk/Rasta attitudes.

To understand it precisely, just think about the different and contrasting names of reggae bands and punk bands: Culture versus The Only Ones; Tradition versus Generation X . . .

It's so clear – the first-generation Jamaican bands of disaffected youth seek their identity by looking beyond their parents' heritage – they seek to understand by probing deeper and deeper into the roots of their cultural heritage for wisdom. Similarly with the music, the rootsier, the better.

In contrast, the punk bands are the lost generation, the misfits, the outsiders, who struggle to forge a new set of rules for life. They want the right to work; the Rastas want truths and rights; where the old generation just asked – have I the right to kiss you?

In case anyone wonders why young black kids have a deeper need to impose some meaning on life, Delroy Washington's lyrics (from his new Virgin album, *Rasta*) say it all: ". . . inna Babylon you're on the outside looking in . . ."

They were brought up on tales of the beauty of Jamaica by parents who emigrated here under the illusion that if the streets weren't paved with gold, they could at least give their kids a better life, and found themselves living on the dole in the cold, cheerless streets of Brixton or Ladbroke Grove.

If you're gonna be poor, you might as well be poor in the sunshine. Not surprising that first-generation English kids of Jamaican descent prefer to hook up with the last bit of the description – especially since this country hasn't exactly welcomed Jamaicans with open arms.

Matumbi's Webster Johnson described to me in almost painful detail the shock he felt when he asked a girl at school out for a date, and she turned to him and said, "What are you – crazy? I wouldn't go out with you, you're black!" Webster's parents had never warned him about racism; they hadn't wanted to encourage him to approach white English people with suspicion.

The Clash, along with Johnny Rotten of the Sex Pistols, have been the most vocal supporters of reggae. Their manager, Bernard Rhodes, used to have a record shop specialising in reggae records in Kilburn, an area of North-West London with a strong Jamaican community. He's watched the growth of reggae in this country with a special interest.

"A lot of it's due to the fact that soul lost a lot of its impact, so reggae picked up more people automatically. There were no other records to listen to. And somehow the two movements have become great friends. Like, bands and people involved have the same identity crises in both camps. To me, reggae gives the emotional rhythm and punks give the dynamic vocabulary.

"But the difference is, at last year's Carnival in Notting Hill, I watched the black kids run along the road picking up bricks, bottles and planks, and while they were running they kept on coming across new sound systems giving out spiritual Jah Rastafari music. So they were getting the spirit – all they needed was the means to carry it out, like the bricks. We've got the means to carry it out but we lack the spirit."

Rough Trade Records in Kensington Park Road is literally the only shop in London to specialise in punk and reggae.

Their mail-order newsletter is instant proof that Geoff Travis, who controls the shop, has an equal love and insight into both forms of music. He's been helped lately by Richard Scott, a long-haired ex-architect, who is, coincidentally, the manager of Third World, the Jamaican reggae/soul fusion band. They're perfectly situated to observe the relation between the two musics since punks and Rastas normally never meet or hang out together in the shop.

Geoff: *You just need to play something brilliant to people with an open mind, and they'll appreciate it. More white people would have listened to reggae long ago, except that so much reggae is released every day and so much of it is completely cornball-ridden MOR that most shops didn't know where to begin in sorting out the brilliant stuff and stocking it. I mean, we've sold 100 copies of Culture's* Two Sevens Clash *album on import from Jamaica and only fifteen copies of Bob Marley's* Exodus . . .

Richard: *Punks are usually quite new record buyers in the twelve to twenty age group. They're an uncommitted market who haven't decided which way to go. But they know they want things that are immediate, honesty, which they don't find in 90 per cent of general releases. So it's very easy to understand why Culture fits in side by side with The Desperate Bicycles.*

Larry Clarke of the Non-Stop Music Centre, a reggae shop in Blenheim Crescent (round the corner from Rough Trade), pointed out that the punks who come into his shop are usually only into the heaviest dub rhythms. "They're just not interested in the commercial stuff."

And it's the heavy, heavy dub that almost invariably carries the message of Jah Rastafari, of spiritual enlightenment. Not that it necessarily falls on receptive ears.

Paul Simonon is the bass player with The Clash. He typifies one reason for the sudden surge of young white interest in black Jamaican music. A former skinhead, he went to primarily black schools – William Penn in South London ("Sticksman [i.e. robber] school dat" observed DJ and film-maker Rasta Donovan Letts) and Isaac Newton in Ladbroke Grove.

"I started listening to ska at the Streatham Locarno every Saturday night with my friends. Everyone of my own age was listening to the kind of ska you heard on the radio, like Desmond Dekker. Then when I moved to the Grove I started hearing reggae again – 'It Mek' and 'Long Shot Kick The Bucket' by The Pioneers. There was only one other white kid in the entire school. That's when I started hearing dub, like Rupie Edwards.

"Reggae, punk, it's not like most of the stuff you hear on the radio. It's something you can relate to, kids your own age – they've got their battles, we've got ours. Black people are still being suppressed, we are being suppressed, so we've got something in common.

"But personally, all that about Rastafari bores me. Kids can relate to us singing about social things, like some reggae does, because they're living it. If we started singing about God, it would be fantasy, like it's all green when you die because you've been good. I don't think there ever would be a God-music punk band, because punks want to tear down everything that's establishment, like Church and police."

Trevor Bow is the lean, skeleton-faced singer with the Sons of Jah, who just scored a reggae hit with "Tell Them Jah Son" on Grove Records. We're sitting round a table in the back room of the Metro Club, an ILEA (Inner London Education Authority) funded youth centre and unofficial Ladbroke Grove community centre just down the road from Westbourne Park Tube station. Trevor strums a guitar and thinks aloud.

"To me, the punks are the conscience of society. That's why Babylon can't stand them. I would definitely play a gig with a punk band, but – me is a man like hear people hail Rastafari. Like when the people clap and things that's nice too, but me like it with the youth down at

Metro seh HAIL Rastafari!" His face thrills in reflex response to the instant spiritual high.

Chaka, doe-eyed guitarist and main singer for Aswad, had been sitting by that same table a couple of hours earlier, discussing the advent of punk music on his life with George ["Ras" Oban], Aswad's bass player.

"The way I check the punks, it's just what were skinheads in a different form, because they used to check for reggae music, too. But at that time many black youths didn't know about Rasta. Now, we've sighted Rasta and we have our culture, we're moving in one direction and they're still trying to find one for themselves. They're the sons and daughters of Babylon – by that I mean they were born in this country – who have sighted up and say, we don't want no more of this. And the only way they can do it is to move completely away, they turn against their parents. Like the Scriptures say, sons against fathers, daughters against mothers . . .

"We want to play more concerts with punk bands [Aswad were the first roots band to do it, when they toured with Eddie and the Hot Rods last year], but you have to be careful to find the right clubs. And then you have to promote it in two different ways – one for the punks and the blacks – so that they'll both know what a go on. But I&I's [the Rasta expression means the individual is part of a wider community] not hypocrite. We want it, that's what we sing about, and so of course we want to do it – one love, one unity."

George, leaning perilously back in his chair, guffaws: "See my trousers now? They're done up with a safety pin and man call me a punk. But it's the same with the holes in my T-shirt – I wear it like that because I haven't got another. The punks do that to be outrageous . . ."

Not always true, but those mohair jumpers with prefab holes do cost £26 . . .

Chaka says "Yes, Rastafari strictly . . . humble, y'know? Discipline. It's opposite ends of the scale. We have to get to the centre of it to sort it out because we're under the same pressure. The directions may seem opposite, but really they're parallel."

Forward on to Zion, Nothing Can Stop Us Now

Whether your destination is Zion or CBGB's, it seems like we're on the way – one thing Rastas and punks are in complete agreement on. The great Jamaican pan-African writer, orator and activist Marcus Garvey prophesied that in 1977, events would come to a head as

Culture described in *Two Sevens Clash*. Unbeknown to them, Joe Strummer was yelling, "In 1977, I hope I go to heaven, 'cos I been too long on the dole . . ."

In other words, 1977 may be the year when everybody will be so disappointed if some kind of shit doesn't hit some kind of fan that they'll do something to make it happen.

Since Rasta Donovan Letts began playing reggae at the Roxy Club, reggae music is the staple dance sound at every punk club. Don says, "That's why punk is so interesting – it's the first white movement I can relate to as a black man without feeling like I'm doing some kind of black-and-white minstrel show."

It was on account of Don that the Roxy was staffed largely by dreadlocks youth. Because there weren't enough good punk sounds for him to play, he started playing the music he loved – reggae – and soon found that the kids were coming up and requesting obscure one-off Jamaican pre-releases, and then started bringing in their own fresh-from-Jamdown discs. It was at the Roxy that many punks discovered that there were more highs than speed.

There's no such thing as coincidence. Elroy [Bailey], the bass player with Black Slate – one of the most aggressive, militant and exciting young roots bands – was drinking mint tea and eating egg on toast in my kitchen when he reminisced about leaving school at sixteen:

"I was learning to do clerical work – it sickens my head now to think of it – then I worked at a brush firm making brooms. It was supposed to be – opportunities!" Elroy laughs, but he sounds cynical as all get out. "There were four different stages. I was in the finishing stage first, then I was supposed to get a break and learn to be a spindle operator, but" – his voice drops to a sardonic whine – "it's an extremely dangerous operation because your finger could get cut off . . ."

Sound familiar? Remember how Mick Jones, The Clash guitar man, was inspired to write "Career Opportunities" after he was offered a post office job sorting through the mail to look for letter bombs?

Elroy continues, "Notice, they put me in the finishing stages first."

Enter the Rude Girls, Having a Good Time . . .

One of the greatest effects of the punk movement is the way it has encouraged women to get out there and play. Siouxsie and her Banshees, The Slits (who, incidentally, were once managed by Rasta Don Letts), Snatch (who are or were – they've just split – the only punk band with a bona fide reggae musician, Phil Ramocon – the jazzy keyboard player who doubles in Rico's band) and X-Ray Spex are four of the most visible examples.

I was always conscious of the fact that there aren't any militant sisters getting out there and playing in reggae, but don't worry – it's coming. Angela [Francis] plays keyboards and Grace [Reid] sings with Brimstone – a reggae band that's just starting on the road.

Grace, Angela and I sat in ballad singer King Sounds' car outside Angela's flat, arguing those same old arguments . . . Rasta is a notoriously sexist creed, not that the punks-in-the-street are necessarily different, and King Sounds proved that he'll be top of the list when the right time comes.

The basic argument is this. Man was first on Earth, according to the Bible. Woman was second, almost an afterthought, and was added for the specific purpose of keeping house and breeding. She's intrinsically inferior, and incredible though it may seem to all you gals in *Sounds*land reading this, there are a lot of bright Rasta women generally known as sisters, or daughters, who blithely agree.

"You can never make me believe I'm equal to man!" Sister Judah, a sparkling, talkative Rasta woman exclaimed in a shocked voice outside the Twelve Tribes of Israel meeting place in South London. All the Rasta men standing round nodded sagely and asked me why I was wearing overalls – did I think I was a man or something? No, it's not that, it's just that they're work clothes, see it? And I work.

No effect.

Anyway, back to the car. I explained to King Sounds that there were two ways of construing the facts set out in the Bible. To me it seemed just as, if not more, likely that woman was the new, improved, streamlined version of man, incorporating all the good points and adding a few more.

Another argument invalidated.

King Sounds was staggered at my cheek.

"But of course women are inferior!" he yelled, as if his whole world was on the verge of disintegrating if he didn't get this sorted out right now (and how right he is . . .). "Women were put on Earth to breed! That's why there aren't more women musicians! They were put on this Earth to fuck! Don't listen to her, girls!"

Grace and Angela turned slowly and stared at each other. Angela said, "I never thought you felt that way. I hope you don't start treating me like that," and started getting out of the car. "Pay no attention to Vivien," Sounds called out. "She's talking from the Devil!"

Angela's neat, perky locks bobbed back through the window. "I don't need to listen to her. I have my own thoughts. But I agree."

Chant down Babylon, sisters.

And the Players of Instruments Shall Be There

Apart from the Letts-instigated tradition of reggae records between sets, the main impetus for punk enthusiasm for reggae is down to the musicians. The Clash definitely lead the way – their cover of "Police & Thieves" is the strongest vinyl evidence to date of new wave sympathy for their black peer group. Even down to the shot of the rioting under the Westway at the 1976 Notting Hill Carnival on their album sleeve, The Clash have always laid their souls on the red, green and gold line. Bernie Rhodes was right when he described them as "a roots band".

Johnny Rotten, turned on by his old friend John Grey, may not have done exactly that, but the influence of his recent Capital Radio interview may well prove to be incalculable.

The shock of hearing Dr. Alimantado's exquisite rhythm and melody as he sings, "If you feel that you've got no reason for living, don't determine my life," was heightened as Johnny calmly told the peak-time listening audience that when he got home after being beaten up in the street, this was the single he put on to soothe his soul.

Dr. Alimantado wrote this song after being knocked over by a bus driver who, the Doc feels sure, psyched right out of the good driver's code when he saw Tado's natty, natty dreadlocks flying in the breeze. The sentiments extended over distant seas and wound up applying to a punk-rock musician with devastating accuracy. Personally, once the initial shock of hearing the Culture pre-release was over, it was a joyful experience simply because it proved how great roots reggae sounds on the radio when liberated from the ghetto stigma of "A Reggae Show" (necessary though they are, what with the crummy backward thinking of all radio bods with the exception of our own Jah Peel).

Johnny was leaning nonchalantly/watchfully against the back wall of The Other Cinema waiting for The Slits to appear, when I went up and told him how great the show had been.

"It's only what I listen to at home, what the great mass of the British public ought to be able to hear but can't," Johnny said, semi-ironic, semi-bitter, very pointed.

"Do you mainly check for dub, militant stuff, or do you listen to the lover's music too?" I asked.

"I listen to everything. I love music and I make very sure I know all about it."

No jestering. I remembered when Rotten had laid into me backstage at the Roundhouse one day for not being up to date because I'd only just reviewed Pablo Moses' "Revolutionary Dream" – just available on British release, it had been knocking around for months on Jamaican (i.e. expensive) pre-release.

Squished up against the wall of The Other Cinema, punks to the right of us, punks to the left of us, Johnny talked about British reggae bands like The Cimarons with a sensitivity and insight that proved he takes his music as a serious thing.

"I don't like the idea of a lot of emphasis on punk and reggae. That way both the musics could get diluted." Johnny is fearful of reggae becoming the latest in thing, a trendy bandwagon: "I've seen how the punk movement was almost killed by the media. I'd hate it to happen to reggae, too."

But I reckon there will always be an underground roots scene. And for the moment, it's a case of reggae bands simply being able to survive, to eat, to keep a roof over their heads, like The Diamonds sing. Besides, they really want to have their music heard. Surely you, of all people, can tune in to that – dodging round the country playing under assumed names because of The Pressure. I'll bet that wasn't how you imagined it was gonna be in the pre-100 Club days. You must be under more pressure than anyone in this cinema . . .

Johnny smiles and drawls, "If you mean, do I get knifed more than anybody else, yes, that's true . . ."

Under Heavy Manners

"We've just come from playing in Scotland and there's a lot of people who want to see punk rock up there, but other people won't let them. That's persecution, to me. That's what tonight's about, too – people being persecuted for looking different."

Billy Idol yelled at the audience at Hackney Town Hall. Friendly strong men stood two-deep, arms linked to hold back rabidly enthusiastic – nay, hysterical – Generation X fans. It was a triumphant set for Gen-X, alarming for anyone liable to be knocked over in the excitement. Meanwhile, The Cimarons were cooling out in a brown leather-panelled council meeting room, thwacking dominoes on the oak refectory table with stylish body movements and warlike whoops – just like back home in Jamaica, where dominoes are played in every back street at night, lanterns flickering on rickety card tables.

The Cimarons sauntered onstage. When you've been playing together for a decade, getting audiences up and cheering from Japan to Germany to Jamaica to the Apollo, Harlesden, you don't get neurotic about following up a barnstormer set.

The sudden adjustment in rhythm and tempo might have thrown some of the audience – for a lot of the predominantly white punk audience, it was their first exposure to live reggae – but it was well cool, the way the pogo people at the front who had been damaging the rather fragile stage with full-frontal hurls started to shift their hips in new rocking beat.

And then a jam, suggested with slight diffidence by Red, the RAR organiser, and enthusiastically received by The Cimarons and Gen-X both.

It started out with just Tony James playing bass with The Cimarons and wound up a wholesale ital stew – Derwood, Gen-X guitarist laying into neo-reggae drums, singer Billy Idol playing guitar, with Locksley Gichie, The Cimarons guitarist, flashing those great horses' hoofs Upsetters ska-style cymbals.

Nobody wanted to stop playing; The Slickers' great "Johnny Too bad" (hear it on Island's *The Harder They Come* soundtrack album), even Tapper Zukie's "MPLA", hit highs of energy, foaming over as the whole hall chanted "black, white, unite".

Tony James lay back on his bed later on at home, coming down slow after the emotional sweep of the gig. "It was so great to be playing along with reggae drums after trying to play reggae bass alone in your bedroom," he sighed, blissed-out.

"I really want to apply reggae techniques to rock and roll. I don't want to be a white guy playing reggae. I want to play our songs but understand what they do with production. Use the way they leave gaps – like you have a switch that applies treble, I'd like a switch to put more gaps in . . .

"From the bass point of view, I love the way they keep up the rhythm – like you're still nodding but the bass player's stopped playing. That's what I wanna be – I want to see punks pogoing but I'm not playing! Because the rhythm's still in your head.

"You know, they're the only guys who are taking music and using '77 production ideas to create something different – like you have a version, and a dub of the version . . . you create some sort of other music from the original, like The Beatles did with the backward tapes in *Sergeant Pepper*. It's real exciting – all I want for Christmas is an Eventide Digital Delay Line . . .

"Only thing is, it's hard to play dub at punk rock speed, 'cos by the time you've left a gap, the song's over!"

Too true, Rasta. I could almost hear the nail being hit on the head repeating itself all round the room, dub-wise.

Over to Carl Levy, Cimarons' organist, to elaborate on the distinctly one-way traffic in punk/Rasta listening habits. That is, the punks listen to reggae, but Rastas never, generally, listen to punk music.

"It freezes the mind, when it hits you. It's suddenly being exposed to total volume all the time. Reggae's more orientated around the bottom, the bass – it's closer to the ground. Punk music is more toppy. That's why there's no way you could get that screechy kind of volume in reggae."

I told Carl about Tony's ideas for using Jamaican production techniques in new wave music. He was silent for a second. He appeared touched, moved even, by the spontaneous gesture of musical respect. It's nice to be appreciated.

"You see, we have a lot to offer, but we're not given the scope, not given the chance. Reggae isn't a trend or a fashion. It's an audacity the way the major record labels have always seen it, pussyfooting around, getting a little thing together on the side. They just – try a thing, instead of investing in it in the right way so the people involved can grow . . ."

Rockers Time Now

Even while Carl was speaking he was aware that times are on the move. After all, The Cimarons have already been offered deals by two major international labels. Although not specifically linked with a black or white militant movement, they've built up a very verbal and enthusiastic white following through having been the first reggae band to play on white territory consistently. Their Gen-X gig wasn't a new experience – The Cimarons made a lot of converts to reggae when they played with The Jam at the Royal College of Art earlier this year.

That RAR gig was the culmination of a series of punk/reggae gigs over the last eighteen months. It started out with Aswad supporting The Rods on that ill-fated tour last year – Aswad claim they were thrown off the tour by their former record company, Island, because they'd blown The Rods off the stage at some gigs, and been treated with hostility by other audiences who hadn't been exposed to reggae and had ears only for Barrie Masters. Plus a certain amount of standing up for their rights with regard to soundchecks and the like.

Then there was the time when Generation X played a hilarious set at the reggae club Noreik to an audience of *Sounds* staffers (the Noreik's just a gob away from Holloway Road) and The Clash – no advertising.

The Cimarons plus The Jam felt good, but it was like – well, here's a reggae band. And now, here's a punk band.

The Slits/Steel Pulse gig at Clouds, a mainly black disco, in Brixton felt very different. Deliberate. Conscious. Both bands knew that in playing together in this particular environment, they were doing something radical. Steel Pulse had already shown an almost uncanny affinity with punk audiences when they supported Generation X at The Vortex, a white punk club. The appearance of The Slits attracted a whole bunch of punks down to a club they'd normally be wary of entering, so that for once you had the unusual sight of a half-black, half-white audience.

The success of the night (which would have been better attended if it hadn't been so extremely expensive to get in) was, natch, down to two extremely hot sets. It looked like it was the first taste of punks for most of the black people there and they were very obviously staggered at Ariana singing refrains from the newest Jamaican pre-release singles between numbers – they weren't to know that The Slits listened to loads of reggae, used to be managed by a Rasta (Don Letts), still had a Rasta roadie and selected this gig as a place they felt they'd actually enjoy playing.

The Slits are (for me, blissfully) the antithesis of the Rasta ideal of a *kinder, kirche, küche* good little woman. They're aggressively free in the way they move onstage, the energy of their playing, and very much a threat to male complacency simply by relishing playing/being with each other at least as much as being with a man.

When Ari screamed "*Under heavy manners and discipline*!" – a basic Rasta catchphrase – bouncing up and down like an ecstatically pogoing scarecrow, the Jamaican male contingent almost dropped their glasses of Red Stripe in shock.

Steel Pulse – even David [Hinds], the militant one – acted like they'd seen a coach-load of duppies (Jamaican ghosts) when The Slits roared into a rather dull photo session, jumping around in ferocious union just like Jimmy Cliff in his gangster suit and t'ing in "The Harder

They Come", like they were all enriched with nourishing marrowbone jelly and Steel Pulse had been stuck with brand x.

By the time photographer Ray Stevenson had finished the shots, Steel Pulse had found the groove, too. Just another instance of the way cultural interchange can be fun, and also result in finer art.

OK, looking back over this article, it reads like there's a suspicious amount of sweetness and light going down in the way of co-operation. In all fairness, every punk and every Rasta I spoke to at least expressed an interest in the counterpart movement, an awareness of some kind of link. But Geoff from Rough Trade also told me that he's had beer glasses thrown at him for playing reggae records at punk gigs.

It's not that I think we'll be hearing reggae sounds that last three minutes of treble-quick time, or punk sounds that vanish and suddenly reappear just behind your left ear.

It's just that something's going on and we might as well try to understand what it is. New young reggae bands are springing up as exuberantly as punk bands, and more and more bands are trying to break down the traditional dividing lines between black turf and white turf. Not to try to imitate each other, just to get a hit off the other's energy. For most of the reggae bands, it's a way of getting the great white record-buying majority to hear their music, for most of the punk bands, it's a buzz to be around the musical energy that gives them a lot of inspiration.

If I suddenly disappear off the face of the planet, you'll know the NF have got me. But I still think that even if there's just a chance that racial barriers can be whittled down even slightly through music, it's worth supporting.

It's like this. When the music hits you, you feel no pain – even if you're purple with orange spots.

And only in *Sounds* next week: a complete (well, just about) guide to all the reggae bands gigging around the country, complete with pix and interviews. Shine up your dancing shoes in preparation and we'll see ya there.

15 16 17

When I wrote this article, I already loved the harmonies of 15 16 17, part of the élite group of lover's rock female singers that included Janet Kay and Carroll Thompson. And how I loved their mentor, Dennis Brown, whose DEB and Yvonne's Special labels with his wife, Yvonne, were in the vanguard of Britain's first indigenous Black music genre.

Maybe it was because I so love harmony singing myself, in my musical hat, but something about this group of people – mastersinger Dennis Brown, Castro Brown and the chatty, cheery, talented teenagers of 15 16 17: Sonia Williams, Christine McNabb and Wraydene McNabb – drew me in so that I wrote this article in a different style, sliding in and out of all of their voices. Digging 15 16 17 was like swapping diaries with your bestie, so you could be absolutely, utterly honest to the person you trusted the most. The heartfelt directness of their vocals felt as if you were sharing a conversation. I still play 15 16 17 and they still soothe my soul.

"15 16 17: Living for the Weekend"

First published in Melody Maker, *20 January 1979*

15 16 17 are the best-known of British reggae's new crop of female vocal trios.

Christine's new beige sandals tap the floor impatiently. Hot and humid condensation splashes from the pipe over her head, wetting the ruffled neckline of her new white shirt. She can feel drops slither down the coils of her white turban; and her nose crinkles up, almond eyes blink, as she shakes her head impatiently.

She looks up. The real dimensions of the room are shrouded in strands of grey mist. The corners appear for a hazy instant, then blur as figures crowd into a new configuration; the only certainty is that the room is very crowded.

Over there are Wray and Sonia. Christine recognises them by the gold thread in Sonia's new mohair jumper. Christine squeezes through tentacled dancers until she reaches her sisters' sides. Actually, only Wray, Christine's older sister, is a direct sister, but Sonia "practically lives round our place, calls my mum Mummy 'n' everything".

Talking to Castro Brown [author's note: the Svengali/Father Figure] again, Christine muses. "Wonder if he means what he says about us coming to the Talent Contest? We deserve to win it – we've worked so hard on our dance steps. We're better than any of those girls they have dancing on *Top of the Pops* – and I'm telling you the truth. When they had The Three Degrees on telly the other night, we danced better than them! And sang their own song better, too!

"I always like to enter competitions, anyway. Any kind of competition. We all do – just ask Sonia or Wray. If we'd only remember to post those coupons lying underneath the table in the front room, we could have all had a weekend in Paris from Honey magazine. I know they said it was only for two, but they'd have to say that, wouldn't they? And there was that car they were giving away on the side of the cornflakes box – I'm not old enough for a driving licence yet, anyway, but Wray is, and we could all pay for her driving lessons.

"I s'pose I could get a Saturday job at Chelsea Girl. They probably give you a discount on the clothes, too, and there's a satin suit – cream, with flowers in the material – that I want to get anyway. You've got to look good onstage. You've got to please an audience. I know even though I s'pose it could seem strange when I haven't really performed yet, not a whole show. But I know what I like. I like songs you can sing along to and that's what he'll want, too – John Public. Truthfully."

But applause is a siren song tugging Christine's ears and, having heard it once, she knows she will hear it again. She did agree to get up onstage and take the mike from the lead singer of The Equators. She'd only hesitated for show; really, she knew she was going to do it as soon as Linda started teasing her, saying that she and Sonia and Wray could sing "Caught You in a Lie" better than they could.

"But it was – just natural. Because, see, I've been singing all my life, really. I come from a singing part of the family. I know I speak English good; maybe you didn't know I don't come from South London. I came over from Jamaica to join my mum and dad, when Grandma and Great-Grandma were getting too old, and me and Wray got to be too much of a trouble for them.

"It's three years since I used to stand up in church and push through to the front, like I'm doing now, squeezing through all these couples, hugging up instead of through scraping rows of wooden chairs. When I got to the front, I'd sing a hymn, and I'd always change the words around, perhaps make it a bit freaky, do my own thing. Or I'd read one of the poems I'd written.

"That's when I started writing stories, too. I'd always be at home writing stories when they expected me for the Spelling Bees at school, even though they thought I'd be there, because they all know I love competitions.

"In a way, I preferred the schools in Jamaica. It never worried me that they used to beat you. 'Lick you,' they called it, maybe twenty times, as many as the teacher felt like. Here, they say if you don't learn, it's your fault and there, if you don't learn they say it's their fault and they'll lick you.

"My gran taught us German. Our family was different than the other families in Jones Town, Trench Town, concrete jungle. My great-grandma is from Scotland, so we're from this side, really. My dad is a real Jamaican and my mother is half – her mother's German.

"Slim Smith [author's note: a Jamaican balladeer of merit, now deceased] was my cousin, you know. He was married to one of my first cousins. He used to come round our yard all the while and that's where I started thinking about singing. He'd be in his thirties now. He'd be an expert, right on top! It was something to do with managers and artists, clients not getting their right amount of money. So he goes mad and conks some louvre windows out. Going crazy.

"Singing didn't really attract me then, I thought it didn't, I thought it was just for fun. But now I know that nothing will stop me. Us. Anything we have, we share. If one has money, three have money. If you pick on one, you got to pick on three. It's always been like that, ever since Sonia's parents brought her round one night when they came to visit our parents. We started dancing to Earth, Wind & Fire in my bedroom, and I laddered my new pair of tights."

When he saw the girls, Castro Brown knew they were something special, straight away. Just what he and Dennis needed, really.

Ever since the Morpheus label collapsed, they'd been working together – brethren before that, still, says Castro. "Now, we're business partners, too. Nobody has ever been a better friend to me than Dennis Brown. When the whole Morpheus thing collapsed, Dennis said to me – and I'll never forget it – 'Castro, as long as Dennis Emmanuel Brown is alive, you will never sleep on the street.' And Dennis has always been as good as his word . . ."

Castro used to run a small independent reggae label called Morpheus – "I used to love the name at first, but then I got to hate it. Morpheus is the Jewish god of dreams [author's note: inaccurate – he's Greek] and I'm not dreaming te blaad claat! Is reality me and Dennis Brown a deal with!

"I've served my apprenticeship in every part of this business. I can promote, I can do advertising, I could go out and just be a compère. I can produce. I made a toasting record for The Dip after the Carnival riots one year, but he sold out all he'd pressed and never done any more. I s'pose I've lost my DJ style a bit, but it's still there inside me, I know that. I know every aspect of this business – I'm not the best at any of 'em, but I'm Jack of all of 'em."

Castro Brown, wide-brimmed gangster hat, three-piece suit an' t'ing, is a professional. Beloved figure on the reggae scene – which inevitably means as much hated as beloved. Gentle, but there's great fierceness within him. His manner towards 15 16 17 his protégés, is tender, then angry, always tinged with elder-brother/fatherly solicitude.

At school, he was a boxer; he's still a fighter and self-promoter. Earns admiration and irritation by featuring himself largely on posters for shows he's compèring, by having a hunger for making his name known. Castro is most fierce, and most gentle, when he cares most. His loyalty to Dennis Brown is passionate; they may not have nicked their palms and mingled the blood, but they're blood brothers still.

"I come here from Jamaica. It's a Sunday, it's cold. I go to school on the Monday; I can hardly speak English. Two thousand kids in the school and I'm the only black one – no one to talk to, no one to understand. It was a terrible experience. I was beaten up. It's not like now – I used to come home with spit on the back of me blazer. I'd been here four years when I had to leave home, my stepfather . . . Terrible life, you know. I been on the street fighting, like I'm fighting today. It's a fight. It's not something I forget, it's something that face me all the time."

Castro cruises on pure energy, a born organiser. His talent competitions at the Georgian Club were the real birth of 15 16 17. He gave them their name, riding back from the competition in a car.

"How old are you?"

"Fifteen."

"Sixteen."

"Seventeen."

Unrealistically, perhaps, Castro wants 15 16 17 – who are now 17, 18 and 19 in "real" time terms – to be called 15 16 17 forever.

Although the world outside may perceive 15 16 17 as teen idols, glamour queen-lings, soft smooch sirens, to Castro, 15 16 17 are an ideal. An ideal to the youth.

He wants every young black kid to look to 15 16 17 and say – yes, there is hope. There is a chance of that cool-flowing, easy skanking existence, sweet consumerism and true romance, and a roof over your head, food in your belly, fire in the winter.

Roots' reggae lovers, usually white, in this country, sometimes look askance at 15 16 17 unable to understand why they dominate the reggae charts so persistently. The same people often used to deride disco, saying that only blues or gospel is "authentic", i.e. worthwhile music.

Have you noticed that middle-class kids run around in rags, while people brought up in poverty tend to be crisply turned out? Rags are a middle-class luxury. No one who was forced to wear rags wants to, as a rule.

The beauty of 15 16 17 is that they have never suffered.

So young that they never grew up in the crippling colour isolation Castro endured, their faces are unmarked, their motivation laser-keen, uninterrupted by fears and neurosis.

From the moment they were "discovered", their way has been clear. Castro has made it clear. "No one would try to put anything over on Castro," the girls tell me.

Sheltered by Castro's armoured wing, the girls know: "We've been quite lucky, because many artists like Delroy Wilson and Dennis Brown have been ripped off so many times. We never had do like other artists: sleep in the back of trucks on the road an' t'ing – fighting for dem pay. We could just do our show and come home again."

You'd think that 15 16 17 were from a different planet than The Slits.

Like Olivia Newton-John, 15 16 17 are nice girls who want to be nice girls. They start out with the traditional entertainment concept: you must gratify the audience. They love to ride in the apple cart Johnny Rotten started to overturn three years ago. They are full of maxims like: "Never turn your back on an audience." Sonia and Christine cluck and get quite disapproving about other girl entertainers who skank round the stage in dreadlocks, who harangue the audience in deep Rasta patois.

We are sitting round in the living room of Christine and Wray's mother; cosy, clean and comfortable, the only sound the bubbling of the compressed air making the plastic skeleton in the tropical fish tank bob up and down. Scandinavian-style smoked-glass cabinets sculpted in stainless steel contain sparkling shelf after sparkling shelf of polished ceramic and blown-glass knick-knacks, the white wool and sheepskin rugs are spotlessly clean, and Christine's little brother asks me politely to take my boots off the rug . . .

Christine's face is a flawless Botticelli oval; the dainty *Primavera* curl of her upper lip is a poem. Even in a blue tracksuit, black turban and perfectly pressed, faded straight-leg jeans. Her skin is the creamy café au lait colour American blacks used to call "high yeller" and regard as the quintessence of beauty.

Sonia's complexion is rich and butterscotch tawny, her smile has just got the cream. She is wearing strappy gold sandals and no stockings in the snow, a surreal touch of summer. She'll take a cab back, too, when she wants to leave. Enters carrying one of Christine's dresses over her arm, in a neat plastic cover as if it had just come back from the cleaners, though it hasn't.

These girls are bandbox fresh, as if they'd absorbed all the books like *How to Be a Girl* and *Growing Up Female* that my parents used to buy me and I never used to understand. They are the kind of girls my mother wanted me to be. They romp and giggle in soft fur coats like high-fashion cover girls.

They are children of the discos. "When we'd get £20, we'd buy three skirts. The next week we'd buy three tops, the next week we'd buy three pairs of shoes, then we'd go sporting. We used to go to Tiffany's in Purley and we had a nice little club round the corner we used to go to every Thursday: we'd have our new clothes on and everybody would look at us. It was fun! You couldn't tell us we didn't look nice – we'd tell you off!"

The difference is that Christine – eighteen – is a born musician, writing songs, poems, singing round the house all her life. When I phone up and say, "Tell Christine I'm bringing a photographer, if she wants to wash her hair" [a joke] the voice at the other end laughs. "Don't worry, Christine's always got her hair washed!"

When photographer Janette Beckman and I arrive, we dissuade Christine from changing into a dress for the photo session; meanwhile, men in tracksuits wander in and out, and kids on school holiday bounce. Christine's mother makes us sweet, creamy tea.

Christine is vehement. She jumps to her feet and stiffens with defiance as she details trying to make the rhythm guitar be more adventurous in its patterns. "I keep telling him to tune his guitar or buy a new one. He'd get the money if he needed it. But they don't take it serious; they're just mucking about! If we had a band like The Revolutionaries or Aswad . . ."

15 16 17 are different from the other disco sweethearts, because when Castro Brown said to them, "Girls, you've got talent. Write two songs and come back and see me," they went home and wrote two number-one reggae hits straight away. One, "Black Skin Boy", originally on Morpheus, has just been reissued as a DEB disco mix. Produced by Dennis Bovell of Matumbi, he also plays all the instruments except the drums (by Bunny Matumbi). It's as loins-stirring as ever, sheer smoky sensuality, teenage trembling, Christine is jailbait, she is Lolita, and the bass line hypnotises even as the song empowers often-under-threat Black Skin Boys (all too often suffering from police harassment and systemic rejection).

Since then, there has been "Emotion", "Girls Imagination", "Suddenly Happiness", "Only Sixteen", "Good Times" – all DEB disco-mixes released in the space of one year, and all but one double A-side reggae chart number ones.

Most of them are soul covers. That's because the girls have been writing songs all year and saving them up for the album of original new songs they're due to record shortly, with Castro Brown producing, as he usually does. Sly [Dunbar], Earl "Chinna" Smith and other crucial JA session men are being flown over by Dennis Brown. If they don't get the band they want, Christine says firmly, they won't make the album.

They're very clear about the deficiencies of the 15 16 17 operation and painfully aware that until their new backing line-up is found, they can't loosen up onstage. They feel now that by the time they've warmed up, they have to leave the stage.

They're all prepared to put money into the band; they want to manage themselves, eventually, and produce themselves by 1980. All three girls are learning to play piano and Christine is starting to play bass.

"I want us to know our instruments good, so when we put on a show we can do everything right. I wanna play some piano, then play some drums – I want to do everything! All of us want to do everything!"

Castro welcomes their urge to independence; he already has the new Black Harmony trio to guide. Black Harmony have been supporting 15 16 17 on their dates.

Speaking as one, they agree, "When we started, we didn't have anyone to play with. It was just 15 16 17 on their own. It has always been just our records pushing us. It's up to John Public."

"John Public is all right!"

Dread Broadcasting Corporation

Had he not died in 2018 at the age of sixty-three, Leroy Anderson of the Dread Broadcasting Corporation, Europe's first Black pirate radio, might well have received one of those government gongs awarded to other once underground Black British media figures (while some, like dub poet Benjamin Zephaniah, rejected them on historical grounds). Leroy's phenomenal contribution to the development of a generation's identity, and the impact he had on British broadcasting, can never be praised enough.

Any UK kid from the 1960s will remember the thrill of huddling under the blanket with a tiny crystal set radio to listen to the forbidden airwaves of pirates like Radio Caroline; and oh, the rage when they would be boarded by police and forcibly taken off the air. They were the only place to hear contemporary music – forget the then stuffy old BBC.

When DBC began operations in 1980, the BBC had woken up to pop and rock, but still refused to play reggae – which at the time was one of the richest genres around, in both Jamaica and Britain. So, in making DBC together with other members of his diverse community, all bonded by dub, Leroy was a great cultural warrior. He risked his life and freedom to make sure the most revolutionary music around got heard on his rebel radio and helped build a community that will endure.

"Tune In If You Rankin: Night of the Living Dread"

First published in New Musical Express, *24 March 1984*

A Rooftop Rendezvous with the Dread Broadcasting Corporation.

The DBC, with its natty merchandising and high rebel profile, is the most vivid face of British pirate radio. They'd only been turned over twice in their four years of broadcasting, till Xmas of 1983. They've now been busted a record three times in the space of six weeks.

Lepke, DBC's Dread at the Controls, says philosophically: "We're not really giving up. We knew it would be a hard, long fight. But being forced to give up through lack of money – that might happen."

DBC are probably the most infamous British pirate radio. Their logo – their "Tune in, if You Rankin'" byword – set international imaginations alight, to the occasional annoyance of their pirate peers.

A pirate's life is obviously fraught with risks. In DBC's case, they broadcast from a West London eyrie twenty-two floors up, entailing an alarming Harold Lloyd-esque crawl up the outside of the building to reach the roof. Would (BBC DJ) Mike Reid be as keen? Throughout their life, DBC's attempted to expand the scope of their music, spanning virtually all black musics minus jazz – reggae, soul, soca, electro-funk, R&B, Afrikan. Apart from worthies like Charlie Gillett, Gary Crowley and Tony Blackburn, there's little enough exposure for this wealth of pan-Afrikan Black diaspora sounds.

From the outset, their attitude was political with a small "p". Lepke was inspired by a visit to his mum in the States, where the selections on the dial taught him that Britain is "a free country with free speech, but no free listening."

The DBC style has always been the nation's most spectacular, its DJs – Miss P (now working for TV's *Ebony*), ex-DBC man Dr Watt (aka the *NME*'s Lloyd Bradley), Lady Di, and freelancers like Gus Anyia and Neneh Cherry – were free to form their own schtick. The result was as rich and surreal as the original Jamaican inspiration, Mikey Campbell's old *Dread at the Controls* radio show – itself banned a long time ago . . .

The station's mainstays are Lepke and his sister Margaret (interestingly, since DBC is the greatest living exponent of Bob Marley's rebel soul, they're Rita Marley's half-brother/sister), and a white ex-public school ex-hippy, Mike Williams. Mike and Lepke went into cahoots when they were both made redundant simultaneously from Better Badges and Honest Jon's Records in the Portobello Road. Better Badges' founder Joly MacFie gave them an old transmitter he had lying around, and DBC began.

Lepke's had a chequered career since he arrived here from Jamaica at age seven. But things started to get tough when his mum left for the States, when he found himself shunted in and out of various homes, getting involved in low-level petty criminality, leading to a succession of stints at Her Majesty's pleasure.

While Lepke was waiting for the last of his youthful indiscretions to send him away again, he was planning for the survival of DBC, which by then was far more interesting to him than his old line of work: "When you're inside, you do a lot of thinking. I saw the way a black radio station would help the community."

To his great satisfaction, the station continued broadcasting in his absence. As Mike points out, "This government's imposed vast amounts of unemployment, which means there's loads of people sitting round doing nothing. They're either going to be entertained in the home through domestic appliances, or they'll be boozed or smacked out. Whatever, they'll be causing trouble. So why not open up the media, give people the right to choose?"

The equation seems simple enough. But with the sudden clamp-down on all the pirates, the government is showing its determination to keep the media in the hands of the authorised, jobsworth few.

Each new transmitter is £300 and having to rustle up an infinity of gear is an alarming prospect, with the best will in the world.

Right now, DBC are launching themselves in many directions – a film is under discussion with interesting major record labels, they're trying to syndicate their DBC Specials, they've already made a record ("Striving to be Free" sung by Miss P plus The Israelites) and a video, and they're continuing live DJ'ing at gigs.

"We want to try and get ourselves a bit more legal, so we can present ourselves more positively – form a co-op, have a broadcasting school teaching young DJs," they say, the ideas tumbling out.

The first time they were nicked, the DBC proudly proclaimed their allegiance to the free radio cause. Four years on, the battle has got hotter. If you like skankin' to the rankin' DBC, you might consider putting your money where your ears are.

Linton Kwesi Johnson

Even at the time, I knew it was an honour to write the first cover story on the man who would become emblematic of Black British resistance culture and forever known as the "Godfather of Dub Poetry". Since then, as a musician, the man they call LKJ (in partnership with producer Dennis Bovell, who, you may recall, also produced The Slits and lover's rock) has continued to fuse riveting socially astute verse with sturdy dub rhythms. The punch of Linton's verse is grounded in hard political facts and the tenacity of everyday activism. In this piece, he is cynical about the rôle of music in the revolution. But his impact belies those words.

"Linton Kwesi Johnson: Poet of the Roots"
First published in Sounds, *2 September 1978*

There's a theory that runs parallel to the "if you can, do, if you can't, teach" maxim that assumes all rock writers secretly yearn to be rock musicians (me, I always wanted to make horror films, but that's another reggae feature . . .). Lenny Kaye has achieved the ultimate in blossoming from rock scribe to rock guitarist when Patti Smith planted the appropriate kiss on his frog/scribe forehead.

Other writers have enjoyed flirtations with the footlights recently – our own beloved David Fudger, for one with his Snivelling Hits escapades (and even he's now retired to the bosom of Virgin Records), Charlie Murray with Blast Furnace and the Expletive Deleteds, Mick Farren's album's just released, Nick Kent's trying to get a deal on some tapes . . .

Linton Kwesi Johnson used to write reggae reviews for *Melody Maker* and has contributed to journals including: *New Society*, *The Times Literary Supplement*, *Race Today*, *West Indian World*, *Race & Class* – he's even written some reggae reviews for us. Plus his two published volumes of poetry, *Voices of the Living and the Dead* and *Dread, Beat and Blood*, probably the most vivid patois explorations of life in Britain's Jamaican community ever to hit ink, some of which has re-emerged musically on his new album of the same name.

But with all due respect to my typewriting colleagues, Linton's the only writer I can think of who's redefined a music, jumped out of the audience onto the stage and slashed the backdrop behind the archetype Jah-chanting rootsical dreadlocks bands to shreds with two disco mixes, "All Wi Doin' Is Defendin'" and "It Dread Inna Inglan'", and one album, *Dread Beat An' Blood* (all available through Virgin's Front Line).

As the backdrop shreds to the floor, we suddenly see that for all their much-vaunted "militancy" (myself included, for sure), most reggae bands over here have not been dealing with truths and rights as unflinchingly as claimed. Only Linton Kwesi (that's a pen name, Ghanaian "day name" meaning Saturday-born).

Linton works at the Keskidee Arts Centre, a converted church in North London tucked away among council developments through line after line of battered, rusty corrugated iron fences, set up to provide a wide range of cultural facilities – theatre workshops, poetry readings, etc. – for kids. Linton teaches the Caribbean Studies course and organises the library.

Inside the Centre, youths were sitting round a table playing a typically raucous game of dominoes. I stumbled in and out of sculpture classes, drum practices, till I tracked Linton down in the long, light library, beneath an arched window, sitting at a desk surrounded by books of black cultural interest, like *The Black Book*, a large-format softback of reproduced black memorabilia of slavery and after.

The brisk, alert man sitting behind the library desk looks like a secondary school teacher – fawn slacks, blue V-neck jumper, red/green/black (not red/green/gold – this means Africa, not Rasta) tam – is The Poet. His words in conversation are crisp, factual, almost academic; his singing is anguished bellows and ominous chants, in English patois writing. Furthering a proud young lineage, it was a poetic extension of the experimental work by Carl Gayle, writing in patois in *Black Music* magazine a few years after Johnson published his first book of poetry *Voices of the Living and the Dead*.

"One wasn't really told about England as such. You had an idea – which is because you were living in a colonial society – England is the mother country. Coming from a colonial society where there's a high percentage of illiteracy, people don't have any concrete ideas of what England is like unless they've been abroad. You didn't have any precise image, you just have ideas – snow, big buildings, lots of white people driving big flash cars. Because all the white people you saw in Jamaica are Americans with big Cadillacs and Pontiacs smoking big cigars. So can you imagine when I came to England in '63 and saw white men sweeping the streets? It was culture shock for me."

Linton is one of the more sophisticated interviewees I've dealt with; blatantly verbal, his control of his own dialogue is immaculate as befits an experienced radio interviewer, not to mention experienced live poetry reader.

While narrating his life story (a classic case of an overachiever making good where a lesser intellect, a lesser will, would have collapsed en route), he displays an impressive recall of the names of his school teachers, local library officials. Every name that's shaped his life gets a brief, graceful credit – every name except for the office stationery factory where he worked when he finally graduated with a degree and couldn't get a job because he was "overqualified" . . .

Linton, aged eleven, arrived from a town and country childhood in Jamaica, having passed a scholarship that automatically qualified him for the Jamaican equivalent of a grammar school.

Linton: *But coming from a Caribbean country, the way the education system was structured, there was no planning provision for people like me; I was naturally put into a very low stream because they assumed that if you came from the colonies you weren't up to it. My class, the lowest class, was pure black – 90 per cent black, with a few Asians and a couple of white kids – so you were put back.*

I was really, really surprised at the amount of prejudice from the staff and from the kids. Like you'd be late for a lesson and you'd be running along the corridor and a teacher suddenly jumps out of his room and grabs you by the collar and says: "Where do you think you are, the jungle!" So he takes you into his room and gives you two strokes of the cane and puts it in red in his little book and you think – my record is stained for life, y'know? I'll never get a job! [Laughter.]

The teachers' attitude was completely different from what I'd encountered in Jamaica. Nobody cared if you didn't learn. What they were concerned about was main-

taining order and discipline, not stimulating your mind to accumulate knowledge. So I think it's a miracle that I left school with anything.

For the first three years I did a fair amount of work. After that it was just gambling and records. Sometimes I wouldn't reach school till 2.00 in the afternoon and I wouldn't go to no lessons, just gambling. Then when I'd go home I'd burn the midnight oil. That's why I wear glasses now – bad light and paraffin heaters fucked up my eyes, y'know? My mother used to work for 2/6 [12 new pence] a week washing people's dirty clothes, cooking their food, scrubbing their floors, to give me what she thought would be a good education so I wouldn't have to go through what my father and her brothers went through . . .

Vivien: *An archetypal immigrant childhood like that makes it very easy to be politicised. Do you have any allegiance to political parties?*

Linton: *Not really. During my fifth and sixth forms at school we had a very good teacher, Mr Winkler, and he influenced me in discussions. He was a Fabian socialist. I was definitely anti-Tory, but when I reached eighteen I realised that I couldn't vote for the Labour Party – it could never be the vehicle for the furtherance of the struggle of black people in this country.*

Vivien: *Why do you think British reggae hasn't confronted British society directly till now?*

Linton: *There has been some attempt made – Delroy Washington talking about the streets of Ladbroke Grove, for example. But British reggae is just coming into its own. It couldn't happen before, but it will happen more and more now.*

Vivien: *There are lots of blood references in your imagery. Do you reckon there's going to be a bloodbath battle between blacks and whites in this country?*

Linton: *Not necessarily between blacks and whites, but between blacks and the police . . .*

Vivien: *Yes, because in* Record Mirror, *the singles reviewer liked "It Dread Inna Inglan'" but said you were anti-white . . .*

Linton: *What a lot of rubbish! In spite of the fact there's no racism anywhere on the record . . . It seems to me that whenever a black person stands up and says anything about black* *people's determination to fight back, people always interpret it as racism. I'm not a racist. I've never been a racist. There's no reference to the black/white situation on the record at all.*

Vivien: *When did you start to write poetry?*

Linton: *About '70, '71. When I was thirteen, fourteen I used to fancy myself as a singer, y'know? [Guffaws.] I wrote songs but I didn't show them to anybody. I wasn't particularly interested in poetry – the kind of stuff you get in school is pretty boring – but I've always had a love for rhythms and words and music. Out of all the arts, my first love was music, literature second.*

I was a member of the Youth League of the Black Panther Movement in Brixton, actively involved in organising concrete issues like police brutality, and they had a library of black literature – history, novels. I read a book by a guy called W.E.B. Du Bois, a Black American scholar, called The Souls of Black Folk, *and that book dealt with the experiences of blacks during the period of the first reconstruction after the American Revolution. That book moved me to such an emotional extent that I felt I had to put down something in response to what I'd read.*

Linton's chosen career as an accountant was shotgunned to hell when his girlfriend became pregnant as he was studying for his A-levels. Being young and in love he reckoned he'd better do the "decent thing", and quit to begin work at Lew Rose, the discount tailors where he used to have a Saturday job, rapidly ascending the ladder from switchboard operator to salesman.

"I used to dress real slick in them times – black tonic 3-ply jacket, double-breasted blazer, brass buttons, fawn tonic trousers, brogues from Brewer Street – know what I mean? Braces, and – what's the name of those shirts?"

Dennis Morris is sprawled in a library chair, collapsing in laughter at the fashion-plate recollections – "Ben Shermans!"

"Yeah, in them days I was a real flash salesman in Oxford Street. 'Good afternoon, sir – nice bit of tonic?'"

From Rose's to the civil service, to the Ladbroke Grove housing scheme consultancy for blacks, all the time Linton was studying at night for his A-Levels and ultimately got accepted at Goldsmiths'

College to read sociology: "It's a waste of time! It's a real wank! So abstract, so far removed from reality . . ."

Reality being what Johnson smashed right into when he couldn't get a job on graduation and found himself walking the streets, hanging out in bookies' offices instead of finding some nice cozy middle-class niche. "Then it was coming on to Christmas and I thought, wife, three kids (two boys and a girl – seven, five and two), time to pull me finger out. So I took this job in a factory in Beckenham, £35 a week. Man, had to work overtime four nights a week and Saturdays to get a living wage . . ."

Johnson left university in June 1976, went to work in the factory in October 1976 and left in December 1976. A mercifully curtailed fit of paying your dues (I speak as one who would loathe to work in a factory). And all this time Johnson was working, till 1975, with a group named Rasta Love, formed at the Keskidee Centre after he presented his first play, *Voices of the Living and the Dead*, there in 1973 – the first thing ever done with live Rasta drumming in this country. He was also interviewing visiting reggae artists like John Holt and Delroy Wilson on Caribbean Radio on the BBC World Service.

"Yes, I was living the artistic life, and as a worker and a student – art, work and student, all over the years."

Winning, much to his surprise, the C. Day-Lewis Fellowship while he was working in the factory meant another extension of Johnson's artistic career and he became Artist in Residence for the London Borough of Lambeth.

"You do things and people begin to take notice of what you're doing. I read one of my poems, 'Two Sides of Silence', on a *Full House* TV West Indian special and people kept on inviting me all over the place to give poetry readings. Everything I've achieved is a consequence of my poetry."

Dread Beat An' Blood can be considered as a new kind of DJ/toasting record, or like poetry and reggae, the way poetry and jazz used to be . . .

Linton: *I always wanted to put poetry to music – I remember when Virgin wanted me to put voices over the rhythms of The Diamonds' first album. But toasting – that's not really my thing; I wouldn't say what I am doing is DJ lyricism. It's in the art of the tradition of oral poetry with music. A DJ takes a rhythm track and improvises words to fit the rhythm. I do both together.*

Vivien: *Are you planning on doing gigs?*

Linton: *If I do one, I'll feel like I have to do a thousand . . . I'm a very ordinary kind of person – I don't want to be a public image living in a hotel room. It's very terrifying to me.*

Vivien: *What do you think about Rasta Repatriation?*

Linton: *I'm not into that bag. I'm not a Rasta, I'm a realist. I understand it as a historical force that began in the anti-colonialist movement in the thirties, then manifested itself in many different ways. Right now, it's the most powerful force in Jamaica. I identify with Rasta because it's about my historical experience, my culture, but a lot of people think that if they play reggae music they have to say Jah to get public acceptance. If that's the price of public acceptance, I don't want it.*

I want to emphasise that I'm not a Rasta. Rasta arose in the Caribbean at a time when people were agitating for suffrage – nobody had the vote then. That was the birth of the independence movement. There were obviously very strong African feelings among particular sections of the Jamaican slaves. It's a positive force in Jamaica insofar as it's brought about a certain pride, dignity in your cultural heritage and so on, and Jamaica really needed that. But most Rastas in this country are just Mickey Mouse Rastas, in my opinion. They listen to the reggae music and smoke marijuana and it puts them in a state of mind where they think, now all I need is a little plot of land down Africa way, and from I have ganja, and from I have reggae music, everything is cool.

It's a mistake to fight against Rasta, but you've got to recognise it for what it is – a historical force, a phase that Jamaica is going through. For the black youth in Britain, it's an alternative to the reality of British society that they don't want to face up to.

Johnson/Poet and the Roots are remarkable precisely because more than any other reggae group working in Britain, they face up to the issues confronting blacks in this country very specifically. Listen to Linton speak about the subject matter of his dramatic narrative songs:

Linton: *"Dread Beat An' Blood" is a poem about a stabbing incident I witnessed at the local youth club in Brixton. "Five Nights of Bleeding" is about a number of incidents of violence which occurred around '73 involving black youth. The poem speaks of the two-faced nature of violence, the violence we perpetrate against ourselves.*

Vivien: *You mean, the self-hatred and paranoia?*

Linton: *Yes, and the violence perpetrated against us by the State. Some of them I heard about, some of them I was there. "Doun de Road" is a poem I wrote round '73, '74, the same kind of theme, the ambivalence of the violence that blacks experience, like the fascist attacks. We take it out on ourselves instead of taking it out on the forces that create it.*

"It Dread Inna Inglan'" is a poem written to George Lindo – I'm a member of Race Today, we're a building organisation, we publish a monthly magazine. There was a campaign of black people in Bradford (Lindo was framed – pressured by fifteen hours of solitary confinement and police interrogation – into "confessing" to armed robbery, although he had alibis to prove he'd been at home at the time the robbery took place) and funnily enough not just young people, but a lot of middle-aged people got involved in the action committee.

I went on the demonstration because Race Today were actively involved in this campaign, along with another group called the Bradford Blacks. Outside the prison, in Leeds, the chant was – "Jailhouse! Ain't George house!" [Weaving, finger-snappin' to the rhythm.] It was a nice tempo. That just inspire me to write – it was a kind of calypso, bacchanal feel to it. We was all jumping and shouting and banging beer cans outside the prison. If you'd have seen it, you wouldn't have believed we were a picket – you'd have thought it was a mas – a carnival . . .

"Come Wi Go Dung Deh" (Come We Go Down There) is about my only visit back to Jamaica in '74, commenting on the situation I saw down there ("Dem a fight fe survive down there . . .") and inviting other people to take part in bringing about some kind of change down there.

"Man Free" is for my good friend Darcus Howe – Darcus had a case where he was up for assaulting a

barrister. He was charged and sent to prison for three months. Our organisation instituted a campaign to get him free, internationally. We picketed Pentonville, we picketed the Royal Courts of Justice. Eventually, they freed him after a week in prison and the poem expresses the sheer jubilation we all felt at him being free.

*"All Wi Doin' Is Defendin'" is a poem I wrote '73, '74 at the height of the police sus campaign, when the special police were on the rampage picking up black youth right and left and charging them with all sorts of things. And the poem expressed how I felt and how I know others felt about the situation – a feeling of determination. F*** me, we ain't just going to stay here and get railroaded into prison. If they f*** us about on the street, come what may we're going to fight them. If you want a war, we're ready for war.*

It's a mistake to try and portray me as a political poet. I believe that poetry don't change fuck all. No art form changes nothing. All an art form can do through the sensitivity of the artist is to anticipate change. You could write a thousand songs about the suffering condition of humanity, but change comes through people's material struggle. Art plays a very strong part, but a lot of artists fool themselves into thinking they're bring about a revolution by singing this and singing that. I have no such illusion. If I have political relevance, it's only because I'm involved in politics and what I write about is what I feel. I didn't set out to write political poems, because then you become a propagandist, not an artist any more.

That kind of art is usually very contrived, very dry and very didactic, but . . . Take a poet like Martin Carter. He's one of the finest poets I've ever read in the history of Caribbean literature and he wrote those poems because he was actively involved in the struggle of the Ghanaian people for liberation. He didn't write them because "This is a serious situation and I think people ought to know." It's very easy for the media to say: this is a revolutionary guy, he's coming heavy with the politics . . .

Dennis Morris and myself were both shouting in disagreement by this time.

Dennis: *You're contradicting yourself. You're talking about that guy who influenced you to write – he's won, that's the whole point. It's about people listening to your music and realising that things are like that out there.*

Linton: *There's nothing I say on any of these records that people don't already know!*

Vivien: *You're wrong. People don't know about these things, just like I wouldn't know about sus if I was still living in Golders Green instead of Ladbroke Grove.*

The Roots, Linton's band, were almost all at school with him. One of them, Desmond Craig, keyboards, is now in prison for a rape he didn't do. A film is currently being made about Linton, at work in the Keskidee, giving poetry readings . . .

As a member of Race Today, Linton is involved with the CDC, the Carnival Development Committee. That evening he was off to a meeting to organise the Race Today mas.

'Cos him a merciless realist and he is not defeatist.
"Man Free" by Linton Kwesi Johnson

CHAPTER 5

The New York Crew

Part 1: Coming of Age Together – US Punk, Hip-Hop, P-Funk, Disco and the Creole Creed

Music happens within a broader social and political context to which it must respond, if it is doing its job. So it was that the vigorous New York punk palette, though less politically active than the UK's, occurred within a much richer tapestry of musix. In London, punk had become the dominant strain, the sound of the town, its often neo-brutalist thrash overwhelming the 1960's pomp-rock dinosaurs (to some young minds, anyway). However, sonic revolution-wise, punk's main contribution was attitude, volume and energy.

However, the New York scene in which punk emerged was an intense, complex cocktail, reflecting the city's many moving parts – the various communities who all had their own musix. In the spirit of the time, they were all rebellious, though designed for partying and dance. Music was NY's loving weapon of choice. Parliament's P-Funk spearheaded what came to be called Afrofuturism, shifting dancers' thinking as well as their hips with masterworks like *Chocolate City* and *Mothership Connection.* Disco was utilising the new electronica in a way that enraged the "straight" world – and grabbed the whole globe. It became the launchpad for the polymath artiste Miss Grace Jones. Manhattan is home to many Spanish-speaking communities; funk, jazz, cumbia, salsa and their sister sounds blasted in uptown and downtown streets – and Kid Creole and the Coconuts synthesised them all. Of course, the hip-hop that did identify with UK punk, like Public Enemy, made up for any lack of activist drive shown by the louche, cool NY punks. And their hip-hop genre went on to become the *lingua franca* – the common language – of all popular music, from then to the time I write.

P-Funk

The first time I heard Chocolate City *was on a Walkman handed to me by Cliff White, a fellow scribe who worked for* Black Music *magazine. We were standing in an English summer garden, but the P-Funk instantly tore the roof off this sucker's maggot brain, and I may have been cosmically aerated ever since. George Clinton's most audacious, unifying and challenging aural and conceptual projections are rooted in the fertile soil of ancestral doowop, and what doowop stands on. Clinton was Afrofuturism, before it was a word. Here is an insight into how he handled more earthly matters.*

"P-Funk: Free Your Mind – Your Accountant Will Follow"

First published in Melody Maker, *25 November 1978*

Pretty soon, the whole Parliafunkadelic troupe arrives in Britain – led by their founder, the black surrealist George Clinton. Vivien Goldman witnessed Clinton's Clones on their recent US ANTI World Tour and talked to the master.

"Let's call it funk"

I dump my bag on the bed. I look around. I grab my bag in confusion. This must be the wrong hotel! It doesn't compute. Check it: if your album's topping the soul album charts, your single's topping the soul single charts and have done for weeks – plus they're both doing just fine in the regular charts – you simply don't stay in a hotel that has cracks on the walls designed with germs in mind and great wodges of ceiling angling tenderly towards the rickety wooden bedstead. Why, the matchbooks don't even have the hotel's name on them.

"Funkadelic is – the absence of plus this or plus that. Absence of bourgeoisie bullshit. Why spend money just because you have some money?"
Bernie Worrell, Funkadelic main motivator/keyboards player.
Welcome to the ANTI Tour.

"Do you want to understand funkadelic? Do you really want to understand funkadelic?"

Onstage, George Clinton, Parliafunkadelicmentbootsy Thang originator wears a straight, waist-length, silky synthetic ash-blond wig. From the rear, catching a glimpse of his skinny thighs slithered into platform boots, his shades just visible behind the flapping screen of hair, you'd think he was an early sixties swinging London dolly bird.

That's how the P-Funk (Parliament-Funkadelic's Pure, Uncut Funk) works – reversal of normal expectations. The only thing you can safely expect is the unexpected. A black man has curly black hair, right? Doing it to ya the Funkadelic way, straight blond hair's the natural thang.

Funk Is its Own Reward: A Potted Personal History of George Clinton
Clinton has claimed that he was born in an outhouse – his mother thought she was taking a crap and little George popped out instead.

The eldest of nine brothers and sisters, George evinced leadership quality from the start: "I had my own baseball team. Anything I could be a leader of, I was attracted to. That's why I went to Motown . . . Style and Cool was your survival kit in New Jersey. You could style your way out of a gang fight. Style has been the key to everything we've done . . ."

At thirteen, George had his first job – foreman in the Wham-O hula-hoop factory, still a student at Clinton Place Junior High School. After that, he formed a doo-wop group, The Parliaments. They rehearsed in the back room of the Uptown Tonsorial Parlor, a hairdressing concern.

Maybe that gave him the inspiration for his own hairdressing salon. When George founded his own Bob Shop, with – legend has it – a nice line in drugs in the back room, he knew all about "conking" – straightening black hair with dye and starch. When he was fourteen, Clinton sometimes made $2,000 a week at $5 a head. The only blacks on TV in those days were Sugar Ray Robinson and Nat King Cole.

But life in Jersey was tough – a good preparation for the hustling George was later to do on the New York streets, getting a recording deal for The Parliaments.

Clinton's street gang was called the Outlaws. He left them in 1956, when a friend had his head blown off by a rival gang, the Mohawks. Clinton's brother Bobby died of a drug overdose at twenty-six, after a life spent in and out of jail. His body was discovered crawling with maggots – the Parliament leitmotif – after three days.

Know your rhythm. George's instinct for a timely exit came in handy when he lost the use of the name The Parliaments after the Revilot label (which released their first hit, "(I Wanna) Testify" in 1967) folded. Clinton was in the process of ingesting large quantities of psychedelics around then, which could be why he renamed his band Funkadelic.

When he repossessed the "P" name in 1970, Clinton simply signed a separate Parliament (he dropped the "s") deal with Casablanca, a precursor of his current elaborate label games. Today, Parliament and Funkadelic have a unique symbiotic relationship.

"In the studio, we can more or less separate the two, conceptually. At the moment, Funkadelic is spontaneous once we hit the stage – everything goes. Parliament is more controlled in the studio, more structured."

Bernie Worrell, Clinton's long-time associate, separates it thus: "Parliament is . . . pop-orientated, I guess. Funkadelic is a conglomerate of funkin' R&B and rock."

Clinton has many, many children, including four "official" kids by his wife, still living in New Jersey. He's got a daughter in college at Rutgers and a son in Air Force college, and George's fatherly advice to them is: "Look and learn from everything. School is basically limited – the streets are a better teacher. But I know school is part of the rhythm."

During the course of his career, George's craziness has manifested itself in a string of the most piercing images vouchsafed us by Black America. The years are a dance whose purpose is to shake the rhythm of the system out of its grinding, all-encompassing synch.

As George's vision evolved, the message had become less overtly threatening to the white majority who quailed at Clinton's jovial "Chocolate City" message. On The Parliament album of that name, George detailed the numerical growth of blacks in Washington D.C., the American capital, till it became "Chocolate City – and its Vanilla Suburbs". His hearty "gainin' on ya" was calculated to inspire rage and fear in the bosoms of every latent KKK member.

"After 'Chocolate City' I had to think of another situation that blacks would just seem very weird in. Because black is commercially successful now. Black is what's happening everywhere round the world, so it would be very stupid of us not to do like any other race and do what we got. Even though some of us would like to be cool and sophisticated like white people; we're attracted to that, too, 'cos we never had it. I realised that the majority of the world was just the opposite – they wanted a real serious n*****. I had to think of another situation that would look very cool and funny to put n****** in, and we could get rid of a lot of live rhythms . . . Nobody could ever conceive of a n***** in a spaceship . . ."

This resulted in the *Mothership Connection* – a mysterious message that purported to interrupt a radio show with the P-Funk – an addictive flow of vamping funk that teased you to attention with chattering criss-cross rhythms and Bernie Worrell's synthesiser doodling an eerie, ethereal background to steamy Fred Wesley horns.

The sleeve showed George, grinning, in a silver spacesuit, climbing out of a space vehicle glowing in the yard of a grey tenement tangle of fire escapes and garbage cans.

The subsequent P-Funk Earth Tour was a $275,000 stage show, featuring a bag of tricks including a full-scale flying saucer, and a gleaming gold pyramid topped by the all-seeing Eye of Egyptian mythology, as seen on the all-purchasing American dollar bill. It established P-Funk as one of the nation's biggest booty-shaker money-makers, so vast that the white media could no longer ignore them, although white audiences by and large still preferred to stay home.

At that time, Parliament were still signed to Casablanca, who were coining it with Kiss's heavy-metal fancy dress capers. Some said that Clinton was obeying edicts from Neil Bogart, head of Casablanca, to start making it by putting on funny clothes. Clinton, of course, knew that he'd been wearing funny clothes before Kiss learnt how to avoid smudging their mascara.

"The record company themselves were thinking we were copying Kiss, but we go out of our way to disprove that – we try to regenerate. The computer can't identify when Funkadelic changed from Parliament. Now we've put on these new uniforms, it sees us as a new group – just when they thought they had us pegged with the *Mothership* [*Connection*]! Yeah, you might say we diluted our message to get it through to more people, but that's cool, too – anything but selling completely out.

"We keep ourselves together by playing ANTI Tours, like we did last night. We just had platinum records two times in a row, we were playing 20,000-seaters two nights in a week with the Spaceship. We're all big stars now, so you don't have nothing but time. Time to get bored with those other five nights – get bored, get high, get fucked up. Most of us haven't even seen what five nights a week of work is like. The ANTI Tour serves the purpose of us being able to play small halls for three hours a night, instead of an hour and ten minutes.

"The Brides of Funkenstein got a hit album out. If we didn't go out, they'd have to go out with someone else. We want them to be in touch with our family.

"It helped us to get our heads together away from the Spaceship and everything – seven nights a week, real cheap and cheesy. We could make a fortune in Madison Square Gardens, but we're getting away from the superstar attitudes. We didn't let nobody ride in the limos last night – we let the roadies have 'em. Just total reversal to what's expected."

Rhythm and Business: The ANTI World Tour

First onstage were The Brides of Funkenstein, Lynn Mabry and Dawn Silva, plus their three backup singers, the Bridesmaids.

They describe their act, quite accurately, as "15 per cent sex, 85 per cent funk". Dressed in layers of white fox tails, like Clinton used to in his Dr. Funkenstein capacity, they sashayed around the stage, in a remarkably wholesome display of sensuality without sleaze. Their set built up to their current US hit, *Funk or Walk* – polished, snazzy, humorous funk played with typical P-Funk fervour – they were backed by Parliafunkadelic players as well as a couple of their own musicians.

On the ANTI Tour, P-Funk have shelved the silver space people *Mothership Connection*-image for reggaematic khaki militant army gear: "It's on purpose. Army uniforms strike up emotions; we don't want to be called terrorists, but we want to get the idea across that we're revolution-minded.

"If you look at the promotional pictures, you'll see we're all wearing roller skates – that's to take the edge off! It was time for a change.

"With 'Flash Light' and the *Mothership* we were at the top – and there's only one place to go. That's down. Groups are designed to self-destruct after a couple of platinum albums – the system has it set up that way – so we figured the only way for us not to keep that date with self-destruct is to change our image and people will begin to see us as a new group."

When the khaki-clad Funkadelic took to the stage – actually, it's Parliament as much as Funkadelic, so let's just call it P-Funk – the Brides, Lynn and Dawn, and their Bridesmaids were among the twenty-eight musicians crowding, but never jostling, the width of the stage. Stars forgot the snotty side of stardom and mucked in with The Parliafunkadelicment Thang's exuberant anarchy.

P-Funk onstage is proof of Clinton's radical approach. Everybody solos, everybody jams. One after the other, voices stepped forwards – top, bottom and mid ranges of penetrating perfection. Over two hours, the P-Funk gave the treatment to ten numbers from all aspects of their doppelganger personae – climaxing in one unpredictable jam, voices piling on voices, instruments crashing, colliding, interweaving.

As with all jams, moments of tedium intersperse the moments of brilliance. That's the way it has to be. As Clinton decrees, the P-Funk do not compute – they are human, and funky, and they follow the awesome, all-embracing P-Funk edict: Free Your Mind and Your Ass Will Follow.

It strikes me as remarkable – from what I can catch between the frenzied bobbing of heads surrounding me, vision obscured by shaking tambourines and party whistles in the audience – that more of P-Funk didn't trip over each other. I had an image of carefully marked boundaries for each of the twenty plus performers, not to mention the kiddies who prance around in the encore. Shades of the Carib Theatre, Kingston, on a Saturday morning, where they always have two or three precociously snazzy dance trios between four and twelve years old, wearing vinyl eyeshades and shorts just like the P-Funk kids. (Strictly roots, you no see it?)

Not so.

George: *This was the first time we seriously did rehearse – that's because we were twenty-seven people. But once we get it completely structured, I'll go against the pattern and cause a little hassle, and you'll experience something new straightening it out!! We take chances on stage like that. Everybody says, "Well, how did they know that?" when the harmonies* *all suddenly meet. It's chaos and order at the same time onstage – controlled chaos . . .*

Dawn Silva and Lynn Mabry view the P-Funk's freedom onstage with nothing short of awe. They met while working with Sly Stone – Lynn is Sly's cousin. Dawn was a modern dance teacher in a California high school until she joined Sly full time. Lynn had sung choir at the Pentecostal Church of God in Christ. Adherents to the Church are forbidden to listen to the radio. Girls must not wear nail varnish, pluck their eyebrows, wear trousers, or skirts above the knee. They were allowed to shake tambourines in church, though.

From this phenomenally restrictive, stilted background, Lynn went to work with cousin, Sly. Dawn's upbringing as a Catholic was less obviously constricting, but neither was it P-Funkentelechy-type loose friendliness.

Sitting on my hotel bed, they interrupt each other, laugh with each other, best friends. Their admiration for George amounts to hero-worship – he's been their Svengali and they appear to adore him as you'd adore someone who released you from slavery.

They joke about Sly's surly, selfish ways, giggle delightedly as they recall how he gave them the elbow for not asking him permission before jamming with George one night.

Lynn: *With Sly we had no freedom. George is so much more open to any ideas we come up with. When we were with Sly, it was black gowns, rhinestone earrings and necklaces, Supremes-type. We were really restricted. Then with Parliament, we can go anywhere onstage!*

Dawn: *George, he's our guardian angel. Everything that he's told us is gonna happen to us, has happened.*

They go on to describe lessons George has taught them. Crucial points like How to Say No and Stay the Good Guy, how to touch emotional wellsprings in the studio.

Then Dawn says fervently: "Whatever level we reach, or whatever direction we take in this business, George is gonna be there. I want him to be there . . ."

Too good to be true? Their sincerity was tangible and their faces glowed with fervour as they spoke of George.

There is a reason why Clinton provokes this reaction. Although he himself protested that "they try to lay (a father figure image) on me, I tell 'em I won't dance with it." The fact is that George's democratic, non-sexist attitude is so rare as to be almost unique. Earth, Wind & Fire's Maurice White takes the same attitude towards Deniece Williams and The Emotions, but it's a comparatively recent trend.

"My main reason is to keep my band members happy by having their own contracts. Otherwise, if I go fishing and come back and say, 'Look what a big fish I caught!' nobody's gonna be happy. They need their own situation to be happy, to be cool. Nobody wants to be a backup musician.

"My concept even makes more money. Top-quality musicians don't mind taking a little ego trip from each other, because I don't do it. I end up having more stars around me, without screaming 'I'm a good guy.'"

Thus the clones of Doctor Funkenstein: the Horny Horns, Bootsy's Rubber Band, Eddie Hazell, Bernie Worrell, Junie Morrison, The Brides of Funkenstein – they're all alumni of the Clinton School of Funkentelechy.

Those, like former Ohio Player Junie Morrison (who was responsible for the band's first hit, "Funky Worm", and all their arrangements), who knew commercial success before hooking up with Clinton, find their record company bankability is enhanced by their association with Clinton's hit machine.

The talent within the P-Funk ranks is extraordinary. Worrell was a child prodigy who played his first classical concert when he was four, played with the Washington Symphony Orchestra when he was ten, worked with Leonard Bernstein, the New England Conservatory Chorus, had private tuition from teachers at Juilliard and the New York College of Music – and only discovered rock and roll through hearing Elvis Presley on the radio.

Junie Morrison's forthcoming *Truth Love and Magic* album is a magical concept record, all the songs, all the voices and all the instruments played by himself.

Though Worrell feels a nostalgic yearning for the wilder days of Funkadelic, he acknowledges it's a relief that the songwriting and arranging of talent has spread out among the band – it used to be between George, Bootsy and himself. Now, he has the time to work on solo projects.

"They thought I'd put all my bands on one label," George chortles. "They thought that if I got big and made a lot of money I'd put 'em all on one label, like Motown.

"But that, to me, would be pimping them too lightly. It works too good the way it is. I'm still going to have my label, but it'll be all new groups. Did you see the Brides last night? They're as good as made. Bootsy was doing that and now . . . what *THEY* expected was corny to me. I got a lot of help from all the members – it's all of us all the way."

Thus, Clinton is in the unique position of having his family funded by several major international record labels – Arista, Warner Brothers. and Atlantic – all of whom channel money and promotional facilities into the P-Funk. George calls it Rhythm and Business.

He has it covered from every angle, although the P-Funk won't appear on TV or radio. Acutely sensitive to the way the media can mess you around by sloppy editing, insensitive scheduling and myriad other ways, the P-Funk have recorded themselves on video, in each of their varied incarnations.

Clinton has achieved the Complete Control ideals of the punk movement, with a flair and thoroughness that only John Lydon's Public Image Ltd and The Pop Group are beginning to conceive of and implement. Clinton may choose to come on like a rapid jive talker, but you'd better listen to what he has to say.

Call me a wacky romanticist, but what makes Clinton's media and business control all the more gratifying to observe is that he uses the power for a good purpose. He comes up with a radical reason for every concept, every lyric, every move.

Even why his former white studded leather and fur costumes have sadomasochist overtones:

George: *S & M and bondage is part of today's womb [he explained cheerfully]. I try to use the part that the System uses, and it works. Part of the commercial thing is to know how to pimp the instincts the System attracts us to.*

Advertising tells us that maybe S & M is the way we can come. We show you that you can use the same thing and not have to hurt each other. You can reach the same intensity as the pain of S & M without taking it all the way. You can wallow in your mind – your mind is the greatest fantasy trip you need.

The System will give it to you in a real jive way, the real knife, the real pimp, till somebody's dead . . .

Vivien: *So you really see dancing as the most effective way to achieve a revolution?*

George: *Dancing is . . . the closest you can get to it without really committing yourself! Dancing's always been the simplest way. You can hyperventilate and get the cheapest high in the world.*

I've seen storefront churches get you so excited, you could funk. They see God, and you know they see something. Like dancing and grooving onstage, you can get to see blue lights. If you hyperventilate, it's a religious experience of the highest order. So somebody introducing a real doctrine to you and showing you how to chant at the same time could introduce you to anything. That's why the funk works.

I can't guarantee the same thing will happen in England, but in the States, the audience clap, shake tambourines, blow whistles and chant along to the familiar, beloved litany of P-Funk chants – "Tear the roof off the sucker", "Funk get ready to rock, funk get ready to roll", "Standing on the verge of getting it on", "One nation under a groove" – it's a parallel effect to massed football crowds unison chanting into ecstasy as their team scores a goal.

It's a legal high and the P-Funk is designed to provoke radical thought, too, even if the audience aren't consciously aware of it.

The P-Funk appears to be an inexorable process. In his typically anti-logic way, George has it un/planned for years to come. In a couple of years' time, when the Brides are established, they'll give the Bridesmaids their own band, which will be signed to another major label and so on . . . and the labels will always want to sign Clinton's Clones, because the music comes from the Pure, Uncut source.

Whenever Clinton and Co. go into the studios, the resulting tracks may be used by any one of the P-Funk family. The massive P-Funk hit, "Flash Light", was originally supposed to be on a Bootsy album – he's sorry he rejected it now . . . the Brides' current hit, "Funk or Walk", is almost three years old, was originally planned to be "We Want Bootsy", a Rubber Band chant.

Every P-Funk family hit is programmed; when Bootsy played

England, he familiarised the audience with chants on the current Funkadelic album – and, on the ANTI Tour, Funkadelic chant "Burnin' Down the House", which will be Bootsy's next chant.

Similarly, they'll consciously release the second-best single first – Clinton was criticised for releasing "Bop Gun (One Nation)" before "Flash Light", but he knew that "Bop Gun" would be a big enough hit to ensure that "Flash Light" would be *HUGE*. It was.

If Clinton's domino effect continues to fall according to plan, the international music business will have to funk – or walk . . .

To examine the cause of life we must first have recourse to death [. . .] My attention was fixed upon every object the most insupportable to the delicacy of the human feelings [. . .] until from the midst of this darkness a sudden light broke in upon me – a light so brilliant and wondrous, yet so simple, that [. . .] I was surprised that among so many men of genius who had directed their inquiries towards the same science, that I alone should be reserved to discover so astonishing a secret.
Frankenstein by Mary Shelley

"At first I thought it was my ego telling me they didn't want us to get so big we meant something. On a business level we were at least such a threat to the industry that they didn't want us to become as big as we were without having more control over us," said George.

George has discovered the astonishing secret of how to make music business moguls dance to his rhythm.

For many years, he had fixed his attention on objects insupportable to the delicacy of human feelings. From rank and raunchy Funkadelic titles like "Call My Baby P-U-S-S-Y" to the new album's lines: "The world is a toll-free toilet, our mouths neurological assholes and, psychologically speaking, we're in a state of mental diarrhoea, talking shit a mile a minute," George has focused on basic physical aspects of human behaviour that drove (seventeenth century satirist) Jonathan Swift to horrified despair.

Clinton claims not to have heard of Wilhelm Reich, the radical therapist who, like activist George Jackson, died in an American jail for his beliefs. Reich's laboratory equipment was smashed by the American government because his researches into how to achieve happiness on the planet – it was Reich who not only stated that orgasms make you feel better, but actually devised items called orgone accumulators that healed wounds and induced states of bliss – were getting too deep to condone, without the government having more control . . .

Like Reich, Clinton has insisted on revealing his physically based view of the truth throughout his two-decade career. "When people get real famous, they get killed. The system is like that," George declares flatly. "If you're a star and I'm a star, the system have it that we ain't supposed to get along. Groups pull the plug on each other – they don't know that if one can make it, we all can make it. In that way they make it so that when a new group comes in, they can take the old group's place and nothing will be done about it.

"The companies do it that way so you'll live up to your self-destruct time of about three years . . . the system made sure that the hippy culture was wiped out in '68, '69. They got rid of a whole generation 'cos they were too subversive.

"But this is a new underground thing, a new version of the sixties working on anti-logic. We're working on something the computer can't compute yet. See, they won't even let a football player become that famous no more if the system has anything to do with it, because you can tell too many kids what to do or think. We're just breaking up their rhythm."

Logic, -n. The art of thinking and reasoning in strict accordance with the limitations and incapacities of the human misunderstanding.
The Enlarged Devil's Dictionary by Ambrose Bierce

For a brilliant man, Clinton has an unusual aversion to the word "logic". It epitomises the world of the "computer" – another word George spits out with distaste. To put it in his own terminology, the vocabulary of the legions of geepies, or Parliafunkadelicment fans: logic + computers = The Placebo Syndrome.

The Placebo Syndrome, in turn, is personified by Sir Nose d'Voidofunk, a repellent character whose Snooze Gun is aimed to sedate the ears, and hence the minds, of the nation with musical pap that's devoid of funk. He is locked in combat with Star Child and his mighty Bop Gun.

All of Funkadelic's artwork, and some of Parliament's, comes in garish cartoon form. Parliament's own sleeves are photos of vivid fairy tales – fantastic projections of the forces Clinton sees mobilising the planet.

For Parliament/Funkadelic followers, and members of the P-Funk family, there is a battle/playground for the forces of good and evil, on a daily basis.

Gradually, a mythology has built up that's as encompassing as Tolkien's *The Lord of the Rings*, or Mervyn Peake's *The Gormenghast Trilogy* – any of the action-packed epic narratives that absorbed the Acid Generation.

George's first band, The Parliaments, was just another New Jersey street-corner combo. But the essence of Parliament, Funkadelic and Bootsy's Rubber Band is a hybrid of street-corner harmony soul – sweaty James Brown funk (both Bootsy and former Parliafunkadelicment person Fred Wesley were Brown sidekicks) and hard acid rock. Those screaming guitar solos don't have their roots in gospel and the wild, occasionally brutal imagery doesn't spring from the herb designed to heal the nations.

George is painfully aware of what it means to be an "acid casualty", your brain so suffused with holy/unholy visions that you spiral off into your own world, unable to communicate with or participate in the general planetary daily interaction.

His view of this supposedly "damaged" mental state is, as you'd expect, refreshingly radical: "I think it's the same as what they did with witchcraft. Like when they prescribe librium, lithium. I don't believe in mental illness. When you go to see a psychiatrist, your fate is in his hands. You're considered nuts, you have no rights whatsoever. If you're on welfare, and the welfare workers come in your house and look in your closet for men's clothes, and they're very disrespectful, if you get upset they consider you have to go to see a psychiatrist. If the psychiatrist says you have to go to a mental institution, it'll take hell and high water to get you out.

"It's an illusion of sanity – that's bullshit. Reality has a lot of different shapes. Reality is an agreement between two or more people.

"The number-one concept in rock 'n' roll these days is you have to be crazy to be hip. That is a fact, but you can also act it out and get the same reaction. Most people that don't realise it's actually just a trap the system put in there, and actually start trying to be as insane offstage as they are onstage. Consequently, you do get tape loop of the head. You just get out of rhythm, start believing your stage image."

This from a man who not only spent many of his formative years running round the stage with no clothes on, but also went out on the street wearing wetsuits, including flippers and goggles.

Iggy Pop wanted to marry George; he said no, but another P-Funker agreed.

Obviously, he doesn't assume a totally different persona onstage; Clinton always comes on a little bit crazy but, as they say in America, he's crazy like a fox.

Public Enemy

As with George Clinton in 1975, the moment I heard Public Enemy was another testament to how fast music can work – locally, domestically and globally – to bind a crew beyond the physical. Clinton's fiery missive from Washington D.C. as Chocolate City *and* Mothership Connection *radically helped to forge a future-bound African American consciousness and identity. It may not have seemed to be my immediate struggle – listening for the first time in that London garden – but it spoke to me, too. That is what art is for and how it works, to link and communicate. Thus, a balmy summer's night on New York's Houston Street in 1988 found me transfixed, listening to Hank Shocklee's harsh, compelling concrète soundscapes for Public Enemy, sounds I had barely imagined and words that roused me.*

Some clarification may be needed for this 1992 piece's closing scenes. The Nation of Islam's Minister Louis Farrakhan is a suave yet divisive African American figure – divisive, because confusingly his different conflicting messages played simultaneously on two tracks at once. Thus, to some, he was a welcome, galvanizing figure, protecting Black rights at a time of conservative backlash; while at the same time, to others, including women across colours, homosexuals and Jews, he was a threatening figure, promoting ideologies of hate with a silver tongue. His seemingly uplifting message was sugar wrapped round poison, helping to distort America's Black/Jewish alliance that had held since the Civil Rights movement of the 1960s. (My own research disproves Farrakhan's race-hate theories. As I write, over two decades later, a New York judge has overturned his $4.8 billion lawsuit against the Anti-Defamation League.)

Timing is always relevant. New York was in the heightened state of racial tension captured in Spike Lee's film Do the Right Thing. *The year before we conducted this interview, the Crown Heights riot had pitted Black Brooklyn against both the police and Jews; and the 1989 killing of Yusuf Hawkins, a young Black man, in a white Italian working-class enclave of the Bronx, Bensonhurst, was still prompting confrontational demonstrations. The mood was explosive. They also refer to the Rodney*

King case, the near-fatal beating of a Black citizen by the Los Angeles police in the street, helping to prompt the Los Angeles riots of 1992.

"Black Noise, Black Heat"
First published in SPIN, *October 1992*

Public Enemy is the nation's fiercest group and, boy, do we need 'em now more than ever. In this year of living dangerously, PE's Chuck D and producer Hank Shocklee tell it like it is, and Vivien Goldman is all ears.

The supposed hook for this meeting with Public Enemy is *Greatest Misses*, a new Public Enemy album containing six new songs and six remixes of past PE material. But there's always something going on to make a comment from Public Enemy timely. The elections are coming into view and the planet being what it is, there will doubtless be some skulduggery somewhere to incite the Public Enemy posse, to fire up the righteous blowtorch of its wrath and direct it at its chosen target.

Public Enemy's Chuck D and producer Hank Shocklee are vivid, commanding figures, blessed with voices so loud they can rock the room with no mike. Both men smite the table with a resounding crash to emphasise a point and delight in picking up on each other's jokes almost before they're uttered. The divine assurance of men on a mission permeates every gesture, the mutual reinforcement of true brothers-in-arms evident.

Each man is equally hunky in sports gear. Chuck was sporting prototypes of one of his new business offshoots – chunky black-and-red high-tops, embossed with the name of his fashion concern, Rapp Style.

Despite misgivings about the "white media" and its understanding of American rap, Chuck got down with the program of our interview. Each time the conversation threatened to explode, Chuck would chuck in a philosophical truth. His instinct about when to steer the discussion is spot on for self-preservation.

SPIN: *The elections are coming up. It appears that many African Americans feel so alienated from the political process that they can't be bothered to vote. How do you feel?*

Chuck: *This is a sports-driven country and if you don't have two popular teams, pretty much no one is going to give a damn.*

SPIN: *Are you going to vote?*

Chuck: *I'm not telling. I can't tell you right now. I can only vote when I'm confident. The one time I voted was for Angela Davis [vice-presidential candidate, 1984], when Ronald Reagan was running. She was running for some kind of communist party! [Laughter.]*

SPIN: *But isn't the ballot box one of the only tools we have?*

Chuck: *This year, voting is making more sense to me locally. To direct you, personally, a lot of people have to register. But the big overall picture is really unclear to me and to a lot of people. Black people are ticking on a trigger. White people's biggest fear is a race riot situation and black people feel they have nothing to lose.*

I travel all over the country, I go to jails, I talk to the brothers, and the average black male sentiment under twenty-five is, "Kill Whitey, 'cause I'm fucked up." I'm talking 80 per cent of the people.

By 1995, if Bush get into office, you'll see the same sentiment among the brothers. They feel just as if they were still at the bottom of the slave ship, lying there with their sisters, sleeping in their own shit. Then, they felt, "If I ever get my hands round that motherfucker's neck, I'll kill him," and that's how they feel now. It's not me, or Ice Cube, or Souljah's feelings – we're just the messengers, and how you gonna kill the messengers?

The best thing about rap is it's a last-minute warning, the final call, like the Nation of Islam paper – a last plea for help on the countdown to Armageddon.

SPIN: *You say, if* Bush *gets in. Does that mean it would be different if Clinton gets in?*

Chuck: *If Clinton gets in, it'll be bedlam by 1997. Obviously, there's more hope with a new face. Otherwise, it's gonna be hell. Shit's gonna jump that you ain't never seen before.*

SPIN: *So what could the government implement to avert it?*

Chuck: *That would be a program and a half. We have to have black schools that teach you how your black ass will survive in America, and the meaning of family. As of slavery, we don't even know if we're related!*

SPIN: *Are you saying that education of blacks has been inferior?*

Chuck: *No, I don't think it's been inferior. It just doesn't teach us the hypocrisies and the double standards, and how to make it as a black person. I can go to college and high school and get the top grades, and when I go out into the job markets, I don't know anything about business. Which means business is a family thing, you know what I'm saying? If you're not family, you're not gonna get that fucking job!*

SPIN: *I was reading recently that the producer-director brothers, the Hudlins [*Boomerang, House Party*], were glad they went to some top school so that they could work the system.*

Chuck: *Yeah, but at the same time, people were looking down at them when they came out of those schools looking for those fucking jobs. People said, "You're still a n*****!"*

SPIN: *So they went off and set up their own separate development, the Black Filmmaker Foundation.*

Chuck: *And they went and looked at each other, and said, "Yeah, we* family, *and fuck everything else." And that's the only way it's going to work here. But black people don't realise they're family and the only way they will is if we get informed that we family. The days of working for the white man are over. We can work with them. Working with someone is something we can do when we have knowledge of ourselves. When we control ourselves, black community will stop drug dealers. They will die from our own hands, in front of a thousand people, as the Nation of Islam teaches us.*

SPIN: *The riots in LA were multiracial, but the media said they were only black.*

Hank: *Yeah! Because the people's intelligence was insulted; forget Rodney King being black, he's a person. And those community leaders – the whole of black America was saying it's the first time we've ever seen them. Who are the real leaders? Ice-T. BDP. Ice Cube. Queen Latifah. They're the people who are sending a message to the kids right now.*

Chuck: *Politicians do less talking than rappers, and their actions are almost invisible. When we started out, [political rap] was not in vogue. The black male image in the mid-eighties was Prince or Michael Jackson, and you were not really defiant. If you was, you was wearing a gold rope and you were a hoodlum. The riots – or rebellion – of 1992 made people look* *differently at that black man and woman.*

SPIN: *Five years ago, you said Public Enemy was on a mission to create 5,000 black leaders. How's it going?*

Chuck: *Like Elijah Muhammad [leader of the Nation of Islam] says, if you want a good leader or role model, look in the mirror and be one. We've gotten a lot of people to the point where there's a lot of better confidence and self-esteem in looking at themselves for a more progressive position.*

Hank: *There's a division happening in the United States. In the sixties, they called it the generation gap. The same generation's happening right now, but the difference is, while you've got conservatives and liberals, you've got this new class – let's call them the ultra-liberals. They're the teenage to mid-twenties group that don't fit in with the rest of white society. They may be white kids, or they may be Puerto Rican or Korean, but the kids got a whole other vibe going on, another culture that's separated them from their parents. What do the kids got in common? If black and white adults don't have anything in common, well, black and white kids do. And what is that?* It's the music.

SPIN: *What does the idea of reparations mean?*

Chuck: *I think after 437 years, black people should be paid back. They shouldn't pay out no tax, because black people worked for free for 400 years. If you look at the state of black America today, we don't own shit, we don't own anything. I still say that the black state has to be repaired. We need to control certain aspects of the media.*

SPIN: *Are you talking about reparations, as in a check dropped through the mailbox?*

Chuck: *If we gave every black family a $100,000 check, and said, "This is in reparation for slavery," you'd probably see $20,000, because you got a $80,000 Benz! [Laughter.] Money is not the answer, control is the answer. Control over curriculums, over education, and no griping about the money afterward or wanting it paid back.*

SPIN: *How long will it take, and what would it take, to heal the trauma of slavery?*

Chuck: *Slavery took place for 400 years, so it might take 1,200. If you take a pin or a knife and stab yourself with it, the initial action would only take a second, but the healing – you're* *gonna feel hurt and pain for two weeks before it disappears. But if everybody doesn't pitch in and understand that we're physically and mentally down in the dumps and injured, there's just going to be hell for everybody. The LA riots were just the tip of the iceberg.*

SPIN: *I went to the East Jersey State Prison one time and I thought there must be a lot of saintly white people 'round here, or how come the whole jail population is black?*

Hank: *It's because black people get processed to the full extent of the law, no matter what the crime is. Everybody sits there and thinks that the law is objective, but there's a whole lot of subjectivity between the objectivity. If you decide it's murder, is it Murder One or Two? Look at Mike Tyson going to jail for rape. To me, the law says, OK, you're not supposed to rape a woman, but aren't there degrees of rape?*

SPIN: *Uh-oh, we're going to have a fight here.*

Hank: *OK, let me qualify that. If the action takes place in a shopping mall, parking lot or car in some secluded street, or perpetrators come into your house – I'm saying there's a degree here.*

SPIN: *Everybody knows you should have a right to go to someone's room and not get raped.*

Hank: *That's true.*

SPIN: *Obviously, Mike Tyson was always a great hero, but he seems to have a history of being unable to handle women.*

Hank: *Yeah, we understand that, but where are the guidelines?*

Chuck: *I think you'll always have a problem when white men judge black men. I'd like to end this one now.*

SPIN: *How do you feel about abortion?*

Chuck: *I believe in freedom of choice.*

Hank: *You should have freedom of choice.*

Chuck: *This is the thing about life. Your parents, your children, your spouses, your friends – everybody else is a visitor to yourself. When you die, nobody says, "Oh, Chuck died, I've got to die with this motherfucker!" [Laughter.] So you gotta be able to have some control on yourself.*

SPIN: *Flavor got a lot of criticism for being homophobic because of the lines in "A Letter to the New York Post" on* Apocalypse '91: The Enemy Strikes Black *– "Ask James Cagney / He beat up on a guy when he found he was a fagney".*

Chuck: *[Laughs with Hank.] Flavor will pick a word that rhymes for the hell of it. "Fagney" was just some shit he drummed up to rhyme with Cagney. You can put a lot of science on some Public Enemy songs, but when Flavor does it, you can't put too much science on it.*

SPIN: *It seems you feel it's not an easy time to criticise other black public figures.*

Chuck: *Right. I don't think it's advantageous for any kind of progress among our people. If you don't control the media, it can only be perceived as confusion. It's not progressive and it's not positive.*

SPIN: *What do you talk about on your lecture tours?*

Chuck: *I speak about rap music, its importance and the change it makes upon our society today – why it's more than what it seems to be. I talk about it as being a form of media conquest. This country is being controlled by the FCC [Federal Communications Commission]; the government monitors the media. To have a radio station, you have to report it to the government. Records just went past all that. I break it down – how powerful it is as a world medium.*

SPIN: *How do you feel about the Nation of Islam publication,* The Secret Relationship Between Blacks and Jews, *that Ice Cube is promoting? [*The Secret Relationship *states that Jews controlled the slave trade – a claim supposedly based on the work of Jewish academics who have all subsequently declared the treatment to be a perversion of their research.]*

Chuck: *I've leafed through it. I'm just going to close on this point: I think all books cannot be read by one person, and I think talking to people is somehow better than reading books because you can't read every book. In this society, it's hard to judge which book is right and which book is wrong because so much of it is controlled by the government.*

SPIN: *Have you seen this book* Jew on the Brain *that [PE's former long-time publicist] Bill Adler put out? It's a refutation of* The Secret Relationship.

Chuck: *Yeah, I saw this. He put Ice Cube on the front. [After the interview, Chuck left the book behind, after saying earlier that he wanted it. On his way out, I passed it back to him. Casually, he said, "Burn this piece of shit," and split without having read it. That was the only moment of my five-year* *fandom of the group that I felt fear of a Public Enemy planet.]*

SPIN: *You mention the holocaust in your lyrics: "[. . .] I got a story that's harder than the hardcore cost of the holocaust," on "Can't Truss It",* Apocalypse 91. *In the* New York Times *recently, there was an article by the chair of the African American Studies Department at Harvard, Henry Louis Gates Jr. He wrote: "And what is yielded by this hateful sport of victimology, save the conversion of a tragic past into a game of recrimination?"*

Chuck: *Number one, it's all in the game of life, and it's being controlled by someone else for more devious methods. I've just got to say that in black people's search for information, they can't be blamed for that search when other information has failed them in the past. They can't be blamed for searching for other religious avenues when the religious avenues in the past have failed us and been hypocritical. The Nation of Islam gets a lot of bad ink, but what else is white America going to say for an organisation that builds strong black men? Fuck what the white man thinks!*

SPIN: *How did you start your involvement with rap?*

Chuck: *We dabble in other areas, but rap's our life. Our mindset is twenty-four hours. Before I met Hank, I dabbled. It was a leisure thing. When I met Hank in October '79 and we hooked up, it became a full-time motherfucking thing. I left school after my freshman semester. I had no direction. Rap actually gave me the direction to go through school. I wanted to apply my design and artistic skills to this new music. So the hip-hop scene and rap became my motive for living.*

SPIN: *We're in the offices of S.O.U.L. Records – your offices. You seem to be developing into quite a corporation. How extensive is your diversification?*

Chuck: *It's hard to say I'm successful at any of these businesses, but I'm trying. I'm looking at getting into merchandising worldwide. I look at it as being bigger than sports, because it's international. Rappers are selling so many things the sports guys are selling; we've sold more, but the sports guys don't give a fuck about us, so I wanted to set up my own, even if it meant failing for two or three years. I know that if I keep on doing it, I'll be all right. I'm calling the company Rapp Style.*

Hank: *S.O.U.L. Records is actually a production deal we have with MCA Records. I'm working with Son of Bazerk, Young Black Teenagers, Dr. Dre and Ed Lover, and a group out of Memphis called Triggerman that is pretty interesting. It gives me the chance to find new talent and develop it, to formalise rap. Even though rap is selling and doing incredible numbers, it still doesn't have a ballpark to work from.*

Chuck: *We also have Pro Division, an extension of Def Jam. We're able to give Terminator a little bit of a breather. It's a tool we'll be working with the next four to five years.*

SPIN: *When does your Def Jam contract run out?*

Hank: *We're in it for life!*

Chuck: *We're one of the builders of that whole place, so . . .*

SPIN: *So you're partners?*

Chuck: *Yeah, and we're looking to be better partners! It would have been us, LL Cool J, and the Beastie Boys, but the Beastie Boys left. So it's the house that LL built and that we put electric fixtures to.*

Hank: *In the next two years we're going to structure rap bigger than sports. Bigger than the NBA.*

Chuck: *They already call Hank "music's worst nightmare". These two n****** here, we're gonna be called the "music business's worst nightmare!"*

Grace Jones

How lucky I have been to get such a ringside view of so many of the world's most brilliant performers. But out of them all, Grace Jones is superlative when it comes to command. Just Grace alone, without the benefit of dancers or wowee props, with just a spotlight, like a benevolent dominatrix, she holds the audience enthralled in her grip. This interview stuck with me, which is why I referred to it years later in "Blues for Betty Davis's Smile", near the start of this book. The issue is representation of females, in this case, both pan-African and both expected to suppress their tender side as if it would dilute some outré image others chose to project onto them. It is as if they could only be perceived as functioning on one level – cheery or wild or avant-garde. Whereas when it comes to proper artists, those who live it in their destiny and DNA, all these qualities interact to make combustible and enduring statements. In Jones's long-distance run at life, she has worn many hats. Her distinctive, ever-evolving music has resulted in a classic-packed catalogue, propelled by riveting images.

Recently, luck led me to swim with Grace Jones in the Caribbean Sea at her frequent haunt: Chris Blackwell's Goldeneye Resort in Oracabessa, Jamaica. Boldly, she struck out to the ocean's horizon, with me paddling behind her – I generally like to stay within sight of the beach. But somehow, there I was, swimming decisively in deeper waters than ever before.

And that is part of what makes Grace so phenomenal. Not just in the sea with me, that one day, but as an artist, she can lead us out further than ever before – and yet make us feel stronger than if we'd stayed paddling in the shallows.

"A Bounding Grace"
First published in ELLE UK, *December 1978*

Black beauty, belle of New York, disco goddess, queen of the night – Vivien Goldman reports on the state of Grace Jones.

"Oh my God, Grace, why must you always do such dangerous things?" The man in the white overalls sighs, shades his eyes against the sun, the unexpected glare that lurks high above the unbreathable fug they call air in New York City.

The air only becomes breathable somewhere around the twentieth floor, where the penthouses start. This particular penthouse belongs to a French artist named Jean-Paul Goude – "He's a genius," adds everyone who mentions his name. Goude is staring at Grace Jones, singer, model, actress, disco goddess.

Grace is wearing a black leotard cut straight across the breasts, help up by two thin straps, nothing else. In an exotic re-creation of the gargoyles of Notre Dame, Grace's lean lines are suspended over the canyons between the skyscrapers; she poises herself over the parapet like an Olympic runner crouching, hunched, at the starting line. The running track before her is empty and blue, punctuated by scudding white clouds.

Grace's close-cropped head rolls round and round luxuriantly, the single flash of gold along the parting glistens. She bares perfect square teeth in Goude's direction, snaaaarls emphatically. She is the image of every wild, dominant jungle woman, every Amazon that men have sighed for in their sleep.

"Don't worry, Jean-Paul, I'm insured. For flying."

If you get your kicks exploding myths, Grace Jones is fun. Myths revolve and collide about her. She is a powerful woman.

"She's a bitch," comments one journalist (male).

Waiting for Grace to send the car back to pick us up at the New York docks, after an Yves Saint Laurent boat party, an aspiring rock star (male) bitches, "You'll have a long wait. I know that Grace Jones, she's a prima donna. She'll keep that limo waiting at her convenience all night."

Next day, the chauffeur complains that no one was there when he came to pick us up . . . which leads on to the more sympathetic comments.

Disco journalist Vince Aletti says, "Oh, Grace? She's a nice girl. You sure won't get bored with her."

And Tony, her road manager, says affectionately, "Nobody realises how maternal Grace is. She's the one everyone turns to if they're feeling down."

But most (straight) men are bound to feel threatened by Grace Jones. At twenty-five, she's blithely conquered milieu after milieu, spanning geographic and artistic gulfs with an athletic stride that any narrow-minded traditionalist would consider unwomanly. At school in Jamaica, Grace broke all school long-jump records. Won medals for the high jump, too, and shows no sign of coming down. "Those are your basic things – using the physical," says Grace. "It's nothing new. But it's the *way* that I do it."

Here is a sample of Grace's way. The first time she took her music show on the road, she entered the tiny discos swinging on a rope, dressed all in black, nothing showing but those all-devouring voracious blood-red lips. Next tour, Grace roared into the smoky night spots on a vicious-looking motorbike.

"Isn't the girl-on-a motorbike motif rather hackneyed now, Grace?"

"Nooooo!" says Grace. Actually, she roars, her accent a cocktail of all of her previous domiciles – Jamaica, Paris, Germany, spiked with a heavy shot of New York. "It's the total combination of the *way* I come on. Dramatic, like a Guy Bourdin fashion photo, a Helmut Newton photo. All that smoke in a small disco, riding a ramp onto the stage . . . and I'm not dressed in leather, like you'd expect. I'm wearing *high fashion*" – an extravagant, translucent black tulle confection, a tutu revealing redwood long legs, with a gold disc perched jauntily to one side on her chignon.

"I regard myself as combination actress, model and singer, and it all comes out in my show. It's like I'm having three different affairs at the same time, but each one is just as important."

Music critics object, say her show is all stylish presentation, image, and not enough music. They don't understand Grace Jones. Music is one among many forms of self-expression and for her, what she sings is not necessarily an insight into her true character any more than the image she projects in a dramatic fashion shot.

"It's great! Because it's like a fantasy on top of the reality. For some people, what they think is the reality is *my fantasy*. So long as I know what it's about, I can handle it."

So Grace has total control over her album sleeves, publicity photos, her live show, and doesn't concern herself with the full spectrum of making her disco hit records – two Island albums to date, *Portfolio* and a new one called *Fame*, both featuring fine sleeves by Richard Bernstein. She leaves the studio technicalities to the expert, Tom Moulton, her producer, popularly known as the creator of the classic disco sound.

Still, when it comes to the singing, she is an artist – one of the few disco singers to flaunt a strong personality over the sheen of metallic disco sound. After months of singing lessons, struggling to acquire technique without losing her own raw urgency, she's perfected her "natural" sound. Now, she discusses voice tone colours as authoritatively as she discusses blushers, eyeshadow. "I've become more aware of my voice. I can make it really bright-sounding with colours – dark purples, bright pinks, pale pinks . . ."

The night I arrived to collect Grace from Goude's penthouse for our official tour of the New York discos, the air was spangled with tension. Grace had just been to the dentist, her whole jaw ached, she'd already done three interviews that day, and besides, she wanted to fix supper for once. Now, here was this journalist come to interrupt her evening, she was in *pain* and . . . muffled arguments from behind the closed kitchen door.

Eventually, we're all in the elevator, direction down. Grace is sullen, her curiously flat eyes stare grimly at the door. We almost make it to the car, when the storm breaks. Grace is huddled, sobbing in the hallway. Wailing. "I always expect people to understand, but no one ever does . . ."

I recollect the snide voice saying, "Grace Jones is just a prima donna," when I spot Grace's white boxer boots stepping into the car. "I've made a commitment and if I say I'm gonna do something, I'll do it."

Later, in Les Mouches, a labyrinthine web of mirrored rooms where Grace launched her singing career, I overhear her say, "Men never understand when I cry. Upstairs I tried to control it, but by the time we left the building I knew I had to let it all out." As we dance in a sudden silver room – lamé pennants drop dramatically from the ceiling to enclose us in lurex twilight – Grace's power pulses back. Languorously, she raises her arms in the classic boxer's attitude or triumph (she takes boxing lessons and boxing is a motif of her new stage act), turns slowly, one boxing boot pawing the floor to the hi-hat cymbal as she revolves.

Now, she's chatting enthusiastically to Sister Sledge, the young four-girl soul group who have just left the stage, complimenting them, hastily adjusting the deep cowl neckline of her draped turquoise leotard – "My tit's fallen out again – that always happens." She's raucous and funny as Mae West; she has harnessed the emotional energy we felt earlier into a Niagara-powerful force field you can sense in a ten-foot radius. Suffering recycled: like Judy Garland, Édith Piaf, both artists beloved of the gay scene, as is Grace. Women who have grown adept at transforming energy, vulnerability, into strength.

Grace's life story reads like a melodrama, or perhaps a carnival extravaganza, starting in Spanish Town, Jamaica. Quiet as can be, the first city established on the island. Growing up in an all-embracing extended family. Preacher father, who loved travel. Childhood ways and games, dominating her doll-playing twin brother (not identical but, yes, he looks as good as Grace. Now he, too, is somewhere in the maze of New York City). The family uproot, move to Syracuse, upstate New York. Drab suburbia, but to get there, the family travelled through Manhattan. "Oh God, it was a dream come true. You can't imagine what it looked like!" Teenage rebel in school – her report card described her as "socially sick" – hightails it to Paris, France, with just 200 dollars. From then on, the story flashes to a high-speed blur, with Grace as Superwoman conquering the capitals of Europe – wild, crazy days and wilder nights.

Here come the myths – a cardinal in Milan shoots himself for love of Grace, she loses her twin brother then finds him again going down an Athens escalator as she's going up, her face in glossy magazines, advertising everything from canned peas to tampons to axle grease from Paris to Marrakesh to Biarritz. Picture this – Grace as Queen of the Night, doing her triumphant, athletic disco dance in mid-air, slowly revolving as she flies across the globe. Grace often dreams of flying. "No plane!"

Grace has lots of dreams. She dreams about animals. Sometimes cats, mostly big animals, like buffaloes. Dominant, threatening animals. Is this because she is genuinely excited by a uniform, an authority figure? I know it is, because she drew in her breath as we pushed through the policemen outside Studio 54 and whispered as much in my ear. She also has frequent psychic flashes, waking and dreaming, foresees trouble or happiness for those she holds dear. The paranormal could be normal if we could all acknowledge human potential as Grace has learnt to do. "I started early and sucked in a lot." Grace's solo flight has been a triumph, but she's taught herself perseverance, endurance. Solo contains lonely. Input she now draws on to sing standard "work is not enough" lyrics as she does on *Fame:* "Fame, what's the use of this game, if I can't have you back with me?"

"I'm not saying all of my life has been lonely, but there are moments I've felt like that. It goes back to the man only being able to experience the successful, aggressive woman in that way, not wanting to experience her emotions." Not only men. People. In fact, all of these people we're walking through, clustered round the blue velvet cordons outside the discothèque Studio 54.

For people who feel they are ultimately insignificant, Studio 54 is the all-beckoning disco mecca. It would be sufficient to enter that broad, high, dark-mirrored hallway they can glimpse through the glass doors. They're thinking of the Girl Who Got In, the one who was refused admission three times and finally got her wish when her friends drove her there in a pickup truck and wheeled her through the door in a bathtub.

Grace knows that the queues outside are there because Studio 54 planned it that way. Restrict the entrance to an illusory "elite" and everybody will crave to be inside. It's only natural – think of Bluebeard's locked room, Pandora's Box. For those, like Grace, who are fulsomely ushered in by the manager, Studio 54 is just another disco; the music's better at Les Mouches, and it's more fun in one of the gay transvestite bars like GG's.

Inside, we enter the perfect setting for the image of Grace Jones. Studio 54 is not a disco, it's a temple of disco, a place where people gather together to worship the style and the beat. Pillars of flashing neon rise and fall to the beat, plunging between the dancers faster than Samson could tumble them. A huge neon strawberry slices the air like a pendulum, almost sweeping the floor. The fragrance of "poppers" – a heart stimulant called amyl nitrate, much favoured by dusk-to-dawn disco dancers – ascends like incense.

Thus, the setting is appropriate for Grace Jones on a variety of levels, not just in terms of image. "I am religious, I believe in magic in a religious way. I believe that you can will things to happen. I look at magic in a positive way; it's very powerful. I actually believe in casting spells, that's what makes it work. Songs cast spells, but you have to hear it at exactly the right time for it to seep in." So Grace shines like a beacon on the Studio 54 dance floor and next morning prays at a church on 127th Street, surrounded by her mother's friends.

If she has, as observers agree, led a charmed life, maybe this is why: first, she made a wish. Then she prayed. She drops her wish, her prayer, written on a scrap of paper, into a box in the church, knowing in her soul that the group magic, group energy will perform the miracle.

Now, Grace is going to combine her "three affairs": next year she's starring, with Olivia Newton-John, in a Metro-Goldwyn-Mayer musical, *Riviera*. She's launching a new line of make-up designed by herself, which people must apply the way she decrees. To date, her dreams have come true.

Kid Creole

My first encounter with Kid Creole and the Coconuts live at a rehearsal had me dancing throughout to their shaking cocktail of hybrid All-New-York sounds: Latin plus funk plus Caribbean. It rarely occurs, but our realities somehow intertwined so that, after this article, we found ourselves becoming actual friends and writing partners on the musical Cherchez La Femme *(it premiered at New York's La Mama Theatre in 2016, got hit by COVID-19, and is still in play!). Engineered by Adriana Kaegi, The Coconuts' witty outfits and dance routines made the band's yin and yang bubble like champagne. Mixed with witty, narrative lyrics made by an English major, for English majors like me and all who are amused by us, I was permanently hooked.*

The Kid's louche lifestyle, idiosyncratic racial terminology and free-wheeling sexual abandon may be shocking, or even just hard to understand from an early twenty-first century perspective. But don't cancel The Kid! During the hedonistic moment captured here – pre-AIDS, post-penicillin and the pill (well, frankly, every era has its own issues) – it was a lot of fun. Not unlike the perverse punk milieu, in Creole-world the more you insulted someone, the more you liked and felt close to them! Divisiveness and separation are being pushed so hard at the time I write, that it is good to be reminded of the inclusionary Creole Creed.

"Kid Creole: He No Pop I"

First published in New Musical Express, *4 July 1981*

And she no Olive Oyl – but Vivien Goldman still meets August Darnell in New York City to learn about the Coconuts' brand-new cha-cha. Colour, culture, sex and music – the Kid threw 'em all together to create the Creole Creed and proved that pure's a bore. On the street with a Kiddy wink, and in the pool hall with Kid, Stony Browder and moon-faced Coati Mundi (the real Pop I).

*

It's all to do with the way I was brought up. Not from the parental point of view, but from the tube point of view. My idols being John Garfield and Humphrey Bogart and those boys – Gable, Spencer Tracey – how they used to dress. Hollywood's idea of style and romance . . . gabardine three-piece suits . . . I used to be glued to that TV set. Beautiful ties. A whole fashion world. In aspiring to be that as a kid, you started to act like that, and the role becomes you. For a while, you know you're playing a role, then as you grow older, the line becomes eradicated . . .
Kid Creole

The short-order cook at the steamy all-night eatery scowled as he slung the fat around the pan, just like Montgomery Clift or Jimmy Dean would have done. He said he would like to be in films, in one of those action movies with lots of murders.

As he spoke, his body straightened, he flung his shoulders out wide: just like those gangsters with groaning pocketbooks, expensive broads and a loveable white-haired mama who will swear in the dock that her boy's the best on the block.

"I don't want to be stuck in this dump for the rest of my life," he said. "Don't you think I look like Bobby de Niro? I figure, well hey, I come from the same block as Lucky Luciano."

He wishes he was a Hollywood hero, he knows he's a star. The trick is making yourself into what you want to be, convincing enough people, and convincing yourself somewhere along the line. It's the Kid Creole way.

August Darnell leans forward and whispers conspiratorially, "Of course, August Darnell is not my real name, but you won't print that, will you, Vivien? Certain information cannot be released. I had to change my name – I'm wanted by the authorities. There are certain organisations that – hey, the tape's rolling. Let's get SERIOUS!"

That day we'd been to see August's tailors, over at the vault-ceilinged palm-potted offices of his managers. (They handle Hall & Oates, too. Daryl Hall was flogging off his old clothes on a rail, but you didn't miss anything groovy, believe me.)

"You'll be wearing braces, of course, and the cuffs on the pants, we can peg them like this . . ."

It's serious business, more dangerous than the dentist. One slip and the cut would be, the hang of the cloth would be – the whole thing would just be a disaster! In America, August Darnell's been waging a one-man zoot suit revival campaign for years. He's a man of style, with an archetypal bedroom voice. Most people seem too stuck on that style, like the stylus in the run-out groove that clicks forever on. Lulled by the cradling cadences of that voice, hanging round haha-ing at the jokes, can take quite some time.

August is lucky – the serious things he has to say he can express through fun, style, entertainment. He's lived by wooing and seduction (just a gigolo) and still does, making records that would charm the pants off you. His musically oblique strategies would alienate the 4/4 majority, if those melodies weren't entrancing. He says he tries to be romantic.

This Kid is so open about personal and sexual politics in his songs that their shock value's sugar-coated with amusement. It's years now since, as Gichy Dan, August authored lines like: "When a man is young he's like a drum, beating off alone" and "Like merchandise, you can't keep a good man down, he's sure to rise" – both ultra-singalong. When he gets the audience to shout that they're all Mr Softees (referring to a song about impotence on his album before last, *Off the Coast of Me*), he's gleefully conscious of the reversal he's sweet-sung them into; he, the hero on the stage, had declared himself to be Mr Softee, that hangdog has-been. The dreaded failure's male self-esteem is reinstated and people can laugh about their sexual incompetence instead of being so worried about failure that they're even worse lovers than they otherwise would be.

August has had more training in the nuances of sexual politics than most. He's the product partly of Montreal, hence the Francophile tendencies of his unusually polyglot paroles, and of the Bronx.

It's one of the boroughs of New York – the territories that surround the sacred isle of Manhattan. The snobbery of Manhattanites towards their neighbours – the Bronx, Brooklyn, New Jersey, Long Island – immediately cuts off valuable input: NY reggae, Brooklyn-based, for example, is unknown to most NY rock fans. The Latin salsa music that happens on hot doorsteps of both Manhattan and the Boroughs is equally ignored – partly because of the communities' self-imposed ghettoism, partly because of a language barrier (salsaniks tend to speak Spanish), at least as much because of white elitism.

August's Bronx – like the East Harlem of his lieutenant Andy "Sugar-Coated" Hernandez's (aka Coati Mundi, after a rodent-like animal spotted by August, Andy and August's little girl in the zoo one day) – is a rich racial mix, where Latin music was the dominant sound.

Kid Creole, Darnell's self-created alter ego (one of three) used to love hanging out on the Bronx's Southern Boulevard when he was twelve years old – a strip where hookers worked twenty-four hours a day. When thirteen, he loved being seduced by all these women in Bronx bordellos. It was, he recalls fondly, a new experience.

"I always thought I was Errol Flynn. Till my lobotomy last year. See how the hair's growing back?"

Songs like "Table Manners" about a man set upon by sexually voracious women craving oral stimulus, on The Kid's new waxing, *Fresh Fruit in Foreign Places,* hark back to those (and other) good old days . . .

"Crazy days of orgies and menages I used to be into before I straightened up. Laughing at it, too, saying how could I have enjoyed those scenes? So demanding."

Fresh Fruit is a clever device. It succeeds both as an album of songs and as a scenario. It's something August was wanting to do all the times he was lieutenant to his half-brother Stony Browder in the Dr Buzzard's Original Savannah Band – that twilight cocktail mélange of big band, disco and Latin vibrations that (via hits like "Cherchez La Femme") bought Coati Mundi the Cadillac that proved he didn't need a Cadillac to inspire respect.

Mundi and August still speak of Browder with great respect, but both make it clear they felt artistically stifled by the band's rigid hierarchy, featuring one Browder on the top like the fairy on the Christmas tree.

Until August met his first wife, Mimosa – Mimi – the inspiration of this musical meandering – he was a philanderer, "a bit of a man about town", supplementing the musical income with handouts from appreciative women. One noted jazz musician was fond of saying he earned an extra $40,000 a year with his extra-musical rhythm; August didn't give an income breakdown, but after meeting Mimi he sent his harem cards saying he was going out of business.

"Actually, I just cut off contact. Stony actually confronted me and asked if I was under a spell, because me being a homebody was so ludicrous. He thought it was some kind of joojoo hoojoo."

[Dear Reader, as our interviewee is deliberately exploring the evolving use of language, specifically the words "Mulatto" and "Creole" in

reference to himself and his friends and family, we are not censoring the usage of the time, both for historical accuracy – and because he himself is making a specific point about this wording.]

"The Savannah Band had the 'Mulatto' credo [all its members were 'half-breeds'] and waved the 'Mulatto' flag. We used to hang around with basically Caucasian women and this turn of mine to a 'native girl' was a slap in the face of the 'Mulatto' creed. Mimi was Haitian, and they were all hanging around with blondes and redheads. When I brought a Haitian girl round, it was taboo.

"Stony had this bizarre idea that we 'Mulattos' had been in the closet for too long . . . the race that was ashamed to speak its name. Blacks had their Say It Loud, I'm Black and I'm Proud, white had always had their movement of the superior race, so Stony said 'Mulattos' should be proud of being half-breeds. They should stand on a pedestal and say, 'Hey, I'm the best of both worlds. I have the black rhythm and the white intelligence.' That's how far out he was."

Coati Mundi remembers being staggered when he first went down to audition for the Savannah Band to see all these half-breed men prancing around in make-up and extravagant gear, but that shock was nothing compared to the kinks displayed in Browder's Enoch Powell-esque racism; applicants to the Savannah Band had to fill in a questionnaire about their blood lineage as if they were racehorses or National Front devotees.

"This was around '75 to '77. It was very sick. The press were alarmed, because blacks started saying, 'We don't want to hear about no goddamn miscegenation.' They said if you had one black parent you were black. Caucasians didn't want to hear about it, because they're ashamed of the fact that plantation owners raped those poor, innocent black slaves and that the result was beautiful children. It was a sick stage in as much as we took it too far. Stony's still doing it – I've dropped the 'Mulatto' approach in favor of Creole music and the Creole Credo. Which is almost as sick.

"I would say this much – the longer we live, the more difficult it will be to find a pure race. What he was saying had its parallels in our music. It was Hispanic, it was black, it was Caucasian. Melodies have come to be associated with the white man's world of Rodgers and Hammerstein, Cole Porter or Gershwin, which is as absurd as only associating rhythm with Africa, saying, rhythm is the dark side and melody's the white side.

"Creole is being used as 'mulatto' once was, loosely to mean a combination of races. Creole is the combination of French and blacks in New Orleans. I use it as a beautiful symbol of the amalgamation of different cultures musically."

All through his post-academic career – August has a master's degree and used to teach/learn from kids – he's been putting all these music into a blender, frothing about men's, women's and youth's voices together with rhythms of all races and places, talking in different tongues. This milkshake's the bubbliest on the block.

Darnell charts his progression thus: "My dad was from the islands, and all I ever heard round the house was Harry Belafonte, then I moved into Motown, then the British invasion, then Marley-ism. It's not reggae – I think Marley was on to something much larger than that. There can be no one to replace him. He alone could have bridged that gap." Marley himself was of mixed-race – a Creole.

Darnell colonises musics joyfully. On *Fresh Fruit*, Kid Creole travels the world in search of his AWOL amour. At the climax of the musical we discover that Mimi has been looking for him back home in New York. In disgust, she has got "married to a man she knew, living on Park Avenue" (i.e. one plush pad).

"With the Savannah Band, each song was a mini screenplay, but Stony wouldn't let me put them in sequence. Finally, I tell him the story of Creole's search for Mimi" – August's first wife, who walked out on him – "much as Jason searched for the Golden Fleece. The journey is just as romantic and covers just as many islands, but it is contemporary. What better way to excuse this many musics?

"Sometimes people get confused when they listen to a Darnell LP – OK, fine, now I'll give you a reason why: Creole is travelling from Africa, which explains the gushing earth drum of 'In The Jungle', through Italy, which explains 'La Dolce Vita' and so on. Each island contributes not only musically, but also to Kid Creole's growth on another level – the journey itself is a *rite de passage* [the literary tradition of novels where the central character journeys the globe, discovering themselves en route through life and lands].

"August Darnell never left New York in that journey. He went downtown, uptown, cross-town and got all these influences – like the other night when I went to see The Clash at Bond's and then went on to a black disco, the Garage, and saw all these black people watching a man perform onstage to a TAPE!"

*

Fresh Fruit is pretty autobiographical. One of the funniest songs is a plea to a woman called Gina. But Gina, the song protests, "he's just a ski instructor!"

This soaringly classist Tatler-ism was composed spontaneously when August took his current wife, dancer, actress and A-1 seamstress Adriana (founder and namer of the Coconuts) out on their first date. She'd been studying dance and acting in New York, and had just become betrothed to a ski instructor on a trip home to her native Switzerland. August just sat down at the old joanna and wooed his new flame with an aptness few could resist. Adriana wound up marrying just the kind of man her mother warned her against. August gained a blatantly ambitious partner who was able to liven up his act considerably with her knowledge of choreography and a typically Swiss bent for hard work and organisation.

Why, Adriana designed and made the leopard-skin bikinis the Coconuts sported in their previous album incarnation; an image that at the very least disconcerted many modern-minded women with its suggestions of Fay Wray rape victims a go-go. Adriana's eyes glow at the memory, however.

"We were acting dumb blondes last year, to attract attention. I'm an actress, you know. We showed lots of flesh. This year people are going to have to see we've got talent. The choreography is much more intricate, we're singing more harmonies. I'm really bored with seeing groups of men playing music. People want to be entertained."

Just as August never questioned the ideology or worth of his Hollywood heroes, checking only the strength in their style, so Adriana never aimed to institute a new style for women's sexuality onstage, relying instead on jokey cartoon-strip eroticism.

Kid Creole's use of women's voices is still mainly as supportive backup, though in their live set, the elegant stick-insect singer Lori Eastside plays the main role for several songs.

At rehearsals, though, it's obvious that the Kid Creoles fulfil that virtual prerequisite of any New Age stepper combo – men and women working together. Apart from the excellent bassie, the Coconuts and Lori Eastside, the mix extends to all skin tones: a Jamaican drummer who sits right over on his kit in the old ska Carly Barrett style; a couple of dudes who would look just right sashaying down the sidewalk in cut-offs and baseball caps balancing a big box (radio/cassette style) – the essential kind of team to cream off Creole Credos.

"I want no more of this," August shouts passionately on "Schweinerei", referring, he suggested, to his frustration with Browder's Big Brothering, and he gives plenty of space to the talents of Coati Mundi. This 32-year-old five-foot-two Creole went into the entertainment business to attract attention. He'd been doing his crazy dancing in public since he was seventeen or so.

"I knew I'd never make it in pro basketball. At school, they abused me because I was small. There's a stigma attached to being small – you're constantly being challenged. People think twice about going up to hit a big guy. If you're small, they say you're a wise-Alecky guy – if you're big, you just have a sense of humour. I couldn't fight a big guy clean. They'd better be ready for anything, like a bat on the head. I learnt all the different things I could in music, to try to get people to look up to me musically, if not physically."

Walking through Central Park, me and Mundi run into a Hispanic family. The father used to play in Latin bands alongside Hernandez, dodging the dodgy shoot-outs endemic to the club scene. The youngest boy's fourteen, wearing a baseball cap though there's a baseball players' strike on.

"You made 'Que Pasa'?" he asks Hernandez admiringly.

Mundi's still new enough to solo fame to smile delightedly and skip slightly at the recognition.

"Que Pasa" is a 12-inch single, Mundi's new baby; witty, characterful series of real-life vignettes like: "When I came from the VD clinic, I thought our love was finished . . .", which gained a deserved following. He also contributed two songs to the new Kid Creole and the Coconut's album, including one featuring ace New York Hispanic musical innovators, Conjunto Libre.

Sensibly, August is not frightened of the competition. At the rehearsal, he scolds like the former school master that he is.

"It shouldn't take more than two minutes to settle into a groove. That took seven," he admonishes. And, "Don't be stationary. I want you all wandering round like a carnival. Put down your instruments and move back and forth, like caged tigers. Act like Puerto Ricans, everybody!"

At a moment of frustration, he shouts: "It's all about listening – about caring enough to listen!"

At the end of the rehearsal, he runs through a list of the songs, giving the band a Pass or Fail on each tune. They scrape through, to this critical ear; this writer had enjoyed the best bop throughout.

After a relationship with the Savannah Band that deteriorated till they had to take rooms at opposite ends of hotels to avoid seeing each other in corridors, Darnell appreciates the camaraderie of the Creole/Coconuts combo. He greatly admires the Coconuts:

"Men don't want to give up what they've worked for all their collective lives. There are intelligent people out there who realise the future is female. Man will have to advance so many light years before his mind will accept taking orders and direction from a female. But that's what's coming. The female mind, generation by generation, is developing faster and coping better with the pressures of everyday living. They are the superior race. All this exploitation – tits 'n' ass syndrome – females are so far above and beyond that, they're smart enough to use it against the people who created it and transcend it.

"A lot of people got into Kid Creole and the Coconuts last year for the wrong reasons. The thighs. The flesh. The devil, the sin of it. So much so that people came to the show to grovel in the dirt at the knees of the Coconuts. That brought attention to the idea, and next year those poor slobs will be back again. But they won't see what they want to see! They'll be forced to hear the music, the progression, the idea. If that's too much for their little minds, then we'll lose those fans. I tell you something – we want to lose them.

"The Creole ideal is in the casting. In the music. It's in the very fibre of my clothes. Co-existence is the only answer, otherwise the planet might as well be reduced to dust. And I don't mean only between races, I mean between the sexes as well. The idea of the United Nations is co-existence, but they don't have the right vehicle. Anyway, adults can never bring about co-existence. Only youth can."

Part 2: New York Punk

Punk-o-philes love to debate about whether the US or the UK was the birthplace of punk. Well, as this collection proves, music mutates and ideas spin round the zeitgeist like wind-borne seeds. There are more connections than divisions. In a previous book, *The Black Chord*, Senegalese artist Baaba Maal described the process to me as the ever-growing tree of music rooted in Africa. The UK Punk Nation was grittier and more political. Rock Against Racism was our crowning jewel. New York punks played harder; no-one has ever contradicted the fact that in our London sub-culture, with our diet of weed and simpler speed, heroin was introduced by the much-admired NY band and famous junkies The Heartbreakers.

Perhaps because they had very narrowly missed Vietnam, NY punks were more about partying and poetry, less about politics. It was more arty; events were often set in galleries and music was more intimately tied up with verse, performance and visual art. In England, we had our poets – John Cooper Clarke, Linton Kwesi Johnson, Benjamin Zephaniah – and visual greats, including Jamie Reid and Linder Sterling. But in New York, the link with punk was more pronounced. Centres of offstage gravity often balanced somewhere between the sex workers of Times Square, who doubled as punk musicians (as some, less, did in London), and the silvery aristo-inclined Warhol scene at Union Square's Factory. The confluence of genders was more celebrated in New York – a legacy from Warhol's revered Factory: an early haven for trans people. That original pop artist's reign held over into punk; CBGB's was just a gob away from Max's Kansas City, his boîte of choice, and The Factory. A blessing from Warhol was still seen as not far off getting one from his beloved Pope.

But while British punks were drunk on Jamaican dub, some Americans tended to be more lateral and stylised, like Talking Heads, with their artful twisted-preppy mien, or The Ramones – a conceptual art piece in themselves, who set out to wrest their sound away from anything blues-based, which so much of popular music was (and may always be?).

One whose contribution may not be sufficiently noted is the poet/musician/memoirist Richard Hell. For it is Hell that is given the accolade of being "First to Wear a Safety Pin" for style as much as function. Of such trivia are legends made. At the time of my article, he and bandmate Tom Verlaine, later of Television, were still quite an item, creatively.

The two men's closeness with Patti Smith would last a lifetime. Together with her intimate friend, photographer Robert Mapplethorpe, when Patti seized New York in the late 1960s, her ascent began in the East Village with Warhol and The Beats. Beyond being the Punk Poet, she has always been a countercultural connoisseur and wise woman. An Anglophile, she and her guitarist, Lenny Kaye, went so far as to found an indie label, MER, to release the velvety roughness of Tapper Zukie's Jamaican DJ toasting, putting her love of dub into action.

As Patti Smith observed when CBGB's was turned into John Varvatos's upscale men's clothing store in 2008, the spirit of punk is more important than the graffitied brick walls now preserved among the top-dollar outerwear. In her connoisseur capacity, Smith related to seventeenth-century French poets, blissed-out scholar beatniks – and the "ghetto" rants of downtown Kingston, Jamaica.

The following three articles, on Richard Hell, the Talking Heads and Patti Smith, were all written within a few months of each other.

Richard Hell

Like his friend Patti Smith, being a self-declared poet, a path he would continue to pursue, made Richard Hell's contribution integral to the avant-garde aspects of New York's 1970s punk scene. His compadre in the group Television, guitarist Tom Verlaine (who even took his nom de punk from a poet!), was a trailblazer in the jagged, scratchy sound that came to typify post-punk guitar. Their blazing intellectual/creative bromance burned out all too soon.

Like the first leaves of spring, New York punk was announced in the UK by two indie 45s, both with a sparse yet gutsy sound: Patti Smith's "Piss Factory/Hey Joe" and "Little Johnny Jewel" by Verlaine's Television post-Hell. Both were top sellers at Rough Trade Records, as was the jaunty "Blank Generation", Hell's first solo cut and also his greatest hit, which helped put punk on the nihilism map. Or nihilism on the punk map. Either way, something clicked.

"To Hell and Back: Richard Hell"

First published in Sounds, *8 October 1977*

"I'm glad my name's Hell, because at least those people at the radio stations are gonna have some idea what to expect. I intend to live up to my name."

Richard Hell is slurring his words, the soft Kentucky accent blurring round the edges. It's 4.30 a.m., after all, and the air in the Coffee Shoppe next to Carnegie Hall isn't exactly Alpine. We're sitting directly over the air vents from the 57th Street subway and it seems like all the pollution of New York City is picketing our Formica-topped nookette. The mini jukebox on the wall is whining, "Hey, did you happen to see the most byootiful gurl in the world . . ." (Richard's choice – also, The Stylistics' "You Make Me Feel Brand New". Ultimate perversity.)

Richard Hell and his band, Richard Hell and the Voidoids, are bound to make it big. ("You really think so?" says Richard, involuntarily anxious.) There's a level of automatic interest simply because of Richard's past associations, all of which indicate an Artist to Watch. He was the former soulmate of Television's Tom Verlaine – "he was a good friend, no, my only friend for years" – and the two new wave culture heroes regularly vilify one another with Romeo/Juliet intensity.

Terry Ork of Ork Records, their initial manager, still has a video tape of the original band. Confirmation of the power of TV's original bionic power source, Tom Verlaine in those days used to move around, even roll on the floor, very physical in a torn T-shirt, while Richard looks bored on bass, occasionally flailing his arms in the air. Edgar Allan Poe would have understood so well; Tom and Richard as chemical doppelgangers, with Tom controlling the balance of energy in the Television unit, spontaneously suppressing Richard's force and moving free with the inspiration of his partner's presence. Richard rebels, Tom says he can't play bass for shit anyway, and Richard departs to join The Heartbreakers.

A classic rock 'n' roll implement, The Heartbreakers still can't fulfil Richard's Gothic/European-influenced vision. Richard leaves, forms his own Voidoids, and everything about his stage presence shrieks body and soul as Richard kicks his left leg out at a right angle like a flamingo on speed. Tom, half of the split atom, is paralysed onstage, his most extreme movement an anguished dying swan crank back of the elegant white neck during a particularly passionate passage of his guitar solo. An obvious case of personality transference, 1977-style.

"I could live with you in another world . . ." Richard sings on "Another World". It doesn't matter that he was unaware of that particular resonance.

I wonder whether or not the bright spark who thought up the new Sire Records slogan Don't Call It Punk realised exactly how spot on he/she was. Take a musician like Richard – he isn't a punk. True, he lives in a highly insalubrious area of New York, way down on the Lower East Side – ideal turf for young punks to hang out on corners and shoot the shit – but Richard isn't there because he's a first-generation American whose folks have just pulled in from Puerto Rico. He's there because he's one of the new generation of artist types flocking to low-rent areas – a process that will inevitably result in rents slowly rising, the scabrous tenements being tarted up till the immigrant families can't afford it any more and have to shift camp to somewhere even less advantageous. Right now, it's still funky in the fullest sense of the word: mean, dirty and low down – just the kind of area your mother wouldn't let you play in.

There, Richard's punkdom (with the possible exception of artistically torn T-shirts) ends.

You know what it's like in England – there's an acknowledged Great British Tradition that musicians shed their middle-class accents pronto, hastily burning any further education qualifications they may have in the process, 'cos if your route to the barricades didn't start in a council block, your credentials are dubious at best.

But over in New York, New Yorkers aren't ashamed to use the word ART. Richard Hell is an ARTIST – or, more specifically, a poet – from an academic/artistic background.

I know that for sure, because I actually met Richard's mother at his Village Gate gigs. She's a professor (I think) of English literature at a university in Kentucky who looks more like a *très chic* elder sister than a mum. Her well-cut pastel suede suit and striped silk shirt were definitely pricier than the clothes the kids in from the suburbs for the weekend were wearing, but stylistically not that different. She made it very obvious that, unlike the archetypal outraged punk parent, she approved of and enjoyed Richard's set. She knows a good bit of art when she sees it.

So here we are in Richard's apartment, feeling fine. Richard started out as a books and words, as opposed to music, person. The metal-clasped trunk in his sparse bedroom is crammed with esoteric literary verse magazines, all featuring the work of Richard Meyers – intense, indulgent word revels. He moved over to rock and roll as a form of personal expression because the teenage rock and roll's adolescent mind is at its most pure. And besides, "poetry's a dead end. Poets are repulsive, bitter people in a confining, disgusting situation."

So now you know.

But on one level, Richard's still more a poet than a musician. His lyrics have the pungent compression that spells fine poetry in neon lights, and his vocal style relies on the way he stresses and colours the words, his distinctive, dramatic phrasing; arts acquired more through poetry-reading than through bashing away at R&B briefs in your dad's garage.

Just to confirm my point, Richard's sitting next to me on the sofa, poring intently over today's mail – the sheet music of the songs on his new album, official copyright confirmation in the U.S.

"See this?" He points to the music notations and yes, there is something slightly strange about them. Instead of the usual circles on the notes, there's a whole bunch of crosses.

"That means they couldn't figure out what note I was singing," Richard says gleefully.

We're examining "Blank Generation"; the people over at copyright control were obviously totally stumped by Richard's singing – nothing but crosses, all the way through.

When you come to think about it, that's very apt. "Blank Generation" has been pigeonholed too glibly as a nihilist anthem. Richard looks at it like this: blank, as in open. He's singing about people who can take it or leave it each time, and everybody's chosen to ignore the "take it".

The message is: don't be too eager to classify. Richard's decided to take it by developing a heavy mystique – as we already know, he's well aware of the potency of his moniker. (Incredible, I know, but the IBA (International Bar Association) over here had to be persuaded to let me use his name in *Sounds*' radio ad; presumably the concept of hell is too heavy for cozy family listening depravity, I guess.)

His chosen mystique is so efficiently alarming that even the folks at his record company approach him v-e-r-y carefully. Richard's got leeway for artistic temperament (which means that he gets that invaluable artistic control) that the slashed-to-shreds Dead Boys will never get, however often they flash their scars. After Richard laid it on the line following some botch up or other, Sire supremo Seymour Stein sent round an internal memo saying that nothing, but nothing, pertaining to Richard must leave the offices without both his and Hell's approval. Makes you want to change your name, doesn't it?

But getting right down to it, Richard's being the perfect attentive host. "What's this?" he says concernedly, swiping my half-finished can of Heineken from the top of the telly where I'd left it while examining the pictures of the band on the wall. "Wasn't it cold enough or something?"

Listen, Richard, back where I come from you've got to drink your beer lukewarm just to stop your blood from freezing . . .

Now he's down on the floor, riffling through the stack of albums and picking out the reggae ones because someone had told him that's what I like. (We settle on Dillinger's *Bionic Dread*, a top fave chez Hell.)

But that's not to say that Hell's menacing image is all a big con. Put it this way – he's moody. Especially round gig time, he'll lock himself away in the small apartment he shares with Ivan Julian, the Voidoids dreadlocked guitarist, and by all accounts he could give Greta Garbo and Howard Hughes a couple of tips about how to be a recluse.

One of those goldarn machines always answers the phone, Richard drawling in that warm, lazy Kentucky voice (with a slight stammer at times of excitement) "UUUhhhh, Richard and Ivan aren't home right now, but if you care to leave a message . . ." etc. If the timing's right, just as you're halfway through whatever convoluted communication you're trying to put over, Richard will pick up the phone. In other words, he was there all along (as if you didn't know). As there isn't a bell on the front door, Richard's got his privacy well worked out.

Myth has it that James Brown requested planning permission to have a moat built round his house in the middle of Brooklyn or somewhere. With a drawbridge. Richard's pioneered a distancing device that's much cheaper to install and runs at least as efficiently.

And speaking of James Brown, Richard has just put his *Hell* album on the turntable. Brown's singing is crazed, anguished: "It's *hell* down here . . ." Richard walks over to the amp, whacks the sound up full. "James Brown is great, he's so cool. Just listen . . ."

We both sit in silence (him chain-smoking low-tar Trues, me smoking high-tar Marlboros, like a couple of nicotine crazies, hitting on our ice-cold cans of beer) on the couch, just synching – or come to that, sinking – deeper into Brown's righteous fury. The visuals fit in just like a movie: through the window, darkness is swallowing up the lines of underwear strung across the dilapidated tenement yard. And on the colour TV with the sound down, masked surgeons are daintily folding back folds of glistening red flesh from a white rabbit on the operating table, their movements controlled as a ritual mercury against the living meat. The rabbit's heart looks puny, but the veins swell and subside in a suitable acknowledgement of the power of the life force.

Richard's turning the album sleeve over, muttering "I don't know when this record was made. Why don't they always put dates on these sleeves like they did on mine? It's gonna be hard for scholars of the future. That's what I think about rock and roll now. It's been going for twenty years. It's really coming up and people are gonna want to know about these things . . ." Told you he comes from an academic background.

Vivien: *So, Richard, is this the way you felt when you decided to switch from Meyers to Hell? Railing at the injustice of the world?*

Richard: *[turns to me and says, quite simply] I just called myself Hell because I felt like HELL and I wanted everyone to know it. I wanted to get started on a new step of honesty, so I included it in my name. I dunno . . . I've always felt so rejected that I never even noticed any difference in the way people reacted to me as Richard Hell. Before I cut my hair and wore ripped clothes and called myself Hell, I was still pretty much of an outsider. It was just, sort of – an acknowledgement.*

Vivien: *You and Tom are really responsible for opening up the whole New York scene, with Television at CBGB's. If you felt that alienated, did you even anticipate the flood of bands that would follow you?*

Richard: *I consciously set out to make it possible for there to be a trend, but it was designed to get a particular message across as well, so it depended whether people would be prepared to accept that message. I wanted it to be popular, but I felt so apart from everything I didn't think it was too likely that there would be many people who . . . it was nice to find out that there was.*

Vivien: *When you realised that a whole new generation of bands had sprung up, did that make you feel less of a loner?*

Richard: *Yes, actually. At the beginning, the new groups definitely made me feel less alienated. I wanted to get something started that would really mean something to everybody and part of it was that there would be a lot of mutual support. At the beginning when there was just us at CBGB's, then gradually there was the Ramones, and the Stilettos who became Blondie, and Patti Smith – it felt great. But then it happened to me in the most intimate way it could possibly happen. That I saw what the facts really were, because it happened to me right in my own room, you know? It turned out that everything was just as competitive as it had always been, and it disappointed me.*

I had thought we had certain things in common, like turning rock 'n' roll into real life and real life into rock and roll, but all the groups badmouth each other the whole time, so it ended up being almost the same thing.

But it's such a bourgeois idea to think that nothing changes and that it's human nature to want to beat out your best friends, but it's . . . I guess rock's bourgeois in its very nature in a culture like this, because ultimately all the groups want as much glory as they can for themselves. It's more powerful than any mission they have in common with other groups.

I respond in kind to that sort of treatment – I'm not a saint, and much as I'd like for there to be an acknowledgement among new wave groups that their common mission is more than their individual glory, I'm still not gonna take any shit from anybody.

Once this record comes out, I know that everybody's gonna be kissing my ass, because I've learnt a lot about what they're like in these few years. I'm not cynical about it, exactly, but I'm not gonna take what people say very seriously . . .

Richard's hands are almost trembling as he hands me the hardback book. "I searched so hard for this . . ."

It's a small nineteenth-century volume, drab green, the complete works of Edgar Allan Poe. If you look at the photo collage on the inner sleeve of Richard's album, you'll see Poe's mournful moustachioed visage prominently enshrined right near Jane Russell (and our own Kate Simon, who took almost all the pix).

Richard: *There's lots of editions that are meant to be complete, but this is the only one I've ever found that has "Eureka" in it. Have your ever heard of it? It's a very long essay, a master description of Poe's concept of the workings of the universe, like his essence, his heart laid bare . . .*

Vivien: *Is that how you feel about this album?*

Richard: *This record is like "Eureka" for me. I achieved it on "Blank Generation". On the next record there's gonna have to be some radical shift. This really encompasses the state of my consciousness right now. I'm not doing that again.*

That state of Richard's consciousness as reflected in his room proves that Richard functions on more levels than rock and roll. His heroes are French poets and novelists Baudelaire, Lautréamont's *Les Chants de Maldoror*, Rimbaud and Huysmans. Edgar Allan Poe, yes, H.P. Lovecraft, no. And then there's Orson Welles – a magnificent publicity photo of Orson in his youthful prime, looking suavely sinister and devilishly attractive, his broad-brimmed hat casting alluring shadows over the overripe, sensuous mouth. Sometimes Richard captures that same presence in photos, a brooding intelligence that's confirmed by his lyrics.

Richard was pleasantly surprised by how accurate the lyrics on the inner sleeve came out, also at how well they read. The only thing that concerned him was whether or not people were going to understand them. In my capacity as random listener, Richard wanted to know what I thought "The Plan" was all about. Well, Richard, strikes me it's about a guy who just couldn't face functioning in the world any more and came up with a scheme whereby he could have a human being of his own to control – sort of a Dr Frankenstein syndrome.

So he calls up an ex-girlfriend and she agrees to join him, have his kid and then split on her own. The benefit for her would be the interesting joy of motherhood with none of the attendant hassles of actually bringing the kid up. The couple didn't tell anyone about their experiment, just followed it through, and sure enough, they had a little girl exactly according to plan. So the hero of the song can do his best to bring the child up with as little of the garbage and bullshit usually thrust upon young people as possible.

Richard: *[ecstatic] That's exactly what I meant!*
Vivien: *Only one thing I don't understand – that line where he says, "I once knew true love – she won't know another". That sounds just like the sort of repressive garbage I thought this scheme was intended to bypass.*
Richard: *[almost stuttering with excitement] No, the point is, she won't know any kind of love except true love because she won't know anybody else except me!*

Aha . . . shades of *The Collector* . . .

Richard: *I'll try and protect her from everybody else except me. This is a plan to create a being with which you can be totally at peace. [Note how Richard unwittingly slips into describing the protagonist as himself – S. Freud.] It's not as fair on the being, if you wanna look at it like that, but it's just as fair* *as any other environment which is imposed on you without your choice because you're a human.*

Richard's getting more and more intense. This song obviously springs from deep inside his own yearnings – he's as near shouting as he gets . . .

Richard: *This is a very fucking nihilistic number here. It's a guy who's absolutely at the end of his rope. He doesn't think anything is any good. He regards it as being the best possible thing that could happen to the little girl. He's exposing her to nothing but the universe that exists within his mind and he wants that to be as beautiful as possible as a substitute for what he had.*

Vivien: *Come on, Richard, all you're really talking about is what every parent has in mind. They think their way is the best and only way and want their kid to conform as closely as they can make 'em. You're just perpetuating a cycle and you're making out you're reaching beyond that.*

Richard pauses, looks at me and grins slyly.

Richard: *Yeah, but they don't bring up their children to be their lovers!*

Richard's putting together his own fanzine called *The Voidoid*. It's currently intended as a one-off, but in more fanciful moments he contemplates putting out one a year for the rest of his life. And re-recording "New Pleasure" once a year for the rest of his life. Just to see how they compare. I told him that that's a favourite pastime of The Wailers and he seemed inspired to actually do it. *The Voidoid* looks all set – he's working out layouts and captions and quotes right now, having fun. The pictures include lots of death images, things like Warhol's electric chair silk screen, pictures of Sarah Bernhardt the actress asleep in her coffin. (Did you know she used to wander off to the land of nod in a coffin? Different strokes . . .)

There's also thought-provoking quotes, like this one from James Schuyler: "Tomorrow is another day. But then, so was yesterday."

And more sage words from Hell, admonitions he's made his own, like "Liars Beware." Strikes me that Hell's far removed from the negative, nihilistic figure you might assume lurks behind titles like "Who Says? (It's Good to Be Alive)". He's a romantic, with chivalrous inclinations. Any romantic with brains is bound to resort to a spot of self-preservation – after all, this is 1977, and nobody's being over-optimistic about 1978, now I come to think of it. What do you say to that, Richard?

"My stance is . . . my stance is like I am on the front of this 45" – pointing to the sleeve of the Stiff release of "Blank Generation" – "with my head to my side and my pants undone. I don't have a stance, I just react. I know that it's not worth writing about anything that isn't distinctly important. To me, being honest is something you take for granted. It's a man's work."

Talking Heads

Post-modernist post-punks Talking Heads, as a unit with their cool keyboard player, Jerry Harrison, connected feet, hips and head together in a surprising, metropolitan and prophetic way. David Byrne has gone on to be among music and performance's key conceptualizers, often along with friend Brian Eno, whose interview opens this book. As Tom Tom Club, Chris and Tina, one of rock's rare cool couples, branded a distinctively playful, brightly-hued party funk. They expressed the singular sound of Chris Blackwell's Compass Point Studios in Nassau, The Bahamas. (Grace Jones, who we met as a disco diva, also invented her original, prowling tracks there, together with Jamaica's Sly and Robbie rhythm section.)

"Talking Heads: Psycho-Killer, Qu'est-ce Que C'est?"

First published in Sounds, *22 October 1977*

QUESTION: *When is a door not a door?*
ANSWER: *When it's the door to the dressing room at CBGB's, which is in reality a blanket nailed to a wooden frame. CBGB's is situated at the corner of Bleecker and Bowery, in New York's Lower East Side. Or is it West? There you go, the streets don't even have numbers like Fifth Avenue or someplace reputable like that.*

CBGB's is the accepted birthplace of New York punk and the first thing you'll notice when you go inside, assuming you've attended any punk gig in a major British city, is that a good 95 per cent of the CBGB's punters look like they're in a time warp from a Middlesbrough Poly gig circa 1969. You get the odd Dave Vanian circa 1976 lookalike, and they look way out.

Infinitely more visually intriguing than les punks New York-style are the bums on Bowery outside. The Bowery is Skid Row. New York winos, dossers and meths-drinkers young and old huddle in the next doorway along from CBGB's, a couple of 'em sit comfortably on chairs, chewing the fat. They act just like a Greek Chorus, commenting on the antics of the young kids who stream out from CBGB's to get some air. The punks and the hobos dress with about equal flair. Who's the punk in 1977?

Anyway, back to the dressing room.

People had always told me about the toilets at CBGB's and the impressive graffiti – "J.D. Is Best", "All the Way with Lenny Kaye", etc. Personally, I was more struck by the adequate supply of toilet paper.

Just upstairs from the celebrated slash city, you get the dressing room. I guess you can dress in it, but a room it isn't. It's like stepping right into some shanty lean-to in the dust bowl.

And there's this beer-befuddled hack plaintively rap-rap-rapping on the wooden post that the "door" (or blanket, as we journalists call it) is held up by. He wants to be let in. He wants to see the Talking Heads.

The Talking Heads are inside; they've just finished their first set of the night.

They don't want to see him.

It's easy to understand why – this gent's truly obnoxious. He's been lurching around, breathing fumes, asking asinine and insulting questions in a spectacularly snotty way.

Chris Frantze (drummer) walks to the door – it might as well be a door; it seems to be keeping the guy outside quite effectively – and says: "I don't think it's really a good idea if you come inside right now." Firmly. And drops the curtain. Conclusively.

While the journalist huffs and puffs his way outside – "Well, if you don't want to be interviewed for *The Voice*, though I can't see why . . ." – David Byrne is sitting quietly tucked away in a corner, retuning his guitar, Tina [Weymouth]'s rubbing a towel across her face vigorously, every line of her compact frame expressing maiden-aunt icy determination, and Jerry Harrison squashes a grin as he packs the instruments away. The Talking Heads know they don't need to take no shit.

Tina: *He was very drunk, but that's no excuse. He asked David, "How do you feel about being in this band, do you like it?" And David quite naturally answered, "I wouldn't be doing it if I didn't." Then he said, "How does it make you feel that your set will make people go out and knife each other on the street afterwards?" I challenged him on it later. I said, "Did*

> *you actually see somebody do that?" And he said [puts on haughty voice] "What are you talking about? You don't know the street! I know the street!" This preoccupation with the street, it's so stupid. Everyone in New York lives on the street every single day . . .*

As far as personalities go, the Talking Heads make the Ramones look like something from an Abbey National pamphlet. The Talking Heads are your average macho rock 'n' rollers. They radiate clean-cut playing fields-of-Harvard wholesomeness, in a unique blend of jock and swot.

And more contrasts. Their songs ought to be cerebral and thought-provoking and deal from the neck up, whereas in fact they're the only new wave band on either side of the Atlantic to have a drummer and bass player who sound like a classic rhythm section, making rhythms that are designed to dance to. That's what drew Seymour Stein, head of Sire Records, to sign 'em. He says that when he first saw the Ramones he knew he was in the presence of true rock 'n' roll, but when he saw the Talking Heads he couldn't believe they sounded so intriguingly oddly new and yet so commercial.

And while I'm writing this, I've got the Talking Heads syncopating through the headphones, unpredictable song structures and off-the-wall arrangements, and even at the typewriter I'm jiggling around like I've got St Vitus' dance . . . *Street /Beat / The Heads Are Neat* . . .

The Talking Heads are an affront to people who think you've gotta be wasted and living on the edge to be real rock musicians. I don't think England's produced a similarly upper-class rock 'n' roll band. Chris's father is a major, Tina's father is a general. Their wedding recently was by all accounts a society affair.

Perhaps the Heads are temperamentally better suited to England than the States. What people could misconstrue as coldness is their version of good old-fashioned British reserve. Tina's haughtiness when faced with people who try to give her a hard time is more threatening than screaming or yelling; it's born of a deep-down awareness of position and privilege, both natural and social.

Tina: *Why should people hide things like going to university, if they have the feeling and the feeling is real?*

Jerry: *This glorification of the working class has been going on for a long time. There's something to be said for some of it, but*

I think that when they do it by trying to write simple songs it's really backward. You'd think they'd wanna talk about the great things in the working class, like they're much more conscious than you give them credit for. Instead they write songs that make them seem banal and pathetic.

Tina: *It's reverse snobbism—*

Vivien: *Do you think of your music as sexual?*

Chris: *I think it's more like when you're having a flirtation with somebody and you lock in with them through a play in words or some kind of bond rather than an actual physical gesture like coming up and patting them on the behind.*

Vivien: *I think it's very sexual. "Psycho Killer" is really erotic . . .*

Chris: *[dry] I suppose it does have its – uhhh – physical moments.*

David: *There are songs about romantic love. It's a very sweet sort of notion of love that's presented. I just felt that's something that's been denied lately. It's presented without sounding namby-pamby.*

Chris: *I was aware, I don't know if David was, that a lot of people are going to get the wrong idea about our sexual orientation just because of the songs we do and because we don't strut around acting real foolish. Some people think that because you don't do that obviously you must be a mama's boy. [Cries of disbelief round the table.] It's true. Whereas in fact it takes some real wherewithal to pull it off.*

Vivien: *Do you think people understand your lyrics?*

David: *Maybe not the first time. Sometimes it takes a few lessons. It's not just entertainment. There is some substance there that would have meaning for some people.*

Vivien: *That's the way Eno operates – he won't lower his standards for some theoretical audience . . .*

David: *I think we'd agree with that, but we wouldn't want to underrate the audience, because I think they would see that and regard us as being condescending. It would be better if we presented them with something that they find a little bit – maybe confusing, and maybe a little bit more difficult to relate to at first, but once they'd got used to it they'd find more in it.*

We're sitting in the Long Island loft where Chris and Tina live. Way out of Manhattan, central New York, it's drizzling outside but colourful and vast inside.

The Heads have provided a veritable feast on the round table by the kitchen area – bowls of seedless grapes, salami and cheese sandwiches stacked up on a big plate, wine.

Sitting round a table is a good chance to observe the Heads; they're marked individuals. David Byrne writes the songs, sings 'em and plays guitar solos. He's tall, lean, with a dark, classically handsome face. He looks like the last of the line of a noble Russian family in a nineteenth-century novel with a hereditary disease, just come off the squash court. A strangely high, quirky voice, sounds like he's constantly on the verge of hysteria. Stutters when he's excited.

Jerry, Bostonian, artistic, looks like a dryad or descendant of Pan. Light brown curls cluster above slanted eyes. Wry.

Chris and Tina – newlyweds. Chris is a constant source of Frankie Howerd-style humour, very dry, very catty, very camp. Tina looks trim and shipshape onstage and off, wears Japanese karate shoes and looks like she's stripped for action. Chaste self-assurance, kind of a friendly Mother Superior.

It's an artistic building. Don Cherry, the great jazz musician, lives upstairs and jams with them sometimes. Chris and David used to share a flat; Jerry and David now share a flat in the city. Tina observes primly, "We still have meetings and get together for social occasions."

When I spoke to the band, the album hadn't even been released in the States yet. Chris and the rest of the band had been talking about what a pleasant surprise it had been to find all their contemporary CBGB's bands' albums actually sounding like grown-up long-players.

"I think we kinda felt, well, we're all local bands, the people who make real records are somewhere else. But it was nice. Almost everyone's sounded like a real record," David enthused.

Chris mused, "It'll be very interesting to see what people say about our record. If their concept of it is different from ours."

"When I listen to it," Davies carries on, "I get the feeling that it's a very happy record, but other people that aren't familiar with my voice might think I'm in pain, you know? Like our parents listened to Elvis and said, 'Oh, it sounds like he hurts, when actually he was having fun' . . ."

A maliciously teasing grin curls Chris's mouth. "Like when David goes AAAAAAGGGGGGG, it sounds like he's in pain but really he's in ecstasy . . ."

"Some of our songs are nihilistic, like 'No Compassion' and 'Psycho Killer'," says David. "But some are very confident. Although some of them are about being confused, most of them are very positive."

Not surprising somehow that David's the only musician I can recall to have written an erotic song revolving round books, writers, lips and tongues and words all meshing together into surreal optimistic Vaseline-on-lensed fantasy – when he finds out his new crush has read the same book, "It hit the soft spot in my heart . . ." and so on and so forth. The Talking Heads are another of these not-afraid-to-be-arty combos. Arty. Intellectual. Adventurous. Avant-garde.

Vivien: *Waddya reckon, group?*
Tina: *We don't think of ourselves as avant-garde. I suppose we are aware of it when we intellectualise, but most of the time we think of ourselves as a band.*
Chris: *We had a general concept and idea about our, uh, image.*
David: *We'd gone to concerts and seen rock bands and I think there were various things that we'd grown tired of seeing and hearing. We thought there were a lot of things that could be fixed. People would come out in elaborate costumes and people would sing in real funny voices. We sort of decided not to do lots of things. There are times onstage I'd like to dance, but I have to play guitar—*
Tina: *It's very hard to do the splits and still do syncopated guitar stuff.*
Chris: *I think it's really distracting when people do all that bumping off each other and bouncing.*
Tina: *It starts to become a real pose.*
Chris: *Let's not use that word in this interview.*

Posey. Hmmm. Sounds like people had accused the Heads of this unpopular stance in the past. I'd hardly have thought it applied, myself. Is immobility posing?

Because that's one of the ironies of the Talking Heads that's always attracted me – they play very physical music standing totally still, heads of the New York Iceman School class, along with Television.

"Oh, gee," said Tina, sounding really upset. "I thought I was moving a lot compared to . . . I used to be too scared to move. Though something spontaneous could always happen that might make you want to throw yourself on your knees."

"Even so," David adds thoughtfully, "if you did it, you might find that if the audience got excited you'd feel like you cheated them. Backstage, you'd know that you weren't doing it for real, so you'd feel bad about it."

Chris: *We're all really concerned about playing right, which might have a tendency to make us look uptight.*
Tina: *But that's when you really transcend, when the whole band becomes very sensitive to one another.*
Vivien: *Do you feel you fit into the punk category?*
Chris: *Everyone sees us as, if not in that category, at least part of that category.*
David: *The similarity is in approach, the fact that when we started we decided there were a lot of things we wouldn't do, and the punk bands decided the same thing. But we came up with a slightly different answer.*

Patti Smith

So dominant in the Sounds *pantheon was poet Patti Smith, right from the start with her indie 45 "Piss Factory", that this brief article simply conveys her word to the concerned, adoring troops on the occasion of a scary accident.*

"Patti Cracks Noggin, Raps on Regardless"

First published in Sounds, *5 February 1977*

Patti sounds plaintive, fragile, over the transatlantic wire. If you can imagine a voice sounding wan, you're near the mark. Reason being: "A swan dive. And there wasn't a pot to catch me." Rock's Queen Poetess dived off a 14-foot-high stage in Tampa, Florida at a gig in a huge amphitheatre. Being a support act, the band hadn't received adequate time to get used to the dimensions of the stage . . . "I didn't have my terrain worked out. Like, it was a new situation for us, a new stage set-up. But I have all my faculties together."

But there you go, despite broken vertebrae in her neck, a cast separating head from shoulders, and the prospect of eight weeks in bed, things could be worse. For a start, it sounds as if Patti's the centre of much love and affection. Her brother, Todd, jumped straight down the 14-foot drop onto the concrete after her, so from the moment she hit ground she wasn't alone. Her boyfriend, Allen Lanier, is with her and when he has to go on the road with the Blue Öyster Cult again, the guys in The Smiths band are rallying round in shifts to keep her company.

"I'm so lucky," she kept repeating. "The doctors can't believe it! An' I feel just like the field marshal, down in the line of duty. I know I'll be standin' soon and in the meantime, just tell the troops to keep fightin' . . ."

Patti asked me what I was wearing. She told me that she was lying in bed wearing an Ethiopian blanket, a grey sombrero and her neck brace. "And twenty-two stitches in my head. But I got a hard head."

"I feel like I've done it. I've seen the angel of death and wrestled with it. Maybe the other guys wrestled and lost and I won . . . It happened when I was spinning like a dervish – you've seen me do that – and just as I stopped spinning, I reached for the mike and just went off the stage. It was the most amazing thing that's happened to me. I'm like the kind of performer that courts risk. I court death, but the way I kept it together was totally relaxed. I saw, like a spiral tunnel of light, and I felt my consciousness draining through it.

"I felt myself going and I said – *GET BACK HERE*! I gripped my consciousness by the throat . . . the biggest battle was in my head, and I won.

"This is all physical shit – I can handle that. And the mental shit is all fine. I'm really happy to be alive, it's great. And, y'know, when they put those twenty-two stitches in my head, they couldn't use an anaesthetic, so I just, like, pretended it was the Civil War, y'know? I pretended I was Robert E. Lee.

"You know how Lenny found out I was alive? I'd just written a poem for Tapper Zukie – it's called 'Tapper the Extractor'. It's the best poem I've written for a real long time. Tapper's poem kept me from losing consciousness. It's all about 'the thread of return' – tell him I'm gonna be sending it to him over the weekend. Lenny's coming over later to type it out for me. Yeah, the thread of return kept me here."

Patti's also happy that Ivan Král is back playing piano with the band. The family's back together again. They've had a coupla weird incidents, like being banned from Boston and New York radio the same time as the Pistols had their spot of media trouble, 'cos Patti said "fuck" on the airwaves. Now, kids are picketing the stations to get them to play Patti's discs again . . .

"This thing has brought us back together and when I'm up, we'll be stronger than ever. WE'RE GONNA COME ON LIKE TANKS!"

CHAPTER 6

Ska and 2-Tone Central

As the eighties rolled in, an audience educated by punk and reggae were well attuned to the emergence of 2-Tone – a jaunty son-of-ska genre that revamped and reconfigured the speedy optimism of independence in 1962, including its haunting jazz strains. Since those times, when Don Drummond's The Skatalites reigned, even after the awful tragedy described in this chapter, ska has become a worldwide phenomenon, signalled by black-and-white motifs as well as music. Successive waves of ska around the world mean that generations of global ska bands and festivals now abound, often springing from the tribe first united by multiracial 2-Tone, but drawing its force from the source . . .

Here is the ska origin story whose tragedy still haunts today . . .

Don Drummond and Margarita Mahfood

The deep research that went into this piece was prompted by conversations I had with original members of The Skatalites, now dead. Naturally lamenting their dead bred'ren, Don Drummond, and his unique take on melding ska and jazz, they would quickly start blaming his lover, Margarita Mahfood, for his death. "If it weren't for her, Don would still be with us," the old-timers would lament. But, given Margarita's fate, I could not help but feel there was more to the story. After interviewing Don's psychiatrist at Bellevue Hospital, I mentioned it to Perry Henzell, the director of The Harder They Come, *who introduced me to fellow researcher, scriptwriter and Jamaican actress Evet Hussey, who also wanted to write a screenplay about Don and Margarita's doomed love. Together we wrote it – and it may or may not hit the screens before or after you read this! But the tragic passion of Don and Margarita, an epic tale (Jamaica's Sid and Nancy), never left me. I felt love and terrible compassion for them both – and, like millions of others, still find ska music irresistible.*

"Blow by Blow"

First published in Pitchfork Review, *2013*

Tears fell on dance floors across Kingston, Jamaica, in the early hours of the first day of January 1965. Enjoying their "jump and prance" to ska – the blithe, speedy sound of independence – partygoers froze as word of the tragedy spread like wildfire from bar to nightclub. The handsome, master ska trombonist Don Drummond, thirty-two, had turned himself in to the police and confessed to killing his great love, the exotic dancer Margarita Mahfood, twenty-five, then known as the Rhumba Queen.

Introverted and depressive, Don clearly benefited from Margarita's breezy, fun personality. It took a woman of Margarita's sensuality and vivacity to unlock him. Her naysayers forget that though Margarita's electric sex appeal tested Don, she, too, put up with a lot during their brief, incandescent relationship.

When I discussed the relationship with Don's former bandmates, the general analysis cast Margarita as a wicked temptress responsible for Don's downfall. And without Margarita and her flirtatious, coquettish ways, Don would still be alive, conceptualising music to propel Jamaica into the future. But it took two to dance that fatal rhumba.

Why should Margarita be blamed for her own death at the hands of a man she had loved and cared for, even when others had abandoned him?

As a founding member of one of the world's seminal house bands, Drummond's name became synonymous with The Skatalites, whom he joined in 1964. The band's name suggests the leaping optimism of the period, when a wave of nations emerged from colonialism and men walked on the moon. New frontiers were being broached on Earth and in outer space.

The double tragedy struck a great blow to the newly developing Jamaican psyche. If there was extra hop in ska's bop, it came from knowing the island, after centuries of genocide, slavery and colonialism, was finally independent.

At that moment, every reveller who came of age with independence realised that ska would never be the same – and neither would they. The pure exuberance of ska would forever be shadowed by the eerie drum roll of innocence lost. Set to immortal dance music, Don and Margarita's co-dependent passion, jealousy, betrayal and obsessive love – not unlike a Caribbean Sid and Nancy – would never be forgotten.

As the story emerged, shocked revellers heard how Margarita had promised to stay home in their two-room shack at 9, Rusden Road, in Kingston's Rockfort area, and wait for Don's return from a show in the country. But the free-spirited Margarita couldn't resist partying on New Year's Eve. Returning early, Don fell prey to manic jealousy. The ensuing tragedy would continue to be debated passionately up to today, much like the grim fates of Kurt Cobain, Tupac and The Notorious B.I.G.

Yet, oddly, Jamaica did not vilify Don Drummond for the killing, even though the gorgeous, vibrant, kind Margarita (the drop-out daughter of a prosperous Jamaican–Lebanese family) was arguably just as loved on the island. It was well known, especially in music circles, that Don was prone to "go and come in the head". He had been diagnosed with schizophrenia. Don resisted controlling his condition with drugs because they stopped him from being able to play. Knowing his own weakness, the great composer, player and arranger, who gave us classics like "Eastern Standard Time", "Green Island", and "Man in the Street", was a withdrawn loner, the archetype of the tortured artist.

Like all newly emerging nations of that time, the island was conscious of its cultural capital and the role its music played in giving the country an identity. Ska was being marketed as part of Jamaica's growing tourist industry.

Yet the rhumba was still Margarita's trademark dance because of the way she shimmied during the salad days of the Cold War. The Berlin Wall went up in 1961, a year before Jamaican independence. And the botched Castro takedown known as the Bay of Pigs happened three years before Don joined The Skatalites in 1964.

Through the global shake-ups, Cuban music had conquered the world anyway, from the congas of American sitcom *I Love Lucy*'s Desi Arnaz to the Congo. But it had a special meaning for Jamaica. As word filtered back that migrating Jamaicans were not receiving warm welcomes in their former motherland, Great Britain, there was a natural urge to seek new allies. Thus, Jamaicans placed themselves on the front lines of the Cold War, through Cuba's links with Russia.

The bond between Cuba and Jamaica was as strong then as it is today. In that era, before the days of all-inclusive resorts for middle-class tourists, the Kingston waterfront was bustling with commerce. Cuban sailors were habitués of the waterfront clubs, bars and brothels in the lost bohemian world of Rae Town, now dilapidated, where much of Don and Margarita's love played out. There, Margarita's erotic dance expressed a social reality, just as Don's plangent playing communicated the depth of the newly independent Jamaican soul.

When I first started covering Jamaican music at the source for the thriving British music press in the mid-1970s, reggae giants like Bob Marley, Gregory Isaacs, Jacob Miller and Dennis Brown, and rapping DJs known as toasters, such as U-Roy and Big Youth, were still active around town. In their "ganzie" cardigans and felt hats, reggae stars could be seen taking meetings with multinational record companies like Virgin or Warner Brothers. (At the time, record companies showed a spurt of interest because of Britain's Punky Reggae Party – the musical bond between two disaffected youth subcultures: punk and Rasta.)

Though they were one generation older, Don's fellow players in the legendary Skatalites – Tommy McCook, Roland Alphonso and Jackie Mittoo – were alive and still playing. Thus, it was through his musical compadres that I first heard of Don and Margarita's turbulent story.

Tommy McCook always swore Don was innocent. Musicians spoke of Don and Margarita in the present tense, as if they were still around – playing, dancing, loving and brawling. At Don's trial, neighbours in their yard described the couple's rapport as "fighting and playing".

Both beautiful and talented, Don and Margarita became an "it" couple as soon as they got together, having met as stars of the Kingston music scene. At just twelve years old, Margarita won the famous Vere Johns amateur show at The Ward Theatre. Still a teenager, she became a regular draw in Kingston's hectic sixties nightlife, with its elegant clubs, such as The Glass Bucket at Half Way Tree Road and the Club Havana on Windward Road. And Margarita was progressive; she smuggled Rasta drummers onto a big performance of hers, though Rastas were still regarded as dangerous and dodgy – and turned the show into a triumph.

Despite her success, Margarita was always friendly, genuine and full of sparkling verve. Petite and fit, with long hair waving around her shoulders, she knew how to turn men on with her earthy energy. Her Lebanese complexion positioned her as a woman desirable to all races. Unlike the statuesque showgirls of Havana's Tropicana Club, who inspired her flouncy, belly-baring, cha-cha-cha costumes, Margarita worked her wire waist and did the splits on those chic dance floors, just like today's twerking queens.

And that was the problem. In those more conservative times, Margarita's blessing was her curse. Her free spirit, talent and sexy moves made her a star – but also caused her strict, abusive father (a wealthy businessman who had made his money in fish) to cast her out of their traditional Lebanese–Jamaican upper-middle-class family. Those magnetic hips drew Don to Margarita – but then made him ban her from dancing in public once she became his woman, plunging their small family unit into poverty.

When Don and Margarita fell in love, Don Drummond was already a hero. Legend has it *DownBeat* wrote about him, and George Shearing named him one of the world's five best trombonists. His distinctive contribution is the melancholy, searching, jazzy trombone solos that add a poignant undertow to ska's cheery gallop. Arguably, it's Don's haunting, witty, sensitive solos embedded in ska's exuberance that give the sound its tantalizing, bittersweet flavour, suggestive of both youth and insight. That frisson gives ska an extraordinary resilience, rising again and again to recharge new generations with its snappy propulsion. Ska has gone through four cycles of popularity.

First, it fired up newly independent Jamaicans, then it energised the mods and skinheads in 1960s Britain. After that it inspired The Specials and other bands on 2 Tone Records in the seventies and eighties. Finally, nineties skatepunks like No Doubt (on the West Coast) and The Mighty Mighty Bosstones (on the East Coast) assumed the mantle of ska. Now, ska and its punk varieties are continuously performed from Japan to Russia and Indonesia. But that moment in Kingston, Jamaica, is where it all began – in the downtown dances and plush nightclubs of an island whose rigid colour and class system was just beginning to shift and a dark-skin downtown boy could capture the heart of a light-complexioned uptown girl.

But despite their differences of class and colour, Don and Margarita had much in common, as well as being leaders in their respective arts. Both headstrong and rebellious, they each flouted the destiny dictated by their upbringing and background. It was Don's mischievous behaviour – possibly shaped by early signs of his incipient schizophrenia – that led his single mother, living in meagre ghetto conditions, to place him with the nuns at the Alpha Boys' School. Thus, misfortune gave young Don a new future. The Alpha Boys' School was virtually the only access to musical training for a fatherless ghetto boy. At school, his brilliance was acknowledged, but even then he was introverted and silent. He heard his own music and distrusted authority.

Before he became a key figure in The Skatalites, Don stood in an individual bandshell wearing a monogrammed jacket as part of the well-established Eric Deans swing jazz band. He was fired for hijacking the show, subverting the anticipated swing rhythms by blasting a ska solo. The crowd loved it; Deans didn't. But Don was on a quest to find his true voice. Rooted in African American jazz (Don's Middle Eastern modal approach owes much to John Coltrane), his musical journey was also directed by another passion he and Margarita shared, as outsiders and seekers – Rasta, the young belief system that had its own black deity in Haile Selassie, His Imperial Majesty of Ethiopia, King of Kings, Lord of Lords, Conquering Lion of the Tribe of Judah, Earth's Rightful Ruler.

Many artists were among those growing dreadlocks and gravitating to the teachings, expressed in the African-derived Rasta drums, used to draw humans close to divinity, aided by smoking marijuana. Jamming with Rasta artists like Count Ossie and The Mystic Revelation of Rastafari helped Don to discover his individual artistry. Don had always heard a different sound in his mind – one that did not always come instantly to his fellow musicians. His producer, the late Coxsone Dodd, granted me a rare interview at Studio One in Kingston. He recalled how during one session, Don was so frustrated at the other Skatalites' slowness in catching the beat that he once pulled a knife and insisted, "Who want to play, play. Who don't, leave," shocking his fellow musicians.

The grey-bearded Dodd's sonorous, deliberate voice had a gravitas suited to his role as reggae's elder statesman. The rhythms Dodd oversaw formed the foundation of Jamaican music recycled by artists today. Many on Studio One's roster of illustrious artists complained about their paltry remuneration; but the sheer scope of Dodd's signings tells its own story, including Bob Marley, Burning Spear, John Holt, Lee "Scratch" Perry and most of Jamaica's great musical names. Over a decade after he'd left Studio One, Marley was still vexed about his lack of money from Dodd. Yet, he would recall his times at Studio One with nostalgic affection and call that period "an education". Don, however, never lived long enough to find that peaceful accommodation.

Assuming the financial risk, producers also assumed they would reap the bulk of any rewards. In many cases, artists were so plentiful that some regarded them as disposable. But Dodd saw the treasure he had in Don. Though Don's music was extremely popular, Dodd had a simple explanation for the money woes that beset Don. "He loved to record so much and he had so much new music always bubbling in his mind that Don would use up his money in advance, by booking studio time," the venerable Dodd explained. Of Margarita, he took a more balanced view than the other Skatalites. Even Dodd was not immune to Margarita's charms. Despite Dodd's admiration for Don, he represented what Rastafarians called Babylon, which is to say he was part of the system that both thwarted and oppressed Don.

Don and Margarita were both drawn to the growing Rasta movement, whose philosophy gave meaning to their post-colonial struggle. The Rasta encampment in the Wareika Hills outside Kingston was a place of refuge for Don and Margarita. Her extraordinary talent and charisma often made her the only female dancing around the flames while the Rastas, channelling Africa, drummed and chanted down Babylon for nights and days.

The controversial Margarita was already both loved and loathed for refusing to go onstage unless she could use Rasta drummers in her set at the famous Ward Theatre. The promoters tried to resist. At that time, Rastas were outcasts, known as "blackheart men", and invoked as bogeymen to scare little kids. It was a bold move that made Margarita even more of a heroine.

Perhaps the pinnacle of Don and Margarita's great love was the Studio One session when he fulfilled her ambition to record. Now readily available online, "Woman a Come" was for many years a rarity, partly because, like Margarita's musical prowess and character, the song was never taken seriously by the musical establishment. The Skatalites regarded the session as a favour to Don and a bit of a joke. But now, Margarita's unconventional, gritty singing sounds avant-garde, a ska Yoko Ono. The Rasta drums and militant womanist spirit make this song an incantation for a more equal future.

Rasta helped to articulate Don's great frustration. His progressive consciousness is clear in his song titles, from "Man in the Street" to songs that spearheaded Jamaican fascination with the Far East, like "China Town" and "Confucius". Involvement with Africa rang out on "Addis Ababa", "Marcus Junior" (referring to the son of pan-Africanist Marcus Garvey) and "The Reburial", a nod to Africa-based Pocomania rituals.

Don was a great artist, eager to progress, yet he was trapped in a rapidly changing but still deeply class- and colour-conscious system. He was trapped as a musician whose creativity greatly outstripped his actual earnings. Above all, he suffered as a man trapped on his island – and in his mind. Because of his medical records as a schizophrenic, Don was not allowed to have a passport.

The greats of America who inspired him – John Coltrane, Charlie Parker, Albert Ayler – were so tantalisingly near, but he would never get a chance to jam with them, as his talent merited. His only freedom was to blow those solos and enjoy Margarita. Meanwhile, Margarita's dancing had attracted attention from American impresarios. But before she was faced with the decision whether or not to leave Don behind and pursue a career on Broadway, she was gone.

Some of Don's peers saw Margarita as a groupie or vampire, but the emotional balance of power in their relationship seems to have been quite different. If Margarita's romantic choice files her under "women who love too much", bear in mind that not only was her brooding superstar musician gorgeous, but also that in falling for a man who could be difficult and rough, against the advice of her friends, she was only gravitating to what she knew. Prior to marrying Don, Margarita married and had a daughter with boxer Rudolph Bent, who was also alleged to have used his fighting skills on her.

Margarita's father, meanwhile, never forgave her disobedience – her class betrayal – in becoming a rhumba dancer and shacking up with a broke black jazz musician. Addicted to each other, neither heeded the warnings. They were blinded by love and need. For Margarita, Don was not only a lover, but also a creative inspiration so thrilling it was worth putting up with his mood swings and recurring disappearances.

When the stress really hit, Don would disappear. Vanish. It was in this anonymous vagabond mode that Evet Hussey encountered him, a fleeting but poignant connection that makes an appearance in our film. As a schoolgirl, Hussey had a summer job at a resort hotel, where she befriended and fed a vagrant, against her boss' advice. After guards chased him from the property, she never thought she would see him again. But some months later, Hussey went to see The Skatalites. To her amazement, the legendary Don Drummond playing the trombone onstage was her friend, the homeless man. She never forgot how he stepped forward and played his solo, looking straight at her.

When he would reappear from one of his walkabouts, before he could rejoin his band, Don usually found himself back at an institution that would become his second home, Kingston's Bellevue Hospital for mentally ill patients.

Like New York's own psychiatric hospital of that name, Kingston's Bellevue is set on the water – but the blue Caribbean, not the grey East River. When I visited the hospital in 1985, it wasn't as grim as similar facilities. I met with psychiatrist Dr Freddie Hickling of the University of the West Indies. When Don was in his care, Dr Hickling was new at Bellevue and starting to implement art-based treatments that led to him becoming a pariah in Jamaican psychiatric circles. Now acknowledged as a leader in his field, Dr Hickling recently went on record as the first Jamaican psychiatrist to discredit the myth that ganja use necessarily leads to insanity.

The sympathetic Dr Hickling showed me an astounding artifact: Don's medical history card. Scrawled in spidery capital letters were the words "Ganja Intoxic."

Professionals like Dr Hickling who are knowledgeable about ganja, the healing herb, insist that people afflicted with mental disorders, such as schizophrenia, must not smoke weed. Similar to acute stress, weed can push conditions that might never have erupted into an explosion that may vanish, recur or remain permanent.

Dr Hickling, Jamaica's first Rasta psychiatrist, clearly revered Don. He explained how the treatments of the early sixties were much less refined than their contemporary equivalents. Don endured crude electric shock therapy and a battery of drugs. When in Bellevue, Don was dispirited, a ghost of himself. Furthermore, regulations meant that he was not allowed to play his horn, a further erosion of his identity.

Despite their differences of class and colour, Don and Margarita had much in common, as well as being leaders in their respective arts. Both headstrong and rebellious, they each flouted the destiny dictated by their upbringing and background.

After the court case, at which Don was defended by future Prime Minister of Jamaica P.J. Patterson, he was condemned to life in Bellevue instead of execution, because of his known mental condition. In previous lockdowns, Hickling told me, Don's main visitor would always be Margarita, turning up with a basket of food for her messed-up man. Those visits may have been some of Don's hardest memories as his infinite sentence stretched out before him.

But Don never served the expected years. He met his unexplained death on 6 May 1969, at thirty-seven years old and in good physical health. There was no autopsy for the cultural giant, whom the authorities saw as a nobody who had killed a rich man's daughter. Friends at his funeral cortège kidnapped the body to examine it. But no report of wrongdoing was ever made and his burial place is still unknown, the subject of myriad theories. So prevalent was the feeling that there was something wrong about the death of Don Drummond that his death certificate states "NO-ONE WAS CRIMINALLY RESPONSIBLE" – a curious caveat.

The riddle of Drummond's death may never be solved. Rumours started to fly. Anybody who loved Margarita – even if they fought with or disapproved of her – was potentially responsible, as if they had organised a revenge hit on Don. Bellevue's staff appeared sincere and hard-working, but their pay was never high. Was someone on the inside paid off – or was Don's death simply revenge by "haters" within Bellevue? Somehow, the unlikeliest prospect of all seems to be the other suggested possibility: suicide.

As I immersed myself in Don's and Margarita's lives, I started to see hints of their doomed love in the many human exchanges around me – happily, however, without Don and Margarita's grim outcome.

Still, I suddenly began to notice how we sometimes try to will those we love into being who we hope they are and often ignore signs that they are actually quite different. Like Don and Margarita, we can betray not just our lovers, but ourselves, too. What is packed in that jumping bundle of urges and needs we call love? How much will we pay for it?

The abrupt snatching away of Don's innovative genius left a vacuum in Jamaican music that still haunts the country's jazz community. Greats who were his contemporaries, like Ernest Ranglin, Monty Alexander, Rico Rodriguez, Vin Gordon (whom they call Don Drummond Jr), and outfits like London's Jazz Jamaica are still here to enjoy. But some will always wonder: What would Don have played, had he lived?

When Evet Hussey and I began writing, I was angry with Don for killing that glorious woman, mother and artist. But as the script and my understanding grew, I increasingly felt the despair and pathos behind his rage. I hope that by discovering the vulnerability behind the tumult, you, the reader, will join me in feeling only compassion for both of these benighted, brilliant souls, doomed to live and die for their lustrous love.

The Selecter

In the beleaguered Midlands, home of 2 Tone Records, factories were coming to a standstill and unemployment soared as this brace of articles was written, in 1980 and '81. They were times in which Britain began being rocked by Black anti-police uprisings that would dominate the coming years, along with the new Conservative prime minister Margaret Thatcher's tussle with the unions. British industry and society was shaken by volcanic change. The transatlantic alliance between America's Ronald Reagan and Thatcher launched the specious economic theory of Reaganomics. Unfortunately, its "trickle-down" theory worked about as well as the hot water gas meters, common at the time, when you didn't have a coin to insert. In short, not at all – unless you knew how to bend the coin slot with a knife, when, if you were lucky, all the collected cash would tumble out. Thatcher went mano a mano with unions that themselves were slow to respond to technological change. End result: a big shake-up of the class system for some and an abyss of economic disparity for others. Though punk never dies, its fashion moment waned as haircut boy bands with touristic videos took over from its social rejects. But the Two-Tone movement extended the rebel punk and Rock Against Racism spirit, and even embedded it in the pop charts. Virtually all its bands mixed musicians' races and ages in a novel way.

With Black and White Unite as a fundamental credo, Two-Tone bands like The Beat and The Selecter harnessed the speed of ska and punk, spiced it with Jamaica-style toasting/DJing, and used it to drive infectious songs of witty social and political relevance that were loved worldwide. Plus, The Selecter's dynamic front woman, Pauline Black (one of those sub-cultural heroes later honoured with an OBE), offered a fresh, somewhat androgynous image of womanhood in her Mod suit and trilby hat.

The story of Selecter told here is one of outsiders finding a way in by helping to create a more inclusive scene than that in which they were raised. As kindred spirits find one another, develop what they call new ska and score several hits, identities shift and clarify. Like Public Enemy and Def Jam in New York, they are like family with their label, 2-Tone, and together they build a new community that they can all call home. Now awarded the OBE, Pauline's 2011 memoir, Black by Design, *fills the gaps in her knowledge of her DNA family she discusses in this article, as the group's considerable fame is consolidated with the release of their breakthrough album* Too Much Pressure.

"The Selecter: Survival Inna Suburbia"

First published in Melody Maker, *23 February 1980*

It took him ages to get the lapel of his jacket off. The scissors kept on cutting the cloth instead of the bits of stitching, but they wouldn't give him a paper round till he was over ten, and that wasn't for another six months. He'd asked his mum for the money to buy one of those suits at C & A, but she said that would have to wait for his birthday, too.

But I can't wait for my birthday! That's not for years! And I've been waiting to see The Selecter play for years, too, ever since I saw them on the telly, and that girl Pauline bouncing around like she was doing tackles and headers and stuff. I think the way they look is great – I want a suit just like the white bloke's.

Hey, I hadn't thought of that – they're the only group where there's just one white bloke, like that, and then one of those black geezers with dreadlocks. I always thought having all that hair flapping round your face was filthy-looking – well, Mum always said that.

My sister keeps on teasing me, but I don't care. I used to go on at her about dying her hair all those stupid colours and cutting holes in her T-shirts and stuff. I used to like her Clash records, but I never liked those reggae things she played; they always sounded too slow, like everybody on them was falling asleep. I like the stuff The Specials do, though, and The Selecter. It sounds a little bit like those reggae records, but it's really fast and exciting. If I see Pauline tonight, I wonder if she'll let me kiss her?

It got to be a strain, being a radiographer and a singer, too. At night you'd get completely exhausted onstage in some place miles away from anywhere, then sit in that freezing van for another three hours till you get home. And when you get back, the room's always bloody freezing and the damp's getting worse, and it's another "in bed at 5 a.m. and in the wards at 9 a.m." job. "I cleared up balls of pus, sick – you name it, I cleared it up. Particularly the posterior end. Barium meals. Enemas."

Which is why, last September, Pauline Black decided to give up her day job and become a full-time member of The Selecter.

Pauline Black onstage utilises the old Judy Nylon method – never leave your audience alone for a minute. She's everywhere, bouncing from foot to foot, diving backwards and just missing (usually) Charlie, the bass player.

On a good night, The Selecter give her back as good as they get. The whole lot of them are in there, bobbing and weaving. I'm told the sparks sometimes fly in The Selecter family. This is undoubtedly because their line-up embraces so many differing cultures, expectations and outlooks. Some members of The Selecter share not much more experience of ska – the music from Jamaica that provides a good 50 per cent of The Selecter's musical base – than the majority of their audience, like Pauline and Compton, the rhythm guitar player.

Charley Anderson, the light-skinned dreadlocks player with a Roman patrician nose and a good build for basketball, heard ska thundering through the town every night, courtesy of Red and Roadie sound system in Montego Bay. Charley went to the Montego Bay High School (along with Mikey Dread, for what it's worth), where he was a good student. Charley cried when he discovered, after he'd arrived in England aged eleven, that the exam nobody had remembered to explain to him or tell him about in advance was the eleven-plus and that he couldn't go to the school he wanted because he'd failed. In the end he had to stay on longer at school, because he'd come top of the class. He was surprised – it wasn't easy to study at home; his father had fucked off to the States, leaving his mother with him and five others. It seemed to surprise all the teachers at school that he'd done so well – they always thought of him as some kind of joker.

As soon as Charley arrived in England, he saw *Ready Steady Go!*, introduced by Cathy McGowan. There, he saw Jimi Hendrix play with his Experience, ribbons flying from the wide brim of his hat. Under the hat, a circular mass of hair grown wild and natural, freaked out, an Afro. Charley's hair was cropped short, but not for long.

He pinned photos of Marsha Hunt in *Hair* to his bedroom wall and spent hours drawing her, extending the corkscrew ends of her Afro into wild, sweeping psychedelic flames that glowed across the page. He was stunned when one of the girls at school told him to fuck off and leave her alone, dirty n*****, and cried and had to switch off the TV when they showed a documentary about the assassination of Martin Luther King. He grew his dreadlocks and became a Rasta when he felt like he'd been sinking down and down till he couldn't reach no further, and had to show outside how different he'd been made to feel inside.

It was strange when other Rastas mistrusted him because his skin was so light, his locks so red. Equally surprising was how when Hard Top 22 – the band that later became The Selecter – played at the little clubs, the black crowd didn't like them because their music was too fast (too much rock and not enough reggae). But now Charley doesn't feel that way any more, as if he can't trust any white people, because there's all these thousands of white kids – and a few black kids, wearing parkas – coming out to see The Selecter play. The way there's black people and white people, natty dreads and baldheads, men and women, working together in The Selecter is the most important thing for Charley.

A British soul group played at Pauline's school dance. After they'd finished their set, they came down into the audience and looked for girls. *See that black chick over there? Hey, you can't miss her in this crowd, man, she's the only one in this whole dump. OK, grab a drink – only soft drinks? You have to be kidding. Hi, babe, you want a drink? I wish it was something stronger, but I suppose you're underage anyway. What's your name?*

Pauline Black was a shy adolescent anyway. Her white adoptive mother – her father was from Nigeria and her mother was half-English, but she's never met them – had taught her to be frightened of black men. When the band all descended on her at that dance, she was petrified and didn't know what to say to these black, threatening presences. It was the first time she'd ever spoken to a black man. When she managed to escape home, to the security of her nice, normal white family, she lay awake in bed and thought hard. Realised again what she'd been realising for years: she had to get away from home.

"I was never a particularly friendly adolescent. Maybe that's why I never had any friends. As soon as I got to fifteen, I became really, really miserable, and it carried on till I was eighteen and left home and discovered drink and sex. I didn't know any black people at all – both my parents were white and all my brothers were. Everyone I ever related to was white.

"Then, when I was fifteen, people stopped patting me on the head and saying, 'What a nice little black girl with pink ribbons in her hair' – because my mother liked pink ribbons, made me look a right prat – but started seeing you as a black mini-woman, who's supposed to have opinions of her own. Then all the prejudice comes flooding in, which people never show to black kids. Then the problems started."

At the time, twenty-six years ago, that Pauline's parents took her into their family, it was a lot easier to adopt a black baby than a white one – as, indeed, it still is. Neither parent had thought there was anything strange about adopting this cute little black (or half-black) baby. Not till her mother began to notice the funny (and not-so-funny) looks she was getting wheeling Pauline down the high street in her pram.

Nowadays, Pauline can see and sympathise with the pressures her mother suffered from the neighbours. "But I still don't think she handled them very well," she says wryly.

Like Charley, Pauline found herself in the no man's land between black and white that the old blues singers sang about – "high yaller". In black American literature of the early part of the twentieth century, there are countless cautionary tales of the hideous fate that befell young "yellow girls" who "passed themselves off" as white. Invariably, the tales end up with the woman being cruelly, dramatically unmasked.

In Pauline's case the process was more subtle. "At school it was OK because you were always good at sport, so you were good for something." The intonation is very cutting. "I was at a school full of white pubescent youths and I was feeling much the same way. But unfortunately, I wasn't quite right to take home to Mum and Dad. So that was a funny sort of period."

Pauline's evolution into being A Singer was slowed down more by her sex than her colour, though Pauline perhaps wouldn't agree – she says she can't see feminism as a struggle outside of the working-class struggle. She saw Mick Jagger perform: "I took it from there that if I was going to be anything onstage, it would at least be something forceful, because that's the way I'd feel, anyway."

"Do you feel you were wasting time studying biochemistry, working at hospitals? Do you wish you'd been doing this performing lark all along?"

"No, not really. It's not so wonderful that it wouldn't be good to do something else."

The thing with this rôle-model business is that it actually works and as Pauline is the first of a kind, she didn't have one anyway. Pauline's desire to sing was triggered by seeing a woman play acoustic guitar in a folk club and the classic realisation that, hey, I can do that at least as well.

Mick Jagger was thrilling, but didn't exactly point to a way that she, Pauline, could be up there singing. "Singing wasn't a thing I set out to do. You either know you can sing or you can't, so you spend half your life humming along to things, being thought of as a person who can sing, but never proving it."

Pauline started going to the folk club regularly, loosening up as the alcohol consumption rose, shedding inhibitions to the extent that she was eventually chucked out for singing an over-rowdy version of "Honky Tonk Women" late one night. By then she'd discovered Joan Armatrading, a great inspiration, and Billie Holiday.

Now that Pauline had left home, "I discovered the glories of beer and the difficulty of having to relate purely as a black person, never having the crutch of being able to run home after school and feeling secure with this white family. Black people started coming up to me and talking patois and I didn't understand a word they were saying. I felt a right prat."

The time was right for her to meet a man named Lawton Brown, apparently responsible for raising a good number of black consciousnesses around Coventry. He was "appalled" at discovering Pauline spending her time singing in folk clubs; they began to write songs together, and he took her to see Hard Top 22, Charley and Neol Davies' band, along with John "Brad" Bradbury of The Specials.

The happy result was an exciting time round the middle of last year, when all kinds of Coventry musicians began to find contexts for their ideas. The Selecter – its formation prompted by the success of Neol Davies' "Selecter" track on the original 2-Tone 45 – is the product of one such conjunction. Suddenly, she discovered herself as a singer and performer.

It appears that the influence of this man named Lawton Brown shouldn't be underestimated. He also had a great effect on Compton, The Selecter's guitar player. He gave them books to read – Pauline remembers Ralph Ellison's *Invisible Man* most clearly.

One of The Selecter's strengths is the apparently effortless black–white fusion, which wouldn't have been possible had Pauline not discovered herself as a black woman, had Charley not discovered himself as a Dread; the early eighties new ska couldn't have happened, perhaps, without the growth of late seventies new British reggae, which as we all know was crucially shaped by the emergence of Rasta.

Compton said, "I was one of those kids. My friends all started going round wearing red, green and gold tams, but you're not sure what you're doing – it's being pushed on you. What Linton Kwesi Johnson did was very important – for a start, recognising that there were kids here who were here to stay. We're born here, we live here, we're British.

"The Rasta thing always had to encircle itself with the myth of Roots, which in the end takes your identity away even more, gives you more hang-ups. You talk to kids, say 'Where are you from?' and they say 'Africa' – but they were born here. It doesn't really mean anything. Linton Kwesi Johnson brought reggae into a British context. Before that, reggae bands over here were playing Jamaican society in a British society . . ."

Which leaves us with the vexing question: what will become of the many sturdy British Reggae bands sporting dreadlocks and tams and a fervent belief in Jah Rastafari as the only self-definition that will help them to survive in an antagonistic society?

Junior Brown, a dreadlocked Ladbroke Grove singer, was bemoaning the fact that gigs are harder to get these days, now that all these white bands are playing reggae . . . I thought of the way Elvis and Mick Jagger both made more money and received more recognition than John Lee Hooker or Ornette Coleman . . . and how psychedelic-sounding reggae groups like UB40, or white bands like Killing Joke or PiL, who have incorporated the far shores of dub into their everyday music, receive more radio airplay than the Sons of Jah ever have or ever will.

This is not only because the Sons of Jah tread over-familiar territory. When Jerry Dammers of The Specials and Neol Davies of The Selecter released the original, seminal "Gangsters"/"Selecter" 45 on a small private pressing, they made a whole generation of musicians appear redundant before they'd even had the chance to express themselves publicly.

Pauline, describing The Selecter sound in relation to The Specials: "To me, they're punk rock-ska-reggae. We're a rock-reggae-soul sort of sound."

Both sounds were born of groups – Hard Hat 22 and the Automatics – who experimented with the rock/reggae forms, first by dividing their sets into punky songs and reggae songs. Now, the musics are fusing, developing – The Selecter in particular – while Davies' great melodic gifts hold out more than a hope that all the "ska revivalist" labels will soon be forgotten.

Among many reggae musicians, the emergence of the 2-Tone phenomenon is greeted with more than mistrust. There's a resentment that occasionally borders on the vicious. Who do these people think they are, coming in and taking over *Top of the Pops* when we've been working for years and still haven't received our just rewards?

The bandwagon's rolling – all aboard! – and maybe it's not such a bad thing. This new ska, new reggae, new rock, presumes a cultural blend that's been worked on and worked on, whipped and whipped, till all the ungainly lumps and frictions, if not eliminated, are at least blended into the functioning mechanism. As such, this music is still ahead of the way society is running and it is a signpost, extraordinarily hopeful in these spectacularly gloomy times.

Meanwhile, the new-fangled rockers – The Specials and the indefinably more soulful Selecter – have apparently been chewing little holes in the stomach/wallet lining of *Babylon Shitstem*. Or so it's been proudly proclaimed.

The situation appears to be this: while Jerry Dammers continues with his magical talent-spotting and hit-creating, Chrysalis are only too happy to have 2-Tone as a kind of unofficial or unpaid A&R department. Not totally unpaid – obviously, if The Bodysnatchers, 2-Tone's latest signing, get, say, 10 per cent royalty, then Chrysalis get slightly less, because some money has to be creamed off into the 2-Tone coffers. 2-Tone aims to set up Coventry rehearsal studios at cheap rates for themselves and other aspiring bands, as stage one of Total World Domination.

The deal is that The Selecter and The Specials are all directors of 2-Tone, though no contracts at all have been signed, except the regular Chrysalis contract. Each band can make singles with ten bands a year, or ten singles; Chrysalis are contracted to release six of them, unless they really don't want to, in which case they don't have to.

Now, with bands like The Selecter and The Specials around, it's hardly likely that ten singles per annum won't be bouncing around. The bands, whoever they may be, sign a regular Chrysalis, not a special super-groovy 2-Tone, contract. If by any freak of chance, all the 2-Tone 45s flop, unlikely though that may seem for at least another half-hour, the deal is that 2-Tone carries the financial can, not Chrysalis. In other words, say The Bodysnatchers get a £4,000 advance and only make £3,000 back, then 2-Tone is in debt for a grand to Chrysalis.

Not that Pauline's easily phased by the business – she and all the others in the band are blissfully ignorant of the contractual side of things.

Compton: "It's crazy, that's what it is, but six months ago we'd never have thought of even getting a partnership agreement and since then, we've all been on the road . . . We were both aiming at the same things: getting our new ska and our kind of identity across, giving Midlands bands a change who normally wouldn't get one . . ."

Who said punk was dead? The ideals – yes, ideals – are flourishing very nicely, indeed; in fact, they're well-entrenched clichés. But ask John Lydon – on this planet, even your best friends let you down. The Specials, The Selecter are chums who have been swept on an unpredictable surge of success and acclaim, before they've had a chance to build a business foundation as solid as the rock-like musical sub-structure that they've honed over years.

But I have no fears for Pauline. That woman is a born survivor if ever I saw one. She nixes the tour bus, walks to gigs. Almost gets run over, skipping in front of a car. Stamps her foot and shouts "Bollocks!" right back when they hoot at her – just being a bit over the top, sometimes.

Pauline, brisk and cheery as a gym teacher . . . "Come along, girls," she says to me and Juliet (another 2-Tone director from the Trigger operation that's been so invaluable in shaping the label's meteoric rise). "Who's going to be first up this hill? Let's have a recce round the corner." Then she's haring off again, all senses alert and buzzing, born to be an explorer.

"I went through eighteen years of conditioning to think a certain way, which gave me all kinds of hang-ups," she says. "When you free yourself from that situation, you come to the realisation that – fucking hell, THEY MAKE ME MAD!"

The Beat

Pauline Black's closing words would be echoed by thousands in the months to come. In the following year, 1981, when this article appeared, Britain was aflame with riots as Black youth rose against increasingly oppressive, racist policing. Action, protest and musix were propelled by tragedies. On 23 April 1979, the National Front overcame a local protest and held a march in the diverse area of Southall, West London. In response, the Anti-Nazi League and local people held counter-demonstrations. The Special Patrol Group (SPG) were called in and amid the fight, a New Zealand teacher, Blair Peach, was killed. The SPG invaded the HQ of prominent local militant Rasta reggae group Misty in Roots, RAR stalwarts, and their Peoples Unite label. Most of their community suffered injuries, including their co-managers, Chris Bolton (white) and Clarence Baker (Black), who barely survived a long coma after the SPG attack. Their heroism became legend, as did the January 1981 New Cross fire which Linton Kwesi Johnson sang of, in which thirteen young Black people were killed by fire at a birthday party. Though widely held to be racist arson, the police inquiry disagreed.

Politics and pop were organically interwoven in 2-Tone bands' music. Two-Tone was a new musical fusion – very British, very urban, they had drunk the punky reggae cocktail and added their own high-energy power pop; an infectious ingredient, as their chart dominance proved. Each had its own anthems, sung like waving flags on protest marches; tunes and words that lifted people's spirits and made them feel optimistically defiant, part of a broader like-minded community. "On My Radio" by The Selecter critiqued media elites. The Specials' "Free Nelson Mandela" helped raise international awareness of South African apartheid significantly. The Beat's irresistible contribution was "Stand Down Margaret", made to ricochet around arenas, sung by thousands. Part of The Beat's mystique (excellent players all) was blending the exuberant youthful energy of their toaster, Ranking Roger, with the authentic, venerable presence of horn player and ska original Saxa (The Beat's parallel to The Specials' own ska horn veteran, Rico Rodriguez).

"The Beat: Heartbeat & Strangelove"

First published in New Musical Express, *7 November 1981*

Vivien Goldman witnesses the subversive pop of The Beat at work in New York against the nuclear age.

With the instinctive gesture of a former literature student, Dave Wakeling reached for *Roget's Thesaurus* when he was looking for a name for his new group. He thumbed through till he found the heading "Music". "Music", according to Roget, breaks down into "Harmony" and "Discord". The listing for "Discord" was headed "Clash". Dave glanced over to "Harmony". Top of the list of alternative words was "Beat".

Dave could hardly believe no one had used the name for a group. Everyone knows that beat's what you need for your dancing feet. Brian Epstein certainly knew when he coined his cuddly toy name, The Beatles. Les Beat honed the name down, and probably had the idea down better than they realised at the time. Because they are. Beat, certainly, in some ways, they can't be (Beat).

The Beat are beatniks. Beatifically blundering into the big time. Their cover of Smokey Robinson's "The Tears of a Clown" filled the audience with the A&R men snapping at each other's expense accounts. Then the little error of recording the bubbly "Hands Off . . . She's Mine", which had sounded so jolly and satirical in the living room, and made militant sister Lesley from the Au Pairs – Roger and Dave's neighbour in Brum – practically give up on the pair of them for good.

This great (ideologically un) sound really did liven up some of the most irksome and regrettable human socialisations, making a glossy commercial for possessiveness and violent jealousy. Why, everyone's going green this year, dear.

The best harmonies sound like discords first time round (check the old Abyssinians for proof) and when The Beat insisted, against all record company advice, on releasing "Mirror in the Bathroom" as the follow-up to "Hands Off", the attitude very much was – well, if we make a mistake, it's our mistake.

Bearing in mind that too much listening to other people's advice instead of your own heart is often the worst mistake considering that part of the game in life is seeing how firmly you can grab hold of your destiny, this bunch of factory workers and organic gardeners and lunatic asylum attendants, unemployed school leavers, ex-shirt cutters and common labourers decided to stick with their feelings and got a gold album.

In a dressing room in Philadelphia, on their current US tour, an American fan who had seemed well up on Beatology shocked Dave Wakeling by saying he'd be proud to fight for his country. The same chap had probably been singing along in the audience to The Beat's explicit anti-war songs like "I am Your Flag". Ear syringes won't do the trick; it's a dub version of certain accepted brain patterns that The Beat would like to see happen – a shift in attitudes. Sugarcoat the serious things with pretty tunes, rhythms and faces, and more people will listen – ah, the old debate: The Beat aren't the first.

Since pop or punk or rock or schlock in Britain started to talk about serious things as a matter of course, we've built up a rapid file of case histories of idealism adjusting to money, or multinational organisations – the perils of playing footsy with Babylon system. All the time, of course, our little moves on the chessboard fall under the shadow of the punitive puppet masters trying to pull our strings and press our buttons for us. But we're the push-button generation, anyway, demanding to do up our buttons ourselves. We're big enough. If there are mistakes, we'd rather they were *OUR* mistakes.

So, the day after a quarter of a million people filled the CND rally at Hyde Park, a bunch of New York chart-followers stomped and sweated and punched their fists in the air, singing and actually dancing to the unaccustomed reggae inflections (dance instructions courtesy of 2-Tone), chanting "Stand Down Margaret", along with The Beat onstage at the Ritz. Whether they understood what The Beat were dealing with is debeatable, of course.

Still, they're living through an international rerun of Stanley Kubrick's spot-on satire *Dr Strangelove*, with the lunatics running the asylum. British people resent the Americans planting cruise missiles on this green and pleasant land, with the finger on the trigger over the water. But Americans have their own daily nuclear headlines, with Russia cast as the big bad wolf. Americans have their own battle lines drawn and Britain is just one dot in the fill-in-the-dots mushroom cloud. Sometimes The Beat sing "Stand Down Ronnie" instead of Margaret.

The audiences sketch the first tentative American skanks, a wrong side of the blanket sideways, off-beat lurch; obviously touched with the tarbrush, but still pogo or preppy, white-ass. The edges of the net of bass culture tighten around a new shoal. A new set of souls. Infiltration, dissemination of information. The Beat play their part.

I think we think too much . . .
"Doors of your Heart" vocal by Dave Wakeling

The Beat are busy. They're in a nice spot now, renegotiating their record contracts in Britain and America with all the cards in their hands.

Those record company meetings – doodle, a giggle. A game The Beat are learning to play now that they're managing themselves, enacting the strategies in person instead of through a non-band spokesperson (formerly John Mostyn). In Britain Arista Records had to cough up a few clauses as well as a few zeros. The Beat haven't yet re-signed with Sire in America.

One of their two days in New York is spent hanging round Sire and ferreting out those funky cheap chic items you can find en route.

The Beat are the only band I can think of with two guaranteed teen heart-throbs as front people. This afternoon both sex symbols – Dave Wakeling (who looks like he's stepped out of an athlete's chic adaptation of *Brideshead Revisited*) and Ranking Roger (whose perfectly curved smile glows like one on a Hallowe'en pumpkin) – have bought presents in Chinatown for their best girls.

I'm attempting to interview Roger, spiffing in his new white karate-style kimono. He's just saying, "After this band, I'm going to be a drummer – a second Sly Dunbar . . ." when Dave walks in, lugging loads of carrier bags. He collapses on the other bed, picks up a miniature Japanese flag Roger's bought to stick in the band of his crown. "A trigram, isn't it?" Dave says, pointing to a Japanese character.

Shuffle, aka David Steele, bassie, slouches in and huddles in a chair, sucking a lollipop. The conversation is general. Roger tells us about moving on from singing in the school choir to toasting with different Birmingham sound systems like Cyclops and Youthman Sound, listening to Dennis Alcapone, Trinity, Dillinger, Clint Eastwood . . .

How did the dreads in the sound systems feel about your working with a white pop group?

"I had cussings over it at first. Some dreads look at me and go, Cho! How dem white man treat you?"

"We treat 'em all fair," Dave interrupts, in a mock-moneybags manner. "We'll put you on £50 a week for the third year."

"Now," Roger continues, gleaming with pleasure, "every dread in the Bull Ring will hail I."

"Is that important to you?" I ask.

"Of course," replies Roger simply. "It's my people."

A lot of people who think back-to-Africa think all black. It used to be hip for black immigrants to hang round with white girls, for example, then Black Power in the sixties, and Rasta now, made it less admirable . . .

"They can go on with what they want. I go out with a white girl from Ireland and I'm proud to walk through the Bull Ring with her. She's my queen," states Roger. "A lot of black people are starting to accept white people since after the riots."

What would Dave like to do, if he wasn't with The Beat?

Well, he's thought about moving to Mauritius, where his girlfriend comes from, then discovered that the island they were planning to move to, Diego Garcia, was being built up as an American nuclear base – part of the Mauritius Independence deal. The original inhabitants, says Dave with a grim smile, were shifted into some slum in Miami . . .

Boy, is it a problem boy?
"Monkey Murders" by The Beat

While the world's longest sausage is wheeled round on the TV screen to the admiration of all, we listen to the new Beat 45: "Hit It" (check the spectacular dub version exclusively, on the *NME Dancin' Master* compilation) and "Which Side of the Bed" – a serious, sensitive piece of sexual politics.

I ask. Which side of the bed did the argument start?
"Which Side of the Bed" by The Beat

Dave the linguist flashes his tennis player's smile. "I thought no one was writing songs for the Young Married set, so I'd do it. My girlfriend says I don't write love songs, only hate songs . . ."

Right about then, I wander off to try to interview Saxa. (Note the try.) In his fifties, Saxa is the group's father figure. Sloping onstage in his paisley cords, propping himself on a stool like early Jah Wobble and Andy Williams, he is the quintessence of the beat hip, trailing cool jazz solos (he goes for big bands and Louis Jordan more than The Beat) like a Pied Piper.

In his absence, band members talk about him with near wonder. The second time they played together, Saxa announced grandly, "You are my boys, and I want to die playing the saxophone with you. That's where I'm closest to God."

I've brought along a bottle of wine to bribe Saxa to talk, as I'd been advised. He doesn't like to give interviews. He's propped up in bed, as he has been all day, chatting with a fan who had dropped in. She's been bitten on the upper lip by a dog but had skipped going to emergency at St Vincent's Hospital in favour of going to see The Beat. I hope I don't get rabies.

"You brought red wine," says Saxa severely, his hands folded across his Lora Logic T-shirt. "Didn't the boys tell you I only drink white?"

It's difficult interviewing Saxa, who has a horror of revealing his personal life, so would rather substitute pretty posies of waffle for information. Besides, he's half an old-fashioned guy and half a little kid, as Roger observed. The result is that he relates to most women with the exception of his wife in a barrage of flirtatious asides and boasty self-advertisements delivered in such a dry, droll way that it's easy to laugh off – at first . . . Overall, Saxa is a loveable eccentric with great panache, who communicates more fluently with his horn than words.

I succeed in establishing a few facts about him.

"I do everything really great. Swimming. Great dancer. Great sex man. No doubt about that. I believe in sex."

Saxa's son is about to start playing with The Beat; Saxa will probably retire from the road. I've never met anyone who has the crusty old curmudgeon schtick so perfectly down; Saxa is right out of Dickens as he groans, "I'm so mashed up with playing music. I want to teach kids to play music. If me live . . ." he moans and shudders, hamming it up.

"You look perfectly fit to me, Saxa. What makes you think you're about to snuff it?" I ask.

"What's the time now?" Saxa props himself up eagerly to grab a watch. "9.15. Probably I'll be dead by . . . ten," he concludes with satisfaction, nestling back into the bed.

Dave Wakeling, twenty-five, imminent father-to-be, meditates on his role as militant songwriter. "Music seems to be the least censored of the arts. I was surprised when TV producers actually asked us to play

'Stand Down Margaret', but the lyrics are the last thing people listen to. The people who make the final decision at the BBC just think music is a horrible racket, so it's a fairly safe, ineffectual way of protesting. It creates a negligible amount of change, just reconfirms people who think like that anyway."

He writes to cheer himself up, he says. "Drowning", for example, was written in a toilet. Dave had barricaded himself into it in a fit of despair on their last US tour.

"It gets rid of poison. It's an alternative to hitting someone or yourself.

"I was writing about things I was obsessed with anyway. People saw it as social comment and we took advantage of it. The biggest challenge is to work out a way of doing it without offending people by ramming it down their throats. To see how much you can get away with and have wide appeal is as much fun as seeing how much you can say . . .

"When I was thirteen, I wanted to be a monk in Japan, because I was reading a lot of Japanese Buddhism. I like the idea of impermanence. It makes everything a lot of easier to handle – you can enjoy everything, because you know that this, too, will pass. It helps with the group, because you don't get carried away about careers or charts, transitory things. It suggests a way people could live together and develop parts we haven't been able to try out . . . Our inherent faults are in everything, not just the political parties – you get Margaret Thatcher because you deserve Margaret Thatcher; you don't like the guy you buy your newspaper from, and Reagan doesn't like Brezhnev . . ."

Dave recalls that in 1978, reggae started to be more lover's rock than rebel music. At the same time punk was "going through what looked like death throes but was actually sorting out what was important – it was becoming apparent that you couldn't change the world by being on amphetamine all your life."

He loved the house parties where the sounds switched between reggae and punk, and was inspired by the Lee Perry production of Max Romeo's *War Ina Babylon* LP, especially the song "Uptown Babies Don't Cry".

"I'd sing along, then I'd realise what I was singing about. The song makes you feel happy, so it puts you in a strong position to say – actually, I agree with that. The more upful the music, the closer to the bone you can be.

"Blockhead (Beat piano person) was round on CND marches in the

1950s, when there was also a quarter of a million people. He thought the world would never be the same, then he saw it all degenerate into backbiting and infighting. He refuses to get involved. But as pop groups get an inordinate amount of press – more than world problems – we should talk about something.

"Most young people are totally uninformed. We worried about it after a fashion – putting lefty causes with transitory pop music. But then we ran a drawing competition and there were loads of kids of fourteen drawing pictures of the world blowing up, with pictures of Margaret Thatcher leering. I read that 59 per cent of young people think there'll be a nuclear war. That's two-thirds of young people! That's enough to make it happen.

"That's why upful music is so important. Wider bubblegum pop appeal can be more subversive. Sometimes I do think music is changing the world, but I tend to dismiss it as a personal thought. The music business is hemmed in, allowed to be subversive, but it's isolated from the powers that control. If we are changing this generation, we'll only know in ten years, when they have positions of power . . ."

This one be your unity rocker, Lord . . .
"Doors of Your Heart" toast

Ranking Roger looks tired on this mid-tour. He still steps onstage, though dancing a manic, double-speed skank, hurtling around, flinging himself about like a hyperactive goalie. The shirt of his immaculately tailored dread ensemble – black with brown cord trim and flashes of The Colours – is sodden by the end of the show and Roger wanders round backstage, bemused by the amount of people wanting to tune into him.

"When does friendship and fandom turn into vampire business?" muses Roger. He didn't leave the house for three weeks. Then he forced himself.

"I found I didn't care as much about people – I was bored with people. I think the American tour turned me that way. New York got on top of me, all the big, massive buildings. I couldn't take it. It's starting to happen again . . ."

Through the slats in the blind, the dawn is creeping up the grey walls of the skyscraper opposite. The thin white light creeps like a slow searchlight scanning the prison wall for escapees. Roger's voice is a low purr, breaking from patois to Brum–Brit mid-word.

His family come from St Lucia; Roger thinks they are disappointed in their lives in Britain, because they've never been able to get work better than the factory jobs they took twenty years ago. The streets were not paved with gold.

"I have to see England as my country, because I was born there, but I have got African blood and I'm proud to be an African. Dave always thinks there will be a Third World War, but the world cannot end just like that, unless God destroys it. Something will happen.

"When I was fourteen I was scared of the bomb, but not any more. If it does go off, there's nothing people on Earth can do to stop it – but people can stop it going off."

We talk for a while about war and peace. Roger says that peace is a must. I say that wars keep on happening at times of inflation because it boosts the economy and reduces the population, making more money to divide among fewer folk. Roger says he'd never thought of it like that.

Roger reads only one book – the Bible. He reads and re-reads chapters and paragraphs – he'll be pretty old by the time he's read the lot, but he should know the Bible very well.

Ranking Roger is a different kind of dread. He brings a breath of a blues dance into a rock and roll show. I feel he is straining to do more toasting, although The Beat have already established a good balance between harmonies and toasting. Roger is a Range Rover, eagerly straining at the leash with new ideas. When it comes to money, he's – Beat.

"I would like to make enough, but not too much. What happens is someone signs a contract, makes it big with one record, then loses it all. One thing I know is that I walked into the music business with nothing in my pocket. Say this whole thing folded and I walked out of fear with nothing, I don't think I'd really partial [worry], you know what I mean? But I wouldn't like to walk out with nothing – I'd like enough to set myself up with something creative. Maybe build a studio.

"I don't think Dave will hang out with The Beat for a very long time. He is going to start a family."

It has been known for people to have a family and be in a group; he'll need the money for the kid, anyway.

"We'll probably have made enough by then."

Enough? I have never heard anyone mention enough money in my life. These people must be bohemians. Everyone knows that when you have got the winning sound, the idea is to milk it till it's squeezed dry.

These Beat-niks talk about retirement, about making enough money and then stopping!

Dave says that The Beat developed so socialistically as much through fear of money as anything else. He's thinking specifically of the corrupting factors of filthy lucre; giving the money from "Stand Down Margaret" to CND was a form of discipline. An act of renunciation from a man who wanted to be a monk and a man who feels profoundly confident that God will step in, like the cavalry in the last reel. We're dealing with people of faith.

Roger says: "I'm glad in a way I got caught up in this. I've always been different. I've always wanted to do what I wanted to do and I don't like people organising my life for me."

CHAPTER 7

Backayard: Bob Marley/Wailers/ Conscious Reggae in 1970s Jamaica

+ Its Roots & Shoots: Mayfield's Soul and Rebel Sixx, Trinibad's Ghetto Prophet

Out of many, one people is the Jamaican motto, and the same applies to its music – a heady brew that has evolved through many forms since the colonial days of Mento's sweet, saucy folk sounds in the 1950s. Along with retained African rhythms, African American soul and R&B gave Jamaican music part of its impetus; Curtis Mayfield was paramount among The Wailers' and many others' inspirations. Marley even adapted a Mayfield track and credited him on his great anthem, "One Love", originally done *à la ska* before the famous cut we all know from the *Exodus* album. The ska we met in the 2-Tone chapter grew into lover's rock, then the conscious reggae made famous by Bob Marley and the Wailers, and on into dance hall, further dividing over decades into a myriad *riddims*. In a violent time, the sparse digital North Coast sound of the early 2020s focuses on "Bad Mind", and Trinidad's Rebel Sixx, the great hope of "Trinibad" music, sings of the sort of betrayal Marley often warned of in his music. But true leaders know that hope must always remain in the mix.

Curtis Mayfield

This brief encounter with Curtis Mayfield stands as one of the most inspiring and uplifting interviews of my life.

"Resurrection of Mayfield's Soul"

First published in the Daily Telegraph, *25 January 1997*

Vivien Goldman meets a legend of black music – back at last after his tragic accident.

The Queen of Soul, Aretha Franklin, is not alone in her sentiments when she exhorts "Go-'head, Mayfield!" at the close of her duet with iconic singer-songwriter Curtis Mayfield on his new album, *New World Order*. She's merely expressing the fervour with which the message man's new recording has been received. The spiritual uplift, social concern, and melodic and rhythmic joy of the album has won it a file-full of rave reviews and two Grammy nominations (for Best R&B Album and Best Male R&B Vocal Performance), to add to 54-year-old Mayfield's existing Grammys for Lifetime Achievement and Living Legend.

Since 1990, when a lighting rig collapsed on him during a free concert in Brooklyn, Mayfield has been paralysed from the neck down. Among the musical treasures lost to himself and the world were the feathery frisson of Mayfield's falsetto and his uniquely concise, oblique guitar style. It seemed that Mayfield, though still accessible as hero and mentor, was lost to us as a musician.

Mayfield's first album for seven years is a resurrection. The fact that, post-paralysis, a fellow human still has the strength to lift our burdens of loneliness and fear is inspiring in itself; but the work's true elevation lies in the most optimistic songs such as "Back to Living Again", with its opening lines: "You just get back up and hold your ground."

"As I wrote it, it was giving me strength," recalls Mayfield softly. Wearing a worn Mickey Mouse sweatshirt, he lies under rumpled sheets on a bed set at an angle in the centre of a book-lined living room. A full-length mirror angled by the bed saves him unnecessary eye or neck movement. Outside the large windows is a lake, one of the reasons he loves Atlanta, along with the "pride among black people" in this New South boom town.

Nowadays, Mayfield has to wait for a musician to bring him an appropriate rhythm track before he can complete a song. He describes how the lyric for "Back to Living Again" was inspired by a line in the film *The Shawshank Redemption:* "You get busy living, or you get busy dying." The idea stuck in Mayfield's head; when his writing partner, Rosmary Woods, delivered a track that fitted the line perfectly, he completed melody and lyrics in an hour.

"After the accident, I wasn't sure whether I could sing. I was quite curious as to what my status was," admits Mayfield mildly. The singer no longer had a diaphragm and his lungs were weak.

"For the heck of it, I went in my own studio and had the engineer put up a couple of tracks, to see if I could sing. It was very disappointing, because I found I didn't have the highs: I didn't have the strength to get through a whole lyric. I left there with tears in my eyes. But in time, all things are for a purpose . . ."

However, he felt able to appear in a video for New York Latin-funk combo Repercussions, who participated in one of two Mayfield tribute albums that followed the accident. "It left a bit of hope. Another year or so went by, then Warners decided they were going to take on the challenge and the risk of investing in my possibly doing an album." Mayfield pauses. Laughs. "I always need a good challenge to push me, or dare me!"

Mayfield found enthusiastic recording cohorts: Aretha, guesting on the lyrical Narada Michael Walden-produced paean to life "Oh So Beautiful"; Darryl Simmons, a prime mover in getting Mayfield back in the studio; Mavis Staples, a friend since their Chicago childhood, whose unmistakeable brio permeates the touching "Ms. Martha"; Roger "Zapp" Troutman; and Atlanta's hitmakers, Organized Noize, of TLC's "Waterfalls" fame. Their stark sound on the crackhead elegy "Here But I'm Gone" echoes Mayfield's urban insights on "Freddie's Dead" from his classic 1970s *Super Fly* soundtrack, the only sobering, compassionate element in a film that Curtis says would otherwise have been "a coke infomercial".

Nonetheless, the cult film is obviously a cultural antecedent to the current gangsta fetish that killed Tupac Shakur. Thinking of the dead rapper, Mayfield poignantly quotes "Freddie's Dead": "But his hope was a rope . . ."

Getting gravity to help his lungs do the work in the studio, Mayfield evolved a system of singing lying down at a slant. His producer's skills used studio technique for precise punch-ins, laying the song down in sections; to achieve the falsetto feel, the tape was sped up. Curtis concludes, "It worked well. For me, the importance was for the listener and the consumer to hear the true intent and honesty of the delivery itself."

Those qualities have always characterised Mayfield, long revered as soul's social conscience. His gospel-brewed harmonics with The Impressions, topped by Curtis's airy falsetto, gave voice to 1960s African America's burgeoning revolutions – both social, on "Keep On Pushing" and "This Is My Country," and amorous, conscious love songs, such as Mayfield's "Woman's Got Soul" and "I'm So Proud", that redefined romance. The assertive "We're A Winner" was so cogent an affirmation of black power in 1968 that, although banned by several radio stations, it still topped the R&B charts, inspiring such artists as Bob Marley, who fondly remembered sitting with Bunny Wailers in the front row when The Impressions played Kingston in the sixties.

"It wasn't hard to keep a trio together," Mayfield remembers, "but trying to bring a compromise to five minds can be tough sometimes. Two of the original five Impressions decided to quit because they wanted to sing more traditional R&B and rock 'n' roll. I was writing songs that were quite difficult for them to comprehend during the early stages of my creativity."

Mayfield went solo in 1970, partly to concentrate on building a record label that would be "worthy of The Impressions". He produced a volcanic album, *Curtis*, that set the seal on his mastery. More appreciative artists eagerly spread Mayfield's word, including Rod Stewart with Jeff Beck, Bruce Springsteen, and reggae artists from John Holt to Chaka Demus and Pliers, who hit with Mayfield's "She Don't Let Nobody". A box set, Rhino's *People Get Ready!*, makes the sweep of the maestro's thirty-five years of work readily available. *New World Order* is the theme for Spike Lee's recent film *Get on the Bus*, about Louis Farrakhan's Million Man March.

It's complicated for Mayfield to move, but the power of *New World Order* keeps the world coming to him. Even before I could leave the house after our interview, another journalist's eager voice was already drifting over the speakerphone and through the Mayfields' sprawling family home.

With his wife, Altheida, and seven of his eleven children and step-children living in this ample abode, the joint is jumping. The extremely comfortable surroundings could scarcely be further from Mayfield's own childhood in Chicago's notorious Cabrini–Green Homes projects, where he lived in one room with his mother, five sisters and brothers. A younger brother was intellectually challenged; he was Curtis's special charge until he died of an enlarged heart at eighteen.

This family home feels full of warmth; one reason why Mayfield is still a great giggler. "I'm not always in touch with my positivity; no one is. But I am mostly. Even if I'm angry or hurt, I like to bounce back. I usually like to keep my spirits high and that has worked good for me.

"With all that love and the respect from my peers and so many folks . . . I can feel it coming in waves," affirms Mayfield ardently. "When that many people pray and hope for you, there's nothing to do but get up and ride that wave as far as you can."

Mayfield credits his poet mother, and her spiritual healer and preacher mother, with equipping him to cope with adversity. "We were quite poor" – Mayfield pauses and chuckles – "but everybody round us was quite poor. We were on welfare. My achievements have really been the success of my mother's dream; she was the artist. But my father left when she was a woman with young children and the time was not right for her. We moved a lot – I went to nine grammar schools. It wasn't easy for her. But she introduced a lot of things to me. She showed me my first little song on the piano, "Clair de Lune".

Early deprivations became the engine behind Mayfield's entrepreneurial vision. He owns his publishing – ever more valuable, as Mayfield is heavily sampled. His childhood instilled in him "a need to own as much of oneself as possible. I used to sleep with my guitar. I'd write five songs a night – a day. When I couldn't find answers, I would write songs. When I was heartbroken, I would write songs. It was my own way of teaching myself."

Thankfully, the lesson is ongoing, and open to the public.

The Wailers: Treasured Trinity

A people's poet, humble Bob Marley sometimes felt almost uncomfortable that he drew so much more attention than his outstanding peer group of musicians – the great generation of conscious reggae, including master-singer Dennis Emmanuel Brown, who we met previously in London with 15 16 17; Gregory Isaacs, Jacob Miller and Inner Circle (now known as the "Bad Boys of Reggae"); producers Niney the Observer, aka Winston Holness, and Lee "Scratch" Perry; and others with outsize talent and personalities. They were vital in brewing the heady musical mix of revolution, spirituality and sensuality that makes this scene still cast a spell decades on. Part of Bob's success was the interweaving of yin and yang, blending his voice with those of his female backing singers, The I Three: Rita Marley, Judy Mowatt and Marcia Griffiths.

Sadly, mass marketing has tended to diminish the vital roles played by Neville Livingston, aka Bunny Wailer, and Peter Tosh, the two other Wailers – bred'ren since their teenage years in Trenchtown. I often found myself in heated debates when it came to the religion side of things, as I was a feminist who sometimes wore clothes or expressed thoughts that more patriarchal rastas found offensive. Such contradictions are typical of so many "revolutionaries" throughout the centuries, whose sense of the struggle falls short of letting women be free. And looking back, I am sorry I affronted so many; but I understand that their concept of orthodox modesty was against my personal religion.

At the end of this article, I join Bob in the studio as he records "Smile Jamaica" – the tune that marked the start of a cycle in which Bob would narrowly escape an assassination attempt on his life, find refuge in London, write "Punky Reggae Party" . . . and record Exodus, *his epochal album.*

"Reggae Part 2: Black Punks On 'Erb"
First published in Sounds, *23 October 1976*

We've got wars and rumours of war . . .
"Armagideon (Armagedon)" by Bunny Wailer

Jamaica is under a state of siege. The roots of the situation lie in the days before Jamaica's independence from Britain in 1962.

Jamaica's two-party system, comprising the PNP (People's National Party) and the JLP (Jamaican Labour Party) were headed by present Prime Minister Michael Manley's father, Norman Washington Manley, and Sir Alexander "Busta" Bustamante respectively. The country was in a state of stagnation as the two leaders alternately led the country, Manley representing a capitalist/Tory view, Bustamante with no hard political line but popular support.

After independence from British rule came in 1962, the JLP had a run of control, until Michael Manley emerged as a force. Educated at the London School of Economics (LSE), Manley assumed the role of a comparative radical and encouraged the support of counterculture figures such as Bob Marley to sweep him to success. Under his guidance, Jamaica moved closer to socialism. America looked on aghast at the prospect of Jamaica allying with communist Cuba, and financial pressure was applied.

A good deal of Jamaica's financial stability was dependent on the bauxite industry. Bauxite is an essential component of aluminium, an essential metal in everything from rockets to pins. Canada and the USA were the largest importers of Jamaican bauxite. The pressure point is obvious.

Bauxite from Guyana, and new technological developments of manufacturing aluminium via electrolysis, led to further financial insecurity.

In addition, Jamaica has another valuable export – grass. That's where the rumours of CIA and Mafia involvement come into the picture.

Rumours of the CIA are everywhere. So Bob Seh: "Rasta don't work for no CIA." Who do you think Jacob Miller means when he sings about "the Roman soldiers of Babylon"?

The truths Toots sang about many years ago are still true: "Time tough, everything is going higher and higher." It's not cheap to live in Jamaica these days.

And you may well have heard of the Gun Court, that forbidding institution where you're sent summarily if found carrying a weapon. It's rather like a South African jail; basically, you're locked away without a trial and left there to rot.

Jacob Miller is an articulate spokesman for the Rastas. We're sitting on the veranda of his luxury pad in the wealthy Beverly Hills area, a crisp white house overlooking gaudy vistas of exotic flowers trailing down the hills. This is where the politicians and the wealthy businessmen live.

Jake is sprawling comfortably in the hammock, doodling on a guitar, totally at ease.

Vivien: *Don't you feel there's some discrepancy between your revolutionary stance and living in this well-appointed house, Jacob?*

Jacob: *If you check it, sister, I sang that "dreadlocks can't live in a tenement" yard. It's good that Rastas livin' up here. People must understand that a dread can live anywhere, even in Beverley Hills. [Jacob's apple cheeks widen even more with a mischievous smile.]*

You no see it. We been down for so much year with slavery. It's just now we try to get up out of the slavery. But each time we take a step forward, we have somebody to try to draw us back down into it, and they "stop us with their guns and brutality". [Jake's quoting his own lyrics.]

True, if I had a weapon now, they'd beat me and shoot me. Even if I don't had a weapon they'd want to do that. [He's surprisingly prosaic.]

So we are the children of Zion, we're crying out, right? Crying out for help . . . some people call him God, but I-man call him – Jah Rastafari. [His voice dropping respectfully at the august name.]

Vivien: *How do you feel about direct political involvement?*

Jacob: *Politics is for the swift and for the generals, not for me. The only politics I want to show all of dem is music. The greatest love of all is music, heavier than every ism. [Meaning political stance or belief.]*

We discuss some breddas that have been harassed by the beast (police), charged without bail or appeal. Jacob's righteous indignation is registered in every line of his face.

Jacob: *Babylon, don't have nothing else to do, mon [spitting angrily]. When dem see a Rastaman now, dem figure seh, well, we can get a stripe, or promotion to be a sergeant or any t'ing, by locking up a Rastaman. Or put a gun into a Rastaman hand or a knife [Jacob's talking faster and faster] and give him five years for it, when dat Rastaman have six mouths to feed the next day. Right? If six of dem [police] go out, six of dem must bring in somebody.*

It's like a competition to see who dem can shot the most. It's like that we deal with, and that kinda dread.

And that's an understatement. The situation Jacob's dealing with is as vicious and explosive as Chile, Ireland, South Africa or Russia.

The next day, I was with Bunny Wailers in the yard at Tommy's. As you would expect, Bunny has a clear-sighted view of the situation. "Politics . . . serious t'ing. Rasta are involved, because even the Prime Minister (Michael Manley) involve Rasta right now. Because he use the name Selassie, saying that he got the rod from Selassie to deliver the children out of the hands of Pharaoh."

That was literally a campaign technique of PM Michael Manley dealing with the Rastas in the hills. Similarly, a phrase from a speech of Manley's – "under heavy manners" (meaning "in control") – is currently a favourite expression among the Rastas.

"So Rasta is deeply involved. He might not recognise it, but these things that are going on . . . I don't understand it, y'know, and I don't get involved with it because it's strange, y'know.

"I don't see where it's necessary. If there are two parties concentrating on people, they should work together then, should concentrate to get a better idea for the people. Whether it come from this side or that side. Then the sense of politics would sound pleasant, but when they say politics now, people get frightened. They don't want to hear it, because it's like giving this man a gun to kill that man, and that man couldn't even vote if you kill him. And politics is men voting for leadership, so if you gonna kill all the people that gonna vote, who's gonna vote for the leaders?"

Quite so. Bob campaigned ardently for Manley at the time of his election (in much the same way as so many big rock stars in the States campaigned for McGovern in 1973 and lost) and it's obvious that Bob is largely responsible for Manley being in power.

Vivien: *Would you ever campaign for a politician?*
Bunny: *Whoever we did a show for, he would win. [Bunny's amused at the thought.]*
But I ain't gonna jump on a political bandwagon: I find that . . . I still have to be careful with my little 'erb spliff, 'cos police gonna look me, mon, though I still don't understand it. If the police get to me, I go to jail too, I go to courthouse too. See me here? Any damn thing can happen.
Vivien: *It's like living on a volcano, really . . .*
Bunny: *Yes. [Bunny's chuckling.] Somehow . . . it's nice.*

Prophetic words, perhaps. Rumours flew around Tommy's yard a few days later that Bunny had been caught with his herb spliff. Seen.

Coincidentally, both Jacob and Bunny made the same point. Contemporary Jamaican music has abandoned, is distanced from the traditional popular music theme of love and romance.

Jacob: *All my life I heard a whole lot of love tunes when I was growing up, but now I understand there's a lot of deeper things than that. Rastas are preaching loving, but not with love tunes. They say you must see God, and God is the greatest love.*

Hence the situation nowadays – virtually every Jamaican song deals either with social conditions, political messages or exhortations to follow Jah and beware Babylon (decadent capitalistic society).

Bunny him seh: *"Reggae does deal in love songs, but it comes from Jamaica, and the depression in Jamaica is very, very great. So a man tells what's happening to him, how he feels, the whole thing. The things that matter. If people would start expressing those t'ing in the old songs, then we would all be living a love song instead of singing a love song. But people sing love songs when they aren't in love . . ."*

While I was in Jamaica, I saw no signs of the notorious curfew. In fact, it was in the wee small hours of the morning that I ran across the equally notorious three o'clock roadblock, as immortalised by Bob on *Natty Dread.*

I was driving back from a house party with Ras Michael and his bred'ren, bowling along an empty country road, when we were summarily halted by the police. Heavy jelly, I thought wearily, but essentially I was too spaced out to be alarmed. Well charge, seen?

We all piled out of the car, while grim-looking hombres with guns circled us. Questions followed, swift and abrupt. Where had we been? Where were we going? Why were we out so late? Who *WERE* we?

Ras Michael exhibited extreme aplomb. Leaning oh-so-casually against the car, propping his chin on his hand, he explains that he is Ras Michael of Ras Michael and the Sons of Negus, and perhaps they remembered his hit single, "None A Jah Jah Children No Cry"?

Yes, indeed. "I got that at home," one man squeals delightedly.

As an irresistible clincher, Jah Mike adds that if they care to switch on their TV this Sunday at eight o'clock, they'll see his new show.

"Hey, mon, can I have your autograph for my kids?" asks an ingratiating beast.

We set off once more, good vibes all round.

Fifty yards down the road, we're stopped again. This time it's army, and they're an even heavier bunch of mothafuggas. In some kind of small tank. *Oy gevalt.*

But Jah Mike, with a weary air, lays it on them yet again. A trifle sternly this time – after all, once a night is enough for any bredda.

And sure enough, the response is identical. Instant switch from hostility to near-obsequious politeness. They even offer to give some of the breddas a lift nearer home. Everyone declines. We go our way, all smiles . . .

The political situation obviously affects the Jamaican music scene in a very direct way.

King Tubby bemoans the fact that his systems can't operate in Kingston any longer.

"It's this amendment, seen? They seem to t'ink that the music in the streets will, like, encourage the people, you know, to violence."

Fred Locks' JahLove Muzik sound system is still in full swing, but that's out in the hills, far away from scenes of potential urban unrest. A bredda called Hugh Boot controls that particular system. In conversation with him one day at a table at the Cafe Attic, digging into banana bread and papaya milkshakes, Hugh offered some inflammatory opinions on another crucial situation of potential unrest. It's equally political, although Jamaica in general has yet to wake up to the fact.

"Man is the powerhouse," said Booty in his curiously soft, lisping voice. His plaintive glistening brown eyes swept over photographer Kate Simon and me, checking our reactions.

"All you have to do is submit to the fact that woman was created for the benefit of man. I know you kinda feel free and liberated" – staring disapprovingly at my shorts – "but that's where the problem starts. It sets the woman against the man."

If all men think along those lines, that reaction's hardly surprising. And, sadly, almost all Rastas that we met – and we made a point of checking this out in almost every conversation – seem to think pretty much in agreement.

One night at Hope Road, I venture to ask Neville Garrick, the very talented artist responsible for a majority of the illustrations – sleeves, programmes, et al. – involving Island's reggae artists, why the chalice always passed right by me as it was handed from bredda to bredda.

Neville is surprised that I ask. "Yeah, it's Rastafari," he explains, "so we don't have any women smoking this chalice. This is for the men, so we can sit and reason."

And what do the women do meanwhile? Not a lot, Neville's look implies. The Bible dictates all Rasta attitudes, and apparently it was written by, for and about men.

As always, Bunny Wailer has a sound, rational viewpoint. He really is a wise man. "Well, the master says, 'Send my sons from afar and my daughters from the ends of the Earth,' so women are equally important."

Most other Rastas we discussed the point with prefer to interpret the Bible rather differently. They conclude that women are unable to attain spiritual achievement, that they're acceptable, even desirable, only so long as they know their place and shut up in society.

The trouble is, it's so easy to be selective when you check the Bible, to tune in to what you want to read and ignore the full spectrum of information. Most Rastas agree that the good, discreet, child-bearing woman's price is above rubies, but who remembers the story of Ruth and Boaz, for example? – "thy daughter-in-law which loveth thee, which is better to thee than seven sons . . ."

A dear woman friend of ours commented bitterly, "Rastas treat women same way God treated Satan." A heavy idea, certainly, but not far off the mark – women as a race of fallen angels.

Even lovely, gentle Fred Locks, an intelligent, thoughtful and spiritual man, feels the same way. "In the form of righteousness, a woman accepts herself as second. She obeys her man, but it doesn't deprive her of the right to speak when she sees him doing something wrong." Gee, thanks, Fred.

"Woman is not really inferior to man, as a person or a human being. But a Rasta woman wouldn't be found babbling with matters that more concern a man."

Gayman from Talent Corporation explained to me, "We don't expect the same things from you that we do from our women, since you are of a different culture."

With that in mind, many people we encountered were patently surprised that two women were doing business daily, without a man controlling their movements. Every woman we met who was professionally involved in the music business was under the auspices of her man, at least nominally. It seems to be a classic situation; the women only become free to function when they're in partnership with a man. "Controlled" by a man is the JA term.

Sometimes it was difficult not to feel repulsed by the gut-level passion of these attitudes. A typical example occurred the day I was leaning next to Tosh against his car, reasoning about this and that. He turned to me and said, almost ferociously, "Women have a certain time that she cannot communicate. All communication is cut off."

Examining me as if I were some dubious lower form of life, and rotting at that, he continued: "That's why a woman is imperfect – she is number six. There's a time when a woman can't even be so close to me. I don't think you are at this psychological moment, but if you are, step far. Don't you know that?" – surprised at Kate's and my shocked responses – "from a medical, physical and spiritual point of view, seen?"

Coming from a culture where the liberating miracle of Tampax is lauded daily in adverts on TV, in magazines, on hoardings, and where menstruation isn't the subject of a frequently used form of abuse – that's a well-drawled "blaaad claat", meaning "blood clot". Unless, of course, "bloody" has a similar connotation? All answers on a postcard, please . . . – our reactions were probably rather similar to what Tosh's would have been if we'd suddenly turned on him and announced that black people are intellectually inferior – in other words, indignation, wrath and scorn in equal parts. Heavy on the wrath.

Perhaps it's naïve, but the Rastafarian movement contains so many good, positive philosophies and attitudes that it came as a shock to realise that while Rasta purports on one level to be a revolutionary struggle for personal freedom, this freedom is sought for only 50 per cent of the population. Even less when you consider the strong feelings against homosexuality – again deduced from the Bible. Homosexuals are called "b**** breddas" in Jamaica. The full import of that term emerges when you consider it in relation to our term for homosexuals: gay. Think about it. Seen?

If well over half the population might as well be walking round ringing bells and shouting, "Unclean! Unclean!", any sensible Western person would feel that a lot of heavy consciousness-raising is called for. All round. Rastafarian certainty that only they understand what is "naturally" correct is infuriating and bewildering. And that's just how Kate's and my attitudes seemed to the Rastas.

The players of instruments shall be there . . .
Bunny Wailer sleeve in JA.

The street sound systems have been hard hit by the state of emergency. Now it's down to private house parties, like the one in Kingston that Ras Michael took us down to. Unfortunately, I was so well charge at the time that in my state of confusion I mistakenly thought that we were at the Grounation (a Rasta prayer meeting) Ras M. had intended to take us to – if we hadn't spent so much time getting well charge . . . seen!

So the finer points of that situation escaped me. That happens a lot in Jamaica, especially when you first arrive and don't realise the near-psychedelic potency of those brown paper cones.

I have a more precise memory of a house party that Jack Ruby, producer of Burning Spear, and Justin Hinds took me to. Jack lives in Ocho Rios on the North Coast, and it was a wild, surreal drive belting horrifically down zig-zagging roads, across the width of the island, to go to a private house where Jack's King Hi-Fi sound system was heading.

Sitting in the back with a quiet U Brown, Jack's excellent toaster (most sound systems have their personal DJ to weave those intricate raps, known as "toasting", over the sounds) the lights bouncing back and forth against the trees, it was like being in a German expressionist film. Except for the Bob Marley studio out-takes on the speakers. Bob's voice echoes in fragmented layers of "Crazy Baldhead" as we search the night mists for the right house.

Eventually we arrive, around 11.30 p.m., and the Hi-Fi sound swings into action. Hugh Brown positions himself, mic in hand, against a wall behind the deck. A couple of breddas sift through the piles of singles and pre-releases, handing the appropriate selection to Hugh.

A favourite sound all over the Island is Leroy Smart's "Ballistic Affair", on the Ernie Hoo-Kim's Well Charge label, emanating from Studio One. Hugh gives it a spin: "Gather round, y'all!" he yells into the mike, then improvises in an even, deliberately paced rise and fall of rhythm, a new set of lyrics that step in counterpoint to the original.

Brothers and sisters step it perfunctorily in the main room, which is stripped for action, bare but for massive speakers positioned around the walls. "Steppin' on forwards, my brothers, sisters, let's go stepping on forwards," U Brown is shouting, singalong, over the system. Knees rise, bottoms shuffle, arms swing. Everybody's getting down. The fridge is well stocked with Red Stripe, the night is young . . .

It's the wee small hours of the morning before the last partygoer leaves the sandy yard, where bred'ren had been reasoning quietly in groups, smoking their spliffs; finally, the most diehard, militantly dressed Rasta-belted brother has abandoned his position right in front of the giant speaker and hit the homeward trail, looking well satisfied with the entertainment received for the dollar entrance fee.

But I did have the good fortune to attend one live gig: the Jamaican Arts Award, held at the large modern hall of the National Arena. And a bizarre night out it was, too. Everything was like one of those faintly twisted Diane Arbus photographs. For a start, most of the people receiving awards didn't show. There was an embarrassing silence when Rita Marley didn't materialise to collect Bob's prize. Gayman, a lanky Rasta with a grin searching as a lighthouse beam, accepted Toots' award on behalf of Talent Corporation.

The main MC was Marie Garth, a diminutive, portly woman with a piled-up hairdo and formal long gown, aptly described by a colleague as "the best-dressed chicken" (that's the legend on an LA-style statue of a chicken in a frilly dress – shades of Beatrix Potter – outside a Kingston fried chicken take-out joint). She carefully articulated her way through the presentations, sounding as if she had a mouthful of a bumper crop of plums to cope with.

She may be JA's most popular announcer, but she sounded tacky as all get out to me – introducing soul/reggae fusion band Third World as "And now, some guys who really know how to put the oomph in their music – yes, siree, we'll do our very best to cheer you up as the evening grows older!" Her sprightly overtures were received with jeers of "Raas claat! Blaad claat! [i.e. blood clot.] Rockers!"

The jeers were caused by Third World's prize. Third World aren't too popular back home – they're not really regarded as sufficiently rootsy, despite winning a gold award for the best musical band. In the event, they put on a weak set, obviously discouraged by the hostility emanating from the audience.

Third World were well and truly blown off stage when Inner Circle appeared. They'd been voted Best Recording Band, but live, they are staggeringly good. Inner Circle are practically the best band I've ever seen.

That night, the band consisted of the Lewis brothers, Roger and Ian, Touta and Augustus Pablo on keyboards, and Chinna on rhythm. And centre stage, the youthful pride of JA, JACOB "Killer" MILLER!

What a star.

Jacob Miller is a roots hero on account of a string of hit singles like "Tenement Yard", "Tired Fe Lick Weed in a Bush", "All Night Till Daylight" and many others. I'd been hanging out with him and the rest of the band during my time in Jamaica, but nothing had prepared me for the tremendous aural and visual onslaught that's Inner Circle live.

Jacob Miller – man, he's outrageous. Bounding onstage with unlimited energy. The atmosphere vibrates as he bellows and moans, his voice vibrating with soul, anguish and that old favourite, lust. Jake's not exactly a skinny little slip of a thing and his gyrations were calculated to leave not a dry seat in the house. He sang all of their greatest hits – "Forward Jah Jah Children" and the others I've mentioned – and never let up for an instant.

Jake's not so much a presence onstage as a visual assault. He's a natty soul rebel. An arrogant, overbearing, irresistible hunk o' punk, combining the fervour of a gospel revival meeting with the ruthless attack of a bulldozer.

Dressed in strictly militant fashion, essential khaki chic, his trouser legs were knotted at the ankle in the latest style. After about three seconds of Jacob ranting, straining, cavorting, leaping and generally grooving like a possessed soul, his trouser legs were undone and billowing wildly at every move. Sweat poured down his plump cheeks, his eyes demonic. Roll over Mick Jagger – Jacob Miller has all the presence and authority you had a decade ago, writes as well, and his voice is better.

The musicianship and visuals of the rest of the band are equally impressive. Roger is a massive man, his hips grinding sensuously behind his guitar like those elephants doing a chorus line in grass skirts in Walt Disney's *Jungle Book*. Serious t'ing, mon. His rock-oriented guitar breaks are another key to the band's enormous potential for international stardom, nay superstardom. Touta's lean LA chic (grey plaited denim, grey suede big-brimmed hat) as he swayed lithely behind the keyboards added a fresh element of excitement (can't you just see the teenyboppers cream?) and Ossie (aka Horsemouth, aka Leroy Wallace) flailed away in a frenetic torrent of the hardest drumming on the island.

The high spot of the set was the moment when, in the middle of a particularly lubricious rendition of "All Night Till Daylight", Jake leapt from the stage to the floor and grabbed *Sounds* photographer Kate in a bump-and-grind dub dance. Kate, desperately balancing her Nikon in one hand, responded admirably. If you thought Jake had intended to spend the night meditating on the Bible, you got the message pretty sharpish.

That gig seemed to be the only one in JA during the three weeks I spent there. In fact, there's only one real venue – the Roots club at the Chela Bay Hotel in Ocho Rios on the North Coast, although there is the odd live set at the famous Turntable Club in Kingston. Other than that, there's a lot of middle-of-the-road dance bands, some featuring excellent musicians, playing at the hotels.

So Big Youth seh: "Every n***** is a star."

Everybody in Jamaica is a musician. However poor a sister/bredda may be, they'll sink all their cash into cutting a 45, to be sold whenever and wherever possible.

So, let's go down to the studio. First, with Ras Michael and The Sons of Negus. Down in Joe Gibbs' studio, Jah Mike (as he's known to his friends) is sitting on a little stool on the floor, flanked by The Sons of Negus, all veterans of the scene, beating deftly on their African drums. Instead of their onstage gear – ceremonial African robes – it's regulation trews and wool hats all round.

On the other side of a sound partition are all the young dudes – Robbie, Chinna, Touter – working together with the unmistakeable rapport that arises from innumerable sessions in as many studios.

Chinna is laying down some fantastic rhythm lines, descending in graceful ripples of notes. He and Robbie control the session to a large extent and everyone keeps on shouting at Touter, "Stick with rockers!" That's because Touter, whose heart lies in rock 'n' roll although he's one of the finest reggae keyboards players in the world, occasionally sneaks in a jazzy lick or two.

To my mind, he's adding a very valuable commercial shade of sweetening to Jah Mike's African sound. Touter answers indignantly, "You check it 'pon dem tape, mon, dey all strictly rockers!"

Things aren't going too well. "Raas claat!" swears Jah Mike in almost unsaintly tone of voice. "We need a raas claat fe dem 'erb back here." i.e., bring on the ganja or else.

"Soon come," coos Tommy Cowan. He's producing and spends most of his time soothing ruffled tempers with unvarying sweetness, while Valerie bops gracefully in the control booth.

It sounds as if Jah Mike's getting a couple hits in the can. He's laying down some hard sounds, all right. The skinny éminence grise of Rasta musicians, his pert face frowning with exasperation, has an ever-broadening appeal.

Ras Michael was largely responsible for the growth of reggae as we know it, via his *Nyabinghi* TV show that spread the roots sound to the entire island. Now he's singing a new song, "No Hoppers (can survive this ride)", which is excellent, bouncy and slightly sinister at the same time.

Jah Mike is well tuned into culture. "Africa, land of the black man," he intones solemnly for an intro, and generations of dust-streaked tribes from the African desert shake defiant spears, or so it seems, even in this thoroughly contemporary studio . . .

Chinna mutters a heartfelt "Serious t'ing," at some particularly meaningful lyric; Rabbi's locks disappear in a cloud of Craven "A" smoke (it's the national cigarette, it seems) and Jah Mike exults "*RAS* TAFARI," then, in an aside, "Blight the Pope!"

Niney, aka the Observer, is one of Jamaica's top producers, particularly noted for his work with the fabulously successful Dennis Brown. I caught him supervising the celebrated Errol Thompson doing a dub; Niney's an imposing figure, a swashbuckling pirate (the thumb missing from his right hand enhances the image), with an ugly/beautiful face and a broad-brimmed denim hat. Reggae's Jean-Paul Belmondo. He encourages Errol as, with two other engineers, they create a dub from the single they've just cut on Dennis.

The three breddas stand lined up in front of the mixer. Obviously used to working as a team, their hands fly up and down, propelling the slide controls in an elaborate game of tag as the bass sinks low, then booms, then fades, leaving only a distant scratching of rhythm guitar.

Then suddenly the vocals ring out for a couple of seconds, and the drums begin to roll and thud . . . it's all over in about a minute, and it sounds just great.

Then there's the formidable Scratch – Lee Perry from The Upsetters. In his Black Ark Studio behind his bungalow, in a control room papered with red and green felt (remember the red, green and gold?) and smothered in *Black Music* magazine centrefolds, the man who boosted Bob to fame is coaxing a better vocal from Junior Murvin.

Junior's "Police & Thieves" single has just scored a giant smash hit in this country as well as in Jamaica. Scratch is pinning him down today. Junior is cutting a follow-up to his hit, almost identical, but with different lyrics.

"Nobody wants to lend . . ." Junior sings, when Scratch flicks a switch and interrupts him peremptorily.

"No *ONE*, not nobody, Junior! Body's a dead t'ing, mon, you put it in da freezer!"

Suitably chastened, Junior gets it right. His face contorts with concentration as he tries to get the right phrasing on the word "razor". It takes about ten tries. Murmurs of "Blood claat," from the breddas sitting round the walls. Chinna, listening attentively by Scratch's side, murmurs "Nice!" as the familiar intro rolls off the tape . . .

Scratch dances with the board while he produces. Flicking switches with a twist of the hips, after a particularly elaborate movement he might spin round twice and clap his hands, and be back in position for the next pull of a slide control. He's aware of his studio audience, but dances in spite, not because of them. It's endlessly fascinating to watch.

Finally, he's satisfied. "Na cool!" he announces. "Super Ape, you got to spin the tape, it get you in the musical shape," he rhymes under his breath as Junior comes in to hear the final verdict.

Certain people in Kingston denounce Bob Marley for being a commercial Rasta (i.e. having sold out), but he certainly doesn't see himself that way. The night before, in the yard at Hope Road, he'd snarled contemptuously about some hapless individual, "I'm don' wanna smoke 'erb, mon, 'im just wanna get high."

Bob knows which is his side of the fence, serious matter. Bob in the studio is a serious t'ing indeed. He records at Harry J's, probably the most luxurious studio on the island. Tonight, Bob's laying down the vocals for his new single, "Smile Jamaica".

Wearing a yellow Spartan Health Club T-shirt, cut-off jeans and the usual broken leather sandals, Bob's tucked away in a sound booth. By this stage of his career Bob's a total mastersinger. He spends three hours or more getting the phrasing perfect, adding a minute inflection here, changing the phrasing of a line there. Concentration is absolute.

There are quite a few brothers and sisters in the studio tonight – including two of Bob's backup singers, The I Three, Judy Mowatt and Marcia Griffiths, wearing ankle-length denim. We all sit round on the shag-carpeted stairs, talking of this and that. Aston "Family Man" Barrett, the bass player, is sitting at the board, rolling an endless series of perfect conical spliffs.

"Too much raas claat noise out there!" Bob shouts through.

Family swivels round to us. "Bob say to be more quiet," he calls to us. "Bred'ren be of one itation!" Pleased with his delivery, he carries on rolling.

In a break, Bob sits down next to me on a bench by the board. Drinking from a bottle of fruit juice, he explains in a low voice, "'Smile Jamaica' is supposed to be what's happening now . . . because Jamaica's a place where when you hear 'Rasta', you hear 'Jamaica'. The outside world people think dat people in Jamaica is Rasta, but only some of de people is Rasta.

"So now that people start to accept Rasta, to deal with Rastaman as a human being instead of somebody you just curse every day, that's different."

Bob pauses, takes a hit off the juice.

"Jamaica need to smile, because in Jamaica everyone really vex too much."

With that, he walked frowning to the board and asked Family Man to play the tape back. He listens to his voice, leaning against the board, the line between his brows even deeper – his face is in a permanent screw. He might have written the song for himself.

"Dat all right?" he enquires anxiously.

Not half, Bob. "Smile Jamaica" is probably the most instantly adorable single Bob's ever released. Funky horns punctuate. He pokes gentle fun at the outside world's conception of the island: "Seems like you're having fun . . ."

It's a message of joy and unadulterated positive vibrations – Rastaman vibrations.

Smile! You're in Jamaica . . .!
"Smile Jamaica" by Bob Marley and the Wailers

By this stage of the recording, Bob has deepened the quality of his singing. Every syllable rings out with meaning and love. As usual, Bob has a new message for his people, one that will be received with rejoicing. "Smile Jamaica" is one of the best singles I've ever heard; it's laughably catchy and impossible not to dance to. A palpable hit.

When Bob finishes, a Rasta mutters, "Strictly curfew, dis – under heavy manners." The hippest praise on the island.

At the end of every sad song is a happy ending, so Jah Bunny seh.

Bunny Wailer

As with all pop groups, fans tend to label their favourites. Thus, in the original Wailers trio, Bob was the tuneful, accessible one, while Tosh was the tough rebel and Bunny was the mystic. In part, it had been Bunny's father's relationship with Bob's mother that had led to Marley growing up in Trenchtown and the Wailers forming. Bunny primarily led to the breakup of the Wailers trio, as he got sick of huddling in a van on damp British motorways with no decent ital vegetarian food to eat or weed to smoke. He returned to Jamaica where, in addition to being a righteous superstar, he was known for cultivating rare ganja seeds. Having led the retreat from the wider world, Bunny outlived his old Wailers bred'ren by several years.

"Reincarnated Soul Makes Year's Best Album"

First published in Sounds, *16 October 1976*

"Why do they regard me with awe? I didn't know that people think of me as superhuman. I've never flown or anything of that type. Ras Tafari did that . . . I'm better at being natural."

Meeting Bunny Wailer (born Livingstone), it's easy to understand why semi-mystical rumours spread around his name. Why people generally regard him with awe, why he is always unhesitatingly put forward as the deepest of the original Wailers trio – Peter Tosh and Bob Marley being the other sweet harmonisers. It seems as if the answer is best put by Bunny himself; he has an extraordinary facility for simply being natural, being closely attuned to the elemental forces, to whatever makes the wind blow.

"I continue to recognise the elements . . . inspiration, sound, vibration." My journey to Jamaica was occasioned by the release of Bunny's first solo album, *Blackheart Man* on Island Records.

After repeated listenings over a period of four months, the enchantment *of Blackheart Man* is as powerful as ever. It's an album made by a good sorcerer, to use Marvin Gaye's category. An album that contains a wisdom and a healing power that becomes stronger the longer you live with it. A cassette of *Blackheart Man* was a constant soundtrack to the time photographer Kate Simon and I spent in Jamaica, invariably acting as an eloquent commentary to the rich flow of input that the island affords.

When collating that input in story form, it was not only appropriate, but also necessary, to use Bunny's words as a frame and structure to the article. *Blackheart Man* embraces and clarifies every aspect of life in Jamaica, Rastafarian life in particular.

Bunny's album was mixed over a couple of weeks at Island's Basing Street Studios in London. Every night there was a crowd of people gathered in the studio, everybody feeling that listening to these magic sounds evolve was the best entertainment, not to say inspiration, London had to offer. The rich, unexpected textures of the synthesiser on "Dreamland", the ecstatic twists and turns of "Blackheart Man", were so absorbing that if you dropped in for a quick half-hour, you'd re-emerge bleary but elated at seven o'clock the next morning. Bunny eliminated sleep until the album was completed.

"It's the best album ever to come out of Jamaica," Chris Blackwell said confidently, glowing from the combined effects of a win at table football and a musical home run. Complexity, subtlety, sophistication *PLUS* roots rocker riddims and thoughtful, heavy message lyrics – yup, C.B. was right.

But at the end of our first week in Jamaica I was as confident of actually speaking to Bunny as I was of stumbling over the Holy Grail in an Orange Street gutter.

Widespread use of the telephone would dramatically alter the entire fabric of Jamaican society; until that day arrives, business is conducted on vibes strictly. The days and nights spent Waiting For Bunny were an enforced meditation, prompting prolonged reasoning as to whether or not he would ever appear, which must have been good for our souls.

When the right time eventually came, Bunny was obviously determined to GET IT ON as an interviewee. We were standing in Tommy Cowan's yard at Talent Corporation, under the big tree, when I approached him. And we stayed right there for an hour. Bunny didn't want to sit down or look for a more relaxed environment. This was IT.

Instantly, another major facet of Bunny sprang into clarity. He may be a master of going with the flow, but what that really means is an ability to focus all of his strength and energy when required. Discipline, as much as self-control. Hence the level reached by the album; nothing spontaneous or haphazard about that creative onslaught. Andrew Marvell said, "Let us roll all our strength, and all our sweetness, up into one ball," and you could say that that's *Blackheart Man*.

That's even borne out by something Bunny said: "Cycles is what goes around, comes around, and I know the moon is round, the sun is round – and yes, records are round! – no ends, no beginnings."

At the beginning of this cycle (since "we are reincarnated souls", Bunny says), Bunny was born Neville O'Riley Livingston on 10 April 1947, in Kingston, Jamaica. He is said to have grown up in comparatively well-off surroundings, by Trench Town standards; at any rate, he's acknowledged to be the most highly educated of The Wailers.

Bunny's is the high voice you hear on the early Wailers recordings, taking lead on tracks like "Who Feels It (Knows It)", dating from their Studio One days with producer Clement "Coxson" Dodd. Bunny was also a songwriter, contributing "Pass It On" to the *Burnin'* album, although it's credited to his wife, Jean.

Many a year has come and gone since those early hits, and now Bob, Peter and Bunny all have albums released within a comparatively short time span.

"People will compare me and Peter and Bob, but that house couldn't be built without the carpenter, couldn't be built without the mason, all those people. All those people have an actual part – you couldn't compare them. One couldn't start, one couldn't work, without the other. So it would be stupid to start comparing the work the carpenter did with the work the mason did. But so it is, people will do these things . . .

"We're still functioning towards the same work, which is Rastafari, so we're together. We might not be together physically, but we're working at the same goal, teaching the same things . . ."

Bunny is small and compact, lean. I hadn't expected his mischievous quality; Bunny has a way of angling his head down, pursing his lips and looking up at you through long lashes, with unmistakeable twinkling merriment. Far from being some elusive mystical presence, Bunny's aura is warmth, conviviality, as well as shrewdness.

When we met, he'd just moved from the pastoral seclusion of Bull Bay to somewhere even more gosh-darned impossible to find out in the wilds. I'd misinterpreted the move as a desire for privacy in order to create – Bunny is shocked at the thought.

"I love to see people! But I'd rather live in the country."

"Why?"

"Wouldn't you?"

He looks good standing there, arms folded, feet planted firmly apart, rooted in his rightful soil. He's one of those people who always looks as if they're in their exact right spot in the plan of things.

When I say "pixie", you should understand it's real Earth spirits from creation I'm referring to, not garden gnomes. Bunny's a smoothly moulded pixie, with gloriously shaped locks; one impressively hefty clump is a diagonal stripe curtaining off half of his face. His eyes peep out quizzically from behind as if through a veil, his beautifully shaped lips twitch at the corners into an infectious grin. With all those mystical signs and portents everyone had rushed to tell me about, nobody had mentioned that he's very cute.

"I'm like a messenger. Sometimes the messenger gets a message, and he doesn't know what's in the message. And sometimes the person that gets the message doesn't let the messenger know what's going on. That's how it is with me, you know.

"I see where people really start reacting to what I've seen and what I've disclosed from what I've seen, and they've really started to go into themselves also. That is important."

The message is essentially the truth of Rastafari. In this instance, Bunny has a clear grasp of what's in the message. It's the story of the Rastafarian, past, present and future (always looking forward), of the Blackheart Man.

Bunny: *That's what we were at first taught, that the Rastaman is the blackheart man. The image den, it was this man that didn't have any family, didn't have any home, didn't have any friend. A lonely man who didn't actually go to no barber or have any form of pleasure – what you call worldly pleasures.*

And then that nickname came up. I don't know where it came from, but it came up. And so you must be careful where you are going. When you pass through gullies, or when you are in lonely places, you have the blackheart man who will take you and carry you away and eat out your heart, and all dem type of t'ing.

So we used to grow with that kind of fear in we. At certain times you'd see him, because wherever a man is, at certain times he must come out and get water to drink or some food. That is the time when some youts see him and then they start to panic, running and all dem type of t'ing . . . till when it grow out and grow out and grow out, that you don't run no more. You stop panic and look 'pon dis man. Check him out and see that he's a man, that he has habits like a man – and eat, too, and drink, too – but him only look different slightly – maybe a man never allow himself to look like him.

And, growing up, you realise – it's like yourself. [Bunny laughs delightedly.] It's like running from yourself!

Even before the hippy style came to England, it was like that with the gypsies, you know, the blackheart man, don't go near them. Same image.

Vivien: *So, Bunny. When did you come to the realisation that you were at one with the Rastaman/blackheart man?*

Bunny: *I saw myself in blackheart man ever since I started to realise myself. The type of impression that I was leaving on my parents . . . they started to treat me like the blackheart man. They look at you and wonder, like they don't know you, like it's some stranger.*

We are the people our parents warned us against, all over again.

Which leads us, quite naturally, to the various messages contained within *Blackheart Man*. First, the magnificent track "Reincarnated Souls". Bunny sings: "A prayer to die before new birth."

Now he says, "We have to be reincarnated souls. It's simple. When man dies, who dies? His body dies. And then it grows into seeds. Don't you have children? Not yet, but you have them there. You have the seeds. That is how it goes – it's as simple as that."

Vivien: *"Reincarnated Souls", "Dreamland" and "Battering Down Sentence" have all been previously recorded. When did you cut them again?*

Bunny: *None of them had been exposed properly. Enough people didn't get the chance to hear it. I started writing "Battering Down Sentence" in '67, in prison. [Bunny spent a year inside, for 'erb.] I learnt self-discipline there . . . "Dreamland" is an old song. All I did was put some other lickle thing to it, some synthesiser.*

We cut the album in Aquarius [a record shop with studio attached]. It's a rock studio, small, hard, nothing escapes. It took us about three months, on and off. Our sound is rock sound, tough, hard music. It has to be hard to penetrate.

Vivien: *Interesting that you should say it's a rock sound. "Follow Fashion Monkey" [a 45 based on a Jamaican nursery rhyme, only released by Island in the States] is actually an attempt at disco music. Not altogether successful, to my ears, incidentally. Does this indicate some hitherto unforeseen direction?*

Bunny: *It is more of a disco type of music, but it didn't do very well in the States. But it's just that one song. See it, there's plenty of things distracting you from what life is all about. If you listen to "Follow Fashion Monkey", it's more like – the shining things. Don't go into them. You can use them, but don't be dazzled or influenced by them. They are there because they come from you. Without you, they couldn't be.*

I've had two albums in mind from before. One I've completed [i.e. Blackheart Man*] and I intend to complete the other. The messages are very close, but this one is more like, ummmm, what you call it now . . .? It's deep, but not deep in the sense of the naturality of creation. It's more of commercial living, how people really living from day to day. There are tracks like "Moses' Children", "Let the Children Dance", "Wanted Children" and "Follow Fashion Monkey". But the whole album won't be that disco sound, it's more a reggae album, but broken up plenty.*

We shall await eagerly.

Vivien: *All those titles refer to children. What does childhood mean to you?*

Bunny: *[quotes softly] "Not until one is like unto a child can he be worthy to enter the kingdom." The reference is because a child is pure, you could say that . . . But growing up doesn't mean that you start getting impure. Those people that control the system, they were children, too, they were pure, too. So who's to blame for them being that way?*

It strikes me that we're back at circles and cycles again . . . Bunny grins broadly, "Yes, that's right."

Bunny means everyone when he says "children". Seen . . .

Vivien: *Both Peter and Bob are on the album. Do you ever feel nostalgic for the days when you all sang together?*

Bunny: *I remember the early days like now. Everything. Mmmm . . . [Bunny tails off in contented recollection.] It would take Bob years just to blank me and Peter out, and it would take Peter years just to blank out me and Bob. It wouldn't work. [Bunny is gleeful.]*

I love all the old songs I did with them. Every one has its t'ing, this one for that reason, that one for this reason . . . But what has happened [i.e. the dissolution of the trio as a regular team] has happened and it is not for the worse. Sometimes in Jamaica we still work together, for the people here are used to seeing the three of us together so much that it would be strange not to see that happen. They would actually drag me out, chuckling. You see [gently touching the Ethiopian cross of finely engraved silver round his neck] if man would realise that this man is that man, just like this tree is that tree, there wouldn't be problems.

You have to respect the tree; the tree has to have you there to eat from you, and you eat from the tree. So everything is like one.

People put things before life. Life is the important thing from where all things came. That should be remembered every time.

Peter Tosh

Peter Tosh was an alpha male of impressive self-confidence. His certainty about male supremacy led to our arguments; but as a wordsmith and political satirist, the dashing Tosh was top. Here, accompanied by reggae's session supremos, drummer Sly Dunbar and bassie Robbie Shakespeare, Tosh is releasing Bush Doctor, *his first record on a deal made with The Rolling Stones' label . . .*

"Peter Tosh: The Bush Doctor's Dilemma"

First published in Melody Maker, *9 December 1978*

Game rules for life: tall people have a natural advantage. Or look at it this way: tall people stand out. They're obvious targets. If you're very tall – or very short – you're automatically called upon to live up to something.

Peter Tosh was the tallest Wailer. Bob Marley – Tuff Gong himself – is the kind of celeb about whom people say, "I never knew he was so short." Peter is a tall karate expert who has consciously groomed himself into being the "stepping razor" – i.e. mobile 'n' dangerous. He is also blessed with one of the loudest voices I've ever heard.

Thus ran my meditations as we sped along the Westway in a car driven by Dr. Winston "Born for a Purpose" Alimantado. Between them their voices rattle my eardrums like a brace of Concordes. Dr Alimantado was driving what should have been a happy team from Manticore Studios in Fulham Road to the Swiss Cottage Holiday Inn, bearing precious cargo consisting of Peter Tosh, 'Tado's best gal Marcia and Yours Truly.

Peter had only touched down that morning and had prudently spent the day resting. Nonetheless, he was as weary as a natty can get, not least because the soundcheck we'd just departed had been a dispiriting affair, generally.

Geoffrey Chung, the dreadlocked Chinaman who's mixing Tosh's sound, is such a perfectionist that he aimed for studio-quality sound at a rough soundtrack rehearsal, entailing hours of balancing and mixing.

Then, a hint of inter-band politics tingled certain members' anger modules – Tosh will persist in playing his admittedly excellent rhythm guitar when the drum and bass section are attempting an individual workout.

The exiled dreads stood shivering miserably round the stage, wearing gloves, scarves and an assortment of the peaked caps that are de rigueur these days. The bigger the cap's crown, the mightier the length of the locks beneath. Only Carlton Smith from the Tamlins, an elegant Charles Boyer-in-Casablanca type, wore a spiffing beret to one side. The Tamlins are one of Jamaica's most beloved harmony trios, with a strong affiliation to the hitmaking factory, Channel One – along with Joe Gibbs, they're the biggest manufacturers of the reggae sounds to rock the nation of Jamaica. The fact that they're doo-wopping behind Peter is a delight, not a surprise; Peter has surrounded himself with the island's most formidable talent.

Drummer Sly Dunbar and bass player Robbie Shakespeare are the cliché of modern reggae; their sound is the rockers bottom for around 50 per cent of reggae reaching these shores. The band is completed by lead guitarist Al Anderson, a Yank who made his reggae debut in The Wailers and whose eloquence is admirably sparse, and session guitarist Mikey Chung, Geoffrey's brother.

Critical observers of Tosh's career have been moved to point out that Tosh has everything going for him except one crucial ingredient. He's tall, handsome, plays great rhythm guitar and has an unusual if occasionally inexpressive voice, and his heritage is impeccable – but his stage presence is lacking.

The obvious contradiction to this oft-repeated thesis is the famous One Love Peace Concert in May of this year, where all and sundry, myself included, hailed Peter as the most dynamite explosion on a bill of Jamaica's Finest.

In fact, it was this show that inspired two members of rock's jaded aristocracy to take the lanky stepping razor under their wing and sign him to their label: Rolling Stones Records. Instant credibility for all concerned – Peter gets an entrée to the automatic market of Rolling Stones fans, internationally; Mick and Keef present allegiance to black music, as they have previously done in taking The Crusaders, Stevie Wonder and The Meters on the road with them.

Thus, the new album, *Bush Doctor.* A sadly lacklustre effort, by general accord. Some blame it on Karl Pitterson's remix of the original

Errol Thompson/Joe Gibbs studio production; the man who successfully sanitised many major reggae bands, including Althia & Donna and Steel Pulse, has never provided Peter with a sound as epic as his lyrics. Immortal lines like "We don't want no peace, we want equal rights and justice" were thrust into the condition of Muzak.

Neither of Tosh's two previous albums, *Legalize It* and *Equal Rights*, catapulted him anywhere near to Marley status. The new single "Don't Look Back" has received the heaviest airplay of Peter's career. And you don't need to be ultra-cynical to believe that it's because Mick Jagger is singing along with his protégé, the man they call the Sun and Moon of reggae.

Despite the vinyl ho-hums, though, Peter Tosh is still a reggae hero. Not only for his vast contribution to The Wailers' sound – his spectacular lean, chopping rhythm guitar influenced a generation – but also because of anthems he's released on his own Intel-Diplo label in Jamaica, like "Mark of the Beast" and "Babylon Queendom", all hard-hitting words and TNT dubs.

Perhaps most important of all, Peter has one of the classic Great Raps of our time. The Minister of 'Erb in person is more fiery, eloquent and truthful than any politician extant, and speaks the truth infinitely more. He speaks like a poet, with rhythm and metre and evocative imagery – even if he's only asking you if you want to roll another one.

He also prides himself on his perfect physical fitness: his unicycle is propped up in the corner of his hotel room. He boasts freely of great supernatural powers; if cornered in argument, he naturally offers his control of the elements as the ultimate, irrefutable defence, whatever the subject.

"I only use singing as diplomacy 'cos it's a psychological way of getting to the people. But if I even had complete control over this record, that is fockery. I want to have complete control over every media so that when I make my record, I put on it what I want to put on it. Not what society wants me to put on it.

"And until I control the media that expose this record, my control over this is nothing. You can't play because of society. Who is society, anyway? Two little baameclaat . . ." Tosh didn't even know that The Glimmer Twins – credited on the sleeve as Executive Producers – are Mick and Keith Rolling Stone. Obviously he hadn't worked it out from the work they put into the album, either. More credit to Robbie Shakespeare, the real guiding hand behind the scenes.

"Me and Robert produce the album together, but you know how the system run already, seen? Those are the kind of things we don't have control over."

Peter says the information on the album sleeve isn't what he gave the record company. I ask him how come he hadn't bothered to check it in advance and he says he can't be "bothered" with that.

"Thousands of people get false information, but me can't bother with that, me dear. Right now it's pure thunderclap me see, and lightning flash and the Earth rock and the whole place a tremble and dance. Truly the Earth is on loose edges. So these little things is fockery to think about. You must think how you're going to dance to the rhythm of the earthquake, because if you cannot dance to that rhythm – oofff, you die. Those are the levels my head is resting on, me dear.

"Me sing all my songs and comes like it's pearls before swine. Because if you sing a song that is a message, society criticises it; if you sing a song for society, roots people criticise it. So what the baameclat amust I do? I'm gonna stop singing and flash lightning and make everybody observe that who wants to criticise. Yes, everything I&I do, them just keep on criticising, and I&I never done anything wrong."

At each of the four trips I have made to Jamaica as a reggae journalist, I have been keenly aware that myself and Kate Simon, the photographer, were treated with a curious combination of deference and insolence from the tightly knit musicians' community of Kingston; artists hungry for publicity were eager to talk to us, yet at the same time, found difficulty treating us as professionals because we were women, traditionally to be flirted with or ignored, not addressed as equals. We didn't cover our hair or wear skirts, therefore we were weird, not proper women at all.

Bunny Wailer dismissed myself and Kate from his studio session one day because we were wearing trousers, so we were not natural women. We must be dykes! We must be dykes, or frigid! We must be on the lookout for a good screw, else why would we be wearing shorts? You no see it, Rasta?

Rastafarian musicians' sexism is more overt than an average rock band's. Although the rock musician's sexism may well run as deep, it's not a central part of a credo that's mulled over every day, as it is in the case of Rastas.

Here's where the trouble starts:

When a woman has a discharge of blood her impurity shall last for seven days; anyone who touches her shall be unclean till evening. Everything on which she lies or sits during her impurity shall be unclean. Anyone who touches her bed shall wash his clothes, bathe in water and remain unclean till evening.
Leviticus 15:19.24

In the autumn of 1976, I was having a casual chat with Peter Tosh in a car park in Kingston. We covered various subjects amiably enough, and in fact at this distance I can't recall exactly what provoked him to exclaim that if it was my Time of the Month, I shouldn't be standing as near to him as I was, i.e. about two feet away.

Here, obviously, we enter sensitive terrain. Should Sikh postmen be allowed to wear their turbans instead of caps? Should Jewish kids leave school at lunchtime on Fridays in winter?

To me, the answer is obviously yes. Yes – freedom to follow religion or not is everyone's inalienable right.

But in order for me to interview Peter Tosh, it's not always possible to arrange that it won't be the "cursed" quarter of the month – I use the word "curse" wryly, of course.

So what's a professional working woman to do? Not interview Peter Tosh for fear of offending his religious principles? Theoretically, yes; practically, are you kidding me?

In the course of the heated discussion in that car park, Peter either caused thunder and lightning to roll and resound over the noontime blue sky, or else timed his imprecations to the elements with astonishing subtlety. Why, the very heavens confirm Peter's righteousness!

Peter Tosh has won many admirers for the vigour with which he condemns the shady practices, the "politricks" by which the "shitstem" of contemporary society works.

His lines, "I don't want no peace / I man need equal rights and justice," were deservedly hailed with acclaim by all right thinkers who heard them. They could constitute a feminist anthem in themselves. Yet, radical as Peter's message was and is, his philosophy is hideously retrogressive to any Western radical's beliefs.

There was one stage in Stokely Carmichael's career as a Black Panther where he stated that women's position in the revolution was "prone". Before his career ended, he'd reversed that line of thinking.

Peter Tosh will not reverse that line of thinking. His identity is a Rastaman, a True African, and as such his attitude towards women will remain as bigoted as a Sicilian farmer who locks his pregnant unmarried daughter up in a pigpen for the rest of her life.

Tosh's business situation right now is riddled with ironies. He has a single, the "Don't Look Back" of radio fame, featuring lots of Mick Jagger, doing better internationally than any previous recording, including his *Legalize It* classic. Yet his album has been unanimously slagged off. By abandoning his gritty, militant stance he loses his militant fans, and he hasn't pleased rock critics either. Most important, has he pleased himself?

At first, the answer is yes. When I say I think the mix sounds far too toppy, Tosh explodes that it must be my system, indicating that the bottom makes his bungalow in Spanish Town all but rock to its foundations.

He goes on to explain that he had to find a company to aid his progression. Mick and Keef "picked up my thought waves, you no see it." And since The Rolling Stones had "some affection for reggae", plus the fact that he was their label's only act, the path was clear.

Vivien: *Didn't Tosh feel strange being, even if peripherally, involved with the biggest heroin case of recent times, considering his moralistic 'erbs-only stance?*

Tosh: *Me can't bother check that, 'cos me don't know how the works set up. 'Erb was invented for I&I&I, white men invented all kinds of different destructive elements. As long as it doesn't come around my temple, I don't get involved. I can't tell Robbie [Shakespeare] not to smoke cigarettes, he cannot tell me not to smoke 'erb. Cow never know the use of him tail till him lose it, and a man have to go on with his destructive thing and receive the penalties of his destruction.*

Vivien: *Was Peter aware that Boots had recently returned a stock of* Bush Doctor *with the infamous scratch 'n' sniff "herb" sticker on the sleeve, because they refused to be associated with a "dangerous drug"? And that his record label had sent another consignment minus the (idiotic) scratch 'n' sniff logo, saying that the Minister of Herbs wasn't referring to marijuana, but to an ancient herbal remedy?*

Tosh: *That's the shitstem I talk about every time. I know that's why they're trying to make me sing the songs I don't want to sing.*

Vivien: *Which are they?*
[He looks ominous.]

Tosh: *Songs like "Don't Look Fucking Back"! I didn't write that! But because of the way things set up out there – imagine . . . things like sniff and smell.*

Vivien: *Whose idea was that, anyway? Would you buy a scratch-and-sniff record, Peter?*

Tosh: *I don't sniff records, mon! Listen, it's just a thing. It's how the world is set up. People like gimmicks.*

Vivien: *Do you feel you are having to make compromises to get your message through to a wider audience?*

Tosh: *Yes. "Don't Look Back" was a Smokey Robinson song, sung by The Temptations. It's dealing with love; people don't look to me to sing a song like that, but people – are not looking at the medias that control everything, the advertising. If I could control my own radio station, I could control the songs I wanted to sing . . . so I have to sing a song where the people, dem a sneer, but – pure airplay!*

Vivien: *So how will people know your real message?*

Tosh: *What am I going to do? Flash lightning and make thunder earthquake!*

Vivien: *Do you feel weird that you're finally achieving international success on the backs of a white rock band?*

Tosh: *It doesn't make me feel any way according to how the shitstem is set up, because the shitstem is set up to make I&I suffer from an inferiority complex.*

At that point, Doctor Winston "Born for a Purpose" Alimantado, who'd been doing an admirable job of restraining himself till then, burst into raucous knee-slapping laughter, jumped up, ran across the room and slapped Peter's palm joyfully, yelling: "Vivien, you no know what I&I talk about!"

So explain already.

Peter patiently explains the obvious: "It's a diplomatic procedure. Because see, my songs is hard stuff which politicians don't want on them radio station because they still want people to live in ignorancy. While all people, especially black people, are divided, the world will keep functioning in fantasy and bullshit and all people do is dead and go to heaven."

Which is where the ironies of Peter Tosh's current situation all coalesce. I firmly believe that Peter Tosh would already have been the respected international spokesman – and star – he deserves to be, if he was white.

It's irrelevant that Tosh's three albums have been given a consciously rock/white-oriented production that's made them unnecessarily floppy; it's irrelevant that Peter is re-recording his old songs, instead of offering new ones – even British reviewers of *Bush Doctor* failed to recognise that "Soon Come" was a hit for Peter in the sixties.

It is important that Peter is one of reggae's major artists – and yet can only be successful by drastically diluting his message, issuing a song that's totally removed from what he wants to sing. It's especially sad that it's this particular reggae musician whose integrity has been brought sharply into question, since Peter, above all, was reggae's fierce and noble warrior. Now, he's lurched to fame on the shoulders of the dissolute, decadent, reactionary capitalists of rock 'n' roll.

If ever a band were a disappointment to a generation, it must be The Rolling Stones, who have dropped all their radical aggression till all that remains are their sexist clichés. Peter's heart seems superficially, still fiercely on the side of the rebel souls.

Apart from its history of super-silky sweet love songs, reggae in the past decade has been (wrongly) taken to be synonymous with aggressive, fighting, anti-establishment music.

That music was largely created by men who were of the Rastafarian faith, a movement designed to raise the consciousness and pride of black people. It is not a racist movement; it asks for equality for blacks, not destruction of whites. It is an intellectual belief, in that it calls for daily study from its followers and daily discussion of its text, the Bible.

Things are going swimmingly. Peter has just finished a vivid description of being picked up while smoking a spliff outside Aquarius Records, facing a patch of green at Half Way Tree in uptown Kingston, waiting for a rehearsal.

"If it was downtown, in the ghetto, that wouldn't have gone on. Uptown, it's just soft-hearted people – dem can barely talk. Downtown, at Randy's, police wouldn't even come near there."

He shows us the tonsure-like bald patch in the middle of his locks and explains the hustles the police pull – "Twelfth of the month, everybody financially broke" – to ensure promotion or some easy money. It's six years since he was last beaten up by the police – he needed seven stitches and had his ribs dislocated that time. Since then he's learnt karate but reckons that offing the Babylon/police who brutalised him this time wasn't worth the inevitable sentence.

My sympathies are all with Peter at this point and we start discussing 'erbs – of course – Peter explaining that he wouldn't smoke the "lickle commercial draw" they grow in England or the States.

I'm responding with some marijuana-oriented anecdote, when Peter interrupts – "I don't like it when women talk too fucking much! You must listen because I created the Earth!" – and continues his dissertation on the evils of ultraviolet light on marijuana.

After a few moments of stunned silence, I venture to ask why Peter is agreeing to be interviewed by a woman journalist when he doesn't approve of women "talking too much" – i.e. voicing their opinions forcefully.

The ensuing conversation is so remarkable that I'm considering bootlegging it for general interest. If I hadn't been present, I wouldn't have believed it either.

Vivien: *You could almost think you hated women . . .*
Tosh: *I!? Hate women!? You think when I go to bed you think it is not woman I kiss, caress and touch?*
Vivien: *That's hardly the point – it doesn't prove anything*
Tosh: *So how can I hate women? Western philosophy makes a woman dominate a man every time. You'd rather I called you a man,* te blaad claat! *This place is run by a queen. I&I don't see no king here. In my house is a king!*
Vivien: *Apart from what's wrong with being headed by a woman, the country isn't actually run by the monarch, anyway. You know that.*
Tosh: *I know that, because of my intelligence, but what happens to the people they call the illiterate and the underprivileged?*

At this point, Peter's voice broke into an uncanny representation of an old-style, musical-hall-type woman-hating homosexual imitating a mincing stereotyped "silly woman": "You want me should sit by you and hug and kiss you?"

Vivien: *Tell me, Peter, what would you do if you had to work with some Rolling Stones Records employee when she had her period?*

Tosh: *[draws himself up to his full, imposing height, eyes flashing] I have things that protect me spiritually when there is things my physical eye does not see.*

Vivien: *Evil elements like what, exactly?*

Tosh: *Evil elements. Did you know that woman is the channel of the Devil? Every time!*

Dr. Alimantado: *[laughs, tries to restore "normality" to the heated exchange] Peter! Cool it, mon! Don't go deh!*

Tosh: *It's true! No, listen! It's the Devil talking through you right now, for you to dominate me! Your sound is like a feedback sound, pure whoooooo, and that will dominate my sound. I never say that you specifically are the instrument of the Devil, I'm saying that woman is easier penetrated by the Devil to get to the man's head, psychologically, from the beginning of time. Who tempted Adam?*

Dr. A: *I man a like join this argument at this point . . . Seen? You see this world? If me and my bredda fight, and you or me a fight or anyone a fight – is not a man and man fight a gwan now [is going on now]. Is not a hooman and hooman [woman and woman] fight. Is not a black man and white man fight a gwan. How come black man siddung [sit down] with you as a white woman and don't kill you? And if I&I should siddung among a white man, we'd sure be dead, even [if] slowly but surely. If only 'cos we want weed fe smoke and dem don't wan' give you weed fe smoke, you no see it? You sit down here with I&I as a woman and I&I reason with the I [and we talk to you] and I no look upon the I colour, whether the I [i.e. me] is black or white. You see Russia and Africa and England and America? Is a MAN AND WOMAN fight a go on.*

Vivien: *But—*

Dr. A: *You no listen no time yet! Hear what I&I have to say. You is supposed to give I&I time to talk as much as I&I want.*

Vivien: *Aren't I allowed any time to ask questions?*

Dr. A: *You get time to ask one question. Or two.*

Tosh: *You see one thing with you? You have some psychological defect that you always misinterpret certain suggestions and take them for a curse, or wars of domination.*

At this point I realise Tosh thinks I'm arguing personally. In fact, I am arguing a principle – his own principle of equal rights and justice, applied in this instance to women, who are as much the victim of Tosh's "Downpressor Man" as is the black man. An old American saying posited that black men and white women were both equally subject; since often the black woman was better able to obtain work in the white world, she had the money/power.

Similarly, in reverse, the white man was the "worker"; white women were, in the middle classes at least, denied access to money/power. In Tosh's eagerness to get his own rights recognised, he's oblivious to his partners in struggle and projects all of his hostility onto a gender that's achieved only as much liberation as he has. The shitstem has until very recently insisted that a woman be conventionally "beautiful" before allowing her to make an artistic statement, and then it's generally under male "tutelage"/protection. And onscreen, they're generally still cast as either virgin, whore or victim, just as blacks can often only get rôles as pimps, pushers or gangsters.

Tosh: *I am just trying to show you the world, but it coming like it casting pearls before swine. It's just the shitstem I beat down aggressively. What the* raas claat *me a hate women for? I was made to rule all things. MAN was made to have dominion over all things. When a man cannot rule a woman, he ain't a man. Seen? Western philosophy is just – women rule. In America, if a woman don't like a man, not once upon a time, right now, she can just scream RAPE – man gone to bloodclaat jail, no hesitation, no asking of what him do.*

Vivien: *Have you ever heard about hostels for battered wives?*

Tosh: *Sometimes many wives deserve battering. Seen?*

While I try to establish whether my ears hear right, Doc 'Tado launches into a refrain enquiring where the concubines that his ancestors used to have "like rice" have gone.

Dr. A: *We have to automatically bow down to a woman no matter how we like it.*

I ask Peter, in his capacity as a man who has repeatedly been battered by the police and hasn't enjoyed it, what circumstances would merit battering a wife. He launches into an extraordinarily precise, all-encompassing list of the traditional clichéd male arguments against women's liberation.

He says that some women like being battered:

Tosh: *Some women are different. You have some women if you don't clap them twice a month they're not all right.*
Vivien: *Would you beat a woman, if she beat you?*
Tosh: *[shocked amusement] A woman can't clap I! The words me use a dominate them, and if I use my hand, that make it worse!*

Tado then steps forward and explains that all Rastamen think the same way – that the expression I&I, which is how a Rasta will self-identify rather than just saying the singular I, refers to the oneness, the unison of attitudes between all Rastamen, not only him and Peter.

An alarming vision of programmed clones emerges and actually, quite a true one.

Dr. A: *I&I make everything that is on Earth. I bring forward a regeneration plan that will forward I&I youth, that is I-man's son, but – [more venom than rage in his voice] – I know what you gwan* blaatclaat *do! You gon' wan' come equal rights up yourself.*
Vivien: *Quite right. Don't you think equal rights refer to women as well as men?*
Tosh: *Equal rights is not man and womanical affairs. That is domestic affairs. That must be kept within the home. Equal rights is a universal struggle.*
Vivien: *Don't you think that personal politics is a microcosm of national politics? Meaning that the state of the home reflects the state of the government. It's just the same.*
Tosh: *[bemused but firm] But that is to be kept within the home.*

I say that it's about time I was going home, because I'm beginning to feel like a down-pressed character in a feminist novel. Tosh is alarmed.

Tosh: *Are you a women's liberationist?*
Vivien: *I thought you'd have known by now – we have argued these points before.*
Tosh: *BAME CLAAT! That's why! [Implication being: That's why I'm having such a hard time.]*

True to his form of spouting a spontaneous list of traditional male-gratification-oriented arguments, Peter says that a woman is not supposed to be equal because she couldn't get a job as a navvy unloading 10lb bags of flour on the docks.

I say that perhaps I am not suited to it, but that's hardly the point. I don't want to go to war with rifles over both shoulders as he suggests is necessary for a person to have equal rights. Equally, I have no interest in being battered.

Previously, Peter had said that a wife would deserve battering if she made her husband jealous, "as 98 per cent of men are". So women should suffer for men's feelings of inadequacy and primitive fears bound up with atavistic urges towards territorial rights? The old hack arguments trot out as precisely as if he'd read them in a book.

Which, indeed, he had – he has read them in the Good Book.

By the end of the interview, I had entered a state of bleak depression.

Peter's reaction was a reminder that it's naïve to label anyone as a Bad Person throughout, let alone when the negative opinions are based on cultural differences so deep as to be near-irreconcilable.

Hundreds of centuries have moulded Tosh's thinking into the reverse of mine, but he was making a human effort to cheer me up. He still didn't understand that my depression wasn't based on anything personal. His attempts at supportive warmth merely reinforced my dislike, in fact, but it is important to realise they were there and that Peter has a kind heart as well as being an obnoxious male chauvinist pig.

Peter describes his new album sleeve thus: "It is a Bush Doctor's physical defence, fighting against spiritual enemies standing in a flame of fire."

The flame will be hotter yet.

Bob Marley

When I met and began working with Bob Marley for seven months as his in-house publicist at Island Records in 1974, he had split from Peter and Bunny and, with the help of bassist Aston "Family Man" Barrett and his drummer brother, Carlton, had enlisted the women of The I Three, Rita Marley, Judy Mowatt and Marcia Griffiths (all stars in their own right and interviewed here), to sing with him instead. Like the rest of the Island Records team and Chis Blackwell, our leader, I was on fire about the mission to spread Bob's message, but also young and unaware of protocol. I would not take a journalist's "No" for an answer and broke every rule by going over an editor's head to a publisher to make sure Bob got heard and seen. At the time, the British media as a whole were not interested in this wild-haired ghetto youth. The trick was to get the publishers to actually listen to the music. Once that happened, the battle was won. Bob wound up on various front covers and his global career began; I left PR for full-time journalism, and our working relationship continued to the last. Bob was very kind to me and he remains my mentor. Thanks to Bob, it is always "Movement time!"

"Bob Marley: Keep On Moving"

First published in New Statesman, *28 May 2007*

Hailed as the best album of the twentieth century, Bob Marley's Exodus *is thirty years old next month. Vivien Goldman recalls the sessions that produced a modern classic.*

The *Exodus* sessions took place in two West London studios: a converted Victorian laundry at the back of the Island Records headquarters in St Peter's Square, Chiswick, and a former church in Basing Street, Notting Hill, parallel to Portobello Road Market. From January to April, from winter to spring, wherever The Wailers worked was crowded with supporters.

At the time, Island was a pioneering independent record label. Unlike virtually all record companies today, its offices housed almost all aspects of making and selling records. I was briefly a member of Island's PR staff in 1975 and I remember the buzz when The Wailers would come in at four o'clock in the afternoon to rehearse for their career-changing Lyceum show. Famous for always being first on the tour bus, Bob Marley often led the way through the loading door in the car park to the very basic rehearsal room. When the phones were quiet, I wasn't the only worker to nip downstairs to the canteen, hoping to peek round the heavy rehearsal room door and get a quick hit of The Wailers.

Later, as a journalist, I spent a lot of time with The Wailers. Perhaps Bob trusted me because he had first got to know me as his publicist. So it happened that I was researching a non-Marley story in Jamaica, when Bob invited me to stay at 56 Hope Road, his gracious great house in uptown Kingston. At this busy Rasta commune, in an elite street right next door to the prime minister's residence, dreads and downtown dons rubbed shoulders with foreign musicians and media. Bob was conducting a social experiment: he described it as "bringing the ghetto uptown".

The day after I left, 3 December 1976, proved to be a turning point. Bob was taking a break from rehearsal for the following day's Smile Jamaica gig, a free concert designed to cheer the island up before the imminent, violently contested election. The mellow afternoon abruptly turned into a nightmare when three gunmen stormed in, spraying bullets. Bob was hit in the upper arm, escaping death by millimetres.

Those bullets ricocheting round the narrow kitchen sent Bob on his own exodus: The Wailers fled to London, which Bob told me was his "second home". There, they set about recording *Exodus*, which would introduce the Jamaican shaman to his largest audience yet. In trying to silence him, his attackers only succeeded in turning up his volume.

Night after night, those precious sessions were attended by a large rotating cast that usually included the members of the young West London reggae band Aswad and their manager, Mikey "Dread" Campbell, King Sounds, the Sons of Jah, Delroy Washington, Lucky Gordon (the excellent Jamaican chef who had won notoriety as Christine Keeler's lover) and Pepe Judah of the Twelve Tribes, the Rasta organisation to which Bob belonged. Bob fed off the energy of that small community. Just as many much-loved Marley lines are lifted from the Bible or old Jamaican folk wisdom, so his quick ear tuned in to snatches of conversation or street slang.

At times, it seemed like Bob had exchanged Kingston's front line for another – that of All Saints Road, a short block away from the Basing Street studio and a centre for black activism. The studio was on the route of the West Indian carnival, which had been founded in the early sixties but erupted into a war between black and white youths and the police just months before the *Exodus* sessions. Inevitably, the stress of the streets intruded at times. Early one Saturday evening, Angus "Drummie Zeb" Gaye, Aswad's teenage drummer, came in seething because he'd just been arrested under the sus law, which had been designed to allow the police to control vagrancy by apprehending people suspected of loitering with intent but was now being widely used, particularly in Notting Hill, to harass young black males. Bob cried, "Come on, Aswad, me gonna mash up all a dem!" and a game of fussball defused the tension.

The broad arc of *Exodus* is an archetypal survival narrative so powerful that it seemed as if the album had sprung fully formed from Marley's head as a strategic, spiritual self-help manual on outlasting conflict and betrayal. Yet when these tracks were cut, there was no idea of the running order, later selected from a cornucopia of material by the producer, Chris Blackwell.

With no road map, The Wailers just kept on recording, in a mood of exuberant creativity. They were always well rehearsed and didn't like to leave the studio with work unfinished; a Wailers session generally had an atmosphere of relaxed discipline. Most of the musicians were trained through years of working in – indeed, helping to create – the fiercely competitive world of Kingston recording sessions.

Many of the rhythms that still shake the world three decades on were built in a single take. Searching for the perfect intonation and inflection, Bob would test each line, shifting the stress on a word or flipping the rhythm of his delivery. This exploration took its time, but Bob never stopped experimenting until he was satisfied.

Throughout the recording process, he kept on writing songs: "Exodus" itself came quite late and there was a fizzing excitement around that track from the moment it was first laid down. The song had so many meanings for all the musicians present, as many of them were exiles. And, of course, the song referred to the common Rastafarian concern with repatriation to Africa, which Bob and the Twelve

Tribes were actively engaged in organising, on land made available by Haile Selassie in Shashamane, Ethiopia.

Bob was preoccupied with movement at that time. "It's movement time!" he would cry when marshalling the troops. "How you feel in life?" he asked me one night. "You feel – movement?" When I affirmed, he nodded, "Good."

This was no time to stand still. Bob frequently debated the events of the day, including the struggles in South Africa and Rhodesia (which was shortly to become Zimbabwe), with the assembled crowd when he wasn't needed in the studio. Not surprisingly, he was usually cynical towards governments and the media.

During one discussion about media corruption, he flashed me a knowing look and said, quite sharply, "Even if you wanted to write more 'bout Africa, [the editors are] probably not gonna print it."

When the night came to finish the "Exodus" track, the Basing Street studio was alive with excitement. From the start, the song had its own impetus. Various pairs of hands – The Wailers bassist Aston "Family Man" Barrett, Blackwell, sometimes even the young assistant engineers Dick Cuthell and Terry Barham – all danced around adjusting the levels of the mix. Every pass sounded superb, but at four o'clock in the morning a moment hit when the whole room knew that this one was it. "Exodus" was militant and liberating, and as we all skanked and sang the chorus, Bob moved as if the track were live-wiring his whole being.

Basing Street was a fine location to road test the track. The area was dotted with shebeens – Jamaican after-hours joints in abandoned buildings and basements. Shebeens were the laboratory for the mid-seventies London sound that remains the basis of so much popular music and that Bob memorably called "Punky Reggae Party". The Clash, The Slits, the odd Sex Pistol, Chrissie Hynde and Boy George were found in shebeens with reggae artists such as Aswad and Steel Pulse. At the Metro Youth Club, right by the studio, Family Man showed up one night with a mix of "Exodus". The mostly school-age dancers – Britain's first home-grown Rasta generation, in red, green and gold tams and belts, the "dawtas" in headwraps and knee-length skirts – started stepping as soon as needle hit wax – the song was speaking directly to them.

Bob appreciated those Metro excursions, but generally hung back in the shadows. He liked to watch how the people felt the music. And over the coming years he would have plenty of opportunity to observe dancers being galvanised by *Exodus*. The album consolidated his position on the international music scene, effecting a transition in both his life and his career. His future took shape during the winter months at those West London studios, which somehow held the whole world.

*

Looking back, this prototypical Peace Concert marking Bob's return to the island after the assassination attempt on his life was, despite everything, a more innocent time. Joy and hope were in the air. In its aftermath, however, leading players were killed, including Bob's good friend Claudius Massop who was shot by the police in the street soon after. An alternate article I wrote at the same time for Harpers & Queen *detailed how I managed to coerce a reluctant cab driver to drive us downtown from the Sheraton Hotel and, with photographer Kate Simon, found PNP don-turned-peacemaker Aston "Bucky" Marshall sprawled across the hood of a 1960s American car in the ghetto streets.* Why is the Peace happening now? *I asked him. A knowing smile crossed his face: "Because we shoot harder." Bucky would be shot dead in a New York City nightclub two years later. Nonetheless, the night of the concert, which assembled Jamaica's finest onstage, remains an inspiration. We still use music as an aid to conflict resolution. It will always be a vital tool in our kit.*

"One Love Peace Concert"

First published in Sounds, *29 April 1978*

Sunday afternoon, Bob Marley relaxed on his front stoop. Everybody is still discussing the One Love Peace show the previous day, on the night of the full moon. Bob laughs. "They said the moon would be red and it was." Pausing dramatically: "It was red-eye!" (i.e. stoned.)

Marley said that all those theories about the full moon driving people bananas were rubbish, as the One Love Peace show proved. I'm not too sure. The moon seemed to be warping my brain cells (I am a Cancer, for what that's worth) and I was soon-come'd into missing some of the bands and then struggling to see what was happening onstage. The festival lasted for the better part of a day. No way you could miss the event fullness of this one. The One Love Peace show reminded itself so regularly that "history was being made here"; it could have been embarrassing if it hadn't succeeded so well.

Music wasn't the most important thing. The concert's true significance was as an affirmation of Jamaican strength, plus a witness to the power that Rastafarian musicians have over the Jamaican consciousness; if Rasta musicians say there will be peace, there is peace. Typical of Jamaica, which at times seems parochial, music, religion and politics entwined tight enough to strangle. An obvious analogy would be a gig to celebrate the signing of peace in Ireland with Sinn Fein and Provo leaders shaking hands with Margaret Thatcher, and Callaghan with Johnny Rotten top of the bill. Intense, right? That's what happened.

The concert was held to commemorate Haile Selassie of Ethiopia's visit to Jamaica in 1966, which Rastas believe blessed the island. It was also held to celebrate the famous Kingston peace treaty forged early this year between street gang leaders/new folk heroes Claude Massop and Bucky Marshall. All proceeds went to the Peace Fund; it was Marley's first stage show since he was forced into exile after an assassination attempt last year.

The arena was built in 1966 for the British Commonwealth Games, ironically enough. It's a functional piece of modern design in spankin' good nick, miraculous by Jamaican standards. Where visibility wasn't that great, the sound was generally excellent. Everyone involved was aware that this was Jamaica's most ambitious gig ever.

The show's format veered awkwardly between the hacked on-off, on-off traditional Jamaican shows and open-air festivals as we know them. The early hours of the afternoon (gate opened at five o'clock, crowd appeared impenetrable by one o'clock) featured a wham-bam-thank-you string of top acts performing one, two or three songs – a tantalising hors d'oeuvres whipped away almost before you're finalised.

Althia & Donna performed "Uptown Top Ranking" rather perfunctorily. Dillinger shone for a brief moment and were gone. Leroy Smart was dapper and incisive as he sang "Ballistic Affair". The Meditations sang their "Woman Is Like a Shadow" classic in graceful three-part harmony before themselves doing a disappearing act. Same goes for The Diamonds. All were backed by the indefatigable Lloyd Parkes and his We The People band.

The mighty Culture also performed just three numbers, "Natty Never Get Weary", "Natty Dread Taking Over" and their Peace tune. As far as the Foreign Press (a new – to me – animal constantly referred to from the stage between sets as if to remind the audience of the importance of The Event) were concerned, a random on-the-spot test indicated that Culture converted the lot. I'm not surprised – Culture's calisthenics-based themes are as attractive as their sprightly waxings, as Britain will be able to observe when they touch down in July.

Dennis Brown was the first artiste to have some time onstage. He sang lots of hits off his *Wolf & Leopards* album and skipped nimbly about the stage in his three-piece suit, but somehow he didn't quite hit the spot, even when singing his very popular current 12-inch hit, "How Can I Leave".

The day was hitting its later afternoon rhythm now and my perception of events from here on was influenced by a string of minor adventures as I was moved on from one vantage point to the next by succeeding front lines of army, police or punters. More of these events next week (I should live so long), but I did get to watch Inner Circle featuring Jacob "The Killer" Miller from the side of the stage.

Jacob is established as a beloved cultural hero and his stage presence is as elusive as the sound of a Concorde passing directly overhead. Whether pulling himself back onstage wearing a policeman's helmet that he'd somehow acquired during his ascent into the crowd or running from side to side of the stage like a chicken with a weight problem in search of the lost egg, he's impossible to ignore.

Audience activity was as heated as onstage activity. The squidgy red running track was permanently criss-crossed by trails of people in search of something to drink, like the sickly "Sky Juice" fruit/sugar drink that you swig out of plastic bags (like drinking the water from the goldfish you won at the fair). An engrossing attempt to buy oranges from the orange lady who peels 'em for you meant that I quenched my thirst but could not see Beres Hammond, popular Jamaican sweet soul artiste. He sings like a classic soul smoocher designed with young lovers in mind.

Come to that, visibility wasn't much better when Big Youth finally made it onstage – they'd been hailing him regularly over the Tannoy – to sing favourites like "Every N***** is a Star", "Hit the Road Jack" and "Isaiah First Prophet of Old". He slickered around the stage wearing white, displaying a very pleasing singing voice. Not as startling as his erstwhile vocal cavalry charge, but characterful and melodic.

Meanwhile, between sets, DJ Errol Thomas (not the Joe Gibbs producer) uttered his unctuous verbal message: "We hear Mick Jagger is here tonight! And Chris Blackwell of Island Records, who's done so much for reggae music!" Two apathetic bursts of near-applause but not half as damning as the storm of silence when Errol Thomas greeted "Carly Simon – if she's here!" Actually, I think he'd got confused and really meant my photographer Kate Simon, but still.

Back to business. One band embodied all the uplifting mottoes hung on placards round the walls – "Build Jamaica with Discipline", "Work together for Self-Reliance", et al. – Peter Tosh and Word, Sound and Power. The only set that reduced me to the state of ga-ga fandom that (unfortunately for critical credibility) I still love best. To say that Peter Tosh is the most aggressive of the original Bob, Peter and Bunny Wailers triumvirate is as daring as saying that Paul McCartney has recently sold many more records than Ringo Starr. I never knew his vocals would be that powerful, blaring pride, complemented by a built-in sneer as 3D as Johnny Rotten's.

Looking mobile in a karate suit, he was almost outshone by bass player Robby Shakespeare (wearing the blue tracksuit with the red stripe). Shakespeare is constructed along the same lines as a Securicor van. He hurtled himself in sudden charges across the stage, his violin-like Höfner bass poised on his shoulder like a machine gun aimed straight at guitar player Al Anderson. As he engaged Al in instrumental combat without losing a fragment of reverb on his thunderous bassline while running, I felt awestruck. Word, Sound and Power consists of the heaviest Jamaican session rhythm section, Robbie Shakespeare and Sly Dunbar, plus the cream of former Wailers sidemen like Al Anderson and Earl "Wire" Lindo on keyboards. I had slight doubts about how much material Peter has. If he has a host of his own good songs stockpiled, he should by rights have monster sales, except that he scares any potential mass audience off by his imposing militancy.

Ras Michael and The Sons of Negus came next, for the authentic drum-bashing Kumina-based roots. The grand old man of Jamaican music and his drummers spread across the stage, well back so that I couldn't see them, transformed the stadium into a campfire revivalist singalong. Bob Marley, looking extremely cheerful, and The I Three gleefully sang an impromptu harmony soundcheck along to "None A Jah Jah Children No Cry" backstage. Ras Michael's continuing success is yet more proof of 1978 Jamaica's craving for roots. Jah Mike's only success commercially is good singalong songs. The sound is purist African-talking-drums style, take it or leave it. He's got soul.

The Wailers didn't sound all that hot. Bob's voice was grindingly off-key at the start and they were the only band to have severe PA troubles. For a Wailers fan, of course, just seeing them perform in Jamaica was interest enough. It made me realise that Bob performs almost entirely to audiences with no idea what he's going on about. "Trenchtown Rock" was delivered with a more easy flowing eloquence to people from Trench Town. They started with an unfamiliar gospel song, which they obviously wouldn't have done outside Jamaica.

Frustratingly, my view was again impeded by the untypical event of a gang of youths making a concerted effort to rip off everything I owned, but I was still aware that musically, the set improved radically around "Jamming" time. From there they went into The Wailers' classic "One Love" (also the name of the show) and closed with an equally emotional "Jah Live". Bob is always magnetic onstage, even though his movements are by now so stylised as to be self-created clichés: the agonised Christ-like raising of the arms, etc. Also present onstage, a remarkably good horn section featuring the Zap Pow horns and Vin Gordon.

People had been expecting Bob, Peter and Bunny Wailer to sing together as they usually do at Jamaican shows. They didn't. The "family affair" aspect of the show was fleshed out by Marley bringing two of his little boys onstage with him, to be present when the mainspring of the One Love Peace show took place. But what mattered most was that Bob called Prime Minister Michael Manley and opposition leader Edward Seaga onstage and got them to join hands with the gunmen. I was standing on the side of the stage, which was so packed that it seemed the entire shebang, and equipment, band, the liggers were so focused on this extraordinary event – is it absurd to think of it happening in Britain? – that emotion didn't give rise to any of the violence feared by pessimists.

Peter Tosh sings that he doesn't want peace, he wants equal rights and justice. Marley is optimistic/unrealistic enough to aim at all three by his action onstage. It was an emotional high point for everyone present and Bob soon finished the set with the full moon shining directly over his head.

*

Back from his exile in London following the Peace Concert, Bob is elated. Enjoying the success of Exodus, *he's living his dream with his own studio in his own comfortable home, surrounded by musicians, family, friends and community. In a wide-ranging talk he reflects on his experience. It is our last interview. All too soon, his gleaming trajectory on Earth will stop – but his star will continue to ascend, ever higher.*

"Bob Marley: In His Own Backyard"

First published in Melody Maker, *11 August 1979*

As you drive through the white-pillared gates into the grounds of 56 Hope Road, the first thing you notice is that the road doesn't have any holes. Even here, uptown in New Kingston, the road surfaces are pitted and scarred, as if someone had scratched their spots; great boulders are kicked casually into the gutter. All the damage, we're told, is because of the recent flood; but the fact remains that in Bob Marley's yard, the tarmac is new, shiny and unblemished.

One side of the house is a big record shop, in an airy room. There are "Babylon By Bus" and "Rat Race" and "Tuff Gong" tie-dye T-shirts hanging on the walls, the most Western-style merchandising techniques I've ever seen in Jamaica. There's even a fanzine section on the counter, selling The Wailers' fan club booklet, including ital recipes, and *Rasta Voice* magazine.

The Tuff Gong outfit is ensconced in what used to be Bob Marley's house. Other Wailers also used to live in the white mansion. The pillars at the front of the drive still say Island House – that's because before Marley took over, it was Island Records' HQ. They don't have a Jamaican base any more; in its place, Marley's own record company.

The yard has become a car park. While the whole island is full of cannibalised cars, bits of cars grafted onto other cars, as car and spare-part import bans reduce the available transport still further, there's a remarkably high collection of new, functional cars – including the BMW, The Wailers' favourite motorised vehicle (just check the initials).

The "straight" world of Jamaica is still making life difficult for the dreads, but here at ex-Island House it's Rasta country. Men and women sit on the steps, lean up against trees; Tuff Gong records is obviously where the action is in Kingston these days.

*

Inside the house is the ultimate proof that Marley, the local boy made good, is bringing it back home. A 24-track studio – there's only one other on the island, at Harry J's. Channel One has only just gone up from four to sixteen tracks.

And what a studio. Very small, but the style . . . Someone says it looks like Miami's Criteria Studios, but my terms of reference tell me that the stripped pine walls are strictly West Coast style. More roots; reggae has gone well international.

In the control room, watching the vertical strips of light that indicate the recording levels on each track flickering up and down, are Bob Marley and his brothers and sisters. Alex Sadkin has flown in from Miami to work with Bob, and Tuff Gong has poached Treasure Isle's engineer, Errol Thompson. They're mixing a new song: "Set it up in (Zimbabwe) [. . .] Soon we'll find out who is the real revolutionary . . ."

Marley takes time out to talk. We go round the house, through a big, beautifully carved wooden door, into an office. And that means a regular Western-style office with new office furniture, even IBM typewriters, and phones with intercom systems.

Vivien: *It's astonishing how much more direct and militant your new tunes are than* Kaya *. . .*

Marley: *This is getting to the point. What they said about* Kaya *is true, but you can't show aggression all the while. To make music is a life that I have to live. Sometimes you have to fight with music. So it's not just someone who studies and chats, it's a whole development. Right now is a more militant time on Earth, because it's Jah Jah time. But me always militant, you know. Me too militant. That's why me did things like* Kaya*, to cool off the pace.*

Vivien: *If you were interested in being heard by an international market, maybe they were frightened off by militant music . . .*

Marley: *Of course, especially the parents.*

Vivien: *Did you feel under pressure to record for the States market, for example?*

Marley: *To tell you the truth, I don't even think that way. I just think more of an inner creativeness. Inna my chest. I don't make a tune specially for this and this; if the feeling comes nice into my soul according to a certain vibration – me no really* *a prostitute. Me just respect people like Taj Mahal and Bob Dylan for how they do with themselves. They respect their own talent – that means where they are and who they are. It's that that people have to want, you dig, 'cos the people don't want to be pleased, they want to please someone, you dig, it goes both ways. So it's no use getting in this mechanical bag, because creativeness leave if you do that. That's why plenty of artists come just for a time and then you hear no more of them, because them no really be themselves. Because when you are yourself – boy, that's it, I think . . .*

Vivien: *Were you ever annoyed at Rasta being used as a sales gimmick?*

Marley: *As far as I'm concerned, the record company might try and show the people a gimmick – we don't think we play at a place and tomorrow everyone is Rasta. It's not like that. It grows. You never can tell which vision you're going to get, or if God is going to call you. So Rastafari is God's new name, Head Creator. Africa is the cornerstone to the realisation of people's unity.*

Vivien: *You just went to Africa for the first time, after trying to get a visa for ages. Was it like you'd imagined?*

Marley: *When I got there it was the same thing I felt about Africa here, the same as I'd always imagined it would be. But nicer.*

Vivien: *How nicer?*

Marley: *Just nicer in terms of living, development, opportunity. When you go to Africa you see how useful you can be to mankind.*

Vivien: *You mean they need a lot of help out there?*

Marley: *Not in respect of the material element. It's like – Africa awaits its creators. It needs a lot of people who know how to do things. This is just a little studio. Africa is capable of plenty studios, but it's up to who really wants to deal with it.*

Vivien: *Some people in England regard Rasta as another offshoot of the colonial mentality, something that holds people down.*

Marley: *What one man thinks is great. But only a fool leans upon his one understanding. The truth is there. King Solomon and King David are the roots of black people and the roots of creation – they are Jacob's people. So when a black man* *says that Rasta is colonialist, he's turning it the other way in a sense of diplomacy. He's putting down his own thing, because he's learnt how to do it. Who teaches him? You dig what I'm saying?*

Vivien: *Just like they say that it's more important to confront the reality in England, for example, than to think of going to Africa.*

Marley: *I could agree with that, but why fight to stay in a place that's dirty, where the rivers are polluted? Why stay in a place where if God shook two earthquakes, all these stones are gonna fall on you and kill you? Africa for Africans at home and abroad. Like England for English people, America for Americans, Asia for the Chinese . . . but we're not saying that people can't mix together. But this world is funny, because you claim you're white and I claim I'm black, and we have a fight, because if you're not sensible, it becomes a barrier. But the truth is the truth, your father's name is Noah and my father's name is Noah and Shem's father's named Noah, so we all three people come from Noah, so we're the same people. But right now it's just a few who search out their roots.*

Vivien: *Do you feel you could exert a lot of power in Jamaican politics?*

Marley: *Me can do a lot of things, anywhere.*

Vivien: *But, for example, after Claude Massop [one of the organisers of last year's Peace Treaty in Kingston] was shot by the police – how did you feel about the Peace Concert?*

Marley: *I&I is RASTA, and the struggle continues.*

Vivien: *But where do you struggle? Do you feel that a Rasta musician should never get directly politically involved?*

Marley: *I don't involve myself. We don't support either the JLP or the PNP. Rasta is different. Claudie was my brethren. And a lot more people. But we know that we are Rastafarians, that we have something to offer. We have the Twelve Tribes of Israel, the Ethiopian Orthodox Church, the Theocratic Government. If a youth wants to go out there and fight politics, he can go. We have something that demands rights if you stand where me stand. If you don't do that, you'll be dying in the streets with your dreadlocks on, because you're not defending the thing you must defend. You can't be strong,* *you must be a weakling. It's just the truth. We defend His Majesty's philosophy. It's not political – it's only words that make it political. It's life – people – action.*

Vivien: *When you sing about militancy what do you expect people to do?*

Marley: *I expect if you're living by the gun, if gun is the fight, then FIRE gun. If where you come from you fight with sticks and stones, then fight with sticks and stones. If the fight is spiritual, then fight spiritual, because everywhere the fight goes on. We don't have any alternatives. If a man fights you with machine guns and you throw stones, then – machine gun for machine gun! So the struggle continues. A lot of people defend South Africa, some secretly, some openly. A lot of white people defend South Africa, and when you keep the black man down in South Africa you keep him down all over the Earth. Because Africa is Solomon's goldmine. So – war! Either I&I lives, or no one lives. You know what the big fight is? It's that black people – and only black people – mustn't say the truth about Rasta.*

Vivien: *I disagree – you can get lots of information about Rasta.*

Marley: *Of course, but say you love Rasta and see a chance whereby mankind can set up something new to live by so that we can all say: THIS is how we want to live – the system won't support that. If all the leaders were to get up tomorrow morning and say they defend Rasta, what do you think would happen? But all of them can get up tomorrow and die. [Rastas reject the concept of death, won't attend funerals.]*

Vivien: *In the mid-sixties you worked in a car factory in Wilmington, Delaware. What was that like?*

Marley: *As a youth I was always active, never lazy. I learnt a trade, welding, so dealing with those things is part of my thing. I enjoy dealing with parts, part-work, and I never really mind because I just did it as much as I wanted to do it. Any time I felt fed up, I didn't really look for a job. I come from country and country is always good. You grow everything. You don't really have to go out there and kill yourself to get a place or have money. You can eat and bathe and make clothes and build your own house, but in a strange land you can't find a place or settle down to find a way to leave. The best way out is to organise and leave.*

Vivien: *Do you regard Jamaica as a strange land?*

Marley: *Jamaica is a place we know, but the system change and it a gets strange. It just change and get strange . . . because I'm tired of saying it. I&I are tired of saying this: RASTAFARI! I&I not trying to push myself; it's just the truth, God knows . . . that's why sometimes I don't even bother to talk because it's just a waste of time, but I still have the urge. But when I talk to people, it seems sometimes we're not on the same wavelength. From Pope Paul's time, we knew we'd be under pressure. White man doesn't have any sympathy with Rasta, but he has to hear that, and perish in his own fornication that he deals with, his own fuckery and his own atomic and his own S.A.L.T . . .*

[Marley's voice sneers – he's referring to the Strategic Arms Limitation Treaty and punning it with salt, which Rastas are forbidden to eat according to their dietary laws.]

Marley: *We haven't really come to save the white nation. But they are some of the people on Earth and they have to hear the truth. The white man has nothing he can give us, you know – only death. That's why I&I is Rasta, because we know death has nothing against I&I.*

Vivien: *But you're working within those white man's systems. Would you have got to be an international star if Chris Blackwell [head of Island Records] was a black man?*

Marley: *Watch me. If I wasn't capable of being something . . . Chris Blackwell didn't help me. I had to work hard, while Blackwell flew out and enjoyed himself. But he had the contacts at the time that we felt we needed, and perhaps we did. But Blackwell did a lot for himself. I remember a time when he had nineteen Jamaican acts signed and before my days he wouldn't touch one. The pressure of the way we had to work was why The Wailers [Marley's referring to the trio of himself, Peter Tosh and Bunny Livingstone] didn't agree, because we didn't get any help, we were out on tour under some steep conditions that first time . . . because if it was my raas claat I'd have blown up the whole Earth already, with its corruption. It's just pressure from all sides – we're born to get pressure, we come upon the Earth to get pressure. You get pressure from your family, pressure from strangers, pressure from all over. So you've got to be mindful.*

Vivien: *One of the biggest pressures on you is being THE international reggae messenger. That's why I felt "Running Away", where you defended yourself against people accusing you of doing that when you left Jamaica for Miami after they tried to shoot you, was* Kaya's *most penetrating, sincere track.*

Marley: *People don't understand that we live in this Earth, too. We don't sing these songs and live in the sky. I don't have an army behind me. If I did, I wouldn't care, I'd just get more militant. Because I'd know, well, I have 50,000 armed youth, and when I talk, I talk from strength. But you have to know how you're dealing. Maybe if I'd tried to make a heavier tune than "Kaya", they would have tried to assassinate me because I would have come too hard.*

I have to know how to run my life, because that's what I have, and nobody can tell me to put it on the line, you dig? Because no one understands these things. These things are heavier than anyone can understand. People that aren't involved don't know it. It's my work and I know it outside in. I know when I am in danger and what to do to get out. I know when everything is cool and I know when I tremble, do you understand? Because music is something that everyone follows, so it's a force, a terrible force.

Someone like me, now – if I want to be a loudmouth, I'm a loudmouth, and someone can come out one day and BOOGAAAA! – shoot me. So, I'm a loudmouth – and then I'm cool. Then I'll come out again. So someone might say, yes, we have to defend this youth, because he deals with the right things, or else I go – wawawawawawaAAAAAA! And one day – know what I mean? But I am a man that can sing any song, because I can never change. I've even tested myself to see if I can change, and there is no change.

Vivien: *I don't know what you mean – everyone changes, all the time.*

Marley: *When I sing a tune like "Kaya", do I change? No. I'm more . . . wickeder! That's how the Earth gets tricked. There are a lot of people just come upon the train and me just say, right, it's this direction I'm going in, let's see who follows me and who does their own thing. So I just say "KAYA!" and everybody just goes so, and now I come back and say "BLACK SURVIVAL!" and – pure idiots, all they do is *follow. Not one of them is a leader – they're all followers.*

So I hear people say, Bob Marley's gone soft, all he is is a traitor to Bob Marley's cause. But how could they know who Bob Marley is and how could Bob get soft? Bob grow inna this thing, the things that Bob sings about are his life, it's how he lives. I couldn't get any education that could change my way of thinking, you dig? I live the way I live.

My struggle can never, ever change. If it could have changed, it already would have, because I've been everywhere. I live in Miami the same way I live in Jamaica. But people don't understand that we're in contact with our own people, everywhere we go, our people come. It's not the place, it's the people. In Miami, my brethren are there, same way. So it's not a feeling like children waiting for Christmas – we're just natural people, soldiers, we just live a war every day. Because just imagine being a Rasta in this world which doesn't like Rasta. We could be enjoying being something else, but no. We say – "WE ARE RASTA!"

Vivien: *How come you're aware of the danger of being assassinated when you say there's no such thing as death?*

Marley: *Hold on, now. You think you can go out there and lay down in front of the car and let it run over you? If I go outside and see the big bus coming and put my head underneath it, what do you think will happen?*

Vivien: *Your head will be crushed. And what will you be then?*

Marley: *[yells] DEAD! This is where people make a mistake. They say that the flesh doesn't value anything, but that's the biggest lie. This flesh is what you've got, what God put inside you is your life. That's the way I think, that's the way I'm organised, because I don't stray from my roots and my roots is God. But, sister, I understand what you're saying. You're saying a man can be dead in his flesh and his spirit still lives, but I respect my flesh, too, and I know my spirit and what it's like . . .*

Vivien: *So when you say you don't believe in death . . .*

Marley: *[firmly] I don't believe in death neither in flesh nor in spirit.*

Vivien: *But I don't understand, because one minute you're saying you don't believe in death and the next minute you say you'll be shot and . . .*

Marley: *Yes, but you have to AVOID it! Some people don't figure* *it's such a great thing, they don't know how long they can preserve it. Preservation is the gift of God, the gift of God is life, the wages of sin is death. When a man does wickedness, he's gone out there and dead.*

Vivien: *Oh, I thought you felt death didn't exist at all.*

Marley: *Death does not exist for me. I truly know God. He gives me this [life] and my estimation is: if He gives me this, why should He take it back? Only the Devil says that everybody has to die.*

Vivien: *Someone from Inner Circle told me that the money from the Peace Show never got to all the right people. Did you know about that?*

Marley: *All I know is that it went to everyone that wanted it. Too much people involved. Too much people have too much thing to say and they don't know anything. So many people go on about how they're roots, and when did you last see them in the ghetto? They hide from the ghetto, they're not in contact.*

Vivien: *But you must find it difficult to keep in touch with the ghetto . . .*

Marley: *[incredulous] Find it difficult? Watch now. You look into my yard. It's a ghetto. This is a ghetto you're looking at. Look out there. I've just brought the ghetto uptown. My thing is, why must I stay in one place every day of my life and all the days of my life I have to run from the police? Look in any other yard along the road and see if you see any one of my brethren out there in any other yard.*

When I lived in the ghetto, every day I had to jump fences, police trying to hold me, you dig? So my job all the while was to try to find one place where the police wouldn't run me down too much. So I don't want to stay in contact with the ghetto, in contact with the ghetto means in contact with a prison, in contact with everything that's bad all the while, not the people. When the law comes out, they send them into the ghetto first, not uptown. So how long does it take you to realise – boy, well, they don't send them uptown, y'know! So we'll make a ghetto uptown. EVERY DAY I jumped fences from the police, for YEARS, not a week. For YEARS. So me get afraid now, me have to make some type of move. You either stay there and let bad people shoot you down, or you make a move and show people some improve-

ment. Or else I would take up a gun and start shoot them off and then a lot of youths would follow me, and they'd be dead the same way. I want some improvement. It doesn't have to be materially, but it can be freedom of thinking.

Vivien: *But the material things have helped you to spread a little bit of freedom out to a few people, but it hasn't helped all the people in the ghetto. Don't you think that only more direct political action can do that?*

Marley: *Something more direct would be if Queen Elizabeth would take her raas away from Jamaica, take away her Constitution, call away those ways of life they have down here.*

Vivien: *I thought that was supposed to happen when Jamaica became independent.*

Marley: *But it never happened. We still have a governor general. No one gives Jamaica people a chance, that's why we say that the Earth is corrupted and everyone has to die and leave we. It's a selfish way of thinking, but . . . [mutters] fuck it . . . how long will they pressure we? We are the people who realise the place where they thieved us from, so we say, AH, you took us from there, AH, this is what we are. But they still tell us, no, no, this is what you are! This is what you must be . . . This yard [house], they call it Freedom Ground. Hardly anything can happen here. The greatest thing that could happen would never happen, so you could say God has we for a purpose and a reason.*

Vivien: *"Ambush in the Night" contains the clearest references you've ever made to colonialism.*

Marley: *[absently] We always try. There's a lot of good music we have in there, a whole heap of good stuff . . . I don't like to talk, because the way I talk, I don't know if I can be understood. Or maybe somebody might understand me the wrong way. There's only one thing we have to say, that is, we are Rastafarian people the same way some people are Catholic. Some people are this, some people are this. They always want to interview I&I, but they don't want to know what we really want to say. It [Rasta] becomes unreal, like something we try and make . . . raas . . . truth is like food, man – when you say food you know you mean food, and when you say truth, same way.*

You know, Vivien, sometimes me no get over too straight,

because you are a woman and you see things . . . Me understand how you see things, but I can't please you by talking to make you feel pleased. Me just have to show you say – you have to be strong.

Vivien: *Since you're always covering old tunes, I thought you should cover the tune "Let Him Go (Rude Boy Get Bail)". It's still so relevant.*

Marley: *Well, Bunny did that in '66, when I was in America, but me did other rude boy songs – that rude bwaoy business, bad, bad music. Only them shouldn't have said "rude boy", them should have said "Rasta". You dig me? But in them times, me didn't know Rasta. Something was going on, you felt it, and didn't know if you were bad bad or good good – then I understood it's good, you're good – it's Rasta!*

Vivien: *When, or what, made you realise it was Rasta, not rudeness?*

Marley: *What is there to benefit from badness? I wondered, I looked at it and thought, boy, bloodclaat, if I thump this man here I feel the contact, too. And then I said, it's the same God that lives in my hand lives in me, and that means that it's not him I thump, it's God I'm really thumping. So I used to wonder about this human feeling business . . . the whole thing is Rasta. The way I tell you, it's a whole experience, but you break it down and it's just – Rasta.*

Vivien: *Did you used to play lots of gigs in the early days?*

Marley: *Not a lot, just like Christmas morning and Easter, we'd be there up at the Carib Theatre. But we was always the underground, always the rebels. We came from Trench Town. So you'd hear about Byron Lee and all that society business, but we came from down so-named WAILERS, from TRENCHTOWN. So we stay, and we're glad of it. You've got to be someone.*

Vivien: *So now you get society knocking on your door . . .*

Marley: *Turn them off. Tell them to come another day.*

Vivien: *Which bit of your career has meant the most?*

Marley: *I love the development of our music, that's what I really dig about the whole thing. How we've tried to develop, really try to understand what we're trying to do, you know? It grows. That's why every day people come forward with new songs. Music goes on forever.*

Before we leave, Marley asks why I haven't tried to interview Family Man (I have tried) or one of the other Wailers.

"It's always me who has to talk," he says, "and I don't dig it either, because it gets me into problems . . ."

The I Three

Like Nigeria's Fela Kuti, who we are about to meet in the next chapter, Bob heard the sense in using female voices. The balance extends the appeal. In the case of The I Three, as he had done in recruiting the island's key players in the Barrett Brothers for the new post-trio Wailers, so he picked women whose singing was already individually loved. The I Three projected the template for demurely dressed and forceful Rasta womanhood.

"The 3 Wise 'I's: The Superstar Women Backing Bob"

First published in New Musical Express, *9 August 1980*

Vivien Goldman checks out the Rastafarian way of feminism with The I Three.

To get into the Mayfair service flat you have to pick your way over the supplies: catering-size packs of rice and kidney beans and pulses, giant drums of oil, more catering packs of washing powder and nappies.

The I Three are going home to Jamaica, where although things have quietened down since the curfew imposed last week (a score of seven dead in the last couple of days is regarded as light), the supermarket shelves stack little else but air.

The I Three are lying in a goodly store, obviously intending to supply not only themselves, but also an extended neighbourhood family. Bob Marley wanders in, bemused at the sight of a living room like a dry-goods warehouse. Rita Marley laughs at him – it's a long time since he's done the weekly shopping backayard [affectionate term for Jamaica], that's for sure, or he wouldn't be surprised at all.

Like the good woman in the Bible whose price is above rubies, The I Three provide for their households diligently, allocating their time between selling in the market, spinning, weaving, and working in the fields and cutting records.

The I Three (remember the Rasta edict that every individual is part of a global unity by changing the first person singular into "I&I"? The I Three are a trio, hence . . .) joined forces to back Bob Marley and the Wailers when the initial triumvirate of Bob, Peter Tosh and Bunny Livingstone broke up to perform their separate works back in 1974. But all three women were in at the beginning of home-grown Jamaican music, when the synthesis of America, Caribbean and African roots was just beginning to whirr round in the blender, frothing the ingredients up into what we now know as reggae . . .

It was an exciting time, leaving school in 1965. Jamaica had become independent three years before and it seemed like the dawning of a new age, bursting like an overripe mango with possibilities.

This particular afternoon, Rita was excited anyway, because that night she was going to a dance. The music in those times, the ska, reflected the mood of the people; fast and exciting, it made you want to jump up, a kind of carnival feeling. The youth were filling the charts with a real Jamaica sound for the first time. It used to be all uptown people before that. Smooth, fancy music from the combos like Byron Lee and the Dragonaires – too refined, designed for people who lived up in the hills, with their swimming pools and guard dogs.

Rita had just come back from the shops, where she'd bought some peroxide and a new kind of hair cream imported from America. You left it in on your head for two hours, put your hair in rollers and suddenly it was straight, and you could pile it up into a bouffant beehive, like the American film stars.

The tourists brought in these new fashions, all cloistered in the new hotels on the beach. People weren't all happy about the tourists. They didn't like the way their swimming and fishing beaches had suddenly become private property, "natives" to be kept out.

Not that Rita liked it either, but since the hotels were already there, she hoped to get a job in one of them. Working behind the desk maybe, smiling nicely at all the guests as they check in their expensive luggage, even more nicely as you pocket the tip in US dollars.

Even though these are booming days, Trench Town is still the poorer side of town, the ghetto. Rita starts to mix the peroxide with water in an empty coffee tin, singing "Simmer Down (Control Your Temper)" as she stirs. She leans against the window, watching the people in the street, and then she sees them.

Rita is always hoping to see them: The Wailers are her favourite group, Bob and Peter and Bunny. Every song a hit and it's no surprise; with Coxsone Dodd at the controls of Studio One, they cut the toughest records in town, tunes like "Simmer Down (Control Your Temper)", "Lonesome Feelings", "It Hurts to Be Alone". Coxsone Dodd makes lots of trips to America, carrying piles of albums back for his artists to choose from – songs by The Moonglows and The Impressions, The Isley Brothers. At every dance Rita goes to, it's always Wailers tunes that get played twice.

There they come now down the alley; Peter, the tall one, wearing a wool cap on his head. It's Peter who Rita calls out to – he's always the one to stop and chat first, the friendliest.

"Look here now, Peter Tosh! So you still don't believe me that I can really sing! Go on now, man, make me go with you to Studio One and introduce me to Mr Dodd. You frightened? I can make records as well as you, you know!"

Peter likes this girl. Her eyes twinkle, she is a tease, but she is definitely far from dumb. He stops for a moment, staring right at Rita; there is even something saucy about the tilt of her nose that makes you want to smile. So Peter smiles back and holds out his hand to the girl in the window: "Come on now."

Rita winds up working with The Wailers. She has her publicity photo taken in a big, wide flounced skirt, as wide as her smile, and the other Wailers all togged up in gold collarless jackets, like those The Beatles wear.

She has her own group, The Soulettes, and every Sunday night they perform at The Ward Theatre, the Studio One audition night, when trios from Trench Town, dressed in their smoothest narrow-trousered suits, sing like soul crooners under a lamp post in Memphis or in a school gym in Brooklyn. Hallways of tenements always add extra echo, make the voices sound full even when they're singing well high, whether you're in Kingston or Brooklyn.

There are The Paragons with John Holt singing lead, Bob Andy singing so sweet he tears your heart apart, The Wailers, The Soulettes and Marcia Griffiths.

In those days, people wanted to put out records. That was more important than money. The ego urge, to have your own record out, to prove you were somebody, the toughest of the tough.

*

Marcia Griffiths – still better known in England for her hit with Bob Andy, "Young, Gifted & Black" than for her more recent solo albums, *Naturally* and *Steppin'* – sits across the room from me. She's a pale-faced woman with a matronly demeanour. "Yes," she sighs, recalling the good old days with Studio One, "it was a musical college – you had to graduate from Studio One."

Judy Mowatt sits on the same bed. She's not a graduate of the Studio One school, but she's taken some hard knocks in her career. She's endured the ignominy of having a tune she recorded, "Woman of the Ghetto", released in Britain under the name of Phyllis Dillon, then a more popular singer; she's been forced to confront serious music/life decisions when, as lead singer with the Gaylads' female counterpart, the Gaylettes, she had to leave because she was pregnant.

"Singing with my pregnancy wasn't accepted then, so I said: OK, it's life I'm bringing. I know that it's not gonna kill me, it's not gonna kill my career, it's not going to take anything from my voice – it's going to add, because it's bringing life into the world, the most beautiful thing one could ever think of."

Outside of singing with The I Three, she had five children to bring up and a farm with goats, chickens and sheep. "I'm trying to collect all the animals that went into the ark . . ."

She also runs a record label, Ashandan, who released a fine Mowatt solo album called *Black Woman* a couple of years ago; the LP will shortly be released via the Grove/Island collaboration. The title track is an invocation of black women's heritage: "On auction blocks we were chained and . . ." It still stands as the most complete, inspirational statement for women I've ever heard in reggae.

To complete her credentials. she's co-author with singer Freddie McGregor of the current reggae favourite, "Jogging". The song came to the handsome couple on their daily early morning jog along the beach in Jamaica; maybe that's why its rhythms make you step in an unusually athletic way.

As for Rita Marley, she's just released her first solo album on the French Hansa Records label; its title, *Who Feels It Knows It*, is lifted from an old Wailers tune. Although it hasn't yet found a British release, the French love it. The cover features Rita looking typically sassy, smoking a big spliff – the first woman for the corniest visual to have emerged from reggae.

The album is smooth – probably too smooth for dub fanatics, for example, but that's its charm. Rita's is a silken, sensuous voice, with a smoky jazz lilt. A grown-up voice.

On the recent Wailers tour, The I Three performed a brief set before their stint backing The Wailers. As usual, their individual personalities emerged clearly, even while they present a unified group spirit. The Wailers thought it would be too much for them, but the trio were determined – they are all strong women. They played their set.

As The I Three sit down together in the hotel room, as they have done so many times before, they all suddenly realise the same thing (you develop a kind of telepathy when you live and work as closely as The I Three): they've never been interviewed as a group before, despite a string of hit reggae singles to their collective name.

I want to know why The I Three have kept themselves so much in the background. It seems to come down mainly to the old Jamaican expression that "nothing happens before the time". Doing elaborate juggling acts between roles is time-consuming in itself.

Then Marcia bursts out: "What we were lacking was the strength and encouragement from the men. When we see that they fail in that area, and that we have to give them strength, this is how we get the courage now to go forward."

Rita: *We were always staying behind the man, being the humblest, but now it's time to step forward.*

They are all very conscious of their roles as mothers. Rita and Judy both have five children, Marcia two. Judy is very serious about explaining to her children that Jamaica is not their home – Africa is their heritage and their future.

Rita: *In this time, the women have to be father and mother both. The majority of men leave women with children and go off on their own ego. You still have to stand firm, you can't go out there and be a harlot or a hustler.*

Judy: *[earnestly] You have to be father, mother, friend, everything for the child.*

Rita is Bob Marley's wife; they married just before he went to work in a car factory in Wilmington, Delaware. The old Wailing Souls label is taken from the two group names: Wailers and Soulettes.

Vivien: *Still, Bob has stated several times in interviews that he is unmarried. How did you feel about that, Rita?*

Rita: *[laughs] Mixed. I sort of understand that in the field of being an entertainer, he might . . . but . . . now I can say, yes we are married. Now it's my turn to speak! [More laughter.]*

Bob got what he wanted to say across, the marriage didn't make no difference. People were very vexed about that article, they said, "Is it because Rita's black?" But marriage is a Babylonian philosophy, it's not important.

We've got beyond that time, or it would have caused fussing and jealousy, and that would be bad for the children. So we operate like brother and sister. We give more respect to each other, not dominating or claiming or being possessive about each other. That's a higher level than the normal marriage.

Agreed. Yet, leaving their marital arrangements aside, the whole question of the way Rasta codes dictate the conduct of man/woman relationships is traditionally very vexing for Western women, starting from the oft-repeated Biblical premise that because women are made from the rib of men, they are automatically second in the running as they were in creation. Add Peter Tosh's remark that women are the channel of the Devil and endless misogynist songs of the "woman is the root of all evil" category (thanks, Wayne Wade), also the asserted "unclean"-ness of menstruating women – it all makes a very disturbing picture to non-Rasta women.

The I Three, of course, all of whose lives have been radically changed to an enhanced self-awareness and pride in their black womanhood through Rasta, have a different view.

Rita: *We know about that – that's part of our religion. When a woman has her periods she's unclean for seven days, you don't deal with your man, you don't have intercourse, you don't cook for him because you have an issue of blood – you separate yourself for seven days.*

Vivien: *But doesn't that make you feel like you're being demoted or rejected or despised or hated or something like that?*

[Laughter.]

Rita: *You need that time, too! That's the only time when the woman's not working. That's our free period!*

Vivien: *But what about looking after the business and the kids and so on . . .?*

Judy: *You look after the kids, yes, but your man is like a kid, too. Man is the first cook, too, you know, they can do everything except have kids, but they get so much more mothering. Women spoil them, too.*

Rita: *Women and Rasta women are two different types. A Rasta woman can be identified, it's significant. Many a woman is devious – through from Eve time, she tempted Adam to eat the fruit. From that time woman is seen as a deceiver that makes man do things he doesn't want to. But I think it's man's weakness, you can't blame women completely.*

Judy: *Yes, even at that time man knew about the apple but woman didn't, so he should have forbidden her to eat this fruit, but he was weak enough to partake of it with her . . .*

Rasta women reasoning, discussing the familiar age-old arguments, ranging through scriptural quotations. Reversing all the old male Rasta misogynist arguments neatly, beating those hateful old arguments on their own terms.

The I Three know little of the Western women's movement. But they are acutely aware of their position as Jamaican women's role models. They are cautious about the songs they choose to cover, making sure they sing only lyrics they can defend absolutely. They encourage younger women and are pleased that more women are now having the opportunity to make records without necessarily having to sleep with the producer.

Rita: *Singing is our career, our profession, our lives, our talent. This is what we dedicate ourselves to, to make a living from the talent God gave us. That's how we eat our bread, feed our children. We try to use the talent wisely.*

We are women, we are sisters, and we speak for the sisters as well as the brothers, and we are the mothers of creation; we start the multiplication of Earth.

The Wailers – Bob in particular – have definitely not been encouraging in the past of The I Three's solo flights. They're more than backup singers, they're a crucial part of The Wailers' chemistry. But now plans are being made for The I Three to record a group solo album in Nassau and Jamaica, backed by Sly and Robbie.

Rita observes: "If The I Three had a million-seller, they wouldn't have the time. We'd be pulling away from Bob as backup singers. But we've been doing it for so long. We figure that now, the privilege to make our own record is there, and we're going to use it."

Rebel Sixx

The most recent article in the book by far, "Ghetto Prophet" took me a year to write – so it took the longest and is the longest as well. Ironically, I have COVID-19 to thank for my base shifting to Jamaica from New York while compiling this book. Poison turned into (journalistic) medicine as, once again, I found myself fascinated by the new Caribbean music. The more I found out about the compelling Trinibad artist Rebel Sixx, the more his fate interwove in my mind with the Marley time you have just read about – the attempted assassination in his own home, followed by his rising with Exodus. *Yet Rebel's fate was less blessed; he became another forceful voice silenced too soon, with too little knowledge left of his philosophy and intent. As Marley had said in our final interview,* a luta continua. *Rebel Sixx's quizzical expression as he sang of what would soon be his own death began to haunt me. I was sent on a quest.*

"Bad Mind Music: The Ghetto Prophet"

First published in Pioneer Works Broadcast, *February 2024*

Only one face was missing from the line-up of Trinibad music's great and bad assembled at George Street in downtown Port of Spain on a July 2020 afternoon to celebrate a peace movement amid gang warfare run amok that had the twin Caribbean islands of Trinidad and Tobago (T & T) reeling from the daily body count.

Present were artists including prankish, baby-faced Prince Swanny, aka Taryll Swan, representing the area of Port of Spain known as Rasta City; and the man from Muslim City, ardent believer Toppy Boss, his career based on singing about the sort of beefs – including one with Swanny – buzzed about on the many online sources for gossip about Trinibad. Reflective of the times, the raw, violent local sound was quite different from the island's upbeat old calypso and soca. Ghetto stars, these young men had known each other most of their lives; battling bards of neighbourhoods at war for the past fifteen years, with local "community leaders" all beholden to one political party or other. Their individual destinies were mostly determined not by beliefs, but by geographical birth; true of us all, perhaps, but for most, a street or so's difference is less consequential.

All present knew the missing individual was untouchable when it came to sophistication, subtlety and depth. In the Trinibad jungle, his was the loudest roar.

So where was Rebel Sixx?

He was a musical original and I had no idea he was dead, let alone the circumstances, when I fell for Rebel Sixx like any fangirl. I thought he was Jamaican as he was so popular there, where I was living as a COVID-19 refugee from New York. Among the phrases Rebel helped to spread was "Fully Dunce", a backhanded compliment. When the expression wound up on book bags and T-shirts, Rebel was accused of spreading anti-intellectualism – whereas he was always encouraging youth to keep studying. His sardonic throwaway had been enough to start both a craze and a controversy.

An old-school reggae aficionado, I was adjusting to the current Jamaican music, oddly bass-free and with an alarming emphasis on the evils of Bad Mind – betrayal by those who pretend to be friends. Realizing my new favourites were by one artist helped; first, the bleak delicacy of his and Travis World's "No Trust, No Love", then others, "Rifle War", "Ghetto Prophet", "Letter From My Heart". Discovering he was already dead by violence at twenty-six disturbed me so deeply I had to find out more.

This was a direct assassination. Two masked men broke in and shot him twenty times at close range at his home in Bon Air Gardens, Arouca, Port of Spain; Rebel hadn't heard them as he was on his PlayStation with headphones. Obviously my new crush had upset some people badly – but his music sang so implicitly of humanity with all of our foibles! Why would people want Rebel killed, even as his art was deepening?

Often, I had been at Bob Marley's side in London and Kingston – through the political dons' assassination attempt on his life in December 1976 (I had been staying at his house at the time); his London exile, in the studio when he transmuted trauma into the epochal *Exodus* LP; and his triumphant homecoming for the explosion of optimism that was the 1978 Peace Concert, although in its aftermath, several leading players were killed, by police or otherwise. Others I had known and loved were also lost in these struggles and I loathed seeing the pattern repeat. This cycle, which I chronicled in *The Book of* (Marley's) *Exodus*, is now being addressed again in the new *One Love* biopic. Rebel's murder hit me with a sort of contact PTSD. The same sick phenomenon of targeting the best and brightest that almost got Bob had killed Biggie, Tupac, Nipsey Hussle, all outstanding young talents whose work was far from done. It seemed to share hallmarks – politically motivated gang allegiances – with Bob's narrow escape. I was haunted by Rebel Sixx's murder.

A wry intelligence in Rebel Sixx's voice allured me. The way he sang it, bloody images became a sad seduction, leading to a contemplation; his sweet-and-sour sound, poetically, cynically recounting brutality with a honey soprano and heavenly timing.

Tall, lanky, he loped laconically through his videos of bullets and betrayal with self-effacing detachment, as if to say – look at the craziness we have let ourselves get into. Along with the music, it was the philosophical sorrow in Rebel's eyes that compelled me to explore his story. Whether in interview or music videos, even when surrounded by a dancing, drinking crowd, his eyes signalled that he was running – making music – as fast as he could, trying to keep ahead of the doom he could sense chasing him down.

But whichever hellhound Rebel had tried to outrun caught up with him. His friendship with the Jamaican producer Squash, aka Andre Whittaker, was the link between the Jamaican scene I was familiar with and this newer (to me) Trini milieu. The 6ix Boss, as Squash was known, was said to be the leader among leaders within the violent scamming, fraud and lottery rip-off community for which his St. James parish on Jamaica's north coast was notorious. However, known to be charismatic and creative, puppy-dog eyes peer from Squash's heavily bleached, tattooed face – the "in" look for "bad boys" in Jamaica – and he posts endearingly on social media with his young children.

But Squash was unavailable. Not only was he incarcerated in Florida on ICE charges, but his HQ, Salt Springs, listed as one of the Caribbean's most dangerous towns, was also impenetrable under police lockdown. The popular music producer, Dindin, had a lead. "Find the one who knew Rebel best, his producer in Port of Spain, Trinidad, El Faltino."

*

Seen over Zoom sitting in the shade of a white-walled building, El Faltino, aka Asim El-Salih Faltine, explained, "Rebel and I met in 2019, the Friday after Carnival, and we were on a musical journey together; I am an elder in the business. I was already working with K-Lion, aka Kwinton Thomas, from my Belmont community and they went on to record a lot together. K-Lion was so young but very talented – one of the few artists we all looked up to.

"I try not to say much, I don't want to mislead nobody," El Faltino continued. "Very small grudges can be turned into big issues because of power and egos. What happened to Rebel is jealousy, bad mind coming from people who are trying to control the youths' thinking. Political corruption in high and low places. His murder is bigger than people think.

"Rebel was the young Ghetto Prophet he sang of, speaking his mind in his humorous way . . . and a lot was going on. He may have offended certain people.

"In Trinidad, each and every one of us have bad friends, even if we not bad," El Faltino continued. "Big businessmen use money to control youths' heads and those who are too sensible to take a buyout may have a problem. But Rebel had the power of the streets without having to use a gun. He planned to build a school in his area, he was developing other artists . . . it was a whole movement. Rebel did not deserve it like that. He was always on a good path."

However, El Faltino insisted that the one I really had to talk to about his final days was Hugh Callender, Rebel's last manager.

From these two friends' narration, I learnt about Rebel's family. His mother was an ardent church-goer and Rebel's soprano was prized in the choir his mother made him join when he had been naughty – he got called Rebel because he was the one always pulling pranks in church. Growing up, he became a star school athlete and sang in a harmony trio, Z-Tech. But his upbringing was not smooth. Like Shane-O, the streets raised him. While Rebel was young, his hard-working mother, a nurse, had to travel a lot and lived for periods in the UK. His father, the singer called El Negro, was not a stable source of guidance or love and moved to America while Rebel was very young, essentially abandoning him.

TikTok features 2020 footage that would have surprised him – El Negro being applauded in a nightclub for singing Rebel's "Rifle War", a much-loved, ironic critique of gun fever, which had recently played in his son's funeral cortège. Comments beneath the post indicate that many in Trinidad knew how little El Negro had been around for Rebel.

So the youth was left to raise himself, in an exciting but treacherous metropolis.

Naturally, Rebel created his own family.

Before he was Sixx, aligning himself with Squash, Rebel was just called Rebel and he projected another identity; typically, one aligned to where he resided. Thus, in their early teenage years in Rasta City, Rebel and Swanny had harmonised together in the trio, Z-Tech. Then Rebel decided to split off. Locals look back nostalgically to that moment just before intra-crew beefs made them and others sub-divide into cliques that sound like numerological codes. Certain "Islam" followers became known as "9". After Rebel left and became a "6", his old crew of Swanny and Rasta City started to call themselves "7" and "4" – as if picking the right numbers could mean a free pass in the lottery of death. Between Rebel and Swanny, a notorious frenemy-ship was born.

To understand the significance of rapprochements between artists from different areas, like Rebel, Prince Swanny and Toppy Boss in Trinidad, or Squash's Salt Springs area in Jamaica and Tommy "Sparta" Lee in its adjacent rival, Flankers, some backstory may be called for.

Trinidad and Jamaica are both Caribbean islands, but in key ways, there the resemblance ends. Jamaica is bigger, Trinidad richer. Jamaica is mostly Black; the T & T population pie is split three pretty equal ways: Black, Indian and everybody else. While both economies are embedded in centuries of unpaid labour by captive Africans, their fates have been carved by geology. Once attached to Venezuela – and still attached, in terms of being an entrepôt for its cocaine and guns and human trafficking – Trinidad's oil resources mean that it has long been awash with petrodollars, depending on the market. In 2020, when much of this story occurs, Trinis earned on average about three times as much as Jamaicans.

Musically, satire has dominated sequential genres of witty calypso, happy, hearty soca and Trini rap, known as rapso. Starting in the 1940s, Trini calypso was so big worldwide that people thought Lord Invader's "Rum & Coca Cola" was actually by the crystal-voiced blonde Andrews Sisters – though their international hit was sanitised of the original references to local sex workers on US army bases.

The famous steel pan chimes the sound of rebellion; forged in the

1940s from oil drums that brought the island wealth, while the drum was banned by British colonisers in the still-turbulent Laventille area of Port of Spain. Since 1986's conscious soca record, David Rudder's "The Hammer", Trinidad has become a much more violent place – along with everywhere else. In pace with "urban" American music, rapso in the 1990s was Trinidad's response to hip-hop; while the current Trinibad crew, like Rebel, see themselves as gangster hip-hoppers reflecting Jamaican dancehall through the prism of Trini creativity.

Above all, the ancestral sexy glitter of Trini Carnival, marking Lent, is still the cultural hub. Its climaxes, like the Carnival Song Contest and Soca Monarch Competition, are calendar highlights that consume the island and magnetise international Trinis to do whatever it takes to get home.

"Liming", an active form of chilling, is a popular Trini activity, and InSight Crime lists party and events promotion among gangs' key activities, along with sex trafficking, money laundering and sandblasting for the endless concrete new builds, funding and thus cementing musicians' links with crime, organised, disorganised and governmental.

A poignant socio-economic distinction can be drawn between Jamaican vs Trini gangs' notorious key activities. Around St. James on the North Coast, Squash territory – dependent on tourism, slowed since COVID – scamming has become an art form. Requiring ingenuity, teamwork, collaboration and acting skills, laundered scam money helps to pay for some of the island's musical output. I was scammed myself and three years on, I am still battling the consequences. Scammers are vampire scum.

Meanwhile, in fatter Trinidad, it is well documented that the biggest local crime phenomenon involves politically aligned community leaders who sideline as gang chiefs (or vice versa), killing to secure government contracts.

When Rebel reinvented himself from being a Rasta City man to identifying with the 6ix, masterminded by Squash from faraway Salt Springs, he found himself a new family at home.

The 6iix were both loved and feared – what was their true identity? Squash was a hit sound creator with a following for his own songs like "Trending" and "Money Fever". Yet perturbingly, he often seemed close to the interests of his late elder brother, a gangster who had been shot by the Jamaican Police Force. He was also perceived to be the face of the G-City gang, whose connections with local criminal organisations were terrorising Atlanta and Miami. As well as posing for pictures with his adorable children, he for some reason chose to show off heavy weapons on TikTok.

Rebel didn't know or care about such talk. When it came to Squash, Rebel was a fanboy. And then – the prize. In Jamaica, Squash heard and loved Rebel's work, and their online exchange led to Squash's visit to Trinidad with members of his entourage.

And this is where we return to our narrators. Suave, serious Hugh Callender and his partner Kyle West at We Love Network strategise corporate brand and artist development ("Just say I'm all-around content production."). They met in 2019, when Rebel turned up at the hip recording studio Hugh managed, as part of Squash's crew. Cracking jokes but working hard as ever, Squash turned the session into a productive party. At the time, says Hugh, the two artists had just met; Rebel had been invited down in his capacity as, "the only official 6 in the country".

"It sounds like being invited to join the Freemasons," I venture.

Hugh laughs. "It felt almost like that. It was the relationship that they have, and how they keep this circle. You feel very safe with the 6, as a creative. Here in Trinidad, you kinda have to cross a lot of mountains and rivers to get to where you want to be. But them fellas move with a kind of confidence that makes you feel like, you know, it have no mountains. It have no river. It's just flat road. Because they have a kind of do anything mindset, in the sense of few limitations between creative and content."

The relationship grew, as Hugh invited Rebel to take part in a project, even filming him at home. Low-key at first, Rebel hung back, but was the only one who responded seriously to Hugh's encouragement: "I have a plan. I want you to manage my music career and platform and help make this dream real." Their collaboration began on Christmas Day of that year. "I have never known a musician work harder than Rebel," Hugh recollects. "He would be in the studio at eight and leave at ten, and write two or three new songs a day. He worked even harder than Squash."

He continues, "Rebel and Squash had a lot in common. They both raised themselves on the streets. The only difference was Squash is very close to his mother and they were often together in Jamaica. Rebel was also close to his mother, but they could only speak on the phone as she was in England. He hadn't seen her since he was a kid. So it felt good that the Sixx family embraced him fully – he was like their extension in Trinidad. That is the honour that they graced him."

It seems Rebel was always looking for a substitute El Negro. In another TV interview, he said, "I talk to Squash every day. He is literally like a father to me. Literally. He is my mentor." Domestically, El Faltino, the energetic hipster, and Hugh, businesslike and eloquent, became Rebel's guides. Grins El Faltino, "He used to call me Fada, even though I told him not to!" In their camp, Rebel became close to another of El Faltino's artists – sparky, witty K-Lion, whose light, skipping vocals were pushing the new strand of Trinibad they were calling Zess. The two recorded and hung out together.

Under Hugh's ministrations, the packaging, marketing and streaming of Rebel saw "Rifle War" soar to number one on the local Apple charts, get playlisted, within four days of its release. "We were trying to smooth up his image for the public but still keep it authentic."

Typically, the more acclaimed Rebel became, the more negative noises he heard rumoured, coming from certain Bad Minds in the vicinity. Encouraged by success, around this time, Rebel moved to Bon Air Gardens, Arouca, a slightly "better" neighbourhood that was more comfortable and was also nearer the studio and his family.

"Residing where he had been residing – in the hills of St. James, a tough area – Rebel had not even realised what a fan base he had till then," Hugh points out. St. James was a close-knit community, with old friends, but it would be nice to have a change of scene – and there would be new acquaintances, like the area leader "Nye", who occasionally booked him on shows. But trouble followed him.

A cop living across the road had turned his security cameras on his new neighbour full-time, which was more unnerving than reassuring, recalls Hugh. Then, to Rebel's distress, El Faltino remembers, some of his old Bad Mind acquaintance followed him to the new neighbourhood, increasing the artist's paranoia. For protection, he started to surround himself with five or six "soldiers" in the new yard.

In the public eye, though barbs had been flung in gossip and song, Swanny and Rebel were still in the same groove, on each other's playlists. Their paths had to cross, differences put aside as appropriate.

Thus, early in Carnival season, Rebel agreed to feature on a requested group recording uniting key Trinibad artists to promote Peace, called "Big Badness". Peace was definitely needed. With COVID-

19 looming, unemployment and fear rising, the murder rates in Port of Spain were raging. Rebel responded to the call for unity.

Carnival offered him a further chance to show support. The government of T & T, like that of all Caribbean islands, has long maintained an official interest in promoting its culture. Trinibad's key figures were put on official alert that they were to disrupt the venerable Soca Monarch Competition, held on 17 February 2020, with a "Zesser Segment" – Zesser being the more user-friendly name for Trinibad popularised by K-Lion.

The addition of Trinibad to the bill marked a changing of the musical guard. A good-times sound, soca now symbolised T & T's artistic establishment. So the Soca Monarch contest held in early February represented a tradition of friendly creative rivalry quite different from the vicious shoot-outs depicted by today's musicians. T & T's entertainment/political complex were clearly banking on Trinibad to sell internationally, despite or because of its lyrical violence.

Elated at making a difference, backstage TikTok videos show the bros laughing, drinking and singing together. But while the talk was of peace, the gang warfare kept going; it had practically become normalised for individual small areas to have at least one murder a week.

Right after the end of Carnival, COVID began to hit the island. Rebel dismissed the "soldiers" patrolling his yard. It was time to hunker down. Still, there was much excitement in the team, as Rebel was booked to play his first show off the island, in Barbados. But a problem irritated Rebel. When the Trinibad crew played the Soca Monarch Festival in February, they had expected to perform their peace tune, "Big Badness". But somehow the release had been delayed. Before leaving for Barbados, Rebel heard that certain artists had never completed their parts and the record was shelved indefinitely. It was all the more annoying as Rebel had only done it to take one for the establishment team – which was now dissing him. It felt sinister.

In Barbados right before Trinidad went into lockdown, Rebel even considered staying. But though it was tempting to duck the tensions of home, he couldn't abandon his folks – he had a newborn son – and the music.

The melancholy lure of "No Trust No Love", the first Rebel track to fascinate me, turns out to have been a premeditated strategy on the part of Rebel and Hugh, in tune with the times.

"We in Trinidad had just left a period of peace," Hugh explains. "There was supposed to be no more bad mind. We made 'No Trust

No Love' on purpose. I said we should work with Travis World. He is more corporate, he has a polished following, a good image and good distribution platforms that we would do well to put ourselves in line with. 'No Trust No Love' was our effort to go fully international. I calculated it was a good number one, and so said, so done."

On the morning of Wednesday, 3 June, Rebel messaged their group chat: "I want to drop 'No Trust' today."

Rebel's unease proved prophetic, Hugh recalls. "One week after 'No Trust No Love' came out, it was number one on the T & T Apple Music chart. Right then, everything was different. On June 10, we heard that K-Lion had died in Miami. He was twenty-seven years old and had seemed in perfect health. It changed Rebel. They said K-Lion had a heart attack playing football, but it was COVID-19 time and there was no autopsy. It seemed suspicious. Rebel broke down in the car when he heard, and from that day forward, it was a totally different Rebel. After that, he moved differently in the sense of not having that many high-risk people around him."

Days after K-Lion died, Nye, the friendly area leader who was producing a show featuring Rebel, was killed. His fate never made the news. Nye's replacement producer, who came from a different area, expected Rebel just to continue as planned . . . but with the death of his comrades, everything had got too hot. Rebel was very uneasy. He knew he was trapped. Whatever move he made would displease someone.

By now, the jollity of February's Soca Monarch Competition had evaporated. Mistrustful of the whole music/political/industry complex, at a moment when COVID had the island on lockdown anyway, as his success soared and the demands on him mounted, Rebel threw himself into a frenzy of creativity. Within three months, he laid down forty new songs – many of which, Hugh recalls, revolved around Bad Mind.

And then came a phone call – from whom Rebel never revealed: an invitation to join a press conference for peace with artists like Swanny, from his old haunt, Rebel City, and Muslim City people like Toppy Boss.

This peace gathering was one of many responding to the Morvant Killings, the 27 June 2020 murder of three men by the police in that area of Laventille whose impact was akin to that of George Floyd's. As gunfire held citizens hostage nightly, the murder rate spiked alongside mass protests for justice and peace. (In 2022, almost 10 per cent of the island's murders occurred in this one area, averaging at least one a week.)

This time, Rebel had turned them down.

Why? It's not as if Rebel didn't prefer peace, but he saw this press conference as a cosmetic charade. He was tired of playing what he saw as a phony peace game, particularly as he had spent the previous months wasting his time trying to fulfil everyone's expectations. He had been jerked around about Big Badness. Now, after the unexpected death of K-Lion, and the unacknowledged murder of Nye, he had lost faith in such performance.

The trajectory of Rebel's career now had a global thrust that looked set to far outstrip Swanny's or any of his other fellow Trinibad artists.

The following day, the rival Trinibad crews gathered for Peace: Rasta City and Muslim artists, Prince Swanny, Toppy Boss, Medz Boss, Lawless, Magic!, Siah Boss, Bravo, Leo King and Leroy. Bold hopes were stated to journalists and the mood was loving elation.

The only discordant note was the absence of Rebel Sixx.

The day after his no-show, Rebel Sixx was assassinated.

It was impossible for the public not to draw its own conclusions, though no one was ever convicted of the crime. The police closed the case after a couple of weeks. Fans raged that Prince Swanny had been seen on social media happily drinking as if glad of Rebel's demise – but he could have been laughing at fond memories. With virtually everyone in the T & T entertainment industry and associated bodies involved, how could anyone be implicated? Or so it seemed to settle.

What failed to feature in Trinidad's articles after Rebel's death was another factor in his complicated, ambitious life. The response to his new song, the 6ix-oriented "868 King", with its steel pans, had been so strong that Rebel was ready to make a change.

"Though Rebel would always love Squash, we were trying to leave the 6ix, this stigma and the box that people were already trying to put us in, and become international now," Hugh explains. If there really was love in their bromance, Squash would understand Rebel's need to distance himself professionally, not personally, drop the Sixx and just call himself Rebel again. Could Squash himself, disillusioned, possibly be implicated? I asked Hugh, who laughed at the idea and stated that such a thing was out of the question.

As if to guarantee that some mystery will always envelop Rebel's killing, there is a dispute regarding the date of the peace gathering held at George Street. Sources said it happened on Saturday, 6 July, the day before Rebel got shot. Others insist that it took place the previous day and that the mix-up is a manipulation – misinformation calculated to make people think that Rebel was killed solely because he was not there.

Whereas several factions were after him; like a John le Carré novel, it was a case of spin the bottle to see who succeeded first. Rebel had been paranoid as he understood twisted Bad Mind thinking. He knew that some would blame him for the death of his pal Nye. Equally, Rebel's refusal to co-operate with his successor from a different team might have made a new enemy. Or could a threat come from someone who hated the 6ix, or loved them and heard he might leave? Rebel's reality was fragmenting as if in a hall of distorting mirrors.

Whichever, on the day the papers reported the peace gathering took place, Rebel had a quiet but productive day at home in Bon Air Gardens. In the afternoon, he had a long phone call with his mother in London. Later in the day, El Faltino dropped by. They spoke of Rebel's plan to move from Bon Air Gardens as soon as possible.

"Certain energies weren't working any more. We were looking for somewhere we could be safe."

"Where did you have in mind?" I ask.

"We didn't find nowhere."

Rebel was pleased to play El Faltino "Badness Cya Done", a new track he had just delivered to Automatic Records. Melancholy, rippling with subdued beats, the "Fully Dunce" phrase he made so popular had now changed to "Fully Paranoid". The lyrics run: "You could win inna music / Still get yuh life lose."

"It was a message," says El Faltino.

The 6ix are scarcely mentioned in the song; but at its close, Rebel once again refers to himself by his old persona, Ghetto Prophet.

We would never know Rebel's next incarnation.

With a bitter half-smile, Hugh describes how, though he was sick, he made it to Rebel's house the night he heard of the shooting, only to be told by the police that the investigation would take its course. "That moment was pivotal for me, because I realised that, yo, these people know exactly what happened. They are complicit in this. They have no interest in doing anything about it, and this is how it's gonna be."

Cruelly, the world was just opening up for Rebel.

Hugh remembers. "In the week before he was shot, Rebel got his first international bookings: two in New York and one in the UK. We got a double fee for one of those as a down payment and after the fact, the promoter said, 'I don't want it back. Keep that money for the family and funeral.'"

One way or the other, peace was part of the mix that slayed Rebel Sixx. Or rather, in true Orwellian fashion, the phony projection of "peace" as some sort of hollow feel-good trope. Now, all our words have become like slippery chameleons and when we try to grab their true meaning by the tail, they change colour.

It might seem like a small story, a local rivalry between musicians; but as Rebel's fate reveals, young entertainers do not work in a vacuum. In a petri dish of talent and Bad Mind, suspended in poverty, an independent-minded artist might be expected to fulfil the agenda of others whose worldview might differ from their own; and to toe a line that keeps wavering and all too often disappears completely.

As the investigation was closed with comparative speed, maybe we will never know exactly whodunnit. But for Rebel's friends, some connection between that peace no-show and his death does not seem self-evident. Despite his best intentions, Rebel had people gunning for him in both high and low places, as El Faltino pointed out, quoting Bob Marley who knew what he was singing about. An optical "peace" mentality seems like the flip side of the same weighted coin as Bad Mind.

"Every time you see a peace concert, just know that behind it is darkness," opines Hugh. "For somebody to openly propagandise and want to showcase that form of theatre, it means they have an agenda."

He recalled others, less grounded in the community than Marley's, half a century ago – like the Amnesty and Peace signing of 2005. "In the weeks following, all the guys who signed the Peace dropped, one after the next. When these events do rise authentically, there are bound to be attempts to cut them down from the powers that be. They don't want positive change that doesn't benefit the establishment, as they see it. In no time in history has it been different."

The loss of both K-Lion and his bred'ren, Rebel, so close together, cut the sapling of Trinibad at the roots. Toppy Boss mourned them in a song that was otherwise all bums and guns. But an infinity of mourning can sap energy needed to make change. Trinidad and the world lost another of its most promising talents before his prime. Is it really too late to give *proper* peace a chance?

"Hope is there!" insists Hugh confidently. "Because Trinibad, like rapso, is the new branch of a legacy that comes from steel pan and calypso. They all represent the decision to go against what is popular or deemed acceptable and choose to carve your own voice and your own way. It *is* a decision, and when those guys make that decision, they almost always accept the rest. It is an attempt to try and leave the situation they have grown in and it is do or die. The irony is, if you do, you might die, too, but you might get a better life and be able to get a house for your mum."

No doubt Squash has long since bought a fine residence for his beloved, flamboyant mum, Shelley Anne Millwood. Through his travails, she has become his spokeswoman. As I was driving to the airport to fly home to New York – and its own lethal forms of craziness, guns and gangs included – news came on the radio that Millwood had just confirmed Squash's release from those ICE charges in Florida. Interested parties can only await forthcoming music and events from Salt Springs and the 6ix crew – with hope.

CHAPTER 8

Fela Aníkúlápó Kuti

You could only get African music at Stern's record shop in London's West End when punk began, and vinyl 12-inches of Fela's *Zombie* were prized. When Joe Strummer of The Clash was singing about London burning with boredom, right about the time the political gunmen tried to kill Bob Marley, the Nigerian military government was burning down Fela Aníkúlápó Kuti's compound and raping his Queens, causing the death of Funmilayo Ransome-Kuti, his celebrated activist mother.

Today's dominant Afrobeats sound sonically differs from its namesake, but its creators made sure Fela's name would mark the consciousness of a new era. Many musicians interviewed in this book owe Fela, like Brian Eno and David Byrne, particularly their album *My Life in the Bush of Ghosts*. In Nigeria, Fela has been described as Africa's punk.

To speak about the links between Bob and Fela, I was invited to Lagos for the annual Felabration in 2013. It hit me how lucky I was to have worked closely with and been influenced by them both. So many parallels connect them, as post-colonial pan-Africanists developing a musical language for their newly independent nations; and yet, they were very different. Bob knew how to switch on the high power where it counted, onstage, but part of his appeal was that of a shy guy, tough but still vulnerable. He liked quietness, to lay back, be an observer and study the people. When Fela entered a room in some amazing, tailor-made, embroidered outfit, magnetic smile flashing, humour-edged voice booming – everyone knew it, differently. In his Alpha masculinity, he more closely resembled Peter Tosh.

Fela Aníkúlápó Kuti

Since the early 2010s, Nigeria's subtle, melodic electronica, Afrobeats, has dominated the dance world everywhere. Don't be misled; the name is a homage to the man, but the sound and meaning are quite different. Fela fused his old/new land's music (Nigeria was just emerging from British colonialism) with the shoots that had sprung from it, like James Brown, and forged the Afrobeats that consolidated people locally and globally, as well as rhythms. There grows Baaba Maal's concept of the spreading tree of Afro-diasporic music again, sheltering us all!

Here, I encounter Fela and the Queens for the first time and am invited into their vibrant extended family – a connection that lasts to this day. This story is also quite a reminder of how empires rise and fall. When this article was written, the American multinational monolith ITT (International Telephone and Telegraph), the focus of Fela's rage, seemed as enduring as the pyramids. Four decades on, sophisticated students on my New York University Fela course have never heard of it.

"Fela Kuti: The Rascal Republic Takes on the World"

First published in New Musical Express, *18 October 1980*
(Interview jointly conducted with Fela's then manager, Martin Meissonier)

Fela Aníkúlápó Kuti plans to become president of Nigeria in 1983.

He's already Africa's most popular musician, with over 100 LPs to his credit. He also has twenty-seven wives.

After another brush with the authorities in Italy recently, he told his incredible story of high life, near-death, CIA plots and political intrigue.

Fela Aníkúlápó Kuti has twenty-seven wives and at least sixteen of them are creating a sensation in The Colosseum in Rome. Perhaps if you released a pride of famished lions among the earnest Scandinavian tourists and nuns shepherding their jailbait flocks along like clucking mother geese, they'd be as big a tourist attraction.

Basically, the seventy-strong folk of Africa 70 don't want to see the Colosseum at all, but ever since their luggage landed at Milan Airport before they did, and 45 kilos of killer Nigerian weed was found, magically, in the first seven cases customs looked at, their time hasn't gone according to plan.

Some people say that Fela, Africa's most prominent musician, leader of the Nigerian MOP (Movement of the People) party and proposed candidate for the Nigerian Presidency in the 1983 elections, would do anything for publicity. But the most cynical PR would think twice before prejudicing his political credibility in such a stupid way.

The seventy wandering musicians were originally invited by the Italian Communist Party to play at their annual L'Unita Festival – a nationwide weeks-long shindig. But as it happened – as it was supposed to happen, Kurt Vonnegut and conspiracy theorists would say – the grass bust shattered all their plans. Their passports were taken away. Fela himself spent days in Milan's Busto Arsizio prison until an American woman "friend" of Africa 70's – 27-year-old Susan Rochelle Findlay – confessed to planting the pot and was imprisoned instead.

By that time, Fela had garnered reams of sensationalist press all over the continent and was forced to cancel date after date. It appeared that, though his name was cleared, his presence was proving something of an embarrassment to the Communist Party (CP).

Right now, while the sixteen or so Queens are prettily posing for stacks of Instamatics, Fela is in the middle of a four-hour confab at CP HQ. He didn't need to fly to Italy to face the dope charge. He could have stayed in Holland, where the news of the grass discovery reached him, but he preferred to face the charges and prove his innocence. At Amsterdam Airport, catching the plane for Milan, Fela announced that he thought the pot was planted on him by the CIA.

It's obvious that when Fela finally arrives to gather his tribe at the Colosseum, he is deeply weary. Apparently, the CP officials were polite, apologetic, concerned even. We're sorry, it's all been such an unfortunate misunderstanding. Perhaps you'd like to try again next year?

Fela, who has now been forced to sink at least £16,000 he can ill afford into this abortive excursion, poses for photos in front of the Colosseum. As photographer Giovanni Canitano begins to shoot,

Fela lifts his arms in the traditional gesture of black power. It's a reflex movement, an instinctive response when the camera is pointed in his direction. But the familiar motion seems to trigger a pre-set response and a new energy seems to pulse through him. Fela looks about him, at the Africa 70 musicians, and suddenly his fist punches the air with great authority, and he flashes a big beacon smile. The musicians begin to smile back.

The Instamatics start to flash.

Them go dey cause confusion, cause corruption, cause inflation . . .
"International Thief Thief (I.T.T.)" by Fela Aníkúlápó Kuti

A shitty story it is, indeed. In fact, you could say this particular chapter starts with ten buckets of the stuff, which Fela and friends smeared all over the house of a Mr Abiola, Nigerian Chairman of ITT (International Telephone and Telecommunications, an American multinational company), leading politician within the ruling National Party of Nigeria, and shareholder in Decca Records.

Fela and Decca Records have a long and stormy history. Anyone who saw *Konkombe: The Nigerian Pop Music Scene*, Jeremy Marre's recent TV documentary, will remember the sit-in staged by Fela and cohorts in the Decca offices when the company refused to pay him certain moneys. It's said that two women gave birth in the managing director's office. The shit-spreading episode, although it was prompted by a further non-payment, has a deeper significance. ITT has links with the CIA, researched in such books as Gary MacEoin's *Chile: The Struggle for Dignity*.

It's a familiar story of destabilisation. A dependency on American funding is set up and when the Third World nation decides to go it alone, the cold turkey throes can be sufficient to drive the nation back to its old supplier. The big multinational companies play a crucial role in this process.

Fela feels that ITT have been particularly noxious in Nigeria – a country that has very little running water, electricity or sanitation, although it supplies oil to the world. He has been very militant in his anti-ITT publicity. Apart from singing specific finger-pointing songs like "International Thief Thief (I.T.T.)", he's also given eighty-three university lectures on the subject in the past year.

Like any good detective, Fela marshals the information about the customs bust to back up his CIA allegations: Susan Findlay, the

American teacher who confessed to planting the "Indian hemp", as the Italians quaintly called it, is actually employed by the Nigerian government, with whom Abiola is involved. Piece together Abiola's involvement with Decca, the government and ITT, then add the crucial fact that he, like Fela, intends to run for Nigerian President in the 1983 elections, and, as Fela says, "the connection is just too tempting".

Up till 1969, Fela didn't occupy his present position as the most specifically political musician working today. Others, like Gil Scott-Heron, are equally direct in their lyrics, but which other musicians, with the possible exception of Linton Kwesi Johnson and the Plastic People, have merged their art and their direct action so incisively?

Thinking back to his pre-political days, Fela says: "Maybe if I'd have known, I'd have shelved the idea. Maybe." He laughs. He's anxious that we understand he's joking.

At the concert in Naples' main square, the audience couldn't believe their luck. Fela and Africa 70's dance music is like a solid fuel injection of percussion, horns and voices. Fela plays jazzy saxophone and keen, stabbing organ. The rhythm guitar carries much of the momentum – it chatters in your ear and won't go away. The bass is sadly lost in the mix tonight, but it's possible to sense it loping deep in there.

It's overgrown salsa, fertilised to Amazonian tropical excess. Almost all of Fela's seventy co-workers seem to be onstage, complete with singing and dancing Queens – it's George Clinton's ideal onstage party pandemonium, seriously wild.

Fela plays for two and a half hours – nothing, a holiday compared to the usual four-night-a-week, four and a half hour sets they play at their Lagos club, the Shrine. Fela had to control his own club. No Lagos club would allow him to play, despite his massive popularity.

Each song lasts over half an hour – churning, ever-changing rhythms that drive the audience to grasshopper-leaping ecstasy. But the Italians are probably missing a good portion of the excitement – understanding those fiery, scaldingly ironic words brands your memory, sugar-coated with pure, uncut Afrobeat. The rhythms remind you that life is fun. You're listening, then you're dancing, and you haven't felt so good for weeks. It's the words that keep on getting Fela Kuti into trouble.

Armed robber him need gun, authority man him need pen . . .
"Authority Stealin'" by Fela Aníkúlápó Kuti

Those lyrics are from Fela's latest scorcher of a disco mix, the first release on his own Kalakuta records label. No pressing plant in Nigeria would touch it, with its explicit references to a recent Nigerian political scandal. They call it "Oilgate" – the mysterious disappearance of nearly three billion Naira (Nigerian currency) of public money. Inside each record is an issue of the Africa 70 broadsheet, *YAP* (Young African Pioneer) News, its motto: "Our challenge is never to suffer again."

It contains a transcript of the "Oilgate" trial in which Fela makes explicit accusations against the Nigerian government, plus a copy of the crucial piece of incriminating evidence: a money draft made out to one Abasanjo, former head of Nigeria's military government, stamped by the Nigerian Medical Association, for 860.15 billion Naira.

Fela pressed the record up in Ghana and had to smuggle it into Nigeria to evade their record import ban.

We meet the day after the Naples show, in Fela's seedy hotel room. He sits in the corner, holding court, dressed in threadbare mauve Y-fronts. The room is full of Queens, lying four to the bed like sensual sardines, and musicians sitting on every available surface.

These are the people of whom Fela's Cambridge-educated lawyer, George Gardner (son of a UN adviser on African affairs), later says: "They have ties stronger than blood. Every person on this tour has scars. Kwesi (Yupe, Fela's political and media adviser) has had his ribs and leg broken twice. He still has bayonet holes in his head. And that's just in the past eighteen months. Every rebel in Nigeria, everyone who will stand up and be counted, is here."

Fela talks fluently for two and a half hours, occasionally looking to one of his people for confirmation. He passes round photos of a meeting of his MOP party, in a sports stadium. The place is packed. Fela's arms are raised in that perennial victorious gladiator's salute. At the last election, MOP was not allowed to register: Fela has plans to bypass the ban, standing independently in the 1983 elections. He calls himself the Black President because, he says, he's more popular than the Nigerian President.

We'll know in 1983. Is it a coincidence that that's the year when the reggae songs say Africa will be free?

Fela comes from an upper-class, ecclesiastical background. His brother's a professor of paediatrics in Lagos and heads the Nigerian Medical Association.

One day, many years ago, the market women came to visit Fela's mother and complained that they were being unfairly taxed. Fela's mother got up from her chair, he remembers, and went to help them, thus starting a career in politics that took her all over the world, even to Russia and, at Mao's invitation, to China. On her way back from China, her passport was seized by the British Government. Like her son in years to come, she was getting to be too much trouble.

Thus, Mrs Ransome-Kuti (as the family name then was) was unable to visit her son while he studied in Trinity Music College, London. Fela lived in Ladbroke Grove, Bayswater, and hung out at Ronnie Scott's and The Marquee, The Flamingo, the Roaring Twenties (now Colombo's), jazz clubs, playing with jazz musicians from all over the place. (Incidentally, his celebrated association with Ginger Baker doesn't date from this period, though Fela saw him play with Cream then.)

Despite maternal and cosmopolitan input, Fela's political awakening began in 1969, when he took his musicians on a frustrating visa-less tour of the US. There, he met with scant respect for African music and musicians (except from producer H.B. Barnum) and was overwhelmed with the size and scale of New York: "I felt like a cockroach."

Fela was baffled by the sudden knowledge that Nigeria's leaders had been hiding the fullness of the twentieth century from their people. He travelled across the States and said, "I couldn't talk, couldn't participate in subjects because I didn't have the knowledge. I saw that the colonial education and upbringing, which America was involved in too, was very badly wild. History starts with Mungo Park 'discovering' the Niger! This pushed me so much I said I would die in the struggle.

"I was singing high-life, jazz, nothing deep. Short, short love songs, stupid, about the rain or something. I wasn't thinking as an African. With the self-insight I got in the States, I vowed I was going into politics. I also saw the power I could have through using music."

His education was intensified by a relationship with a Black Panther woman in Los Angeles (who shocked him by revealing she'd been in jail for kicking a policeman at a demonstration) and he started to try to write African music, first by copying the rhythms of a pioneering London-based Nigerian musician called Ambrose Campbell. At that stage, Fela was a political innocent. "I didn't see any opposition at home. I thought any African who heard this idea must buy it. I didn't know I would start a lot of trouble."

*

The trouble began almost imperceptibly, when the police stopped him from playing his new pan-African militant music in a club he part-owned.

He won that court case.

Then, on 30 April 1974, the police raided his house and tried to implicate him in a big grass bust. He wound up spending time in prison till his name was cleared. "In that prison, we had order – a president, an attorney, a sanitary inspector. The place was so crowded, but the prisoners set up the order. They called it the Kalakuta Republic – 'Kalakuta' means rascal, it's an East African word.

"I used to think criminals were just – criminals. In jail I found they were intelligent people, who wanted to better their lives. I told them I would rename my house Kalakuta Republic, not knowing I was bringing real trouble and confusion on my head . . ."

The police raids were systematic now. One morning, just before Fela was due to pick up the band's passports for a Cameroons tour, the police broke into his bedroom and planted him with a spliff. Fela grabbed the joint, swallowed it, washed it down with a swig of whisky and lectured the policeman about how wrong they were to persecute him when he was trying to fight for them.

Nonetheless, they attempted (unsuccessfully) to wash his stomach out in hospital and then locked him up again for three days to observe his shit.

Fela ate lots of vegetables. At night, when the guards were sleeping, other prisoners passed him chamber pots and then hid the contents. When he finally sat down to deliver on the morning he was due to go back to court, he remembers proudly, "I gave them a nice, clean shit."

This incident is commemorated in his song "Expensive Shit". The cover of that album shows the barbed wire fence that now surrounded the growing Kalakuta Republic, its tentacles creeping down the road as more and more people wandered into the house and decided to stay on, camping outside. The original wooden posts were replaced by barbed wire, Fela electrocuted the barbed wire. When the authorities really decided to smash up this offensive state-within-a-state, they would have to switch off the electricity in the whole neighbourhood – but that was still a couple of years away . . .

In the meantime, the Nigerian press was full of clashes between Fela and the police. He was raided for any and every reason, repeatedly taken to court, jailed and beaten, till the Chief of Police decided to meet Fela for himself. Fela describes him as "a thoughtful man", though it does seem as if his thought processes lagged slightly in Fela's case. At any rate, finally convinced of Fela's integrity, police harassment suddenly ceased for two years, till 1977.

At that time, the Nigerian government's military powers made our sus laws seem like a summer holiday – the army were entitled to pick people up and beat them at random in the streets, for traffic offences and the like.

But while the official Nigerian Arts Festival – Festac – was going on, the soldiers began to pick up foreign journalists and visiting artists. Not surprisingly, many of these visitors began to gravitate to the Kalakuta Republic. When Africa 70 staged their own mini-Festac at the Shrine, its success aggravated the regime still further. They were already vexed at the initial appearance of *YAP News*, although, as Fela explains, "It was a heavy manifesto, not an attack, so they couldn't hold me for sedition."

The serious trouble, the trouble that people who've hardly heard of Fela Kuti know about, began when one of Fela's people was badly beaten in the streets. He made it back to the Kalakuta Republic, but as Fela was organising transport to hospital, the army arrived demanding to arrest the beaten man. Fela refused. War broke out.

The carnage was almost inconceivable. Fela pauses even now when he remembers and shakes his head. "It was terrible . . . terrible . . ." His mother, 78 years old, was thrown from a second-storey window and died soon after.

Later, Fela and followers used her mock coffin – Fela wanted to use her actual corpse, but the rest of his family wouldn't agree – for a protest. They left it in a window of the burned-out Kalakuta Republic, in the heart of Lagos, with a sign saying "This is the spot where justice was murdered." When the military regime handed over to an equally dubious, according to Fela, coalition government, they left the coffin as a silent protest in front of government HQ. She would have approved.

Almost all of Fela's wives were raped by soldiers. One had broken bottles sewn into her vagina at the hospital. Aleike, Fela's most loquacious wife, remembers the high jinks they played in prison that time, fooling the wardens by hiding precious cigarettes in toilet rolls in their vaginas – just like prisoners in Irish H Blocks today, discovering all kinds of new anal functions.

When the army burned the house, they also burned the soundtrack for a film Africa 70 had just finished. Fela crossed to Ghana, to try to salvage the remains.

There, he found a government even more repressive and vicious than the one he'd left behind. It only took three months for Fela to be deported; the official reason was that he had taken the side of some market women in a street argument. But Ghanaian students had been using Fela's anti-military song, the hypnotic "Zombie" – "It's against the kind of mind that takes orders without thinking" – as a rallying-call.

With the help of Kwesi Yupe (then the only outspoken editor in Ghana, whose *Catholic Herald* was repeatedly raided by the police) till he had to flee with Fela to escape worse, Fela met with student leaders and encouraged them to close down the universities. Under the circumstances, it's perhaps surprising Fela was there as long as three months.

"I have to keep passing the message of pan-Africanism wherever I am. They were annoyed . . ."

It was these events that decided Fela to marry the women who'd supported him through such extreme tribulations – twenty-seven of them, including his original wife, British-bred Remy. She comments, "I didn't mind. Before that, he used to have lots of girlfriends. Now at least he's honest."

The marriage took place in the Ifa religion, a traditional African religion Fela has been rediscovering as part of his pan-African quest. Anyway, it's traditional in African culture for a man to have as many wives as he can afford to buy from their parents and support.

"Doesn't that imply women are just a piece of property to be bought and sold, even if the sum is nominal as you say, Fela?"

"Aha, now you understand," says Fela mysteriously.

She go do anything he say / But lady, no be so . . .
"Lady" by Fela Aníkúlápó Kuti

That's one of Fela's old big hits, wherein the approved cultural African woman knows her place – *kinder, kirche, küche* (children, church, kitchen), as the Nazis were so fond of saying.

Here, we're confronted with the anomaly of "radical" people intent on finding their freedom through rediscovering traditional cultural habits that many people were thrilled to see the back of. Men are usually quite attached to these traditions that ensure a non-stop mother/nurse/cook/cleaner figure, unpaid.

Fela's Queens share a cheery, girls' dorm, sisterly rapport. Fela explains, "My affinity for sex helps keep them together. I sleep with two or three a day, so none of them gets too neglected." Long faces among the Queens often indicated, if their teasing is anything to go by, that the Queen in question has somehow got stuck on the rota and is anxiously awaiting her turn.

If a wife is "unfaithful", the other Queens are dutifully supposed to report back to the King. Despite nasty rumours about wives locked in rooms, they themselves say his punishments are not too severe.

Admittedly, Aleike is a favourite Queen, and as such has little cause for gloom, but her view of the multiple-wife structure is very positive: "If he was a harsh man, none of us would stay with him." Only fifteen or so have left to date – and there's doubtless a queue of potential Queens.

Everyone in the family finds it quite reasonable. If any Queen is dissatisfied, she's free to pack her bags and go marry someone else, just like that. It's a disturbing thought, though, that after a period of intense involvement with, and economic dependency on Fela, a Queen might have some difficulty in finding a new niche.

Aleike is bouncy and bubbly. She used to be a fashion model and is still pleased to pose for the snap-happy tourists.

She comes of a "colonial" family – father a judge, mother a nursing sister – who gave her a proper convent education, then cut her off when she went to live with Fela in her late teens. Fela taught her to be an "African woman" and to overcome Western indoctrinations like jealousy. Western feminist conceptions of what constitutes freedom appear irrelevant to her; she has found her freedom through Fela, she says. "Fela trusts us. I pray we will never let him down."

If you're intent on retrieving African identity through reabsorption of traditional customs, apparently "tradition" is a virtue in itself. World Health Organisation statistics say that about five million young African women a year undergo the clitoridectomy operation; their clitorises are either cut or removed without anaesthetic. Aleike says that this (to me) absolutely horrific operation is OK: it's cultural. Kwesi, Fela's radical political adviser ("I'm a political animal") endorses it, too. Speaking from personal experience, he says that "cut" women are more sexually sensitive and responsive. Not surprising, since they've been mutilated so that they can only receive vaginal sexual pleasure.

Still, back home in Lagos, the neighbours who insulted the raped women as whores now respect them as "Fela's Queens".

Sometimes the terms "radical" and "colonial" seem to blur around the edges.

Aleike tells me stories of how people who've abused Fela's generosity often meet bad deaths, as if by magic. "Many people say he's a god, sent to do things for the African people."

It's five years now since Fela changed from his slave name, Ransome-Kuti, to his new name, Aníkúlápó Kuti. It means a traditional hunter, who controls death with the magic amulets he carries in a pouch by his side.

I ask Fela why he thinks he hasn't been killed yet.

"They like me. It's a bundle of contradictions. They beat me a lot, but they don't see the point in killing Fela who makes music."

I never did find out what's in the leather pouch Fela always wears round his neck.

*

For many years, this next article was my favourite article of all. I couldn't help it – the story is just so sensational, so exotic for anyone from anywhere, that the night I describe was never forgotten by those present. But its surreal exhilaration gave way to sadness, as understanding grew that the relationship between Fela and Professor Hindu, aka Kwaku Addai, was toxic. The association caused despair among Fela's friends, family and musicians as he fell more deeply beneath Professor Hindu's spell and became increasingly erratic. In this instance, Fela's urge to redefine African-ness after years of British colonialism would harm him severely. The yearning to penetrate true African science would compel Fela ever more intensely, even as the brilliant leader largely withdrew from the world as the effects of the AIDS, whose existence he rejected, consumed him. Undoubtedly, a lifetime of torture, near-death beatings at the hands of Nigeria's army and police, and repeated imprisonments also contributed to the early end of a complex, flawed but magnificent man. But even after death, Fela proved unstoppable; his musical and activist influence, unending.

"Resurrection Shuffle"

First published in New Musical Express, *14 January 1984*

About 200 people turned out last weekend at the Country Club in North London, for a benefit to prevent its closure. Entertainment was provided by Nigerian musician Fela Aníkúlápó Kuti's spiritual brother and sorcerer, the Ghanaian Professor Hindu.

No one knew what the entertainment would be, exactly, but Professor Hindu's feats are legend. He'd already cut one boy in Lagos to bits and reassembled him at a later date, and burned another then scattered his ashes on the sea. Fela's wife Sewa told me she'd seen the sea judder, then give up the now-intact human torch.

Thus, on Friday, 6 January 1984, we all watched as the professor cut a man's throat and buried him outside the club. Two days later on Sunday, 8 January, we gathered round the rough grave for the resurrection. The buried man's brother had stood guard in the meantime.

"I can't believe this is happening in Camden Town," breathed one awestruck youth standing next to me. Fela Kuti in the kind of massive fur coat that rhymes with Cadillac and his son, Femi "The God", casually dressed in embroidered gold-and-ivory robes, stood solemnly at the other end of the grave.

We were all waiting for The Resurrection. Professor Hindu, the Ghanaian man of magic, was stalking the sodden soil, jabbing a finger and spouting incomprehensible incantations.

The 200-odd assembly was shivering, barring the professor himself. As if to show his disdain for the material world, he was wearing only red-and-blue underpants, long socks and Italian shoes.

The earth was pulled away. Then, just like the end of *Carrie*, a limb appeared. Amid mass gasps, the body was pulled out. Soon, the limp, dirty body was being carried into the shelter of the Country Club. He was a sorry sight, a far cry from the inarticulate but still normal character who'd stood by Professor Hindu two nights before, meekly offering himself in all good faith to the magic man's powers.

It seemed a safe enough bet. Fela's spiritual brother had already magicked several gold and silver watches from nowhere that I could see, and reassembled shreds of fabric into a pretty striped dress and skirt for a young female he'd pulled from the audience. I ran into her later in the ladies and she seemed completely dazed.

"The skirt's a bit big," she said, tugging the waistband.

A woman stood beside her saying, “This could mean great things for you. TV, theatre. Just leave your name and address.”

“I will,” the girl breathed back.

Professor Hindu is a jolly chap, with well-muscled legs and a protruding navel. His habit of shredding his tongue, laying the slivers on a piece of cotton wool and then firmly re-slotting them into place has left his tongue with an irregular shape but no scars. Though it does strike this particular Western eye as unhygienic, to say the least. I saw him drop a piece of his tongue on the dirty stage and not even wash it before putting it back.

Stomping round, blood dribbling down his bare chest, the professor sharpened knives and machetes, then sliced fabric swiftly to prove their point. The prof cut the geezer’s throat, all right. Blood was everywhere, the wound gaping. A piece of cloth was tied round his neck and the poor sod was carried out into the rainy Hampstead January night and interred in the deep hole that had us all guessing, by the entrance.

Unfaithfully, I felt sure that when our backs were turned, the bloke would leap from the grave, or else, even more uncharitably, that he’s stay there for eternity, as no one would bother to check the Resurrection out.

But the Sunday was even more crowded. As a crowd-warmer, the prof showered the room with watches then called another audience helper. He already had a nice suit, so the professor, having previously shredded and reassembled his tongue like a Meccano set, created some smart underpants from scraps.

I cornered him later and asked: “Well, were they from Marks and Sparks?”

“No,” replied the impressed young man. “It’s his own label inside. Professor Hindu underpants.”

After the disinterment, the body was laid out on the stage, only the merest rise and fall of the chest hinting at possible life. The professor was rough with his resurrection. Being awakened from a three-day sleep by shouts of “Ho!” and swift kicks in scalp and chest isn’t my idea of a wake-up call.

“Pollutina! Hezekina!” the professor proclaimed.

Fela had previously explained that the professor, though a great spiritualist, was lacking in book learning and English as a language.

“When I bury this person, many people say, ‘This is London, not Afrika! You’ll get trouble.’”

The mud-caked body shuddered more and more, rousing slowly from its trance.

"But Brother Fela wanted my capacity through the One-ness to surprise the European!"

The body trembled more forcefully, as if an earthquake were rousing its cold bones. A couple more kicks, then the Experiment rose to its feet, looking, as you can imagine, well out of it – red eyes that could scarcely open, limping, the works.

"Now it's not a body, it's alive!" exclaimed the prof, ripping off the bandage to reveal a red bruised-looking neck but no scars.

As the resurrected man was helped off, the Professor advertised his abilities: "I can help a person with any problem! If you want promotion, business, to roll a baby, I can help you! Call me at the Hotel Russell! And buy these magic rings, only £5!"

A few more agreeable hours were spent, bopping to the African disco of Jumbo Earthworks, when who should approach me on the dance floor but the undead himself, Mr Vivisection. Now spruced up and wearing real outerwear, he was still not a pretty sight: wandering, odd eyes, a big scar down his face; in fact, everything but a bolt through his neck.

Although his English is minimal, I understood he wanted to dance. I preferred to talk.

"Were you really under the ground?"

He nodded, halfway between Harpo Marx and Lurch from *The Addams Family*.

"Did you stay there for three whole days?"

Mr Vivisection shook his head.

"You mean—" I continued, when he interrupted.

"I love you. Come to my hotel," he said and began waving a key in my face.

"No," I said, "I'm busy. So did you—"

"But I have money. Plenty money," he retorted crossly.

"That's not the point. Now, what happened—"

"So find me another woman. Look, look."

"Find your own bloody woman," I answered and stalked off. Being resurrected is no excuse.

Next day, my phone rang a few times – all folk who'd been at the Club wanting to know what had happened. No one could make it out, least of all me. Even if Mr Vivisection only had his throat cut a bit and stayed underground for six hours, not three days, he made a remarkable recovery. And those Professor Hindu underpants can't be bought in Kensington Market and really belong in the Victoria and Albert Museum Costume Collection. If the prof had raw liver secreted in his mouth and didn't slice his tongue at all, how come his voice sounded so normal?

Sadly, by the time you read this, Professor Hindu will have winged back to strife-torn Lagos. But before he cuts out, maybe he can do something about my phone bill.

*

Fela's relationship with his glamorous, talented Queens was unusual, possibly unique. Even regular polygamous marriages, like some Queens' own families, weren't like Fela's domestic arrangements. There was always plenty of drama and excitement going on, not unlike a girl's dormitory at boarding school, as well as creative sisterhood. I fondly remember hanging round with them, lounging together on every available surface, all of us inventively painting our faces – me following their bold lead. Suffice it to say that the Queens really loved Fela – and if they wanted a change, they left, no problem. But most stayed and wanted to be by his side even when he was terribly sick. So dazzling and energetic was their onstage presentation – visually, musically, their dance – that it was good to discover what lay behind the Queens' performance. As with Bob Marley and his I Three backing singers, Fela also picked his female singers and dancers well. As you might expect, Fela had a lot to do with their artistry – but not everything.

"Afrobeat Aesthetic and the Dancing Queens"

First published in Fela: From West Africa to West Broadway *by Trevor Schoonmaker. Basingstoke: Palgrave Macmillan, 2003.*

The Shrine, Lagos, 1985: Femi Kuti was onstage, passionately performing a song about institutionalised African anarchy, "Madness Unlimited". Behind him, the horn section that usually backed his incendiary father, Afrobeat creator Fela Aníkúlápó Kuti, wailed as if in protest of his forced absence. Two backing singers, their second-skin African print minidresses cinched with beads, undulated on high heels behind him. Their faces were dotted with red, yellow, blue and white dots that swirled like crop circles or aboriginal art.

Wearing a narrow red suit embroidered with abstract designs, Femi was carrying the message forward to an international audience for "Lagos Jump", a documentary I co-produced for Channel 4's *The Tube*. All the aesthetic manifestations of a radical philosophy were being continued as the son played in living tribute to yet another jail term in his father's thirty-year struggle with a succession of Nigeria's military regimes. This time, Fela was imprisoned on trumped-up currency smuggling charges and it was up to Femi to hold the operation together, though he was already making his own music. Later, Fela's convicting judge admitted he'd been forced by the military government of General Buhari to convict Fela.

The set was gripping: a stripped-down, sustainable mini-version of the full-on Fela experience. That spectacular groove machine overwhelmed and literally entranced with its explosion of thunderous rhythms, challenging lyrics and extreme physicality. The elaborate, graphic make-up, the catchy choruses of songs like "Lady", "I.T.T.", "Shuffering and Shmiling" and "Zombie" were a pounding package of sensory stimulation designed to push Fela's anti-colonial pan-African message.

Fela's creativity was as deep as the oil wells of the Ogoni and Igbo states in southern Nigeria, the main source of Nigerian wealth and conflict, in a country crudely welded from some eighty tribes. That he chose to use this talent as a weapon in the struggle for his people's liberation and enlightenment had resulted at this point in the dissipation of Fela's entire fortune. Onstage at the Shrine he would strip to reveal the scars and burns covering his body, inflicted by the army and police. His fingers were broken to try to stop him from playing the saxophone. Somehow, Fela's indomitable resilience enabled him to write a song about any and every atrocity, passing the word on to his followers, where television would never reach. There was plenty to write about and Fela pressed on endlessly. Once a song's immediate moment had passed, he would never perform it again.

Fela may have been absent, but the dancers were still grinding in their usual spot, large cages suspended on the edge of the seats that had been a feature of every Shrine since the first club, then called the Afro Spot, was opened in 1969 after Fela's trip to the United States. They suggested a retro world of go-go girls in 1960s discotheques – the type of club Fela frequented and played in during his early Grand European Tour days, when he had his jazz band, Koola Lobitos. It was a period in which he was making incredible discoveries about the wider world beyond Nigeria. As he told me in a 1980 interview,

"I couldn't talk, couldn't participate in subjects because I didn't have the knowledge. I saw that the colonial education, which America was involved in too, was very badly wild. This pushed me so hard, I said I would die in the struggle."

Part of his re-education came via an early 1970s relationship with a young African American singer and activist, Sandra lzsadore, who exposed him to Black Power ideas and lit an already smouldering fuse of revolution.

"Fela put the girls in cages because it made the show more glamorous and exciting," says Izsadore, whose vocals on the pulsating "Upside Down" are an essential element of Fela's canon. "He was the only one doing it in Nigeria; it was part of the new ideas he brought forward."

The cages and their occupants certainly affected our British cameraman. Lithe movers, wearing a twist of a halter bra, the dancers' firm thighs flashed erotically beneath their blue micro-skirts and waist beads. One dancer stared intently into the lens, as if challenging the cameraman to hold her rapidly flickering undulations steady in the frame – which he did, for what was probably the longest take in the entire shoot. The primeval pussy power conjured by Fela was working as planned, even though he was in prison, far away. Many of those compelling moves did find their way into the eventual broadcast.

But while they unleashed erotic fantasies, the most drooling voyeur had to be aware of another meaning at work. The circular swivels and percussive thrusts of Fela's dancers' hips represented the ultimate yoni – the Earth Mother and the Fertility Goddess, Mama Africa.

Like every other aspect of Fela's mighty seventy-person show, the style of dance was closely controlled by the great bandleader himself and was intended to be as purely African as possible. Of course, Fela's uxorious ways were well known; but the primal pelvic geometry of the Queens' hip moves also testified to his devotion to the reimagining of Africa both ancient and modern, and the reconstruction of the continent's identity after the collapse of colonialism.

Regal and serene, Alake Kuti was one of Fela's more articulate and mediagenic Queens. The well-educated daughter of a judge and a nurse, she was part of the mass departure from Kalakuta in 1984. Alake states emphatically, "Fela designed everything. He instructed. Everything was his own. There was free style and then there were special dances [to go] with his music. It all came from him. He taught us himself and engaged choreographers. I had three teachers for my voice."

Each step of the dance was rooted in the old African way. "Fela's dances come from village ceremonies and rituals. In Africa, rituals, costumes are a way of life; painting and powdering the face, the mud, if that's the case," explains Wunmi Olaiya, the award-winning contemporary Afrobeat artist, costumier and choreographer, who was raised between London and Lagos. "That's what Fela brought together – the traditional and what was happening right now."

But modern 1960s Lagos was scarcely a hotbed of such quaint rural pastimes as traditional music and dance – widely regarded as old-fashioned village activities with little contemporary relevance. The enthusiast had to seek it out (rather like The Rolling Stones digging up rare blues records in Lagos' old coloniser's capital, London, during the same era). A weekly programme on Nigerian Radio 4 featured traditional music and Fela urged Femi to listen to it. Fela's daughters Yeni and Sola were members of the Calabar and Igbo dance troupes and trained at her school, New Era. Generally, academia preserved and taught the ancestral dance forms marking the ancient cycle of reaping and sowing, wedding and dying, birthing, growing and all phases of fertility.

"Both Yoruba dances and the Congolese use a lot of hip control. I call it isolate and control of the midriff – the mid-portion of the body," explains Olaiya, who teaches African dance. "It's just about going further with it. The dancehall girls in Jamaican ragga do it too, and more. It's all about total isolation and control of each hip, being able to release one cheek from another. Dancing from that section releases much more than just jumping. It's a fantastic, liberating feeling for a woman. But in Nigerian dance it becomes eroticised, because it's such a sexual part of the body, and when you see how the woman can control it, so smooth-ooooh!" she shudders deliciously.

"Everything is sexual and sensual, and it has a lot to do with fertility. It's a celebration of life," adds Sandra Izsadore. "Some of the African countries' styles are 1:11 or leaping and acrobatic, but Nigerian women always did the grounded type of dancing. What I liked about it was the freedom. Other dance had to be ladylike, and that was so restrictive. Nigerian dancing really opened me up and I lost a lot of inhibitions."

Fela's first dancer was known simply as Dele. She was the muse hymned in the vamp of "Lady": "African woman go dance, she go dance the fire dance."

"Dele loved to dance to that one," recalls Femi fondly.

Izsadore remembers her "long gyrations and movements I'd never seen before. She would make her whole body vibrate and the audience would go wild."

Fela's original drummer, Tony Allen, confirms "She was the best. There cannot be two of her."

Dele danced solo, but that all changed in 1978, when Fela married twenty-seven women in one traditional ceremony. Fela felt the need to formalise and make public his bond with these women, who had just survived with him the army attack on his extended family home, the Kalakuta "Rascal's" Republic. In their brutal response to Fela's popularity among the foreign VIPs like Roy Ayers and Stevie Wonder attending the international Festac concert of 1977, Fela's 78-year-old mother, the pioneering activist Funmilayo, was thrown from a window. She died shortly after from her injuries.

A devoted son, Fela was devastated by the loss of his inspirational mother; the first woman in Nigeria to hold a driving licence, the respected co-revolutionary of Mao Tse-tung and Kwame Nkrumah. Finding a way to channel his absent mother's spirit and wise advice became a central preoccupation of his life. Fela's many women had also suffered severely. Some had been raped with bottles by the soldiers. So the marriage took place and in a mega mom-mom-mom-and-pop operation, the Queens became his troupe of female singers, dancers and *animateuses* (as the French call those who lively up a scene). They were Fela's feminine principle, to crib from Jung.

"Fela had someone instructing the dancers, but he would come up with routines and was always looking for them to have a better outcome. He was always telling them how to dance, trying to make them more African," Femi remembers.

The sole dancer in the early 1970s, Dele began grooming the Queens but left to join the organisation of juju musician Ebenezer Obey, while the compound's initial communal vibes disintegrated into acrimony. "When Kalakuta got really crazy, she left," as Femi put it.

Reflecting on the eventual dissolution of his father's multi-marriage, which paralleled the dilution of his father's pan-African principles among his extended family, Femi laments, "The dancing started out with Dele as free expression. But towards the end, those dancers were really just like striptease."

The mass marriage lasted until 1984, when Fela emerged from a jail stint on trumped-up currency charges amid rumours that some of his wives had adopted Fela's inclusionary sexual ideas for themselves. Their departure marked the start of an intense and largely solitary period of communion with the ancestors, an introspective spiritual search that led Fela to explore the philosophies of people like Professor Hindu, which lasted till he joined his ancestors.

It was a deeper concentration on a permanent quest. To implement his continuing process of reimagining the future of Africa, Fela spent over three decades seeking the touchstone of historic authenticity. He moved far beyond his own immediate heritage, which represented a web of compromises and accommodations to the heavy hand of British colonialism and imperialism; his father was a missionary and his grandfather wrote liturgical music for the Anglican church. Each generation's choices traced the societal convulsions that shook Nigeria. For Fela, the customs and culture of tribes like the Hausa, Igbo and Yoruba were key to a quest that led him through the Kabbalah and ancient Egypt.

As a pan-Africanist, Fela did not restrict his researches to his own geographical area. The idea of the decorative make-up that became a trademark of the Afrobeat aesthetic swelled from various sources.

"Fela started going to lectures at the university and at the same time he was enriching us with his knowledge," explains Alake. "He came across this book about ancient Egyptian make-up. The Yorubas believed strongly they migrated from Egypt to where they are now. I don't know which book; so many of them got burned when they destroyed Kalakuta. The make-up became part of our costume, especially when we were doing comprehensive [full-scale] shows. But when the group became Egypt 80, we always had to make up."

If he encountered resistance, Fela used the texts as ammunition in his culture war. "What he was trying to portray was the African way," observes Femi. "Someone brought Fela a photo book of Kenyans in the village wearing heavy make-up and Fela said, 'You see these people? They didn't take it from me, so this MUST have existed in Africa! What is everybody [complaining] about the make-up for? Now I insist MAKE UP!'"

Whether relaxing at Kalakuta or on the road, travel permitting, the Queens took their time getting into the day and preparing for the night's show. Hours of the afternoon would pass with them lounging across the bed or sprawling in the armchair, intently anointing themselves with tiny, perfectly positioned spots of white, yellow or red. The pointillist swirls pivoted from or echoed key features, like a particularly elegant line of the cheekbone or jaw. Each Queen looked different and each one's vision expressed her highest self. Fashion designers and make-up artists like Zandra Rhodes and Vivienne

Westwood, skaters, crusties and ravers would all flash off the Queens' individual self-painting. As one Queen, Olaiya, puts it, "The make-up calls us to be really different and funky. We're decking it out."

To play with painting their faces, the Queens reached back to their foremothers and went shopping among the great heaps of pigment powder piled on cloth on the ground among the spices in Lagos' big markets. "We would think back to Cleopatra and Sheba. I know my great-great-great-grandmother painted herself during the festivals," says Alake. "We also used those old pigments for our make-up, like Osun, which is made from wood and comes from the ground, like chalk. My grandmother was a trader. She travelled for days to the market in Lagos and she sold everything: fish, clothes, honey, kola nuts. She showed me gold dust once, piled into her hand. She made up with different sorts of white powder that we mix with water, like Efun. She always put on her own powder, Tiro. [Years later, Tiro was considered a health risk as it could cause infant lead poisoning.] We have colours like yellow, and indigo for blue. The Hausa tribe use another powder, Lali. Women use them to paint designs on the face, hands and feet, just the way the Indians do with henna. Each tribe has their different way of doing things."

Alake now lives in London with her son and is a children's storyteller; wearing full magical make-up, she encourages the kids' face painting. "Sometimes when I start making up," she muses, "I feel like I've won the world."

w"When Dele started to dance, she had no costume, and when the first Shrine opened, the Queens wore skimpy outfits, like go-go queens," says Izsadore. "Then one of the Queens, Sewa, started to do her own designs in the African tradition. I loved her first outfits, with the leather straps and the buckles up the leg, and her cute little picket fence skirts. After Mother passed, Sewa became the head Nigerian female at Kalakuta, the strongest and most respected."

Fela's commitment informed every facet of living. Within the Kalakuta household, Fela encouraged the use of chewing sticks rather than the Western-style toothbrush and toothpaste, and he insisted that everyone use local black soap. Certain of the less hardcore residents hid their own imported white soap, much to Femi's annoyance. Fela's philosophy was consistent with the advice Marcus Garvey gave about spending your money within your own community. Femi explains, "Fela wore those clothes because if you buy African fabric and give it to the tailor, already you're helping the society. You're helping your mothers in the market by providing them with money, instead of just buying jeans.

"If I look at it objectively, Fela's life was his mission. Maybe he had to go through everything, even the beatings, for my generation to be brave enough to take the next step. People in the record industry, people in authority, so many people listen to Fela. He laid a very solid platform for Africa to build on."

Femi Kuti

When a great musical innovator and thinker like Fela dies, if his work is not extended to future generations, the loss is compounded. A loving, if strict, father, he expected his children Yeni, Femi and Seun to work, and they have fulfilled his intent. Fela's sons, Femi and Seun, have sustained and extended the spread of the tree of pan-African music described by Senegal's Baaba Maal. Daughter Yeni, a popular broadcaster and producer, spearheads the giant-size Lagos Shrine which closely resembles the previous one – on steroids. The careers of many Afrobeats artists, including the African Giant, Burna Boy, who trumpets his connections with Fela, have been launched in the New Shrine.

The immense yet intimate venue is the fulfilment of the dream Femi talks about in this article, while he recreates his father's classics with hip-hop activist and visionary drummer Questlove and The Roots – rounding out the harmony of the pan-African Black Chord that connects music throughout the diaspora.

"African Son"

First published in SPIN, *February 2000*

Femi Kuti, looking fly in an indigo batik tunic and trousers, picks at the native delicacy of the strange city where he's recording: a fragrant, greasy, oozing Philly cheese steak.

"What is *this*?" he asks optimistically.

The Nigerian saxophonist/bandleader is working at the Studio, a recording space founded by various legends of the 1970s Philly Sound. Kuti might recognise those disco-soul classics if he heard them. But nostalgia is not why he's a hero. Local fans and modern-day hip-hop heroes The Roots are remixing the simmering "Blackman Know Yourself", a track from Kuti's new LP, *Shoki Shoki*. The album reinvents the lethal slow burn of Afrobeat – the funk style coined by his legendary rebel father, Fela Aníkúlápó Kuti, in the 1970s – with modern DJ flavour, and it has been torching international dance clubs for months (it hits the US this month). Although raised in Nigeria playing his dad's music, Kuti, now thirty-five, still knows how to digest what he likes, be it jungle, techno, hip-hop or – as he is bravely proving tonight – Philly cheesesteak.

The Roots' beat scholar, Ahmir Thompson, aka Questlove, his huge Afro skewered with two picks cues up "Time Is Running Out Fast" from James Brown's *The Payback*. "This is the track James recorded after he heard your father play in Nigeria," he says to Kuti, who grooves on the similarities. Then, sitting on a stool in the darkened studio, Thompson meditates on the boho-jazz groove he's building for "Blackman Know Yourself", tugs up his T-shirt and records a percussion track by steadily patting his Buddha-like tummy. By the time he's finished, the song has, well, a somewhat different swing than the original.

Left alone in the studio to lay down his saxophone track, Kuti has trouble locking into Thompson's downtempo groove. "I'm so used to playing this my own way," he laments after a take.

"No, man; that's really good," Thompson says, looking up from his laptop in the control room. "Stick with it."

Kuti's eyelids tremble as be goes off into a flurry of circular breathing, teasing a storm of emotions out of a small phrase over and over again. After he nails it, Kuti says with a cheeky grin, "I want people on the dance floor to listen and say, 'Who's playing that saxophone?'"

Like the cabalistic vision of time, the process of cultural exchange in pop music is an infinite loop that keeps on moving. Fela fed his head with American contemporaries like James Brown and Miles Davis (whose polyrhythms stem from Africa); Femi has been hanging in house and jungle clubs in Europe and America. That vibe is channelled into *Shoki Shoki* with help from his band, Positive Force, hotshot French producer Sodi and British audio engineer Mark Saunders. Meanwhile, American artists and DJs are diving headfirst into the sea of Fela reissues, thanks to two European box sets of vinyl and assorted CDs. "Those reissues have made a whole new generation of sample madness," Thompson laughs. "The race to use the tracks has started already: Q-Tip, Lauryn Hill, D'Angelo, Black Star, Mos Def and myself. Afrobeat is the next crop of funk to get appetised."

The Afrobeat sound is original African American: ancestral Nigerian percussion igniting with fiery jazz and good-foot funk.

Its sprawling urban synthesis expressed Nigeria's radical sprit – in sharp contrast to the smug, if sensuous, patron-praising songs usually performed by Nigerian pop artists such as King Sunny Adé. And the form is synonymous with Femi's father, whom he adored.

Born and raised in Nigeria and schooled for a time in London. Fela Aníkúlápó Kuti was, to quote Bob Marley, a real revolutionary. He was politicised by an affair with Sandra Iszadore, a Black Panther, in 1960s Los Angeles. By the mid-1970s he had changed his name from the Westernised moniker Ransome-Kuti to Aníkúlápó-Kuti (roughly: he who carries death in his pouch). He also reprogrammed his music with incendiary lyrics that celebrated pan-Africanism and attacked Nigeria's successive military dictatorships. Not surprisingly, he got into frequent conflicts with the government and spent a significant amount of time in jail. Yet, his music and message made him an international hero despite infrequent touring. (Not surprisingly, few promoters wanted to deal with the logistical nightmares of bringing Fela's twenty-plus band members and extended family out on the road.)

But a father's shadow can weigh heavily: just ask Julian Lennon or Ziggy Marley. Perhaps inevitably, Femi has long been on a quest to forge an individual identity. You can see it in his personal life. Fela was known for his mighty consumption of weed – he especially enjoyed a marijuana extraction known as *goro* or "Jam", a sticky, black-brown paste that can restructure your innards. Femi doesn't smoke (he gave it up along with cigarettes as part of a spiritual cleansing in 1984). His father was generally held in awe for simultaneously marrying twenty-seven women in a traditional ceremony – in addition to his British-born wife, the gracious Remi, mother of Femi and his sisters Yeni and the late Sola. Femi's a one-wife man and he keeps her close. "I have my wife Funke in the band with me," he points out. An arrangement "which controls my sexual powers and makes sure I'm not a maniac on the streets."

(Of course, old-fashioned faithfulness is also a preventative measure against HIV. Fela died of complications from AIDS in 1997, shortly after having been roughed up – yet again – in a Lagos, Nigeria, jail. Fela allegedly had sex some three to five times a day and, like Sting, was a fan of tantric forms of sexual control. Fela felt he didn't need condoms; according to his daughter Yeni, he thought Africans were immune to AIDS, that it was a white man's disease. It is remarkable that of the innumerable women he bedded, only two are known to have had his kids and, to the best of Femi's knowledge, none of Fela's wives have tested HIV positive.)

Musically, Femi is also his own man. Like Peter Tosh and Zack de la Rocha, the politicised Fela wouldn't sing about love on principle; Femi's first single, "Berg Beng Bang", is an audio Kama Sutra banned in Nigeria for its frankness. While Fela's tracks thundered on free-form for an hour or more, Femi's are punchy, in synch with the rhythm of modern attention spans. "I used to get bored playing long songs," he says during a post-production pool game at the studio. "The problem was cutting them down and not having problems at home!" Femi chuckles, imitating Fela: "'So! You're not playing Afrobeat any more!' I still wanted to be a part of my father, y'understand, but doing Femi Aníkúlápó Kuti."

Both father and son had much in common. Fela was regal and Femi, the teenage prince, could exhibit the sort of aristocratic haughtiness that causes peasants to revolt. It has mellowed with age into a playful warmth, a tender sense of social justice and a practical spirituality. The two men loved and were intensely proud of each other, but Fela could be overbearing and hated disobedience. Though Femi's dad was supportive of his solo career, young Femi had to earn his place in the band, with little help from Fela other than his famously brutal criticism. (For example, when producer Bill Laswell remixed Fela's "Army Arrangement", while the musician was incarcerated, Fela commented that what Laswell had done to him was worse than any of the tortures he'd suffered in jail.)

Although this is the first time Femi Kuti has received this much global attention, he's been laying its foundation for almost two decades. After Fela was jailed in 1984 under the General Buhari regime on trumped-up currency charges and Fela's then-manager, Pascal Imbert, was also jailed, a 21-year-old Femi ran his father's nightclub, the Shrine, took over the band (then dubbed Egypt 80) and became a forceful frontman.

During yet another of his father's jail stretches, Femi again handled the band and club – so well that Fela wanted him to continue after his release. But Femi refused. "I had developed too far musically; I wanted to do my own thing," he explains. "It was the best decision I ever made in my life, even though my father and I didn't talk at all for a good five years."

An unplanned meeting between Fela and Femi in a Lagos club in the mid-1990s led to a reconciliation, which irritated members of the family who, for reasons of influence-wielding, preferred them to feud. The perversity continued: after Fela's death, his old band members, in a cruel anti-colonial twist, refused to play with Femi because he was not a full-blooded African. (His mixed African/Native American maternal great-grandfather moved from the States to England in the late 1800s, played trombone in a band in London and married an English girl. Their daughter Sadie Eileen was a trumpeter who married a Nigerian named Taylor in the 1940s; their daughter, Remi, is a pianist who married Fela.)

"I nearly cried," says Femi, frowning, recalling the band's reaction. Fela's musicians now play the old repertoire in Lagos clubs with Femi's sixteen-year-old half-brother, Seun. But Femi's mind is on his own mission. "I'm fighting for my people, I'm fighting for the world," he says, eyes flaring. "I believe the sin in life is not to try."

As their limousine crawls through a Manhattan traffic jam, Kuti is being dragged across the carpet by his sister Yeni, Funke and fellow dancer Shade Alalade. Once he's floored, they pelt him with cushions while he writhes around, giggling. "Help!" he cries. "Sexism! Domestic violence!" Life with the Kutis tends to be one long preadolescent roughhouse session – "stupid idiot" is a favourite term of endearment. This skittish, cuddly Kuti is the flip side of the militant Kuti, the fiery musician who critiques oppression over pulsating polyrhythms, and Kuti the sex god, who gets cheers when he takes off his shirt onstage in Paris, London and New York City.

Through the limo windows, the scene is not unlike Kuti's frenetic hometown of Lagos – the New York City of Africa, with its notorious, hours-long traffic jams and skyscrapers looming over shantytowns. Back home, Kuti lives with his wife, sister, mother, grandmother and various kids in an ample family home in Ikeja, a working-class neighbourhood.

"I've been working with my sisters for thirteen years and there's nothing better than when you have people not afraid to tell you when you're wrong," he admits. Both Yeni and their sister Sola worked with Kuti's Positive Force until Sola's death from cancer, shortly after Fela's death in 1997. Yeni remains the band's choreographer. As with most great African bands, the women who sing backup and dance with Kuti are integral to the music. They tease the rhythm, dialogue with the players and beam into the groins of the audience with low, winding hip moves. Decked out in hoochie-coochie beaded headdresses, bras and ra-ra waist beads that would make Donatella

Versace swoon, their glamour and personality are a big part of the live Kuti experience.

With its deep-groove rhythm section and the cumulative brio of Kuti's rampant dancing and circular breathing-charged sax work, the band has been busy making converts. In Paris, a *très chic* crowd waiting for headliner Maceo Parker wound up on its feet, cheering. At a show in Nice, Kuti noticed that old showman Mick Jagger dancing in the wings. (They exchanged bows.) In New York City, Kuti's set was the main attraction of the opening-night party at the CMJ MusicFest, the city's biggest annual new-music conference. He killed it, and his 2 a.m. set the next weekend at the TriBeCa house mecca Vinyl left a packed room of house heads, African American intellectuals and African expats begging for more. The same week, he chatted at length with Stevie Wonder at the celebrity-magnet bistro Mr. Chow's and was humbled to register that his limo was as big as Wonder's. Fela's gigantic, unwieldy crew always travelled cheap; this was plain weird.

But Kuti keeps his perspective. He has more important things to deal with. In 1998, he launched a youth-targeted political organisation called M.A.S.S (Movement Against Second Slavery) on his late father's birthday, 15 October. And at the moment, his greatest preoccupation is the reopening of the Shrine nightclub. It is an almost holy mission. Just as music is more than entertainment in Africa, where it marks every passage of life, so the Shrine was always more than just a hang-out; it was the spiritual home of Fela's pan-African message. When the military raided and burned down the Kalakuta commune in 1977, raping many of Fela's dancers and throwing his mother, Funmilayo, out of a second-storey window in the process (she would later die from her injuries), the neighbouring Shrine on Agege Motor Road was shuttered and Fela was effectively banned from playing anywhere.

Fela finally found a new location for the club in 1979: Pepple Street in Ikeja. Architecturally, it was minimalist: a dance floor with no walls, a partial zinc roof supported by painted pillars, murals of dancing figures and inspirational slogans on the walls. Big cages for go-go dancing queens ringed the place, shrouded with torn chicken wire to protect the booty-shakers from probing fans, while backstage, paintings, newspaper clippings and photos on the walls told the story of the Kalakuta raid and the club's painful birth.

Throughout the years, the Shrine always found a way to stay open until Kuti closed it for good in January 1999, after considerable harassment from the landlord (who had an ongoing row with Fela). But with money from the release of Fela's back catalogue, Kuti plans to reopen a new version of the Shrine later this year. It's a symbol of both continuity and change for him. He imagines it as a place where African artists and those from the diaspora can perform together – in essence, a place where he can remake history.

Idealistic, yes. But people are responding. After recording with rapper Common Sense and spending time with D'Angelo (who wanted input for a cover of Fela's "Water No Get Enemy" with Lauryn Hill), Kuti had a revelation. "In Africa, we identify with America and forget who we are: and no one in America knows Nigerian artists. But in the studio with D'Angelo, I felt a missing link," he says. "When I played him Fela, his reaction and smile was a spiritual communication. I felt there has been a complete misunderstanding between America and Africa. I feel that Fela's legacy, and now me, can help change that and build. D'Angelo wants to come to Nigeria, and so does Thompson. So when we reopen the Shrine, we're going to make a very big festival. We're going to make Africa great again."

*

Formal and social, Fela's cosmopolitan musical education in Lagos, London, New York and Los Angeles resulted in the synthesis of Afrobeat. Fusing and mutating by their new context the strains that had shaped him, Afrobeat drew on unusual rhythms and sounds from instruments Fela found in remote bush villages, used in rituals. The disciplined big band of James Brown was always a strong influence – Fela was a strict and decisive bandleader. But throughout, American jazz was part of Fela's own creative foundation. It permeates Afrobeat, from the drums up to the crowning glory of Fela's and his co-players' horns. And when he rehearsed every day, alone at home in the Kalakuta Republic, it was often to American jazz legends like John Coltrane, a friend of his fellow jazz genius Ornette Coleman.

CHAPTER 9

How to Be Harmolodic

With its syncopated, liberated reach for spirituality, jazz music has elevated successive generations of artists. In terms of the arc of this book, jazz particularly influenced post-punk. Playing those few chords at volume can get tired after a while, and the wild frontiers of jazz beckoned, with their infinite possibilities. Proximity to jazz greatness shaped local punk artists, like Patti Smith, who was a regular at Ornette's birthday loft parties. To many, New York was jazz central, home of the free feeling to which most committed musicians aspire, whether they show it or not.

Every step of jazz's evolution was rapidly absorbed by players globally, including those in Africa, like Fela Kuti. And since Ornette Coleman kick-started it in the early 1960s, the system he calls harmolodics, more generally thought of as free jazz, has been known as the ultimate liberation music. Profound, intuitive compatibility, arrived at through extreme rehearsing, allowed for previously unknown room for individual expression within a multiplayer format. In an era when so many colonised nations were attaining independence, this organisation of sound felt emblematic of a new order's possibilities.

Riveted by jazz, newly independent Jamaica's ska musicians forged their own style, known as Jazz Jamaica; Don Drummond, who we met in Chapter 6, was a prime exponent. As I write, the genre, both British and Jamaica-based, is still expanding.

Key to free jazz thinking is the harmolodic system Ornette Coleman devised. Unlocking the 4/4 bar cage of predictably structured songs, which represent most of pop, harmolodics lets energising air into the rhythmic equation. And it is actually more than a musical approach – it is an open-hearted attitude to life as well. As is only right, Ornette was unique but still part of a community; he also inspired others to form orchestras to make music in his disruptive yet healing spirit, with their own individual angle on how musical structure can communicate.

But back in New York, where the Texan Ornette refined his harmolodics, foremost among those bold jazz adventurers was Butch Morris, creator of the Conduction theory of music. I was also glad here to quote the thoughts of pioneering writer, musician and bandleader of the Burnt Sugar The Arkestra Chamber and movement leader Greg Tate.

A theme of this book is the interconnectedness of the branches on the spreading tree of musix rooted in Africa described by Senegal's Baaba Maal; how the allure of certain musix forms its own tribe, separate from other aspects of the absorbed one's identity. In all areas of creativity, aware arts lovers of the 1960s had their thinking, work and approach to living shaped by the sound, feel and philosophy of free jazz. Among them was cheeky Brit Ian Dury, turning his polio-survivor's limp into a swagger. His quirky ascent to stardom with vaudevillian, satirical tunes was powered by the sense of expansiveness induced by total absorption in the work of Ornette Coleman, Don Cherry, Miles Davis, Albert Ayler and their fellow sonic explorers.

Ian Dury

Perhaps only punk could have been such a welcoming micro-genre for jazzhead Ian Dury to sign up for, with its inclusionary emphasis on people perceived as misfits and outsiders. Older than the rest and already an art professor, visually distinguished by his polio-caused limp, Ian was matchless when it came to quick wit and saucy, Cockney-flavoured banter. Dury lived harmolodically; that is, he blended foresight with spontaneity and awareness of how to ride life's rhythms. A cultural firestarter, the 1981 tour he arranged became a living musical bridge, connecting The Slits and Ornette's trumpeter, Don Cherry. The gigs first introduced Cherry's daughter Neneh (who we met twice earlier, both with The Slits and solo) to London's teenage she-punks, who she promptly moved from Sweden to join aged sixteen. Not only a cultural connector, Dury may have been the wittiest punk.

"Ian Dury: Wide Boy Wonder!!!"

First published in Sounds, *15 October 1977*

"I wonder what would happen if I drank this? Might do me some good," Ian Dury says grimly.

The dressing room is full of the band relaxing pre-set. Wreckless Eric is wandering around looking like a rabbit just emerging from a hangover, clutching a bottle, and Ian's clutching a bottle too. But Ian's bottle is horse-laxative size and has a florid Edwardian label on it saying "Hair Restorative". Its official function is to add that extra bounce to Ian's short top and long sides coiffure, but the roadie's just been round to say they're on in three minutes and Ian's lost his voice. At this stage, anything goes. What can you say when it's the first time the guy's been onstage for a year and a half, he's lost his voice and he's the lead singer?

Not much, except something vaguely optimistic and reassuring, like "I'm sure it'll come out of the hat." So that's that, I said, and I honestly wasn't surprised when that's what happened. The tumult that clogged the airwaves between "Blockheads" and "Plaistow Patricia" was as the tumult of a town hall full of people from High Wycombe going ape.

We were rattling round in the back of the bus, cat's-eyes striping the 2 a.m. road to Oxford, when the girl sitting opposite me said: "If you'd patented the idea of putting a safety pin through your ear, you'd be a millionaire by now."

That's not why I tune in to Ian Dury, but his impeccable punk pioneer credentials make it satisfyingly apt that he should be making his return to the public eye in today's Age of Punk. Like a film that ends up neatly back where it started, like waking up from your nightmare in an EC comic and finding yourself back at the beginning – only this time it's real . . .

Gawd, that makes it sound like dealing with Ian Dury is a nightmare. Other way round, mate. I've never come across a musician who's got so many people round him eager to point out that they're working their little tushies off for the aforesaid musician for love, and will continue to do so until forced to stop by the arrival of the big bucks (and hence, pay) that said musician's art will undoubtedly (if there's any justice on the planet) bring. Remember that phrase, "The Common Touch"? Whatever it is, Ian's got it. People just love him . . . that's what he's talking about when he says "I've never struggled. I've had everything laid on."

"No, there's always been people rushing round me all the time ever since I was about four, even before I got polio when I was seven. Because I'm bright." Ian is categorical, his wise monkey face (see evil/hear evil/speak no evil?) mottled with an interesting selection of shadows from the table light. We're sitting now in their motel room, one of those sublimely neutral environments done up in orange and brown. Open the door to the room and you can't tell whether you are, in fact, halfway to Oxford, or in Akron Ohio, or in the new motel on the moon. That's how you can tell you're on the road.

Just to put you all in the picture: it's the morning after the night before, the night when Ian pulled it out of the hat and thrilled, where by all normal expectations he'd have bombed. We haven't slept; Ian and party wisecracked their way through the ride to this motel (situated in prime blasted heath location), and Ian continued to goof through a flaccid, shrink-wrapped motorway salad and gruesome red-and-yellow trifle ("Mmmmm, lovely . . ."). And the specific reason why we're gathered together (with Ian's particularly warm, gracious bass-player girlfriend Denise Roudette and Frances, who's prowling round the room taking pictures) is The Stiffs tour and Ian's new i-fficially five-star album *New Boots and Panties!!*.

Ian's comments about having everything laid on are not strictly true. Apart from the obvious resilience Ian's needed to overcome the physical disabilities he's worked with since his childhood bout of polio, he's gone through a slice of angst in the year and a half since he last performed . . .

Vivien: *Have you felt frustrated about not doing shows?*

Ian: *No. Well – yes. One misses it, but then one doesn't miss it if one doesn't have a reason to do it.*

Vivien: *Last thing I remember was all the papers saying you'd never be able to play again, you were gonna vanish from the public eye into rock and roll mystery, leaving only a memory of Kilburn and the High Roads behind.*

Ian: *That was a lot of mary went down there. All I said in print was there was nothing wrong with me. I went skint and I got, like, a bit mental last year. Also a bit run down. You only get run down when one side of your system doesn't work properly. I was depressed 'cos I was working too hard – one can bang one's head against a wall for a considerable period of time, as long as one thinks one's gonna bash one's head through the wall. I didn't think I was at the time.*

The way Ian views things, it's all all right if you've got the spirit, and that's what pulled him through. It's because he reckons his spirit's all right that he thwacks the drums with such vigour through Wreckless Eric's set and similarly, because his spirit's all right he's been writing with Chas Jankel every day he's been "off the boards": "I met Chas last year and he taught me how to make things I wanted to listen to. I haven't made an album I wanted to listen to before. In a way I can listen to it and quite dig most of it because musically it's incredible, so I don't really listen to myself."

Musically, what goes on is rock/jazz, as opposed to jazz/rock, e.g. Weather Report. Also, a lot of music hall/carnival/fairground-sounding music. A nifty synthesis of Ian's roots. Remember, he used to be an art teacher, went to the Royal College of Art, at a time when hardcore jazz was the current inspiration for those with ears.

"Charlie Mingus and you – well, you were made for each other," Ian enthuses. "You should get every single one he's ever made – *Tijuana Moods, Charles Mingus Presents Charles Mingus* – that's the best one, with Eric Dolphy on it . . . You know, Ornette Coleman said that playing music was awful in clubs, because you were playing for guys picking up chicks and chicks picking up guys and people smoking joints and all that, not for people to listen to, and Ornette is – oh, bollocks to what he is. He's Ornette and there's a load of people like him you never hear about.

"This bloke came up to me after a gig and accused me of putting it on. Mostly I'm never putting it on, I'm hiding things. Nor does Wreckless Eric – he hides things. It's more a question of controlling your outbursts in some kind of semblance of reality, otherwise there wouldn't be any point in having an outburst.

"Those people like Ornette have the outbursts. There's an awful lot of people in the world who do things for pure love, so much so that nobody ever hears about them, nobody ever knows what they're doing except themselves. I'm just a wanker. I'm doing an interview and I'm on the road and I'm having my picture taken, and I love it, don't I?

"So in a way, I feel like I compromise. Because I know a lot of those guys. And if I'm meant to be a little more real than most rock and rollers – though there's loads of people who are much more real in rock and roll nowadays – there's loads of people who are much more real than us working in the complete darkness. You're being nice to me, you're talking to me, and maybe people will buy another ten albums. And a lot of people who read what you write will come up to me . . ."

Ian tells us how some geezer came up to him – Wreckless Eric, and Ian's sidekick/ mentor/inspiration/soulmate Fred "Spider" Rowe (a jovial, burly guy, no hair and all tattoos, looks like a cross between a stevedore and a headmaster; he's got class) – and recognised them at Barbarella's, so he played spoons with 'em during the set. All I can say is, if you're surprised by that, I'm surprised. "I dunno . . . it seems a bit weird. I said I wouldn't do any more interviews because it all seemed a bit boring, all the same."

Ian cocks his head enquiringly to the side, raises a curious eyebrow. Instant journalist. "Do you like the album?" he asks daintily. "Well,

I'm not going to make any more . . ." he says and laughs raucously, slapping his skinny knee.

"Well, that's all silliness, isn't it?"

"If you make a record, if you do anything, you should try and do something that amazes you, otherwise what are you trying to do? Are you trying to amaze somebody else? If you're trying to amaze somebody else, I think you're a wanker really." Ian goes on to qualify the statement, but the essence of it still holds – he's a perfectionist, in a warped kind of way. "I was doing something else before I was a rock and roller that was more valuable to my spirit because there wasn't anybody clapping me on the back."

Similarly, when Ian started out in da biz, he could never take bods materialising from nowhere with management contracts quite seriously. "I thought it was a joke, a bit of venom. I don't really think that you can tell people things – people do what they want to do." I don't think that's strictly true . . . Ian interrupts me, breaking into a soft, staccato, music-hall, quickfire delivery.

> *. . . Get your teeth into a small slice, the cake of liberty . . .*
> "Sex & Drugs & Rock & Roll" by Ian Dury

"I don't say: do you really want to work here forever? I can't come out and say: don't work in this factory no more, you're being ripped off, it's inevitable that in a bit of time you'll stop doing that because a machine will do it for you. Who wants to hear that again?

"See, I don't want to put a message out 'cos I ain't got no answers. If I had an answer, I'd tell everybody. But I'd be treated like a dementoid, 'cos who's got the answer? If I had the answer, I wouldn't be a bloody rock and roll star . . ."

A point to ponder here, ladies and gentlemen. I recall interviewing Sex Pistols manager Malcolm McLaren at the (now) historical press conference when the Pistols signed to A&M Records. Malcolm explained that he didn't feel in the slightest perturbed about advocating Anarchy. He never claimed to offer an answer – he just enjoyed creating the situation. The Clash essentially do the same thing, except that they suggest answers. Ian doesn't even pose the questions on a Pistols/Clash level of literality, but they're all there, implicit in his songs, like "Blockheads". I thought "Blockheads" did give a message, namely that you are no better than the blockheads and the blockheads (thickos/yobs) are no better than you. Ian didn't agree.

"It's just describing blockheads quite accurately and attacking people in a certain area beautifully accurately. 'Imagine finding one in your laundry basket,'" he sneers snidely, just like he does on the record. "I could measure you with sugar to that! I know exactly who'd shiver to that, and I hope it gets right up their pinafores."

His voice is savage.

"That's not a message, that's just having a pop. Messages is for Western Union, baby . . ." he said, slipping into a mock-Western voice.

That's one of the album's chief joys – Ian's delivery is always on. Every word shrieks its fullest meaning just because of the way he sings.

"That's acting, right? A kind of acting. The words are quite easy to say and they're nice to read. The Kirk Douglas thing. I like old Kirk . . ."

"You mean the old cleft chin vibe?"

"No, the straightforward kind of thing."

Aha! Straightforward. A key word when it comes to Ian Dury. He sings about blockheads, about lawless brats in council flats, he sings directly about his dad on "My Old Man" ("did the crossword in the *Standard* / At the airport in the rain" – there's a line for ya), and he sings about beat-up whores like Plaistow Patricia and crafty wide boys like Billericay Dickie. And he uses the same approach to each – conveying emotion, feeling and caring without sentimentality by clinically spot-on observation/insight.

And another thing Ian's dramatis personae have in common is that they're all "The undernourished. There's a lot of songs about undernourished people on the album – most of them. 90 per cent of everything is undernourished, so I think the album's got a fair share. Then there's a couple of beauties to brighten the day a little – there must be, otherwise we'd all go spare, wouldn't we? 'Wake Up and Make Love with Me', that's humorous, isn't it? Quite nice as well." Ian chuckles quietly. "I get embarrassed. That's why I made it humorous. I wouldn't like to project myself as some guy who can wake up properly all the time."

That's the same approach you use in "I'm Partial to Your Abracadabra". It's a way of saying, "I think you're magic. I Love You" without you having to blush – that flippant coyness that still doesn't obstruct the information.

"I f***ed that one up, didn't I. I wanted to make that hermaphrodite – no, hermaphrodite implies something sexy, or some duality. It just seems to me that inevitably the human race will evolve eventually into one sex. Women will have their babies in a nice box and we'll all fancy each other for what we are instead of what we like or what we're supposed to be – or tits or all of that old bollocks . . . Hey, that's quite a nice line, isn't it? 'Tits and all that old bollocks' . . . Denise! Are you paying attention to all this? I'm making a right kipper out of myself, and it's all going into Vivien's article . . ."

Denise looks up from her magazine on the bed behind me, laughs.

Vivien: *Perhaps I'm so strongly drawn to your album because even while it's chronicling losers/undernourished/deprived people, it's still very positive.*

Ian: *"Plaistow Patricia" has got a happy ending – she meets that Chinese person and she gets a nice showroom, and – I don't want to talk about heroin at all . . .*

"Everything's all right as long as you don't get hepatitis" [he mimics satirically]. It's like a five-part song that's constructed round a whirlpool. It's not that each chapter is unrelated, but it goes like that as she gets older. The original version of that had a man ringing her doorbell and then she ended up walking into the Thames. I wasn't very positive then. I changed the ending because it made a thing that had a beginning, middle and an end. It's really about Davey Payne playing saxophone. He really knows how to make the sound swell. It's about spirit, it's working, it's in tune and it's in time.

I'm always pleased when someone I'm interviewing comes up with some comment that seems to sum up all of my favourite qualities in the individual and the music they make. Ian just did it. He's about spirit, he's working, he's in tune and (luckily for us) he's in time. It's probably got something to do with his cross-class background (father a bus driver, mother a university professor). Probably got something to do with the vitality that's enabled him to overwhelm physical handicap (just like Gene Vincent, who Ian sings about respectfully and lovingly on the album, being bandied about homes in his childhood and surviving). And certainly it's a lot to do with what Ian's talking about now:

"I don't want to die. Who wants to bleedin' die? It's all right if Johnny Rotten" – Ian's a long-time J.R. fan, incidentally – "doesn't survive. If he doesn't, it's because he doesn't want to. I think we're quite close to living forever, actually. That might sound a bit out of tune, but Stanley Kubrick thinks it as well. I do believe in evolution. I'm an optimist, although I can't prove it and I still don't want to send messages.

"I think it's wonderful, I think there's a lot of it about and as long as everybody washes their hands, it'll be OK."

Don Cherry

Don Cherry's life was an incessant quest for the perfectly imperfect chord dancing in his head. Watts, Los Angeles, could not contain him; he was always restless and, as he makes clear here, ready for life and music's next adventure. Now a site of pilgrimage, the magical home that his wife Moki created in the southern Swedish forest, Tågarp, proved a genuine crucible, its young students now leading actors and musicians; not least his children Neneh and Eagle Eye. As discussed, the Cherrys' artistic line continues. Neneh's daughters all became musicians: Mabel, Tyson and eldest daughter Naima, who is also the guardian of her grandmother's legacy. Moki's mythic, witty multimedia work is now acknowledged, with major solo exhibitions in museums around the world. A twinkling sprite of a spirit, Don Cherry's eclectic, playful and imaginative work is transcendent.

"Don Cherry: Black Gypsy, Folk Dreams"

First published in Melody Maker, *22 September 1979*

Probably the only person who isn't surprised to find Don Cherry playing on The Slits' tour is Cherry himself. Since his apprenticeship with free-jazz guru Ornette Coleman, the trumpeter has pursued a fascinating multi-ethnic career that centres around his house in Norway. Vivien Goldman watched him work and play.

One of trumpeter Don Cherry's various musical involvements is with a group called Old and New Dreams – an evocative enough name for the group of former Ornette Coleman co-players.

The following conversation took place more than once while I saw them in Oslo recently between Cherry, lean, lithe and bouncy, and Charlie Haden, the bass player. Charlie would be sitting in the back of the car, dolefully balancing the double bass over the back of the seat. "Old dreams, that's what we are," he'd say.

"No, Charlie, no!" Cherry replied, rubbing his hands gleefully, fidgeting excitedly in the front seat. "*New* dreams. Always new."

Cherry refers to himself as a "black gypsy". The man's in his forties, but you can safely say he's forever young; when he concentrates, he's a kid still, straining with all of his being to understand where the musical ball's going to fly next – to field it soaring, in mid-air, and bounce it back in a graceful arc of inspiration.

At supper, Haden and fellow band members Dewey Redman and Ed Blackwell (the drummer whose kidney condition necessitates Old and New Dreams' tours being structured around access to hospital kidney machines) quietly sit round chewing over the day's events with the fish stew. Cherry bursts through the swing doors, twitching for action.

"Where's the disco? Who wants to go to the disco? I want to dance."

We're in a big, bare studio in Oslo, and Old and New Dreams are recording their second album.

Things are going well – put it this way, things *have* to go well, since unlike rock musicians, jazz players can't afford the luxury of studio experimentation as a general rule. It took The Slits, to name a recent example, seven weeks to record their *Cut* album; Don, Charlie, Dewey and Ed knock their second Old and New Dreams opus off in three days, two for recording and one for mixing.

ECM's Manfred Eicher is at the controls. A tall, thin, gangling man, with a moustache that looks like he's grown it to appear older, he makes sporadic efforts to be friendly, but warmth does not come easily to him. He likes there to be no one in the studio but himself and the musicians. I pretend to be a microphone.

Being used to dub-style mixing intricacies, Eicher's methods seem staggeringly simple. He gets a sound, then whams straight through – and on to the next tune. No time for niceties, except when Haden's unhappy with his bass sound on his spectacular tribute to the whales track.

Whales have been recorded talking to one another underwater; Haden has uncannily recreated the whales' conversation on bass – anguished bellows, wistfully rising to a shriek. It's eerie, all the more for being overwhelmingly emotional. The shrieks and wails rise to a hubbub. Haden sawing furiously on his bow and the sound of strings slapping against wood makes you *feel* that you're on board an old wooden whaling ship, the whale's tail thrashing, threatening to crack the boat in two . . . It's almost a relief when Blackwell's drums flurry in. And the horns drift a melody you suddenly realise was implicit in the whales' cries all along – that's all part of the way Old and New Dreams play, in accordance with the theories of their mentor, Ornette Coleman.

Haden, whose roots are in country music (his parents played at the Grand Ole Opry in Nashville, Tennesee, and that's where he made his pre-teen debut), told me that until he met Ornette, he'd never been able to express himself fully – to "free up", as Jamaicans say.

Later, when I ask Cherry if he'd had the same experience, he says: "I've been open to learn all my life, but Ornette's particular concept of music is where you're reaching for pure sound. I'm not thinking of style, because style's a straitjacket, in a way, because it means you've always got to sound the same way to be recognised. To reach a certain quality, there's got to be a sameness of something that's always going on; the change in the cycle of night and day is something that's always going on, music is something that's going on just as steady as that. But only if it's quality; there's something relative in the quality of John Coltrane playing something and a great African musician playing. It's something to do not just with the person, but with the spirit of the music coming through him . . .

"Ornette's harmolodic system . . . when Old and New Dreams plays a composition, it's very bright and brilliant in *form* and *swing*. Swing first, then form. For Ed Blackwell, with his conception of rhythm, he can hear a sound and know what to do with it to make it swing. That's a special state a musician must reach for. The melody's brilliant enough that when you come to improvise after playing it, the music keeps rising. That's the whole concept of the music."

"Just because I come from Watts, I don't have to talk the same way they talk in my neighbourhood."
Don Cherry

Cherry arrives later than the others on the day they're mixing the album. He saunters in, lighting the first of a string of Gauloises, looking ready for a stroll on the deck of a luxury liner: crisp white jacket, open sandals, a red T-shirt emblazoned with "Don Cherry – Organic Music" in black velvet, around a symbol that looks vaguely mystic and oriental – it's one of his wife Moki's designs. The elegance is misleading – far from travelling with a lavish wardrobe, Cherry just packs a small red knapsack – *très* Beat. You feel he plays pocket trumpet because it's so portable.

Cherry says I should try to visit his and Moki's house in Tågarp on Sunday, that every Sunday they have concerts there. Since 1970, they've lived in a rambling old Swedish schoolhouse, all slats of red wood, way out in the country. That's when he's not in his Long Island, New York loft, right above his pals the Talking Heads.

Cherry is constantly enthusing about other musicians: Africans or Orientals with unpronounceable names he forgets to write down for me, an American blues musician living in Italy who had to quit the States "when they were trying to denigrate the Black Panthers, which they could never do."

He also expresses a love for certain rock musicians, notably the Talking Heads, Ian Dury and Lou Reed – he played on Reed's last album, *The Bells*, and played with him at New York's The Bottom Line. The Happy House Band that's currently backing him on The Slits tour are Reed's New York musicians. Cherry starts dancing wildly when I play him a tape of Lora Logic's next album – "I love the way she *sticks with it!*" he cries after one prolonged sax riff.

Cherry's eclecticism began when a cousin in the marines brought home Afro-Cuban discs. By now, it demands varied outlets, hence working with Reed's rock musicians, releasing an ethno-jazz album called *Codona* with Colin Walcott and Brazilian percussionist Naná Vasconcelos, and cutting a harmolodic jazz album with Old and New Dreams – all in the space of two months. So it's no surprise when the Swedish band playing in the next hall to Old and New Dreams in the tiny Swedish community centre the night after the studio inspire him. "Check them out, man, they're great! I've asked them to play at home tomorrow!"

The next day's a Sunday, concert day. By the time I wake up the garden's full of Swedish hippies in clogs and peasant skirts, their blond children swinging from tree branches.

The regular Sunday concerts get a lot of coverage in the Swedish press, where the Cherry's efforts to make Tågarp into "a working free space, also a platform for a lot of things going on in the arts in Sweden," are duly noted. The old schoolhouse is a school again and Swedish TV is just recording a series of shows featuring the kids – notably Cherry's sharp and sagacious eleven-year-old son, Eagle-Eye, cast as a detective in shades and a big hat.

The band has fourteen people and they play a very Cherry-eclectic series of sets, one after the other – a folk set, a funk set, a Latin set, with varying approximations of authenticity. The folks mill around eating Swedish pastries and drinking cups of tea. It's halfway between Glyndebourne and Woodstock – no mud, though.

Before dusk, the guests disappear into the forest in Volvos, and the house guests eat garden-fresh veg before retiring. The whole day has brought to life the childhood memory Don tells me about the next day: "It was a community happening, which jazz has always been."

"I left America because I was never, like, ambitious to be the Number One Trumpet Player. I always wanted to develop in music and I thought of the trumpet as a voice. I'm not a great musician, never will be, but I feel to play – sing – on the trumpet, I feel for the trumpet to fly with movement, like I know it can with sound."
Don Cherry

This is how Don Cherry remembers his childhood, a tale from a secret garden:

"The first instrument I played was a drum I made myself out of a barrel, and I'd beat on the drum and sing. I had a strange little life, because I was raised next to a vacant lot with a big eucalyptus tree, and I had a tree house, and we had tunnels in the vacant lot . . . I had a Huckleberry Finn-type life, trying to catch rabbits. That has a lot to do with me listening to ethnic music and playing guitars from Mali and instruments of bamboo and wood . . ."

Cherry was raised in Oklahoma. He's part Indian (Choctaw tribe). His grandfather was "an educated black man in his community, he worked being able to fill out certain papers and do bureaucracy for the American Indians and blacks in the community."

Later, Cherry moved to Watts, Los Angeles' black ghetto.

"Our institution, where we got educated, was the streets," Cherry says. Specifically a record shop run by a saxophonist called Charles Cunard, who'd let all the budding musicians listen to the old Charlie Parker Dial 78s, Thelonious Monk, Bud Powell, Dizzy Gillespie, Fats Navarro, Stanley Turrentine and Billie Holiday records for free while they bought reeds for their instruments.

The other vital institution was, of course, the Church. "Gospel music, from the beginning. The main thing is that everybody in church would feel it and go into what they call speaking languages" –

i.e. talking in tongues – "where the Holy Ghost takes over. Being able to play like that is what you're reaching for."

Old and New Dreams' recent US tour played to mostly white audiences. This depressed Cherry slightly; he saw it as proof that black America isn't checking its culture, its roots.

"Everyone in music plays one thing all night, whether it's free or funk or what. I like to play different things – that's when it's fun."
Don Cherry

The evening after the concert, we're back in the big schoolroom. Moki Cherry is an artist, she works with fabrics. Poles hang from hooks set overhead and Moki suspends different hangings like stage sets from the arched wooden ceiling – a different environment every night, if you want, a fairy castle or a pillared hall.

We've finished supper and before Don puts Eagle-Eye to bed, he's having a drum session with him on the kit in the corner. The Cherrys' fifteen-year-old daughter Neneh is a punk bass player, his son David plays keyboards and tuba, and another daughter, Jan, plays violin.

Firmly, Don leads Eagle-Eye to double, then fracture the pace, then add cymbal frills. He tells Eagle-Eye again how Blackwell makes rhythms by playing it one way with one hand and backwards with the other. He directs him towards interplay between hand and foot cymbals. He tells him, earnestly: "Everyone has their own rhythm, but the essence of what I hear – I always hear the *shuffle* first."

Ornette Coleman

Here Ornette and his harmolodic team are in one of my favourite phases of his always fascinating, shape-shifting career – the double bass, double drums full-on head charge of Prime Time. There are certain intense moments when listening to the ferocious, full-frontal double-barrelled thrust (double rhythm section!) of the album, Dancing in Your Head, *is a serious necessity. But then the same applies to other Ornette works from the dazzling breadth and depth of his canon.*

"Ornette Coleman: On Human Feeling"

First published in New Musical Express, *10 July 1982*

Ornette Coleman's harmolodics brought about the musical change of the century. After his New York comeback last year, the legendary tenor man talked to Vivien Goldman about race, religion and all that jumpin' jazz.

The Big O originally hails from Fort Worth, Texas. He has been a fighter and an outsider all his life. His fragile frame is a walking contradiction of equations of brawn with strength.

He is invariably polite: call it being a nice guy, or the humility of true genius; call it the survival mechanism diplomacy of a man who had to accept racist insults with a smile, in the South, with his life on the line. Whichever, it's fascinating to see an artist keep his ego on the leash.

He listens attentively, head slightly to one side. After you've finished talking, he says in a tone of wonder "Is that so? Is that right?" with such a devastating appreciation that you're forced to reassess what you said. Is he sincere or sarcastic? If he's pleased, he adds: "*That's good, that's good*."

When I think of Ornette Coleman, I remember the phrase, humble lion. The achievements of this sensitive, querulous man are awesome.

He's one of the few people this century who've readjusted our ears, jogged our receptivity and rhythm sensitivity.

In 1945, Coleman was overjoyed when his mother gave him his first saxophone. She had reason to rejoice, too; by the next year Coleman was supporting the family on the money he was earning playing at extremely rough Southern gambling juke dives.

In an extensive interview in A.B. Spellman's fascinating book, *Four Lives in the Bebop Business*, Ornette recalls crying on the bandstand one night, wearing the tuxedo he'd hired to take his then best girl to her graduation dance. The chance of a job had come up, and Ornette had to blow the date and work instead. As he played, drunks flashed knives on the dance floor. Ornette was crying because he didn't want to be there, couldn't understand why his music was encouraging violence. That night a couple of guys got cut up, one killed.

It seems unlikely that Ornette's music was really prompting violence, but as soon as The Big O cut loose and began to follow the lines of music dancing in his head, beyond the stated melody line – an extension of the melodic improvisations in certain sections of a song that characterised bebop, the music that dominated when Coleman first began – he provoked a remarkable violence for such a charming, courteous, non-macho presence.

Frequently, the violence was physical, gangs of men outraged by his unfamiliar musical vocabulary waiting outside the stage door to mash up musician and instrument. Later, the violence changed to savage criticism and rejection by all but the close-knit band of musicians (Don Cherry, Charlie Haden, Ed Blackwell, Charlie Moffett, Dewey Redman) who trained with Ornette and never left him, spiritually.

So what was all the fuss about? It's only music.

But hearing is a means of perceiving the world, of organising information. If you start to hear differently, it's as radical a change as starting to see things differently, and of course it's a threat.

Ornette once told me that he first conceived harmolodic music when he was playing in a church group and listening to the choir, who were, by conventional standards, duff. But he realised that all the voices pursuing their own melodies made a different kind of unison, unregimented. It wasn't off, it was *on*.

It's a great communication challenge – talking eloquently and listening intently at the same time.

Ornette coined the term "harmolodic" to describe the process whereby each instrument, each voice, pursues its own melody in song, ignoring the established set structures (bars, keys, chord changes) that will amputate inspiration for the sake of a neat middle eight, with everybody compulsorily shifting gear at precisely the same time.

Since Ornette began to develop his harmolodic stratagems in the early 1950s, nobody has superseded the scope of his vision.

Of all musics, harmolodics most explicitly deals in liberty and respect for each individual's (potential) contribution. The arrogant titles of his early albums – *Tomorrow Is the Question*, *Something Else!!!!*, *The Shape of Jazz to Come* – must have outraged all those who lost their way in the unaccustomed maze of so many individual sounds and self-expressions sliding alongside each other.

Accustomed to receiving music in pre-packaged bite-shaped segments, hearing all the tastes flood in at once, proved to be a sensory overload for most. Hence the cries of "charlatan" and "fake" that Ornette endured simply because he heard one step beyond. Conventionally attuned ears just hear a horrible noise, till the melodies start to unravel; then it's an earmakable/remarkable exhilaration – like suddenly breaking out of a traffic jam and winging wildly down an open road.

This interview took place last year, when Ornette, who hadn't played in America for years, played two sets for two blazing nights at Joseph Papp's Shakespeare Theatre in New York.

Ornette, always a natty dresser, had some exquisite suits for the occasion, made out of special jewel-coloured fabrics he'd found in Chinatown.

Prime Time, Ornette's group that matched the splendour of his suits, features a spectacularly sizzling rhythm section of Jamaaladeen Tacuma on bass (hear his new *So Tranquilizin'* 45 on Rough Trade) and Denardo Coleman, Ornette's son, drumming (often in the company of another drummer). Denardo had great fun playing on his father's *Ornette at 12* album when he was twelve years old.

Like so many of Ornette's moves, Denardo's colourful, rumbustious drumming drew all kinds of flak from the critics. Wisely ignoring the words of cloth ears, Denardo has progressed till now he expresses the state of the art in drumming in the age of the drum machine. The beat, the regular thump as reproduced easily by technology, is implicit; instead of stating the obvious, Denardo's drums dance with and beyond the rhythm, with subtlety, authority and humour.

Ornette says he appreciates the "good taste" of Denardo's drumming.

At the four spectacular Prime Time sets at the Shakespeare Theatre, I also appreciated his endurance. At the beginning of the first set, Denardo slashed his hand on a cymbal but continued playing with his usual vivacity and wit, even though his yellow satin jeans were so blood-spattered they looked like early Clash "Jackson Pollock" gear.

Drummers who go along with the new rulings of the Musicians' Union against electrical manufacture of sound should check out Denardo – he's the proof that drum machines actually liberate drummers to do more interesting and human rhythms.

Ornette's album title *Dancing in Your Head* has become a catchphrase and it's a good summary of the effect of Prime Time live, which combines attack and passion with the sensitivity that comes from listening to other people's desires as attentively as you listen to your own. It touches the body and the mind at the same time, unusual for dance music.

Sometimes it seems that bodies and minds wave hopelessly at each other across a widening chasm. It's another elevating aspect of harmolodics, that healthy music, that both bits of our being get a good massage when Prime Time play.

We met the day after the concerts, the archetypal triumphal return, in Ornette's hotel room.

Every time I'd seen him before in New York, it had been in his enormous loft in the Bowery; with the hieroglyphic painting from the cover of his *Body Meta* album on the wall and enough equipment for a group rehearsal sitting where the three-piece suite would be in less bohemian surroundings.

But the hotel room is uncluttered. Ornette, who is abstemious and would rather eat a little than a lot, offers me mineral water. He isn't feeling too well, something like a cold. As he sips his mineral water, I encourage him to go for hot lemon and honey. Something about Ornette's expression of patient suffering – the man is tired, he's just done four intensive shows on the trot – brings out all of my maternal instincts.

Vivien: *Why are we in a hotel, not at home?*

Ornette: *[sighs] For some reason, me being somewhere is like having the approval of the people that want me to be there. Because people harass you. I was on the Bowery and people*

> *kept on calling the police on me. Wagons coming every five minutes with a big blast. On July 4 1980, someone called the cops on me when I was rehearsing – and I was on the Bowery [the most low-down winos section of New York]! How can you disturb someone on the Bowery!?*
>
> *That's why I'm taking my time in finding somewhere to put my investment and time. I've gone to places before; spend lots and lots of money and get the same reaction. I went to the Bowery because at least I reckoned someone would let me do my work there. I'm in the process of acquiring a school to do some teaching. Maybe whoever feels they're my enemy won't feel that way about that.*

I tell Ornette that Bob Marley used to have the same problem in Kingston; he solved it by investing in a large property uptown and moving his extended proletariat family right in there in the heart of the *haute* bourgeoisie.

Ornette digs it. "At least he'd get some protection that way. But I can't afford to live in the richest neighbourhood, and probably they don't want me to come round them, so I'll play it by ear and see how it works . . . I find it very hard for music and the music business to agree together, but it can be done."

Ornette's coming-out/return gigs after what he calls "one of our little slink periods" of public silence and private writing are prompted on one level by an association with a man called Sid Bernstein, who began managing Ornette in 1980. "Till then I'd been road manager, repairman, everything." Further fruits of the new liaison are a deal signed some time after this interview took place with Island Records. Since the collapse of Artists House records, with whom Ornette released *Body Meta* and *Dancing in Your Head*, Ornette had been sitting on some Prime Time tapes (digitally recorded, no second takes), now released by Island as *Of Human Feelings*.

About the projected school (no age restrictions), Ornette says: "The thing that's so profound is that teaching to exist and teaching to keep something that's in existence is two different things. There's so many people that have not had the opportunity to learn to exist, as well as to learn how to do something that's already in existence."

Is it difficult to teach something you hear in your head to other people? Ornette has always worked intimately with his musicians, sharing houses with them, woodshedding for months. As he did with James Blood Ulmer and Don Cherry, he's done with the new generation of Prime Time . . .

"There is a way of getting the sounds that you want at the place when you want them with the results that you want. They are available, it's just how to go about travelling that road to find them; some rhythm sections eliminate the right to think and therefore you have to lock your ideas into [their sound]. Some people think this is a very good discipline for music, that you have a strict order of logic and you show how many variations this logic can mean to you emotionally. That's all it's ever gonna do. It's not gonna free you from the cause of not needing.

"There's too much beautiful music and too many creative people to be bound to that limited concept. It doesn't have to change, all it has to do is to grow.

"I have that problem, because when you're playing Western music in the form of a unison, and we've all been told what that unison is supposed to do for our heads, when you hear more than one unison you can't deal with it. It's not true; because just like we all have five senses, there are sounds that appeal to many other senses and the Western world would be very healthy to allow those sounds to amalgamate with those other senses.

"That's where the sanity and insanity lies, because no one wants to admit that they don't know how, where, why to do it, and where it is; but they all admit there's something to be done, whether it's a music professor, critic or what.

"I have tried my best to show the people that are playing with me how I approach it when I try to achieve my goals. I'm trying not to have a logic that's limited by the only source of unison. No matter if you have a hundred or a thousand unisons, somebody's gonna hear somebody they don't like. So if they are gonna hear somebody they don't like in one unison, why not have something they don't like in a thousand unisons? Since it's all you, like or dislike.

"It's just plain logic that if human expression is going to mean something other than the repetitions of patterns, that everybody should participate in it to create or eliminate the patterns – or, to let what there be exist [as it was], before the logic of patterns.

"Learning music is not the same thing as learning to manipulate a machine or doing something where the skills have to be always to the exact state in order to ensure the healing, like a doctor or mechanic, the perfection of the instrument being the expressed state. That's not a pattern. That's knowledge. The pattern comes from the logic you use to describe the logic. And music has been put into a mechanical pattern that has limited the use of what logic would mean, without having to think of a pattern in sound.

"One reason why it's like that is because Western instruments are built into a certain logic that goes – but it doesn't mean it's the ultimate expression of sound in music. That's why styles have been created, because of decorating those logic sounds. To me, that's what harmolodic will mean; one day it will free you from having to have a style or create a style that's different from all the other ones."

Ornette's speech is a soft Southern burr; he places odd emphases on letters and vowel sounds, jumbling the expected rhythms, and talks in spirals of meaning that can be as startling when you first meet him as harmolodics are when you first hear them. I only succeeded in following certain steps of Ornette's reasoning when I had a chance to play the tape back, in fact. When you unravel the words, though, they're a deep dance.

I ask, "Ornette, why do you think people get hooked on a rhythm? Like reggae, say, the pleasure of familiarity. Is it a feeling of stability or security that people crave?"

Ornette says straight away, "I think it's the tempered scale; the thing we call the tonic."

A tempered instrument is any instrument you can tune; a non-tempered instrument, the reverse. You can, of course, detune and thus de-temper even a piano, that most restrictingly linear of instruments.

"The thing that lets you think you can repeat it, or the thing that is unison. It has a tendency to consume and be mentally stimulating; at the same time it's always played with some purpose. If I play a certain line, or a guy plays a line with me, it all fits the same purpose; but the content of it gets a different result.

"So I would think that the rhythm structure of sound is the basic of what causes that to happen. *IT* doesn't always cause that to happen, but it does stimulate the same motives.

"What I'm saying is, if you take the rhythm out of notes, you don't have that. Like in classical music, what you have is the major seventh, coming down on the third and the fifth, and tonic at the same time. In the major seventh you don't have to use the rhythm, it's kind of resolved anyway, but any other note it takes some kind of rhythmic figure to get it to an expression of motive. The major seventh motive is already set up, it's going to a time; and you don't have to use rhythm to do that. But other sounds you have to use rhythm so that the note can rise those rhythms to the destination they're gone.

"I think basically what you're saying is the rhythm of logic that makes the rhythm exist, as opposed to the repetition of notes. See, rhythm always sounds like rhythm, but no thing always sounds like rhythm. Intervals always sounds like rhythm, but no thing always sounds like rhythm. Rhythm always sounds like rhythm. That's why when it plays well, it's found a way to resolve both without having to get in each other's way.

"That's what I try to do – not what I *try* to do, what I *do*: I am exchanging rhythm for notes and notes for rhythm, and give them equal position. Sometimes it's challenging to do it, because the rhythms don't have to be resolved. The notes seem to always want to be spelled out."

Abruptly, Ornette, who's sitting with legs primly crossed in the armchair facing me, asks, "If you wasn't singing in any language that you know, and you were singing, how would it sound?"

I'm not accustomed to thinking in Ornette's metaphysical musicology. Unexpected? "Free, or something?" I say hesitantly.

"Well; that's a good word to use, free; but how would it sound? If you weren't singing in any language, how would it sound? You wouldn't have any reference other than what you'd heard and you'd have to make the comment after the experience. You couldn't conceive of making a comment before the experience.

"That is what happens in emotional experiences. The person finds themselves having an experience that they neither had motivated, had a reason for experiencing, or had a need for a desire for it. And yet those experiences bring things to a higher level. That emotional experience, they don't know what caused it to happen, and yet it happens.

"Sometimes in sound it opens up those types of avenues. Sound sometimes lets you have the experience that you wasn't prepared for, that enlightens you more than one that you want to approve of: like, yeah, I like this or I don't like this. It goes beyond that sometimes and enlightens you.

"I think every person that breathes has that within them in some degree of something that they do. It's just a matter of how they find a way of expressing without it being harmful to them.

"But with music, it covers so much emotion and expression in people that the person starts becoming . . . like, what they say – a fan. To me there's only one thing, and that's the music thing. When a person starts saying "Are you into so and so?" that means you're not into something else. Well, it doesn't make any sense. I have never really disowned anyone who's liked what I've done. I just see them as another person enjoying themselves, and something that I do makes them feel good about being that way. Therefore, I would rather for them to feel better about what *that* is than to make them feel like they're a fan. In Western culture, value is its own reward."

I ask, "When did you start finding out about cultures that weren't Western?"

"I think my first real experience was in the South," says Ornette. "I mean it was racial. But when I started not thinking that everything had a racial motive because someone wanted you to be with less, I went on an Indian reservation and saw some American Indians participating in their own culture and it awakened, fulfilled me. Then the person spoke about this, they didn't want any white people there. And I assume that though I wasn't white, I also wasn't Indian, so I was intruding on their personal belief. The thing that really touched me more than anything was how they were praying to their own god that didn't have nothing to do with any religion I've ever experienced. And not only did they know what they were doing, they knew why.

"In the South, I had had that same experience, but it always presented itself in a racial issue. I'd see a white person doing something that I want to participate in, but I couldn't, because of segregation. I'd see something a white person was doing that I hadn't had the experience to know as a kid. It was so *strange* growing up like that.

"When I was playing in church bands it gave me a real human interest in all those human things, like most people believe that people are equal. Then you realise that basically, most people see equality as something that gives them security in their environment, more than something in their heart that they want everybody to experience. But what can you say? I'm sure these things have already been said in the same way by millions of people.

"I think the same thing that separates human beings and races is the same quality that separates love and creativity. What I'm saying is that when someone finds that you do something and know something that they don't know, and you're in a lesser position, they have to try and destroy you. It seems like that's the pattern.

"Even in education, if someone has developed something they do that is much more individual and more in control of the person than the persons that are in possession of the things that he needs to excel in their own field, they usually annihilate. Kill. Because society hasn't allowed the creative man to change the will of someone that is better off. It's not because the people that are better off feel any different about those that aren't. It's just that they assume that they have a right to the place where everyone wants to be; and that's where they think they should be, if they're there already."

[While I was working on this anthology, I spoke to Denardo, Ornette's son, as some readers had found Ornette's communication too elliptical. He chuckled, because he understands every word. Ornette is commenting on the sad fact of what has previously been described in this book as "Bad Mind". Said Denardo, "Ornette's not necessarily talking about the classroom. It's people who think they are intellectually superior to others, who try to make sure that any other ideas, which can outstrip theirs, are going to be squashed. Like how some bandleaders won't hire anyone who sounds better than them."]

Ornette's expression and use of language is individual, convoluted and yet lucid, like an official philosopher. What was his education like?

"I grew up with a family of schoolteachers; not my mother, she was a housewife." [Ornette's father died when he was seven.] "But sisters, aunts, cousins, uncles, they were all in education.

"When I finished school, I got about ten or twelve scholarships to go to college. At the time I had a band, I was playing, I was making 200 dollars a week. If I was getting paid that in proportion to what I'm doing now, I'd be very wealthy. But it just had something to do with the fact of the need of what you were doing. I was playing in this kind of syndicate type of thing, where I played in white clubs on Wednesdays and Fridays and the Mexican clubs Thursdays, and the crowd was always large.

"So I was making a comfortable kind of living as a young teenager, for my mother, because we were very poor. It wasn't till I was twenty-two or twenty-three years old that I had my own room. At that point it was just my mother and sister and me, and I still didn't have my own room, so you can imagine how big the house was.

"So I decided to go down to a college and see. When I got there, the guys were starving – they were in worse conditions than I was! So I said, I can't go to college and not be able to support my family right. I decided that I would return home, since I realised I was going to be paid for something I learnt to do, and since I had already found something that I could do that I could get paid at. I took that security.

"It wasn't till deep in the late years of bebop that I realised that in classical music, there was music that hadn't had an applied result to it; just to be music."

[Again for this anthology, I discussed Ornette's quote, which had caused some confusion, with Denardo Coleman. His response: "Bebop was part of a designed environment which Black people were included in, whereas classical music wasn't specific to any one environment. It was just music, for the creativity. Ornette was commenting on Black and white and the different freedom you can have to express yourself. Bebop is really advanced, but bebop wasn't free. Then on the other side, you had this other music that could exist (anywhere), for music's sake. Because it's not just music, you've always got a backdrop of the environment. Are you really in a free environment? Ornette raises questions about identifying when you're not, that you have to understand it, and it is something to move towards. Environment and mind need to be free."]

"I began to realise that there was what you call culture and those kind of things. Because I've always thought that those kind of things was just people being human beings and I didn't never think that culture, wealth, poverty was something that had been done by design. I thought it was just a person.

"No one is born knowing that they're not rich or poor. When you was a baby, you didn't know that. So it's by design. That's why I don't understand those words called socialism or communism. Those kinds of things are really design. They're designed to instil you with the very thing that [they're] supposed to free you of. What it would be if that design didn't exist? But they took the design from the design.

"The only thing that I have literally tried to join that I thought was good is religion. I really think that real religion eliminates the need of you having to design someone else's behaviour, because you don't want to trust them. You don't have to design someone's behaviour if you have a religious feeling. All the other things are designed because of human behaviour . . ."

Vivien: *But don't you feel restricted in established religions? They have a very rigid code*

Ornette: *Only because of the fact that they challenge your will of who you are, not what you can do and what you got. If you want to be a good person and that's what your goals are, then it doesn't matter what your religion is, what it is* *that you want to achieve with your living, because that's the highest goal, to be a sincere, good person. Once the patterns are applied, then you are restricted like you say.*

Vivien: *It's almost as common to see jazz musicians wearing the Muslim skullcap as it is to see a reggae musician's dreadlocks. Since you grew up in one of the most overtly racially hostile areas in the world, you've lived through many phases of growing black consciousness, a lot of which have been religious. How did you feel when your friends started taking African names, for example?*

Ornette: *I hadn't really thought about all the problems of social prejudice, because I didn't think that some particular race had caused my parents to become poor. I didn't think of it racially; I just thought of it as being poor. Where I grew up, there was no segregation – well, there was, but because there were no white people I didn't realise it was segregation. I didn't see other races.*

Vivien: *So when did you start to relate to white people?*

Ornette: *I saw them, but I wasn't socialising with them. The conversation I have with you, I couldn't have with them. When I went to California in 1950 or '51 was the first time I had a conversation with a white person without thinking another white person was gonna come up and say, "You can't do this." But all of those scenes came to my mind a different way than just black and white. They came to me according to what you could say was a territory.*

In my hometown there was a black man who had a bank, and then you'd go up the street and see a hillbilly in a worse condition. But you still couldn't talk to him, so it was always strange to me to understand the motive of what that system really meant to white people.

Changing your name . . . your religion, doesn't change your race. Sometimes people think you change your race by religion, but regardless of what religion you're going to accept, if you're black and look in the mirror, you see a black. I think a lot of minority people have changed their social and religious structures to try and find more individual freedom for themselves. Whether they do that, I don't know, but it seems to bring a certain respect to the minority. I think that if human beings didn't have to be bothered with the category of being a lesser being among someone else, they wouldn't have to change anything about who they are.

Whenever a white person becomes religious, it's about him getting closer to his identity. But with minorities, it gives them more relationship to being accepted on a cultural, religious concept. You've got to understand that in Western society, the concept that we live and struggle in is by someone's design, and you know it's not your own.

Vivien: *What do you mean, Ornette? Are you thinking about conspiracy theories, multinational corporations pulling the strings of puppet politicians?*

Ornette: *Is that what you think? [Asks in polite surprise.]*

Vivien: *I see it as a crucial whodunnit and I haven't read the last page.*

Ornette: *You already have over 200 million people; whether they're a corporation or not doesn't matter. For one thing, you don't have to be a part of something to know you have the privilege of doing something that someone else doesn't have, if you're a part of that mass imagery that we call human beings. In this particular, Western, environment, the darker-skinned people are in a lesser position. I guess, I've heard, only because of numbers – not concepts or intellect, or ability, just a minority because of numbers.*

Vivien: *You've worked with lots of people outside jazz – from Yoko Ono to The Master Musicians of Joujouka. What kinds of things did you learn from them?*

Ornette: *I've got on with most people involved in music; all they really want to do is their best. But to solve that problem is so hard to do. I think Yoko has always had an instinctual feeling to her, to make an impression on Western culture, and I think she found a way to do that in the non-black side of Western culture. The Joujouka people have been omitted from Western culture, and they're not even black!*

So what I've learnt is that in Western culture, the struggle is for the individual to relate to the masses, not for the masses to relate to the individual.

Vivien: *We're back to that whodunnit . . . plots to keep the lowest common denominator going, so that people aren't encouraged to think.*

Ornette: *You mean – the idea of keeping somebody with less? . . . maybe that's true, too, but what I'm saying is that the difference between living to make something that you are trying to achieve become valuable in your lifetime, as opposed to letting things that are outdated make you feel that you are inferior to whatever it is you're trying to achieve.*

Vivien: *What are your goals now? You've succeeded in making a lot of people think, as well as making their lives more pleasurable . . . what seems most important to you now?*

Ornette: *What I'd like to do is to continue to advance the concept of living without being affected by anyone [answers swiftly and firmly] as long as the motive that you have will be advantageous to people. That for me is much more noble. No one wants to be unhappy or unsuccessful; everybody wants the same thing, more or less. I would like to continue to get better and have less problems about how I get to do that.*

*

The harmolodic family, buoyed by their creativity and stimulating community, had a verve and passion for life and art that added an extra infusion of energy into a movement – and a room. Fourteen years later, for the Village Voice, *I was able to re-visit them when Ornette finally found a more stable home, his first since the free-wheeling 1960s SoHo loft days. This time, I could more fully introduce the brilliant poet, performer, publisher, record label head and my mentor, Jayne Cortez. Along with Don Cherry's then wife, the Swedish multi-media artist Moki, I was lucky enough to receive from these two women – and the men who loved them – liberating lessons in the artist's life. Key to it all is owning your intellectual and creative property, and somehow finding a way to grab a physical space you can use to further your work, with players or associates you can weld into a team. Combine your skill sets, control production of your work, build your team, so if and when you do business with a more significant, even corporate, entity, you deal from a position of strength.*

And above all, keep going, no matter if challenges arise. Discipline and rigor are a given, or why even bother.

"Harmolodic Harlem: The House That Ornette Coleman Built"

First published in the Village Voice, *3 September 1996*

The Lee Building is an unlikely art deco remnant of a more elegant age, stranded among garish Harlem fast-food joints. Its eau de Nil façade and silver numerals are shaded by the elevated train. Inside, that all-too-rare breed, a human elevator operator, ropes you up past a methadone clinic and into the studios of Harmolodic Inc., the house that Ornette Coleman, inventor of the harmolodic concept, built.

After forty years of battles – racists in his native Texas, traditionalists pelting him with rotten eggs onstage, business associates ripping him off, supportive record-label executives resigning mid-project – Coleman's music and relationship to the industry are both at a peak. In the space of one year he's released three records, all on his own label steered by his son, drummer, producer and manager, Denardo Coleman, and sensibly linked to PolyGram in jazz-mad France, through Verve in the States.

It's about time. Prior to last year's eclectic *Tone Dialing*, the first Harmolodic Inc. release, the legendary saxophonist had not had a record out in seven years. Says Denardo, "My father would rather sacrifice without working than feel he has compromised himself."

These are busy days at Harmolodic, which is issuing its first group of records: two hardcore harmolodic CDs from Ornette, *Three Women* and *Hidden Man*, jointly titled *Sound Museum*; and *Taking the Blues Back Home*, by pioneering poet, artist and activist Jayne Cortez and her group The Firespitters. All the releases so far are produced by Denardo, whose skills have brought a needed clarity and balance to harmolodics and free jazz, thus clearing him of any taint of nepotism – after all, he's Cortez's son, too.

As the 1996 US elections approach, it's time to invite Ornette Coleman, who's done so much to promote democracy in music, to the White House. Coleman describes his harmolodic mission as to "remove the caste system from sound". As Ornette wrote in *BOMB* magazine, "In music, the melody is not the lead. The lead is a sequenced unison form which requires anyone to transpose all melodies note for note to their instrument." Linked by a groove too deep for the ears to hear, harmolodic musicians perform their own individual tunes, with simultaneous subconscious synchronicity. Harmolodics is a jailbreak from those 4/4 prison bars and a holiday from rigid rhythmic expectations. It's as natural as thinking about a few things at a time. If you're from a family in which everyone talks at once, but communication is always achieved, you're already hooked on harmolodics.

Harmolodic Inc. is no mom-and-pop operation; however, it offers evidence of the civilised harmony that can be created despite the dissonance of a past divorce. A lifetime ago, Coleman and Cortez were teenage sweethearts who married, then divorced ten years later, after a period of living apart. At no stage have they worked together artistically. Indeed, Cortez's husband and occasional collaborator has long been the eminent sculptor Melvin Edwards, whose soulful art graces Cortez and The Firespitters' *Taking the Blues Back Home* CD cover.

Denardo's upbringing included shuttling between protest marches in the Deep South with his militant mother while staying with his dad on St. Marks Place in the 1960s. He made his drumming debut in 1966 at age twelve, on Ornette's *The Empty Foxhole*. The son is well aware of the artistic qualities the parents share. "The good thing they have in common is they both want whatever they're doing, whether it's music or poetry, to be to the point. They really try to get below the surface, and immediately identify and dismiss anything trite or superficial and go on working. It's all got to be approached with a certain edge and I like to play with that drive. You've got to fire up; it's got to be urgent, even if it's relaxed."

The thunder of the Metro-North train hurtling past Ornette's office window jogs a blues gene, as Jayne Cortez rehearses "Taking the Blues Back Home" inside the studio. The urgency is palpable as Cortez commands the music with her characteristically deadpan, ferociously sardonic inflection: "I'm still the owner of the secrets in the blues, from a long time ago." In this incantation, imperiously claiming her birthright, Cortez summons deeper, darker forces; the dust from which Cortez comes and will return is evidently the earth of Robert Johnson's crossroads.

These rehearsals are for a particularly significant tour – of South Africa. Cortez has a long history of activism. In the 1960s, she worked with the SNCC (Student Nonviolent Coordinating Committee), observing voter registration in the South and reporting her findings back to Los Angeles. She has worked with members of Nelson Mandela's African National Congress. Discussing the band's set list for the Azania (Free South Africa) shows, Cortex finds history has caught up with her 1990 prophecy. Of her popular political anthem, she cracks, "We can't play 'Mandela Is Coming', because Mandela's already come!" The group listens attentively to her ideas. All agree with Cortez's emphatic "We've got to play something positive and optimistic, to encourage the people."

Encouraging the people has been a life's work for Cortez. Whether she claims the title or not, Cortez – whose tenth volume of verse, *Somewhere in Advance of Nowhere* (Serpent's Tail/High Risk Books), has just been published – is the godmother of the contemporary spoken word scene. Her commitment to the interaction between voice and musical instrument, and art and politics, is vindicated by the rebirth of the genre. She's an inspiration to such poet performers as Dana Bryant and Tracie Morris, the latter of whom comments admiringly, "Jayne even dares to discuss the people who give you the blues!" The subtle empathy between word, rhythm and sound that she has evolved over eight albums with her group – Denardo, guitarist Bern Nix, saxmen Talib Kibwe and Frank Lowe, and bass player Al MacDowell – remains unique. You can hear it on the risky improvisation of "Talk to Me" – a tender, edgy, free-form cut on *Taking the Blues*. It is dedicated to the late musician Don Cherry, whom Cortez used to educate with Fats Navarro records while he was a kid living down the street in Watts.

Cherry's free spirit also hovers over Coleman's two new CDs: "Three Women" and "Hidden Man", both dedicated to Cherry and the late drummer Ed Blackwell, who was in Coleman's quartet in the 1960s.

Ornette is a metaphysician and student of the Kabbalah. He's received many honours, including a 1994 MacArthur Foundation "genius" award, a recent doctorate from the New School for Social Research, and honorary degrees from schools in Pennsylvania, California and Boston. He deserves another award for his dapper dress. For his current PR shots, Coleman sports a jacket with scalloped lapels accented by buttons; naturally, it's designed by Coleman and custom-made in India from special silk.

The two sets of *Sound Museum* mark a return to futures past that's prompted in part by the release of the Ornette box set, *Beauty Is a Rare Thing* (Rhino). Sifting through memories to select the compilation, Coleman decided to regroup his band. He toured Europe last year with Prime Time.

Thirty years ago, Coleman used the quartet format to implode jazz expectations. He then went on to explore symphony orchestras in *Skies of America* and his spine-chilling soundtrack to the movie *Naked Lunch*. He used double bass and double drums in Prime Time, and assembled a panoply of assorted talent (including body-piercing fakirs, philosophers and African dancers) in his landmark performance at 1994's San Francisco Jazz Festival, freaking out some of the audience, who left.

But Coleman says he wanted to return to a traditional format and hear his music played by "great younger musicians". Thus *Sound Museum* features a quartet comprising a new family generation: Denardo, Charnett Moffett – whose father, Charles, played with Coleman back in the day (prophetically perhaps, Charnett's named after Charles and Ornette) – and pianist Geri Allen. Allen's not only the first woman player in any Coleman band, but she's also the first keyboardist in thirty-five years. "Back in the fifties when Ornette got rid of the piano, that was a revolution, because now you couldn't follow the chords, which meant you couldn't follow a formula," Denardo explains.

Sound Museum's resulting chemistry allows perhaps the most radical statement yet of the harmolodic concept. While *Tone Dialing* explored genres not usually thought of as harmolodic, like Caribbean music and rap, *Sound Museum* plunges right in to present no less than twenty-six takes on the same motif. Like the discovery of infinite meaning in a single mantra, the de/re/con/structions of *Sound Museum* cast such drastically different lights on the source material that there's no sense of *déjà entendu* (i.e. been there, heard that).

"When we were working on the record, it became apparent that there were many great interpretations of the compositions," says Coleman, who, despite suffering a bad case of media fatigue, agreed to answer our questions by fax. "We had recorded continuously for days and days. We decided it would be good for people to also hear the directions these compositions went in, particularly as all the musicians were exploring the music harmolodically. So what resulted are not outtakes, but interpretations. As we decided to release two discs, I felt that these two paintings that were on my walls reflected the feeling of the music. We specifically put the individual selections on the disc that felt closer to the visual image."

It might not replace Windows as an organizing system, but the mood-picture method works. *Three Women*, by a North African artist named Zohra Azzoug, and its companion, *Hidden Man*, by Bob Thompson, are both densely coloured, somewhat Fauvist pieces, evocative even in the vastly reduced reproductions of the CD artwork. Perhaps the titles were unduly influential, but after repeated listenings, *Hidden Man* seems more introverted, while *Three Women* has a lighter, more extravagant feel.

Coleman's involvement with the visual arts has a poignant history. "I was working at Bullock's department store in L.A. in the late '50s as an elevator operator. On my lunch hour, I walked past an art gallery. And in the window was a painting of a woman. I will never forget her expression. Even though in the painting she was surrounded by luxury, she seemed not [to be] in that environment. She was in a different place in her head, and seemed sad to be where she was.

"I realised this was how I felt. Being an artist is very hard, and I realised that artists need to be supported. So at that moment I decided I would dedicate myself to helping artists, any kind of artist, any way I could. Soon after, I wrote a piece called 'Lonely Woman'." The song became a classic, whose exquisite melancholy helped establish Coleman's reputation for brilliance.

Ornette began collecting art seriously in the '60s. Like Cortez, who frequently organised her own poetry readings and drama groups, Coleman took the promotional initiative; by the '70s, he was running Artist House, a gallery and performance space on Prince Street, where both *Sound Museum* pieces were originally shown. Ornette lived upstairs. "The space was used by many different types of artists and musicians before Soho became what it is," he reminisces. Longtime Coleman guitarist James Blood Ulmer wryly adds, "It was bad luck, because Coleman was the first person who was into art, who got evicted because of it. I lived upstairs with him for a year, and the neighbours didn't want to hear the music."

Like every other New York artist, the harmolodic crew has moved frequently, one step ahead of gentrification. From Soho, they moved to an old schoolhouse on Rivington in Loisaida. Now, in the spirit of successful African Americans like writer Quincy Troupe reclaiming Harlem as a spiritual home, Hamolodic Inc. is firmly ensconced on 125th Street.

Coleman is the first to say that his career has bloomed since Denardo's intervention. But Denardo knows who to thank. "I love playing the drums, but I needed to make sure there was a musical environment to play in. I'm sure I got that from my mother and father, both people who decided they needed to do something, so they created a vehicle to enable them to do it. Don't wait for the call, just go ahead and create."

Butch Morris

Closing this section with Butch Morris and his Conduction method reminds us that Ornette was not alone in his quest to break the sound bar barrier. The two composers, each with their own distinct yet somehow complementary visions, would have failed in their mission to make us hear and think differently had they not, like Fela, seeded future players. Denardo Coleman, Ornette's drummer son, has made international harmolodic events and gathered orchestras in Cuba and Africa. The Lower East Side's NuBlu Orchestra still performs Butch's special technique. Often, it was conducted, post-Butch, by our friend, the great cultural commentator, artistic provocateur and musician Greg Tate, a disciple of both Butch and Ornette. As I was writing this, Greg was awarded a posthumous Pulitzer Prize. As adept at expanding the musical as he was the written language, Greg also succeeded in establishing teams of musical collaborators. Extending the legacy are cohorts like fellow visionary, guitarist Vernon Reid (co-creator of the revolutionary Black Rock Coalition).

A true roots community was built that endures and ensures the continuation of groups and collectives like Greg's Burnt Sugar The Arkestra Chamber and the commitment to this free-thinking tradition. Now harmolodic habitués like Vernon Reid, cornetist/composer Graham Haynes and guitarist Jared Nickerson continue Tate's own twist on Conduction, like the medicine it is.

"New York Stories: Vivien Goldman"

First published in the Daily Note *at Red Bull Music Academy, New York, May 2013*

A post-punk professor remembers an electric bandleader of the Lower East Side.

This is a song for a spirit. A fickle, tempestuous trickster that flits from one place to the next, one player's horn to the other, sprinkling giddy freedom. Maybe that euphoria can never be a constant state, but while you feel and live it, it's as joyous as it gets. So what can a poor human do to reliably provoke that sensation?

If musicians improvising together only play what they feel, without listening and bouncing off their cohorts – well, it's not the best anarchy.

In the East Village that sense of release was regularly obtainable at a venue that has survived the tsunami of gentrification: Nublu on Avenue C. Bliss was often provided by the *boîte's* resident genius Butch Morris and the musical style he devised: Conduction. Impish and sagacious, the dapper Butch dressed in bright, floppy clothes. Face framed by a soft grey Afro nimbus and fulsome goatee, he was a two-tone spats or sandals sort of fellow, an original boho boulevardier.

Naturally, Butch's style and honey personality made him a familiar figure around the villages of Alphabet City and the Lower East Side. Its streets gave him a haven, as they had fellow jazz-improvising horn men before him, like harmolodic dude Don Cherry, one of whose classics is named "Brown Rice". Cherry was fond of the tofu scramble at the Life Café on Avenue B at Tompkins Square Park, facing Charlie Parker's old pad, but the fine wines and French cuisine of the Casimir bistro on Avenue B were more Butch's speed than vegan fare (in that sense, he was a bon viveur of the old school). He owned the Lower East Side and was a mascot of local haunts like Arcane and Lucien. Casimir's neo-Parisian ambience was "Butch's office".

His frequent collaborator, cornetist Graham Haynes, observes, "In this country we live to work. Butch knew how to work and take time out to live. You have to live so that you can be at peace and happy. Then you will have a story to tell in your art."

Perhaps it was a knack for art/life balance that enabled Butch to come up with one of music's greatest balancing acts: his Conduction method, short for Conducted Improvisation. But surely, you say, that's a contradiction in terms? Not so. Rather like free will, which all too often bumps up against some pesky limitation, or a free lunch (which rarely is), free-jazz improvisation itself is not quite as free as you might think. If you only ever improvise alone, it's a bit like always playing badminton against yourself. After a while, humans want to bounce their notes against others, and not just hit the wall of their own fabulousness over and over again.

But how?

Ornette Coleman, aided by Cherry, came up with the solution of harmolodics. Busting the four-bar barrier, harmolodics involves many rehearsal hours to attain the level of empathy necessary for players to flow together. People jam to their own spontaneous tunes, inspired by an underlying melodic motif and interacting with fellow musicians; everyone is united to form a greater, unpredictable whole. Harmolodic players walk a musical tightrope on an invisible wire of skill and communication.

Butch's solution was the reverse. Butch was the visible wire on which all the musicians walked. He was the Wizard of his own Oz – though Butch never hid behind a curtain. To perform Conduction, the musicians did not even need to have met each other before. The common denominator is that each player had to understand Butch's visually coded language of signs, indicating by facial expressions and gestures when players should change their speed, volume, tone. They all simply started responding to some sound or tune thrown at them by Butch and took it from there. Butch developed Conduction as a benevolent dictator of musicians glad to be subject to his will.

"I always knew I was going to learn with Butch," says Haynes. "The way Butch heard music was very precious – his attention to silence, dynamics, and negative and positive space. I wasn't getting that from anyone else . . . and I work with a lot of people."

Like a few other jazzmen of his generation, the young Butch, a native Angeleno, had served in Vietnam. Afterwards, he bopped about the planet quite freely, creating and collaborating with multimedia artists and big orchestras on both coasts, and in Europe and Asia. When Nublu's anonymous façade, with its single light and no signage, opened on Avenue C, it was a reason for jubilation – now, Butch had his own live laboratory close to home. Before Nublu opened, Alphabet City was still largely Hispanic, known as "Loisaida". Local nightlife scenes like the World and Pyramid had closed. What would become John Zorn's venue The Stone was still the Golden Dragon Chinese Takeout – eat there at your peril.

At a tipping point, Loisaida's graffitied squats were about to be razed for condos; soon enough it would be easier to find a wine bar than a Santeriá botanica [store for spiritual needs in the Yoruba-based faith popular in Cuba and around the Afro-Caribbean-diasporic world] on Avenue C. Just a block away from the East River, Loisaida felt like it was not just on the edge of an island, but also its own freewheeling fringe world, one in which Butch was a creative king. But that Loisaida was starting to be squeezed out along with the squatters and candy stores. Naturally, Butch still reigned among the hipster set, but many of his local *compadres* were leaving the area involuntarily. Says Butch's good friend, producer Brian Bacchus, "Nublu seemed like a rebirth of all the wonderful chaotic creativity of the 1970s and '80s, which Giuliani and gentrification had almost squelched in the '90s."

"There's always a vibe working without written music."
Brandon Ross

Much as the 1940s bebop clubs around 42nd Street were venues for musical sparring, so was Swedish–Turkish musician Ilhan Fredrik Ersahin eager to create a downtown locus for DJs, improvisers, and a dancey avant-garde when he opened Nublu in 2002; three years later, Butch's Conduction sessions there formalised into the Nublu Orchestra.

Many of his best-known Conductions are numbered, but Butch's first Nublu sessions were so experimental they were off the grid. Still, relaxed as he was socially, when it came to Conduction, "Butch was a monster!" Haynes remembers. "He would terrorise people if he thought they made a mistake." But Haynes, Butch and guitarist Brandon Ross were musical soulmates. Those who couldn't take the fire, left.

"You had to leave your agenda at the door," says Ross. "You had to put your concentration and whatever resources you had available at that moment with Butch. That's what Conduction summons of people, what Butch asked of people."

I also went to hear Butch to submit. Overlapping waves of feeling induced by the shapeshifting music would sweep me along like a serene or stormy river. In the course of one Conduction concert I would feel a gamut of emotions, as if Conduction were a group therapy session. And this from a random bunch of bodies, all obedient to Butch's baton. Whoever turned up to play would get a fifteen-minute briefing from Butch and the gig would proceed to be whatever it was, like a tasty soup cooked with whatever's around.

It was always delicious. And felt nourishing. In the course of one Conduction concert, I would taste a gamut of emotions.

"There's always a vibe working without written music," comments Ross. "Butch might grab something he heard when the band was setting up and start to sing from that sound. The music was exciting because you really did not know what was going to happen."

Butch later spread his workshops, projects and musical-collective sessions to other East Village haunts like Lucky Cheng's, the Bowery Poetry Club and The Stone, but Nublu was where he was able to stretch out over a period of time. It was also just a short stroll home from Nublu to East 7th Street, with his hat jammed down tight and his oversize coat flapping against the cold dawn wind on Avenue C.

Conduction was one man's musical concept, but time tells us that it's taken root. Before Butch died, he had the felicity of seeing other Conduction ensembles flourish, including the Burnt Sugar collective founded by Greg Tate, who used to play guitar with Butch at Nublu.

"Conduction lives because we're all Bozos on this bus! And therefore wanna keep standing next to the fire of a postmodern pan-Afrikan master of the universe who walked it like he talked it. No Sell Out," Tate notes in an email.

So this is a song for a spirit. As I said, it's a trickster and can be fickle; it likes to flit about. For some luminous years, it alighted on Butch Morris and Loisaida. If we call out and listen loud enough, it might alight right where we are.

CHAPTER 10

Finale

After a lifetime of pondering music, I often find it best to heed the advice of a wise old Trinidadian calypsonian – in this case, let me leave you with the words of the Mighty Sparrow.

Before reggae became the rage worldwide in the 1970s as the Caribbean music of choice, it was Trinidad's witty calypso, with its salty political satire and folk wisdom, that carried the swing.

Previously in this book we touched down in Mighty Sparrow's Trinidad in 2024, to try and discover who killed the powerful artist, Rebel Sixx. The sound he helped establish, Trinibad, was a harsher time's response to the brand of cheerful musix like calypso, where violence could erupt among the "Bad Johns", the "rude boys" of their day, but musically the weapon was sharp-edged satire. Revered among the heritage of classic calypsonians will forever be The Mighty Sparrow.

Much has changed since the following article was written. The anger roused by the Windrush scandal that brought Sparrow to London at the time is being channelled into a different awareness. Whatever you may think of Brexit, and its far-reaching consequences fuelling future struggle, Sparrow's central message is crucial and eternal.

His call for unity and peace is the ultimate message of this lifetime of interviews with inspiring musicians.

Mighty Sparrow

"The King of Calypso on Freedom, Windrush and Oral Sex"

First published in the Guardian, *26 November 2018*

He inspired Bob Marley's political awakening, survived a coma, and has sung about everything from sex workers to Khrushchev. And at eighty-three, the calypso great still wants to turn the news into song.

"Can you put on the TV news?" asks Slinger Francisco, aka Mighty Sparrow.

While the photographer sets up in my living room in Queens, New York City, the 83-year-old calypso originator scrutinises the screen, where the US midterm elections offer gold to this instinctive satirist.

Watching Sparrow watch the news, eyes narrowed in concentration, is a reminder of the decades of conflict he has processed into poetry – from the impact of US naval withdrawal on Trinidad sex workers, on the infectious 1956 song Jean and Dinah, to the space age and cold war on 1963's Kennedy and Khrushchev. More recently, he has hymned a pre-presidential Barack Obama and railed against Russian oligarchs on Neurosis of the Rich. "If you have time to look at the news," Sparrow observes, "you see where most of those songs' inspiration comes from. There's no question about it." The concept of fake news is anathema to him. "Certain people are telling the audience: 'Don't believe what you see, don't believe what you hear or what you read.' But I do believe."

Rather like today's verbal argy-bargies between rappers such as Drake and Pusha T, early twentieth-century calypsonians also elevated barbed banter into a showbiz art called picong, and locals would gleefully look forward to calypsonians' response to every scandal and row. The rivalry between Sparrow, Lord Kitchener and Lord Melody, for example, gripped the calypso fans known as Bad Johns and Saga Girls – edgy dressers who danced the reel and quadrille in the carnival tents and were Sparrow's constituents. "We used to put on a show!" he chuckles.

According to the Trinidadian writer and broadcaster Isaac Fergusson, "Even politicians were afraid of Sparrow and what he would reveal about them in a song. Until he came along, most calypsonians were semi-professional. People paid them with rum and food – a treat, rather than a salary. They survived on the gratitude of the people. Sparrow changed all that. He wore a suit like a businessman and insisted on being paid. He could be demanding, but musicians loved to play with him, because he treated them the best."

Despite conflicts with the establishment behind Trinidad's fabled carnival (1957's Carnival Boycott documented his strike for fairer pay for male calypsonians), Sparrow is nevertheless an eight-time winner of each of the carnival's Road March and Calypso Monarch awards, and is often dubbed Calypso King of the World.

The lyrical sting of calypso and the instrument associated with it, the steel pan, may be pop's most embedded form of resistance. Starting in 1740, the legal banning of the African-style drum (made of wood and animal skin) under slavery and colonialism encouraged the invention of the steel pan. Hammering industrial metal into tempered scales, steel pans were made out of oil drums from the island's chief export; this was music made by any means necessary, to defy those who benefited most from the island's resources. Calypso's lyrics, too, became a forum for thrashing out the issues of the day, reporting on anything from industrial disputes to sexual peccadilloes.

Colonial-era education and studies of the English poets remain foundational for Sparrow. "We always wanted to belong to the English side of things, because that's all we knew," he says. "As we grew up, America became a second part of us. But going to England felt like going home." Throughout our conversation, Sparrow sings to make a point. "Remember this?" he asks, before breaking into "Rule, Britannia!": "Britons never, never, never shall be slaves."

When his mother Clarissa Francisco brought the eighteen-month-old Slinger and his elder brother on a small boat from their native Grenada to Trinidad, they were moving from one UK colony to another. Though both islands like to claim him, his ancestors were involuntary immigrants. Sparrow's gripping track "The Slave", from the 1964 album *True Life Stories of Passion, People & Politics*, set a template for how Caribbean music could interpret its bloody history. Fergusson recalls his friend Bob Marley confiding: "When I heard the Mighty Sparrow sing 'The Slave', I knew what I wanted to do with my music." Over a propulsive Afro-Cuban jazz rhythm, Sparrow's pointed enunciation and swelling attack on the chorus builds a narrative that foreshadows Marley's later "Redemption Song". "Every time ah tink 'bout de whip an' dem dogs, meh body does start to shake" ("The Slave"). As Sparrow soars into the line, "Oh Lord, I wanna be free!" the track stops so abruptly that it feels as if the listener is leaping from a cliff into the ocean to escape the slave-catcher's dogs at their heels.

Sparrow's life since has reinforced these creative imaginings. Few people have survived a coma to perform again; in 2013, he hovered between worlds for two weeks. Even fewer have teased those writing them off, as evidenced by 1970's "Sparrow Dead". And not many descendants of stolen Africans have managed to make the return journey, but Sparrow did. Inspired by a visit to Nigeria in the 1970s, he has recorded in Yoruba, as well as Creole French, Spanish and Dutch. Despite the military regime, Sparrow found Lagos a paradise. "I never thought I'd reach there – it was like the Garden of Eden. They basically did everything like we do in Trinidad." Sparrow met the firebrand Afrobeat creator, Fela Kuti, and was honoured with a title, Chief Omowale of Ikoyi.

But he had already toured Africa in song, taking a fantasy trip on one of his most beloved numbers, 1964's hilarious "Congo Man". Opening with a lusty chuckle, it finds Sparrow revealing his envy of a cannibal who has enjoyed eating two white American girls, one cooked and one raw. Despite the song's popularity, it was banned from local radio till 1989. In my lounge, Sparrow sings the familiar verses and even enacts a typical audience reaction: "I never eat ah white meat yet, except" – a beat, eyes twinkling – "all right, just one time in Canada!" Cue the audience, corpsing. Well-versed in calypsonian double entendres, they understood that he was skewering not so much racism or cannibalism, but another taboo: oral sex.

The reason for today's interview, however, is more serious. Sparrow has been called to England to perform at the London jazz festival's Windrush celebration, curated by Anglo-Trinidadian poet and teacher Anthony Joseph, and featuring Calypso Rose, Cleveland Watkiss, Gaika and others. It is a strategic reminder, after the recent scandal in which some of those Caribbean immigrants were redefined as illegal by the

Home Office, of the defining contribution that Afro-Caribbean artists have been making to British culture ever since Sparrow's frenemy Lord Kitchener walked off the Windrush in 1948 and sang "London is the place for me" into a Pathé News microphone – a catchy line that heralded the arrival of multicultural Britain.

Contemplating Brexit, Sparrow mutters: "I wonder why that happened?" He has confronted such divisions and dashed dreams of solidarity before, in 1959's Federation, with his comment on the crash of the post-colonial ideal of a united Caribbean. "We were trying to benefit [from independence] and we wanted to get all these islands together, create a federation where we could bargain better and benefit by all being together," he says. "But once individual prime ministers in the Caribbean had tasted power, nobody wanted to give it up. Suddenly, before you could really get together, it's all broken up. What do you do? It was terrible.

"In a way, it was similar to the scandal around the Windrush," he continues. "Suddenly you are told you are a non-person, not to be treated with any respect. They say they don't want you."

Sparrow has succeeded in translating his witty island authenticity to the world, in a one-man demonstration of the role that culture plays in uniting humankind. Having seen and heard so much and compressed it into so many searing songs, as he anticipates performing to symbolise the beleaguered, resistant Windrush generation, how does Sparrow think we should approach the future?

"What would I like to see? People get together and get involved with fixing things instead of just having everything severed," he replies. "We have to just hope that the younger ones step in and get involved as early as they can, to make things better. You know, singularity is not a thing that we want too much. We don't want to be singular, as time goes on. We want to be together."

Mighty Sparrow performs in Windrush: A Celebration, at the Barbican, London, tomorrow, as part of the EFG London Jazz festival.

Quoted Material

Song Lyrics

p.12 "Sea Song" by Robert Wyatt (Virgin Records). Lyrics by Robert Wyatt © 1974 (BMG Rights Management LLC).

p.15 "Signed Curtain" by Matching Mole (CBS Records). Lyrics by Robert Wyatt © 1972 (Domino Publishing Co. Ltd.).

p.21 "Team Spirit" by Robert Wyatt (Virgin Records). Lyrics by Robert Wyatt, Bill McCormick and Phil Manzanera © 1975 (BMG Rights Management LLC/Universal Music Publishing Group).

p.37 "He Was a Big Freak" by Betty Davis (Just Sunshine Records). Lyrics by Betty Mabry © 1974 (Higher Music Publishing Inc./ Betty Mabry Music Co.).

p.40 "If I'm in Luck I Might Get Picked Up" by Betty Davis (Just Sunshine Records). Lyrics by Betty Mabry © 1973 (Higher Music Publishing Inc./Betty Mabry Music Co.).

p.40 "In the Meantime" by Betty Davis (Just Sunshine Records). Lyrics by Betty Mabry © 1973 (Higher Music Publishing Inc./ Betty Mabry Music Co.).

p.41 "Anti Love Song" by Betty Davis (Just Sunshine Records). Lyrics by Betty Mabry © 1973 (Higher Music Publishing Inc./ Betty Mabry Music Co.).

p.42 "Don't Call Her No Tramp" by Betty Davis (Just Sunshine Records). Lyrics by Betty Mabry © 1974 (Higher Music Publishing Inc./Betty Mabry Music Co.).

p.54 "Dreadlock Don't Deal in Wedlock" by Jah Wobble (Virgin Records). Lyrics by John Joseph Wardle and Wayne Jobson © 1978 (BMG Rights Management LLC).

p.55 "Dan MacArthur" by Jah Wobble (Virgin Records). Lyrics by John Joseph Wardle © 1979 (BMG Rights Management LLC).

p.63 "Poptones" by Public Image Ltd (Virgin Records). Lyrics by John Lydon, John Joseph Wardle and Keith Levene © 1979 (Warner Chappell Music Inc./BMG Rights Management LLC).

p.64 "The Heathen" by Bob Marley and the Wailers (Island Records). Lyrics by Bob Marley © 1977 (Fifty-Six Hope Road Music Limited/Blackwell Fuller Music Publishing/Universal Music Publishing Group/Peermusic Publishing).

p.69 "The Flowers of Romance" by Public Image Ltd (Virgin Records). Lyrics by John Lydon and Keith Levene © 1981 (BMG Rights Management LLC).

p.69 "Go Back" by Public Image Ltd (Virgin Records). Lyrics by John Lydon, Keith Levene and Martin Atkins © 1981 (BMG Rights Management LLC/Warner Chappell Music, Inc.).

p.70 "Phenagen" by Public Image Ltd (Virgin Records). Lyrics by John Lydon and Keith Levene © 1981 (BMG Rights Management LLC/Warner Chappell Music, Inc.).

p.70 "Banging the Door" by Public Image Ltd (Virgin Records). Lyrics by John Lydon, Keith Levene and Martin Atkins © 1981 (BMG Rights Management LLC/Concord Music Publishing LLC/ Warner Chappell Music, Inc./Universal Music Publishing Group).

p.80 "One of These Nights" by Eagles (Asylum). Lyrics by Glenn Frey and Don Henley © 1975 (Universal Music Publishing Group/Cass County Music Co/Red Cloud Music). Cover and lyric change by Jam Today.

p.98 "I Heard It Through the Grapevine" by Marvin Gaye (Tamla Records). Lyrics by Barrett Strong and Norman Whitfield © 1968 (Sony/ATV Music Publishing).

p.102 "Lovers of Today" by The Pretenders (Real Records). Lyrics by Chrissie Hynde © 1980 (Peermusic Publishing).

p.111 "Private Life" by The Pretenders (Real Records). Lyrics by Chrissie Hynde © 1980 (Peermusic Publishing).

p.117 "Twisted" by Neneh Cherry (Circa Records). Lyrics by Neneh Cherry and Cameron McVey © 1992 (BMG Rights Management LLC).

p.142 "Punky Reggae Party" by Bob Marley and the Wailers (Island Records). Lyrics by Lee Perry and Bob Marley © 1977 (Fifty-Six Hope Road Music Limited/Blackwell Fuller Music Publishing/Universal Music Publishing Group/Kobalt Music Publishing Ltd.).

p.144 "Brothers in Trouble" by Delroy Washington (Virgin Records). Lyrics by Delroy Washington © 1977 (BMG Rights Management LLC).

p.148 "1977" by The Clash (Columbia Records). Lyrics by Paul Simonon, Mick Jones, Topper Headon and Joe Strummer © 1976 (Universal Music Publishing Group).

p.150 "Born for a Purpose" by Dr. Alimantado (Greensleeves Records). Lyrics by Winston Thompson © 1979 (Jack Russell Music Limited).

p.174 "Come Wi Go Dung Deh" by Linton Kwesi Johnson and Poet and the Roots (Front Line). Lyrics by Linton Kwesi Johnson © 1978 (BMG Rights Management LLC).

p.176 "Man Free" by Linton Kwesi Johnson and Poet and the Roots (Front Line). Lyrics by Linton Kwesi Johnson © 1978 (BMG Rights Management LLC/EMI Virgin Music Limited).

p.182 "Chocolate City" by Parliament (Casablanca). Lyrics by George Worrell, George Clinton and William Collins © 1975 (Kobalt Music Publishing Ltd.).

p.189 "Promentalshitbackwashpsychosis Enema Squad (The Doo Doo Chasers)" by Funkadelic (Warner Bros.). Lyrics by Garry Marshall Shider, George Clinton and Linda Lee Brown © 1991 (Kobalt Music Publishing Ltd.).

p.198 "A Letter to the New York Post" by Public Enemy (Def Jam/Columbia). Lyrics by James Boxley, William Drayton Jr., Gary Rinaldo, Cartlon Ridenhour and Stuart Robertz © 1991 (Reach Music Publishing/Shocklee Music/Universal Music Publishing Group/Terrordome Music Publishing LLC).

p.200 "Can't Truss It" by Public Enemy (Def Jam/Columbia). Lyrics by Carlton Ridenhour, Gary Rinaldo, Hank Shocklee, Stuart Robertz and Cerwin Depper © 1991 (Reach Music Publishing/Shocklee Music/Universal Music Publishing Group/Terrordome Music Publishing LLC).

p.207 "Fame" by Grace Jones (Island Records). Lyrics by Jack Robinson and Gil Slavin © 1978 (Universal Music Publishing Group).

p.215 "Gina, Gina" by Kid Creole and the Coconuts (ZE/Island Records/Sire). Lyrics by August Darnell and Ronnie Rogers © 1981 (Night Notes Music/Raineyville Music/St Swithin's Songs).

p.216 "Schweinerei" by Kid Creole and the Coconuts (ZE/Island

Records/Sire). Lyrics by August Darnell and Adriana Kaegi © 1981 (Raineyville Music).

p.216 "Que Pasa" by Coati Mundi and Kid Creole and the Coconuts (ZE/Island Records/Sire). Lyrics by Andy Hernandez © 1981 (Rainbowphonic Music).

p.220 "The Most Beautiful Girl" by Charlie Rich (Epic). Lyrics by Billy Sherrill, Norris Wilson and Rory Michael Bourke © 1973 (Sony/ATV Music Publishing LLC).

p.221 "Another World" by Richard Hell and the Voidoids (Sire). Lyrics by Richard Hell © 1977 (Dilapidated Music/Doraflo Music Inc./Quick Mix Music Inc.).

p.227 "The Plan" by Richard Hell and the Voidoids (Sire). Lyrics by Richard Hell © 1977 (Dilapidated Music/Doraflo Music Inc./Quick Mix Music Inc.).

p.235 "The Book I Read" by Talking Heads (Sire/Rhino/Warner Records). Lyrics by David Byrne © 1977 (Index Music Inc./ Warner Chappell Music, Inc.).

p.262 "Doors of Your Heart" by The Beat (Go-Feet Records/Sire). Lyrics by Andrew Cox, David Steele, David Wakeling, Everett Morton and Roger Charlery © 1981 (Concord Music Publishing LLC/Sony/ATV Music Publishing LLC).

p.263 "Monkey Murders" by The Beat (Go-Feet Records/Sire). Lyrics by Roger Charlery, Andrew Cox, Everett Morton, David Steele and David Wakeling © 1981 (Beat Brothers Ltd./Sony/ATV Music Publishing LLC/Concord Music Publishing LLC).

p.263 "Which Side of the Bed?" by The Beat (Arista Records). Lyrics by Roger Charlery, Andrew Cox, Everett Morton, David Steele and David Wakeling © 1981 (Zomba Music/ Beat Brothers Ltd.).

p.270 "Back to Living Again" by Curtis Mayfield (Warner Bros.). Lyrics by Curtis Mayfield and Rosemary Woods © 1996 (Warner Chappell Music, Inc.).

p.272 "Freddie's Dead" by Curtis Mayfield (Curtom Records). Lyrics by Curtis Mayfield © 1972 (Warner Chappell Music, Inc./Todd Mayfield Publishing).

p.275 "Amagideon (Armagedon)" by Bunny Wailer (Solomonic Records/Island Records). Lyrics by Neville Livingston © 1976 (Peermusic Publishing).

p.276 "Tenement Yard" by Jacob Miller (Island Records). Lyrics by Jacob Miller and Roger Lewis © 1980 (Sony/ATV Music Publishing LLC).

p.276 "Forward Jah Jah Children" by Jacob Miller and Inner Circle (Sweet City). Lyrics by Jacob Miller and Roger Lewis © 1974 (Universal Music Publishing Group).

p.287 "Police and Thieves" by Junior Murvin (Wild Flower/Island Records). Lyrics by Junior Murvin and Lee "Scratch" Perry © 1976 (Universal Music Publishing Group/BMG Rights Management LLC).

p.289 "Smile Jamaica" by Bob Marley and the Wailers (Island Records). Lyrics by Bob Marley © 1976 (Fifty-Six Hope Road Music Limited/Blackwell Fuller Music Publishing/Universal Music Publishing Group).

p.294 "Reincarnated Souls" by Bunny Wailer (Solomonic Records/Island Records). Lyrics by Neville Livingston © 1976 (BMG Rights Management LLC).

p.299 "Equal Rights" by Peter Tosh (Columbia Records). Lyrics by Peter Tosh © 1977 (Universal Music Publishing Group/Royalty Network/Sony/ATV Music Publishing LLC).

p.320 "Zimbabwe" by Bob Marley and the Wailers (Island Records/Tuff Gong). Lyrics by Bob Marley and Mathieu Andre Boogaerts © 1979 (Fifty-Six Hope Road Music Limited/Blackwell Fuller Music Publishing/Universal Music Publishing Group/Kobalt Music Publishing).

p.350 "Badness Cya Done" by Rebel Sixx (Attomatic Records). Lyrics by Kyle Roberts © 1979 (O/B/O DistroKid, ONErpm, Unison Rights S.L.).

p.356 "International Thief Thief (I.T.T.)" by Fela Aníkúlápó Kuti and Africa 70 (Kalakuta Sunrise/Knitting Factory Records/Liberator Music). Lyrics by Fela Aníkúlápó Kuti © 1979 (Fela Anikulapo-Kuti Estate Kft/BMG Rights Management LLC).

p.357 "Authority Stealing (Pt. 1 and 2)" by Fela Aníkúlápó Kuti and Africa 70 (Kalakuta Sunrise/Knitting Factory Records/Liberator Music). Lyrics by Fela Aníkúlápó Kuti © 1980 (Fela Anikulapo-Kuti Estate Kft/BMG Rights Management LLC).

p.362 "Lady" by Fela Aníkúlápó Kuti and the Africa 70 (EMI). Lyrics by Fela Aníkúlápó Kuti © 1972 (F.K.O. Music/BMG Rights Management LLC/Royalty Network).

p.389 "Sex & Drugs & Rock & Roll" by Ian Dury and the Blockheads (Stiff Records). Lyrics by Ian Dury and Chaz Jankel © 1977 (Templemill Music Ltd./Warner Chappell Music, Inc./ Sony/ATV Music Publishing LLC).

p.390 "My Old Man" by Ian Dury and the Blockheads (Stiff Records). Lyrics by Ian Dury and Steve Nugent © 1977 (Templemill Music Ltd./ Warner Chappell Music, Inc.).

p.414 "Taking the Blues Back Home" by Jayne Cortez and The Firespitters (Harmolodic/Verve Records/Virgin Records). Lyrics by Jayne Cortez © 1996 (Bola Press).

p.427 "Rule, Britannia!" by Thomas Arne. Lyrics by James Thomson, 1740.

p.428 "The Slave" by Mighty Sparrow (Island Records/RCA). Lyrics by Francisco Slinger © 1963 (Railroad Town Music / Zalytron Music).

p.428 "Congo Man" by Mighty Sparrow (National). Lyrics by Francisco Slinger © 1965 (Railroad Town Music/Zalytron Music).

Quotations

p.38 Maycock, J. 'Betty Davis: The Witty, Wicked World of Betty Davis'. The *Daily Telegraph* and *Pride* magazine, April 2002.

p.74 Vonnegut, K. *Cat's Cradle*. New York: Holt, Rinehart and Winston, 1963.

p.189 Shelley, M. *Frankenstein; or, The Modern Prometheus.* London: Lackington, Hughes, Harding, Mavor & Jones, 1818.

p.190 Bierce, A. *The Enlarged Devil's Dictionary.* London: Doubleday, 1967.

p.200 Gates, H.L. Jr. 'Black Demagogues and Pseudo-Scholars'. The *New York Times*, 20 July 1992.

p.218 Maal, B. Quoted in Corio, D. and Goldman, V. *The Black Chord.* New York: Universe Publishing, 1999.

p.228 Schuyler, J. 'Bleeding Gums'. *Hymn to Life.* New York: Random House, 1974.

p.271 Darabont, F. (Dir. and screenplay). *The Shawshank Redemption.* Castle Rock Entertainment/Columbia Pictures, 1994. Adapted from King, S. 'Rita Hayworth and Shawshank Redemption'. *Different Seasons.* New York: Viking Press, 1982.

p.292 Marvell, A. 'To His Coy Mistress'. *The Oxford Authors: Andrew Marvell.* Oxford: Oxford University Press, 1990.

p.413 Coleman, O. 'Tone Dialling'. *BOMB*, 1 July 1996. Available at: https://bombmagazine.org/articles/1996/07/01/tone-dialing/ [accessed 31 July 2024].

Acknowledgements

My foundation, my Big Sisters Judith Slipacoff and Susan Godfrey, who still teach me about sisterhood. Their generous lessons extend: mega lenswoman and schwis Janette Beckman; Eve Blouin (Viva Chantage!); Mariane Pearl; Nina Ritter; Adriana Kaegi; Denardo Coleman; Oberon Sinclair; Graham Brennan; Ann Minahan, The Hair Goddess @riah; Alexis Adler; Denardo Coleman; Monifa Fergusson; Isaac Fergusson; Oberon Sinclair; Graham Brennan; Evelyn McDonnell and Jana Martin (Fictionaires 4eva!); Eve-Marie Kuijstermans; Liz Pelly; Pete Shelton; Graham Brennan; Robert Katz; Danny Bentley; Gina Birch and Mike Holdsworth; Caroline Coon; Neneh Cherry and Cameron McVey; Jeannette Lee; Geoff Travis; Andrea Oliver and Garfield Hackett; Dennis Bovell; Johnny "T" Taylor; Yeni, Femi and Seun Kuti; Mykaell Riley (I owe you a platinum watchband!); Jenny, Hollie and Paul Cook; Chris Salewicz; Don Letts; Jon Savage; Paul Bradshaw; Spencer Style; Martin Meissonier. RIP our party-starting songbird, Angela McCluskey.

For bringing me back to making music which helps my writing sing: Martin "Youth" Glover and YouthSound; Richard England and Cadiz Entertainment; Alex Kassner and all at Kassner Music; Markus Detmer and Staubgold Records; Dunia Best and Aram Sinnreich of the VG3; Felice Rosser of the group Faith; Andy Caine; Phil Painson; Ryan Burvick and AudiopicturesNYC; Magnus Fiennes; Camila Alvarez; Isa Schwarzenberg and Tapete Records; Lilia Ohls and HowdyPartner Booking.

Marvin Taylor of Fales Library, NYU and the Vivien Goldman Punk and Reggae Collection; Dr Jason King (forever my Pygmalion and I your Galatea); Nick Sansano, Dan Charnas, Jenny Brown and my fine colleagues at the Clive Davis Institute of Recorded Music, Tisch School of the Arts, New York University, my scholarly perch since 2004; Jesse Lauter and the Reggae Seder; Everton Valentine Hoo.

This book would have been just too daunting without the diligent and creative stewardship of Barney Hoskyns and Mark Pringle and all at Rock's Backpages, who saw value in that crumbling print.

And to my editors who commissioned these pieces: Nick Logan, Richard Williams; Alan Lewis; Neil Spencer; Sally Brampton; Ann Barr; Caspar Llewellyn-Smith; Ben Beaumont-Thomas; Trevor Schoonmaker (thanks Amanda Zarate); Brandon Stosuy; Kandia Crazy Horse; Mark Kemp; Piotr Orlov; Jeremy Larson; Ray Rogers; Liz Pelly.

These articles were originally illustrated by photographers whose work is now regarded as classic, and I am proud of our association: Janette Beckman, David Corio, Dennis Morris, Kate Simon, Adrian Boot and Ray Stephenson.

For extra help Getting It Together: Nathalie Martin, for digging in the vaults with me, scanning and organising; Kim Evans and Dave Hucker who tracked down that elusive Grace Jones article; Stephen Chivers and SoundsClips on X, formerly known as Twitter; Tom Vickers, fellow Funkateer; Matthew Worley; Nigel Copsey; Richard Nelsson. "Rebel Sixx, Ghetto Prophet" would not have been possible without Hugh Callender; El Faltino; Dindin; Maxine Walters; Joshua Jelley-Schapiro, Mirissa Neff and all at PioneerWorks.

For making this book exist: my agents – Roisin Davis of ROAM and David Grossman of the David Grossman Literary Agency, thanks for your faith, efficiency and good sense. Lee Brackstone, Sophie Nevrkla, Susie Bertinshaw and all at White Rabbit Books. My fams J.C. Gabel, Sybil Perez and all at Hat & Beard Press. Thanks to Brother Lemi Ghariokwu for gracing the jacket with your distinctive vision and Alexesie Pinnock, for both my author photo and for helping make my life in Jamaica possible.

Most of this book was written in Jamaica, where my life was made possible and pleasurable by Chris Blackwell, Marika Kessler and all at Goldeneye Hotel and Resort, Oracabessa; Mr. Brown; Charlie Wilson; Andrea Barron and Gregory Roberts; Wayne and Brian Jobson; Joseph Issa; Ann Hodges and the whole Hodges-Smikle clan, Steve, Ronny, Samora and Rico. This book was assembled over the COVID cycle, a terrible winnowing time in which I lost many of my closest bred'ren, including Hodges-Smikle's estimable patriarch, Colin Smikle. We will continue the work he loved with the Trench Town Reading Centre (www.TrenchtownReadingCentre.com). Readers, please visit and contribute. Other crucial brothers gone: DJ Dave Hucker; DJ Femi Adebayo; writers Stanley Mieses and Greg Tate; photographer Jean-Bernard Sohiez, who shot the cover photos of my 1981 tune "Launderette"; and three major bassies who welcomed me into the reggae family: Aston "Family Man" Barrett, Robbie Shakespeare and Aswad's George Oban, with whom I wrote "Launderette" in one glorious flash.

If I missed anyone out, I am so sorry and hope to rectify.

To all my students, past, present and future – thanks for the lessons. Just don't test me.

And thanks again to Jenn Pelly, who got me thinking years ago by saying my old articles were too good to be locked away behind a paywall (oh, vanity! Let's hope you agree, fierce reader . . .).

[illegible]